A POLITICAL SOCIOLOGY OF THE EUROPEAN UNION

MANCHESTER
1824

Manchester University Press

EUROPE
IN
CHANGE
SERIES EDITORS: THOMAS CHRISTIANSEN AND EMIL KIRCHNER

The formation of Croatian national identity
ALEX J. BELLAMY

The European Union and the accommodation of Basque difference in Spain
ANGELA K. BOURNE

Theory and reform in the European Union, 2nd edition
DIMITRIS N. CHRYSSOCHOOU, MICHAEL J. TSINISIZELIS, STELIOS STAVRIDIS AND KOSTAS IFANTIS

From integration to integrity: Administrative ethics and reform in the European Commission
MICHELLE CINI

The transatlantic divide
OSVALDO CROCI AND AMY VERDUN

Germany, pacifism and peace enforcement
ANJA DALGAARD-NIELSEN

The changing European Commission
DIONYSSIS DIMITRAKOPOULOS (ED.)

Supranational citizenship
LYNN DOBSON

Reshaping Economic and Monetary Union
SHAWN DONNELLY

The time of European governance
MAGNUS EKENGREN

Adapting to European integration? Kaliningrad, Russia and the European Union
STEFAN GÄNZLE, GUIDO MÜNTEL, EVGENY VINOKUROV (EDS)

An introduction to post-Communist Bulgaria
EMIL GIATZIDIS

Mothering the Union
ROBERTA GUERRINA

Non-state actors in international relations: the case of Germany
ANNE-MARIE LE GLOANNEC

Turkey: facing a new millennium
AMIKAM NACHMANI

Europolis: constitutional patriotism beyond the nation state
PATRIZIA NANZ

The changing faces of federalism
SERGIO ORTINO, MITJA ŽAGAR AND VOJTECH MASTNY (EDS)

The road to the European Union
  Volume 1 The Czech and Slovak Republics   JACQUES RUPNIK AND JAN ZIELONKA (EDS)
  Volume 2 Estonia, Latvia and Lithuania   VELLO PETTAI AND JAN ZIELONKA (EDS)

Democratising capitalism? The political economy of post-Communist transformations in Romania, 1989–2001
LILIANA POP

Europe and civil society: movement coalitions and European governance
CARLO RUZZA

Constructing the path to eastern enlargement
ULRICH SEDELMEIER

Governing Europe's new neighbourhood: Partners or periphery?
MICHAEL SMITH, KATJA WEBER , AND MICHAEL BAUN (EDS)

Two tiers or two speeds? The European security order and the enlargement of the European Union and NATO
JAMES SPERLING (ED.)

Recasting the European order
JAMES SPERLING AND EMIL KIRCHNER

Political symbolism and European integration
TOBIAS THEILER

Rethinking European Union foreign policy
BEN TONRA AND THOMAS CHRISTIANSEN (EDS)

The European Union in the wake of Eastern enlargement
AMY VERDUN AND OSVALDO CROCI (EDS)

Democratic citizenship and the European Union
ALBERT WEALE

Inclusion, exclusion and the governance of European security
MARK WEBBER

Jay Rowell and Michel Mangenot
EDITORS

A POLITICAL SOCIOLOGY OF THE EUROPEAN UNION

Reassessing constructivism

MANCHESTER UNIVERSITY PRESS
Manchester and New York

*distributed in the United States exclusively
by Palgrave Macmillan*

Published by Manchester University Press
Oxford Road, Manchester M13 9NR, UK
and Room 400, 175 Fifth Avenue, New York, NY 10010, USA
www.manchesteruniversitypress.co.uk

Distributed in the United States exclusively by
Palgrave Macmillan, 175 Fifth Avenue, New York,
NY 10010, USA

Distributed in Canada exclusively by
UBC Press, University of British Columbia, 2029 West Mall,
Vancouver, BC, Canada V6T 1Z2

British Library Cataloguing-in-Publication Data
A catalogue record for this book is available from the British Library

Library of Congress Cataloging-in-Publication Data applied for

ISBN   978 0 7190 8243 6 hardback

First published 2010

Typeset in Minion with Lithos
by Action Publishing Technology Ltd, Gloucester
Printed in Great Britain
by CPI Antony Rowe Ltd, Chippenham, Wiltshire

CONTENTS

List of contributors   *page* vii
List of figures, tables and boxes   ix
List of abbreviations   xi
Preface: Revitalising EU studies through constructivism   xiii
Andy Smith

Introduction: What Europe constructs: towards a
sociological constructivism   1
Michel Mangenot and Jay Rowell

Part I The construction of European fields
  1 Making top civil servants: Europeanness as an identity and
    a resource   25
    Didier Georgakakis and Marine de Lassalle

  2 The invention and transformation of a governmental body:
    the Council Secretariat   46
    Michel Mangenot

  3 Lawyers as Europe's middlemen: a sociology of litigants
    pleading before the European Court of Justice   68
    Christele Marchand and Antoine Vauchez

  4 The emergence of 'European' careers in subnational French
    administrations   88
    Marine de Lassalle

Part II The social construction of European problems
  5 Constitutional activism and fundamental rights in Europe:
    common interests through transnational socialisation   109
    Laurent Scheeck

  6 The construction of a European interest through legal
    expertise: property owners' associations and the Charter of
    Fundamental Rights   128
    Hélène Michel

7 A constructivist–institutionalist approach to EU politics: the case of Protected Geographical Indications for food 146
Andy Smith

8 The European Parliament and the politicisation of the European space: the case of the two port packages 164
Willy Beauvallet

Part III Constructing reality through policy instruments

9 From integration by law to Europeanisation by numbers: the making of a 'competitive Europe' through intergovernmental benchmarking 185
Isabelle Bruno

10 From instruments to the instrumentalisation of 'European opinion': a historical sociology of the measurement of opinions and the management of the public space 206
Philippe Aldrin

11 Expert measurement in the government of lifelong learning 225
Romuald Normand

12 The instrumentation of European disability policy: constructing a policy field with numbers 243
Jay Rowell

Index 263

LIST OF CONTRIBUTORS

Editors

Jay Rowell is researcher in Political Sociology at the CNRS and director of the Centre for European Political Sociology, Strasburg.

Michel Mangenot is senior lecturer in Political Science at Sciences Po Strasburg and deputy director of the the Centre for European Political Sociology, Strasburg.

Authors

Philippe Aldrin is Professor in Political Science at the University of Nice and member of the Centre for European Political Sociology, Strasburg.

Willy Beauvallet is a post-doctoral fellow at the the Centre for European Political Sociology, Strasburg.

Isabelle Bruno is senior lecturer in political science at the University of Lille 2 and member of the Center for Politics and Administration.

Marine de Lassalle is senior lecturer in Political Science at Sciences Po Strasburg and member of the Centre for European Political Sociology, Strasburg.

Didier Georgakakis is Professor in Political Science at Sciences Po Strasburg, holder of the Jean Monnet Chair of European Political Sociology, and member of the Centre for European Political Sociology, Strasburg.

Christele Marchand is a post-doctoral fellow in Political Science at the University of Picardy.

Hélène Michel is Professor in Political Science at Sciences Po Strasburg and member of the Centre for European Political Sociology, Strasburg.

Romuald Normand is senior lecturer in Sociology at the University of Lyon.

Laurent Scheeck is lecturer at the Institute for European Studies at the Université Libre de Bruxelles.

Andy Smith is *Directeur de recherche* at the French Fondation Nationale des Sciences Politiques and member of the SPIRIT research centre in Bordeaux.

Antoine Vauchez is a Research Fellow in political science at the Centre National de la Recherche Scientifique.

LIST OF FIGURES, TABLES AND BOXES

Figures *page*
3.1   Jurists' standings before the ECJ   72
3.2   Newcomers in the Euro-litigation arena   78
3.3   Euro-lawyers' seniority before the ECJ   80
5.1   The normative sources of the ECJ and the CFI, 1998–2005   118
9.1   Competitiveness pyramid of the EU   192
9.2   Steps in the benchmarking process   194
9.3   R&D intensity   199

Tables
1.1   Directors-General by nationality (1958–2005)   30
1.2   Number of years of DG's directorate by nationality   32
1.3   Number of years of the DDG's directorate by nationality   33
1.4   Average types of career according to types of employer
       and nationality   38
2.1   Development of Secretariat staff   53
2.2   'A' rank officials in the Commission and Council Secretariat   54
3.1   Actors of the Euro-litigation arena (1953–1978)   70
3.2   The 10 major actors before the ECJ   74
3.3   International and European legal capital   82

Boxes
10.1   J.-R. Rabier, the entrepreneur and his enterprise   217
10.2   The structural pro-Europe effect of Eurobarometer surveys   219

CAG	Competitiveness Advisory Group
CAP	Common Agricultural Policy
CCP	Product Conformity Certification
CDU	Christian Democratic Union
CFI	Court of First Instance
CFSP	Common Foreign and Security Policy
CNH	National Housing Council
COCOR	Commission of Coordination
COREPER	Committee of Permanent Representatives
CTS	Continuous Tracking Survey
DG	Director-General
	Directorate-General
EAGGF	European Agricultural Guidance and Guarantee Fund
ECB	European Central Bank
ECHR	European Court of Human Rights
ECJ	European Court of Justice
ECSC	European Coal and Steel Community
ECT	European Constitutional Treaty
EFTA	European Free Trade Association
EHF	European Housing Forum
ELO	European Landowners' Organization
ENA	*Ecole Nationale d'Administration*
EPC	European Political Cooperation
EPP–ED	European People's Party–European Democrats
ERA	European Research Area
ERDF	European Regional Development Fund
ERT	European Round Table
ESDP	European Security and Defence Policy
ESF	European Social Fund
ESP	European Socialist Party
ETF	European Transport Workers' Federation
EUL	European United Left
FEANTSA	European Federation of National Organisations working with the Homeless)
FNPA	National Federation of Farmland Owners
GAC	General Affairs Council

GATT	General Agreement on Trade and Tariffs
GEFI	*Groupement Européen des Fédérations intervenants dans l'Immobilier*
IALS	International Adult Literacy Survey
IGC	Intergovernmental Conference
ILO	International Labour Organisation
IMF	International Monetary Fund
INAO	National Institute of Designations of Origin
IR	International Relations
IUPO	International Union of Property Owners
LSE	London School of Economics
MAPROC	*Mission d'Appui aux Programmes Europeens*
MIT	Massachusetts Institute of Technology
MLG	Multi-level governance
NPM	New Public Management
OECD	Organisation for Economic Cooperation and Development
OMC	Open Method of Co-ordination
PAPE	Politics and Public Action in Europe
PGI	Protected Geographical Indication
PIP	Priority Information Programme
PISA	Programme for International Student Assessment
PPEWU	Policy Planning and Early Warning Unit
PSC	Political and Security Committee
SF	Structural funds
SPD	Social Democratic Party of Germany
TQM	Total Quality Management
UNICE	Union of Industrial and Employers' Confederations of Europe
UNPI	*Union nationale de la propriété immobilière*
WEU	Western European Union

Andy Smith

Preface:
Revitalising EU studies through constructivism

Since the late 1990s, 'social constructivism' has slowly but surely been introduced into the study of the European Union. Drawing upon 'the
constructivist turn' in International Relations (IR), a series of scholars
announced new and exciting ambitions for the generation of knowledge
about the politics of European integration. In particular, this 'promise' of
constructivism was advanced in order to shed new light on two aspects of this
process. First, the authors involved claimed that the application of constructivism to this subject area would produce more information about the way
interests are defined, aggregated and defended within the EU. By moving
research away from the assumptions, questions and research methods of
rationalist intergovernmentalists or functionalists, these early 'EU constructivists' considered they would be able to better capture the social 'thickness'
and interdependencies behind EU negotiations. Second, these pioneering
scholars sought to emphasise the importance of identity, or rather constructions of identity, within European integration. Where rationalists had
assumed identities in Europe to remain predominately 'national', neo-
functionalists claimed to observe the emergence of supra-national allegences
and functionalists downplayed the very importance of identity for politics,
EU constructivists sought to reframe it. They did so by studying the construction of identities in Europe as both a means of understanding the
development of the EU as a political project on the one hand, and, on the
other, the difficulties experienced in legitimising this enterprise and the
governmental organs it had created.

Nearly ten years on from the launching of this collective intellectual
endeavour, individual EU constructivists have certainly produced a number
of important publications (Parsons, 2003; Checkel, 2003; Jabko, 2006).
However, taken as a whole, constructivism as applied to the EU has thus far
been largely unsuccessful as an intellectual project in two ways. First, it has
not developed a pervasive influence over the study of European integration or
even, more modestly, the study of the way the EU operates. On the one hand,
the so-called theoretical debate in this field about 'the nature' of European

integration is still dominated by a cleavage between intergovernmentalists and neo-functionalists. Most publications in this area, not to mention teaching, still devote much of their 'theoretical' sections to these viewpoints on the EU. On the other hand, scholars who claim to be more interested in the 'Europeanisation' of national and intranational polities rarely frame their analyses using constructivist concepts and research methods. In short, as the content of any EU Studies conference or the dominant journals (*Journal of Common Market Studies* and *Journal of European Public Policy*) clearly testifies, for nearly all scholars of the EU constructivism remains an exotic 'cuckoo in the nest'. Second, EU constructivists have largely failed to build bridges with the rest of constructivism in the social sciences. This is particularly clear in France, a bastion of constructivism but also a country where the vast majority of its proponents have thus far shown no interest in studying the EU.

These failures cannot simply be ascribed to the hegemony of positivism and rationalism within Western societies and their respective social sciences. Although this remains a massive barrier to the spread of constructivism, EU constructivists have hindered their own cause by invariably taking on positivist and rationalist doxa with both hands tied behind their backs. Specifically, there have been two major problems with the way in which constructivist ambitions, premises and questions have been imported into the study of the EU. The first, and overarching, problem concerns the type of constructivism from which this importation has generally been sourced: 'social constructivism' as defined by theories of IR. Although steeped in epistemological reflection, ironically these writings ultimately lack clarity as to the aims of constructivist research. More precisely, once one has set out constructivism's differences from positivism, rationalism and functionalism, most EU constructivists rather lamely claim only to want to add insights to those generated by other approaches (Zürn and Checkel, 2005). Above all, they have failed to equip themselves with intermediary concepts – i.e. tools for mediating between an ontology and empirical investigation – which would enable them to unpack processes of construction such as those which shape and cause EU decision-making. Consequently most EU constructivists end up neglecting the full, and exciting, scope of a genuinely constructivist standpoint and research perspective.

The second problem is one of research methods. As Moravsick brutally but fairly pointed out in the *Journal of European Public Policy* special issue of 1999, early EU constructivists were particularly vague in setting out the solid research techniques which could have enabled them to transform their questions and hypotheses into systematic research protocols. Unfortunately, little progress appears to have been made on this front in the last decade. Instead, if anything there has been a *fuite en avant* which has generally entailed the use of fragile discourse analysis, survey and questionnaire generated statistics (Trondal and Veggeland, 2003; Schimmelfennig and

Sedelmeier, 2005). Unlike constructivists who ally theory to the sociological method when analysing national or local politics (Dubois, 1999; Pinson and Sala Pala, 2007), EU constructivists have thus far rarely generated systematic knowledge either about how actors have been constituted or about what precisely these protagonists have constructed, how and why. As with the problem of theory, this methodological underspecification has ended up delegitimising, and even trivialising, constructivism within EU studies.

In the light of this unfortunate trajectory taken by constructivism within EU studies, this book is particularly timely for two reasons. First, it brings together a group of political scientists who are all convinced that the original constructivist project in social science was justified, rigorous and relevant to the analysis of politics. Second, these same researchers all consider that constructivism should, and indeed must, be introduced with vigour and confidence into the study of the EU. However, to do so their respective research also shows that EU studies must be prepared to 'begin again', and this by abandoning vague 'social' constructivism in favour of an alternative version of this approach firmly founded on institutionalist concepts and the sociological method. In summary, both the individual chapters that follow and the book as a whole, constitute a sustained and systematic challenge to existing approaches to the EU. I for one look forward to following and taking part in the exchanges and debates it will undoubtedly spark, both amongst scholars of European integration, but also amongst social scientists in general interested in making good on 'the promise' of constructivism.

Bibliography

Checkel, J., 'Going Native in Europe? Theorizing Social Interaction in European Institutions', *Comparative Political Studies*, 36 (1–2), 2003.

Dubois, V., *La vie au guichet. Relation administrative et traitement de la misère*, Paris: Economica, 1999.

Jabko, N., *Playing the Market: A Political Strategy for Uniting Europe, 1985–2005*, Ithaca: Cornell University Press, 2006.

Parsons, C., *A Certain Idea of Europe*, Ithaca: Cornell University Press, 2003.

Pinson, G. and Sala Pala, V., 'Peut-on vraiment se passer de l'entretien en sociologie de l'action publique?', *Revue française de science politique*, 57 (5), 2007, 555–597.

Schimmelfennig, F. and Sedelmeier, U. (eds), *The Europeanization of Central and Eastern Europe*, Ithaca: Cornell University Press, 2005.

Trondal, J. and Veggeland, F., 'Access, Voice and Loyalty. The Representation of Domestic Civil Servants in EU Committees', *Journal of European Public Policy*, 10 (1), 2003. 59–77.

Zürn, M. and Checkel, J., 'Getting Socialized to Build Bridges: Constructivism and Rationalism, Europe and the Nation-State', *International Organization*, 59, 2005.

MICHEL MANGENOT AND JAY ROWELL

Introduction:
What Europe constructs: towards a sociological constructivism

Over the past two decades, the European project has come under tremendous pressure and has changed substantially.[1] Not only has the number of member states more than doubled since the Single European Act, but the range of its policy competences has greatly increased, the institutional architecture has been overhauled and new procedures and methods of government have been introduced to accommodate these changes. This process was regularly punctuated with political crises (such as failed referenda, the resignation of the Santer commission, recurrent political brinkmanship at many European summits and a slow reaction to the financial crisis) against a backdrop of rising Euroscepticism as measured by Eurobarometer, low voter turnout at European elections and the continued perception of a 'democratic deficit'. During national referenda campaigns, national and European elites systematically warned that a 'no' vote would bring the EU to a grinding halt, whereas editorialists regularly prophesied the impending demise of the EU in the immediate aftermath of each European 'crisis'. And yet, despite the gloom and the assertions of doomsayers, the EU has shown great resilience and a capacity for adapting to ever-changing internal and external conditions. This institutional capacity is not new, as the European project went ahead despite the rejection of the European Defence Community by France in 1954 and accomplished customs unification ahead of schedule despite the 'crisis of the empty chair'. Today, despite continuing criticisms, less than enthusiastic public opinion and leaders in many national capitals whose public commitment to the EU has been tepid at best, European institutions nonetheless continue to churn out compromises, directives and policy which, even if they are more a reflection of 'muddling through' than a fervent proclamation of a bright European future, have had an ever-increasing impact on the daily lives of European citizens. How can this surprising resilience of European institutions and their capacity to adapt and adjust to the daunting political and institutional challenges be explained and understood?

There is a somewhat flippant answer to this puzzle which would consist in saying that the capacity of EU institutions to pursue 'business as usual' following each crisis is proof of its lack of responsiveness to citizens' concerns and provides grist for the mill to those who regularly denounce a Brussels bureaucracy functioning in a closed circuit, cut off from the people and territories whose interests it purports to represent. People working in European institutions are of course acutely aware of changes in the political climate and public perceptions, but this type of answer, when redefined, raises real questions which become the starting point for this book. If organisations bend and sway without breaking or disintegrating, it is because they are the product of a long process of institutionalisation providing them with the necessary consistency to weather the many storms that have swept through the EU since the 1990s. However, as Neil Fligstein has recently and convincingly argued, accounting for the ability of European institutions to grow and develop requires going beyond the study of the visible tip of the European iceberg to look at less visible and routine processes below the waterline (Fligstein, 2008: 9).

While rationalist accounts of the solidity of European institutions have taken into consideration the constraining effects of past decisions (on 'lock in', see Pierson, 1996) and the emerging character of national preference formation in negotiating arenas, they remain empirically centred on the 'big decisions' such as treaty revision and intergovernmental negotiations and fail to capture the often invisible, but essential, day-to-day interactions and institutional drift and socialisation processes which continually transform anticipations and representations. These long-term processes have firmly anchored European institutions as a 'given' around which actors deploy their activity, even when formulating ostensibly national preferences. As such, the sedimentation of decades of institution-building has anchored the European polity in a web of mutually supporting legal and social institutions and conventions: treaties, jurisprudence and criss-crossing norms (both 'soft' and 'hard'); specialised administrations and agencies working at multiple levels; public policies which generate new categories of action firmly rooted in policy instruments and woven into several levels of governance; professional careers and interest groups which are horizontally linked and gravitate around the European polity; a range of policy instruments and discourses which have constructed Europe as the natural and legitimate scale of regulation in a growing number of areas; finally, social and political representations in which even the most critical Eurosceptical voices rarely challenge the existence of the EU but seek rather to redirect its form or finality. This brief and non-exhaustive enumeration of the different forms of institutionalisation points to an inclusive conception of this notion which will be explored throughout this volume.

Institutions are here defined in a wide sense and are not merely reduced to formal organisations, their internal structures and processes of internal socialisation. In this sense, institutionaliation takes on a broader meaning than in many other strands of European studies. First, institutions are not just finite organisations or points of fixation of interests as neo-functionalist accounts often portray them. Nor are they bundles of norms with discrete boundaries which define procedures in negotiating venues as in intergovernmentalist accounts. Institutions are not just contextual elements which externally bind the rationality of strategic actors, as in rationalist or principal/agent accounts of European institutions (Moravscik, 1998). While these conceptions of institutions form a basis for analysis, a more Durkheimian conception of social institutions is required to better understand the dynamics of incorporation of procedures and external structures into social practice and in turn, the transformative effects of social interactions and strategic action on procedures and organisational configurations. Institutions are therefore interiorised norms which limit the scope of possible action following a logic of appropriateness (March and Olsen, 1989: 26). However, they also offer possibilities for interpretation and can be selectively mobilised by social agents, thereby bringing into play a dynamic process alternating between incorporation which reinforces institutions through socialisation, and transformation through shifting configurations and power relations. Norms, habits and specific ways of doing things are progressively inscribed in individual and group identities and define legitimate representations and weigh on anticipations and strategic action, both among actors within European organisations and among actors more or less subjected to the 'gravitational pull' of the EU polity. In this sense, this volume seeks to build upon the growing body of literature centred on expanded institutional perspectives as well as more recent, but growing research centred on socialisation processes (Cini and McGowan, 1998; Checkel, 1999) and actor-centred political sociology (Georgakakis, 2002; Smith, 2004; Vauchez, 2008).

Rather than theorising individual agency as an ontological property held by strategic actors seeking to maximise their interests or denied to actors exposed to the normative pressures of appropriateness, the sociological approach offered in this volume theorises agency as the ability to recognise and pursue individual interests, which varies according to the quality and types of resources held by social agents, pre-existing dispositions more or less adjusted to dominant norms in a given context of interaction and finally the changes in the configurations and structures of power relations which create opportunities for a strategic reinterpretation of norms. Institutions will however not be handled as an abstract bundle of binding norms, nor reduced to a set of procedures defining logics of appropriateness in specific bargaining arenas, but will be examined in their diverse and often very material manifestations. As such this volume will seek to go beyond the often ritualised incantation of 'institutional effects', 'institutional context' or 'hard and soft norms' to analyse the socialisation effects specific to Europe ('going native'). It will thus seek to examine the nuts and bolts of what institutions are made of, historical processes of institutionalisation and how a sociological approach to categories, discourse and social agents can help bridge the gap between norms and practice to help explain the surprising resiliency of EU institutions.

Studying institution-building as a dynamic and ongoing process of sedimentation logically excludes an intergovernmental and rationalist approach, as this epistemological stance has so far refused to consider much of anything beyond national preference formation and bargaining dynamics in bounded settings, thereby leaving the thickness of institutions outside the realm of empirical enquiry. The development of institutionalist perspectives in European studies has brought focus to the essential question of socialisation and identity constructions in their capacity to structure practice through the internalisation of meanings and compliance to social norms. However, to a large extent, this strand of research has centred the scope of enquiry on the conforming effects of European socialisation to the most central actors of the European policy and has examined only the relationship between the intensity of interactions and the appropriation of common norms and values (Checkel, 2005). This picture appears adequate to understand institutional resistance to change when a group of actors sharing a common set of norms and identities 'circle the wagons', but does not adequately account for the idea of resiliency which includes adaptation, and therefore the transformation of group norms and practice.[2] Furthermore, while this literature has made important inroads in understanding the transformative normative pressures exerted on individuals, much of the debate remains focused around an 'all or nothing' opposition which has traversed European studies since their inception: between, on the one hand, intergovernmentalist perspectives in which national preferences and values remain dominant, if not exclusive, and, on the other, supranational conceptions of the EU which presuppose the existence of an elite already having 'gone native'. If intergovernmental theories are of little help in explaining the institutional strength which EU institutions have demonstrated, much of neo-functionalist and neo-institutional literature has placed its empirical eggs in one basket by restricting enquiry to a limited number of settings at the heart of European institutions.

Largely theoretical debates in European studies have crystallised around oppositions between the degree of agency, the types of institutions examined, and the driving force of integration, producing what some authors have called 'complementary perspectives masquerading as incompatible rivals' (Peterson, 2001: 290). Despite attempts to bridge gaps (Checkel and Moravcsik, 2001) and propositions to hybridise opposing theoretical propositions (Jupille, Caporaso and Checkel, 2003), the metatheoretical landscape in European studies remains divided. Controversies are often fought far from empirical fieldwork and are to a large extent influenced by political oppositions on the nature of the European beast as a supranational, multi-level or intergovernmental entity (for a recent overview, see Cini and Bourne, 2006).

Towards a sociological constructivism in European Studies

The introduction of constructivism into European Studies a decade ago sought precisely to move beyond these increasingly sterile theoretical (and political) oppositions and propose new avenues to understand the 'thickness' of institutions, identity formation and the emergence of a partially autonomous European polity (*Journal of European Public Policy*, 1999; Christiansen, Jorgensen and Wiener, 2001). While this collective endeavour has created an increasingly diverse body of research, in many ways it has yet to fulfil its programmatic promise and transform the intellectual excitement it initially generated into a comprehensive framework sufficiently robust to redefine the way we think about Europe and empirically engage European dynamics. As a result, constructivism has been added to the increasingly long list of metatheories on Europe which coexist, but it has remained relatively marginal and has so far failed to significantly alter the way we perceive and study Europe.

Despite the unfulfilled promises, a constructivist perspective, taken in a broad sense, appears to provide the theoretical framework with the most potential leverage to address the initial puzzle which brought together the authors of this volume. In light of the weaknesses which have hindered the uptake of constructivist perspectives in mainstream European studies, it will first be necessary to address these objections and propose empirical and methodological avenues to put a general constructivist perspective on a more solid footing.

The problem of ideational exclusivity
While recognising the important contributions of constructivist perspectives to understanding processes shaping institutions and policies in the EU, the contention that ideational factors, often reduced to discourse, are the very fabric of Europe tends to reduce the empirical focus rather than widen it. To paraphrase Thomas Kuhn's interpretation of paradigm changes, the constructivist project correctly identified empirical anomalies in the 'normal science' approach to the EU, but in its application, the reliance on ideational forces has addressed some of these anomalies while also creating new 'blind spots' by blending out organisational dynamics, the strategic action of individuals and the existence of material interests. The contributors to this volume all consider a constructivist perspective to be essential to their work, but remain dissatisfied with the sociological and empirical underspecification which characterises much of the literature subsumed under the banner of constructivism. The often narrow focus on ideational factors has largely failed

to provide an overarching picture of the interplay between ideas, institutions, actors and interests.

To take one example, Martin Marcussen's study of the social construction of economic and monetary union is one of the most ambitious and solid attempts to operationalise the constructivist agenda (Marcussen, 2000) by inscribing the emergence of a new European field of action in a plurality of national and social spaces over a twenty-year period. If Marcussen pays attention to the diversity of actors who formalise and impose the new economic policy paradigm (economists, central bankers, ministers and Jacques Delors' advisers), the theoretical argument of an ideational life-cycle and a diffusionist theory of ideas give the new discourse a structuring force having a life of its own, largely disconnected from the institutional, social and political context of its elaboration and reception. As such, little attention is paid in this book, as in other research projects labelled as constructivist (Diez 2001; Hay and Rosamond, 2002; Kallestrup, 2002), to the specific resources and legitimacy of certain strategic actors who seek to impose new cognitive frames and group norms, thereby missing the essential problem of authority, symbolic resources and power relations which are as essential to the 'success' of an idea as the intrinsic logic of its causal story (Stone, 1988). Focusing uniquely on the most visible and institutionalised discourses also raises the problem of seeing failed attempts to contest or impose new norms, which can be as instructive as the study of 'success stories', for they bring to light powerful mechanisms of domination such as gate-keeping and agenda denial (Bachrach and Baratz, 1962). Failed reforms or problem definitions in the past often leave few visible traces in the present, but can have lasting consequences as shared, but largely implicit lines that should not be crossed, thereby limiting the strategic possibilities of policy entrepreneurs. The empirical dependency on visible texts and discourse to identify ideational forces therefore tends to leave out tacit norms which can be all the more binding as they 'go without saying' on the one hand and 'hard norms' such as institutionalised procedures, rules or cognitive categories inscribed in policy instruments.

As Schmidt and Radaelli have argued, discourse needs to be situated in institutional 'riverbeds' to produce change (Schmidt and Radaelli, 2004). In other words, research on ideational factors needs to both take into account the diversity and performative capacity of different types of discourse (as an intersubjective speech act, a finalised result of exchange such as a white paper or a Commission communication, an interview etc.), and systematically recontextualise ideational constructs in the configurations of their emergence and transformation into social practice; constructs which are always subject to interpretation and adapted to specific settings. Ideational constructs are the product of social agents who are not interchangeable, work in specific institutional and social contexts, pursue particular goals and therefore need to be sociologically embedded.

Methodological and empirical underspecification

With a few notable exceptions (for example, Trondal, 2002), the constructivist research agenda has focused on qualitative research techniques heavily centred on discourse analysis. As such, it has been subjected to the same types of criticisms as other qualitative post-positivist theoretical frameworks, such as its failure to produce refutable results; the representativeness of empirical material based on a small number of cases; the difficulty in measuring the actual 'power' of ideas and their capacity to generate social practice; the problem of discourse as an *ex post* rationalisation not always reflecting core beliefs; or the difficulties involved in ascertaining bias between what is said (or can be said) and what is done. Another problem more specific to working in contexts where most actors possess superior cognitive skills and are in constant contact with expert knowledge, is the circularity between social science knowledge and 'indigenous' cognitive categories, or the 'looping effect', where individuals under scrutiny share many of the analytical categories with social scientists (Hacking, 2000: 9). This seems to be particularly true in European Studies where social scientists and European officials share a quest to qualify and understand the specificities of this set of new institutions (White, 2003).

Beyond these common objections to qualitative research which reflect the great methodological and epistemological divide in the social sciences, much of the constructivist literature has hurt its own cause by failing to formalise the conditions of its empirical validity through robust protocols for fieldwork. This would have helped allay the criticisms of all but the most positivist and quantitatively oriented members of the scientific community. Fuzzy methodology, sparse information on the criteria of selection of the corpus, and failure to differentiate between different types of discourse have cast a shadow over the validity of findings in many constructivist studies.

Three possible paths to increasing the methodological and empirical reach and solidity of qualitative constructivist research seem possible. The first, which will not be followed in this volume, would consist in drawing on the more formalised methodologies of text analysis which would include a more rigorous and explicit definition of a corpus. This would provide clearer indications on potential biases and allow for a reflexive analysis of the empirical validity of findings. Without necessarily resorting to lexicometric analysis, such a research strategy would provide a better grounding of discourse analysis in its temporal, spatial and institutional context.

The second path, followed by several authors of this volume, is to harness the power of combined research methodologies and diversified empirical sources in order to increase the solidity of findings through empirical triangulation. This implies first and foremost a differentiated treatment of discourse produced or collected in different contexts or through different techniques. In other words, texts found in policy papers destined for a wide public, internal documents, or discourse generated through an interview or a questionnaire, are not interchangeable and can only be analysed when replaced in the configuration of their enunciation. A second form of empirical triangulation consists in multiplying the points of view and varying methodology and the types of sources to tell a more complete story. Several chapters of this volume demonstrate the empirical leverage provided by bringing together text analysis, interviews and biographical data, both quantitative and qualitative, with more structural and configurational frameworks to create a more complete picture of the links between ideas, positions, dispositions and resources which social agents possess on the one hand, and social and institutional configurations which both constrain and create potential spaces for a strategic appropriation of norms on the other. This leads directly to the third possibility which consists in specifying the sociological and institutional coordinates of ideational factors which we will discuss in more detail.

As we have already mentioned, debates on socialisation and agency have centred on the duality between national identities and preferences and the hypothesis of the emergence of a supranational European identity (see for example Hooghe, 2001). However, as research on epistemic communities and specific policy sectors has shown, there are also more specialised professional and sectoral logics at work which include an ever-greater number of stakeholders. (Petersen and Bomberg, 1999; Guiraudon, 2003; Richardson, 2001). In a nutshell, social agents who have pursued a career in public administration possess different resources and ways of thinking and doing things than agents who have worked in the private sector; agents with training in legal professions need to be differentiated from agents with training in economics or public administration, etc. These sociological cleavages go beyond the national/supranational dimension, and are in many respects as important, if not more so. This brings to light the limits of a theoretical debate reduced to an 'either/or' or an 'all or nothing' proposition and sheds light on the plurality of conflicting logics and norms, the complexity and imbrication of arenas, and therefore the difficulties in assigning identities based on preformed theories on the effects of socialisation or strategic action. The sociological 'hardening' of constructivist perspectives proposed in this volume is therefore based on answers to a few simple questions. Who is producing the discourse being analysed? In which institutional and social context is discourse produced, and for what purpose? What are the procedures and explicit and implicit rules governing discursive acts? The answers to these simple questions are of course complex and far-reaching, but they open avenues which are often ignored in much of the existing literature. As Andy Smith points out in the Preface, such questions generate tools for mediating between ontological claims and empirical verification capable of opening the black box of identity and institutional construction which shape EU decision-making and broader processes of institutionalisation.

From a methodological standpoint, the reconstruction of institutional and social spaces of action generate a dialectic where discourse can be used as an indicator of positions and power relations as a means to specify the context of production and appropriation of ideas. Conversely, the empirical reconstruction of social spaces and networks in which there is a constant tension between cooperative moves to create common values and competitive moves to gain individual advantage (Richardson, 2001: 15) allows for a more reasoned selection of the discursive corpus and objectifies the positions of dominated players who are often left out due to their lesser visibility and the normative pressures of a consensual style present in many European arenas. Ascertaining both the sociological properties, dispositions and resources of actors and the sociological oppositions which structure a given policy sector around specific bones of contention has several advantages. This perspective recasts the existing debates around an 'all or nothing' proposition opposing a more or less static reading of national policy preferences and an often angelic reading of consensual policy-making in the EU where the shared use of 'Eurospeak', a conscious depoliticisation of issues and the proclaimed adherence to an overarching 'European interest' is taken at face value. Such a 'literal' reading of what goes on masks asymmetric power relations, unequal access to the most central policy arenas and the specific resources and forms of authority which dominate in each context. The power to contribute to the setting of norms and to transcribe unwritten norms into institutionalised forms, the ability to reinterpret existing norms, to fit discourse to the specific requirements of different situations and audiences or to harness their authority to further individual strategic aims is not evenly distributed.

In the end, discourse-centred constructivist perspectives and socialisation theorists have largely failed to precisely study the mechanisms, instruments and social dynamics which generate and reinforce institutions and norms, which in turn create specific and partially autonomous organisations, practices, policy styles and instruments. Paradoxically, constructivism as it has been practised, like rational choice theories, has tended to treat individuals and groups as asociological, decontextualised units of analysis: universal utility maximisers on the one side and more or less passive recipients of group or institutional norms on the other. By taking up Giddens' dialectic of constraint and agency in institutions and through institutions (Giddens, 1984), the question moves on from an ontological level to a more empirically based question on the configurations, contexts and social properties and dispositions which explain differential capabilities to pursue strategic aims which transform existing group norms or on the contrary promote institutional 'lock in' in the interests of the dominant players. As a result, social and professional status and trajectories, the unequal distribution of resources and knowledge, controversies on the legitimacy of specific actors and their claims and context-specific forms of resource mobilisation will be central to the analysis of the dialectic of the conservation or the transformation of institutional arrangements and power distributions.

This volume will therefore examine the theoretical and empirical benefits which can be gained by mobilising different strands of sociology to 'harden' constructivist perspectives and make them more robust.[3] The idea of an empirically 'grounded constructivism' has been widely discussed and has given rise to a series of theoretical propositions and hybrid denominations such as sociological institutionalism (Checkel, 1999), social constructivism or structural constructivism (Kauppi, 2005). The use of 'sociological' as an adjective has come into vogue over the past years in constructivist, institutionalist and international relations derived literature (Rumford, 2002), but remains most often either a highly abstract programmatic declaration or applied to highly aggregated entities far removed from the sociological properties of individuals and groups who build European institutions in their daily interactions.

The aim is not to join the fray of labelling theoretical currents by proposing a new hybrid theory or synthesis, an exercise often verging on theoretical hair-splitting,[4] but which has contributed little to a better cumulative understanding of what Europe is and does. This book will be centred on problem-solving and will take up a series of interpretative debates on the EU and test, somewhat experimentally, the possible contributions of different strands of sociological enquiry which are rarely mobilised to study European political processes.

Going on where constructivism has left off

Rather than considering European institutions and policies as a social construction limited to norms and discourse, the authors of this volume make the assumption that European organisations, actors, rules and policies are something more than ideational constructions; that their study should go beyond discourse analysis and should therefore not be limited to perceptions, anticipations, discourse, policy framing and other terms used to designate cognitive constructs and 'soft' institutional norms (Campana, Henry and Rowell, 2007). The emergence of European problems (Smith, 2004), the idea that Europe is a 'natural' space of regulation in an increasing number of policy areas, and the seeming irreversibility of the process of institution-building is in part shaped by ideational configurations, but the authors of this volume will seek to understand these processes by integrating power relations between collective and individual actors and providing the sociological flesh which avoids many of the over-generalising pitfalls of metatheories on the 'nature' of the European polity and 'European' actors.

This assumption leads to the further central structuring argument of this book which in some ways picks up where many constructivist studies leave off. Instead of framing the question in terms of the social construction of Europe (of monetary policy, foreign policy, etc), the argument adopted here consists in asking 'What it is that the European process constructs?' – not only in the sense that institutions frame problem definitions and norms of appropriateness through discourse, but perhaps more importantly the way in which they reconfigure the legitimate arenas of discussion, policy making and implementation and thereby transform group identities, resources and power relations. The three parts of the book will thereby take a sociological and empirically grounded constructivist tack on studying three 'outputs' or by-products of the European process: European fields, European policy problems and specific policy instruments.

The construction of European fields

The first part of the volume, subsumed under the general theme of the emergence of European social and institutional spaces, will highlight the productivity of combining constructivist perspectives with structural sociological methods of enquiry (Georgakakis, 2008). Part of the problem of discourse-centred constructivist literature is that the diffusionist theory of ideational influence often fails to identify and explain the social and political conditions making new discourse not only possible, but also 'contagious'. Relatively vague references to a general 'ideological context' or the dominant role of a few key players are not sufficient to establish a solid explanatory mechanism, thereby creating an interpretative tautology (an idea succeeds because it is either adjusted to the 'esprit du temps' or because it is the best answer to the cognitive uncertainty of central actors or institutions).

The construction of specifically European social spaces, often cutting across organisations, will be apprehended by mobilising what could be termed an actor-centred structural constructivism. Within this general framework, the EU will be studied through the lenses of the emergence of particular careers and career interests, forms of socialisation and interaction which define a *habitus* particular to an emerging 'post-national' European elite. In doing so, we will seek to specify institutional and sociological oppositions which determine the boundaries between arenas of action and interaction. Much of the empirical work in this section is theoretically grounded in the sociology of elites derived from Bourdieu's field theory (Bourdieu, 1998).

This is most explicitly the case in Didier Georgakakis and Marine de Lassalle's analysis of the Directors-General of the Commission in Chapter 1. The creation of these 'European' positions within a European civil service is certainly one of the most tangible expressions (and at the same time one of the driving forces) of European institutionalisation, yet it remains unclear in what way these posts are 'European', as well as if and how they are becoming more so. Based on a biographical database retracing forms of socialisation prior to entry in the European civil service and the painstaking reconstruction of career paths, the authors provide precise empirical data on the Europeanisation processes in careers and shed light on a series of cleavages which do not just differentiate 'national' from 'European' profiles. By looking at patterns over the last fifty years, the chapter provides some answers to the Europeanisation of political and administrative careers and shows that if certain long-term trends can be identified, it is far from being a continuous and standardised process across all positions, nationalities and European political sectors.

In his socio-historical chapter on the Council secretariat, Chapter 2, Michel Mangenot analyses the contribution of an actor-centred sociology to study both the process of institutionalisation and the critical junctures where the role of the secretariat was redefined. Through the study of this institution which plays an important, if discreet, role in centralised coordination, which has largely escaped the attention of scholars in European Studies, Michel Mangenot places under scrutiny the path dependency hypothesis and demonstrates that if there are perceptible institutional paths derived from initial choices, it is the changing profiles of the members of the institution that explains the processes of institutional innovation and inflexion. Therefore, the essential question is not whether the institution adapts to change or not, but if and how new actors adapt to the existing institution, and how this differential adaptation, which depends on prior experiences and dispositions, can serve to explain the institutional drift of this core institution.

The two following chapters explore the processes of institutionalisation of European careers and professions in less obviously central arenas of the European polity: the transformations of the legal profession around the European Court of Justice (ECJ) in the first three decades of its existence and the more recent emergence of 'European' careers in sub-national administrations.

Antoine Vauchez and Christèle Marchand's analysis of the Euro-litigation field in Chapter 3 shows how the existence of new venues of legal action promoted the creation of a structured space of European litigation specialists. Although incidentally referred to as essential to the emergence of EU domains of regulation through test-cases, litigation or legal consulting, Euro-lawyers have never garnered significant attention among scholars. Based on a data set that includes all 503 lawyers and the 744 cases they have pleaded before the European Court of Justice between 1954 and 1978, this chapter analyses the genesis of this specific European elite and identifies some of the factors that favoured their successful integration in this area of legal practice: early involvement before the European Court, essential to building a professional reputation; geographic proximity to EC institutions; belonging to the higher strata of national legal professions; and active membership in the various transnational learned societies and professional associations.

In the fourth chapter, Marine de Lassalle retraces the processes of the emergence of 'European' careers at the sub-national level. The vast body of literature on multi-level governance developed over the last ten years has provided a more complex vision of the process of Europeanisation by opening new avenues on what was previously thought of as an essentially 'top down' phenomenon. However, despite this vast body of research, there has been little grounded empirical research on the local and regional transformations of administrations and forms of career specialisation in European affairs. Using France as an empirical example, the chapter shows that while the administration of regional funds and the conception of projects financed by the EU has engendered a 'market' and career opportunities for specialists of Europe at the local and regional level, the impetus of this movement is to be found not only in the 'pull' factors of EU policy, but also in the dynamics of competition between the state and sub-national actors on one hand, and between rival sub-national administrations on the other. This dynamic of emulation and competition has nonetheless produced a highly segmented market. Contrary to assumptions of 'vertical' integration and career fluidity theorised by the multi-level approach, the case at hand demonstrates that career corridors remain segmented and rarely imply moving 'up' and 'down' the chain of institutions.

The social construction of European 'problems'

The second section will examine the co-construction of specific policy fields and *Europeanised* definitions of policy problems requiring some form of *European* intervention. The extension of European policy competencies has carved out new spaces of action and opportunities for interest groups and national and sub-national political and administrative actors by providing new venues and by promoting a change in the scale and contents of problem definition and resolution. This phenomenon has simultaneously created new policy spaces and stimulated the transformation of interest organisation and articulation. These questions have spurred on a vast body of research, much of which has gravitated around the concepts of multi-level governance and Europeanisation. While both concepts have been productive in addressing the emerging forms of policy interaction and regulation, they have also created a sort of methodological exceptionalism by implicitly assuming that dynamics within the European polity differ ontologically from policy dynamics in other more stable and bounded policy settings such as nation-states (for a critique see Hassenteufel and Surel, 2000). This section will reconsider questions related to input- and output-related legitimisation of Europe (Scharpf, 1999) and the particular dynamics of depoliticisation and repoliticisation of policy problems (Smith, 2004).

The chapters will therefore closely examine a series of European policy fields (maritime transportation, property rights, food labelling and the dynamics of interwoven European jurisprudence) and seek to specify the possible contribution of political sociology frameworks to more established cognitive approaches in European studies such as agenda-setting, frame analysis or constructivist approaches to particular policy fields (for an overview, see Campana, Henry and Rowell, 2007). However, contrary to these perspectives which remain largely based on discourse analysis, the theoretical and empirical innovation proposed by the different chapters will meld discourse analysis with a sociological analysis of group mobilisation within policy-making forums.

If the consensual and often technical style of decision-making in the EU has most often been explained by voting rules and norms of appropriateness cemented through time, Laurent Scheeck's chapter on the relationships between the European Court of Justice and the European Court of Human Rights (Chapter 5) draws attention to the importance of taking into account both the institutional configurations in specific fields and the sociological dynamics of interaction to understand the sociological underpinnings of the interwoven and mutually supporting jurisprudence of the two courts. Scheeck explores how lawyers and judges established a transnational epistemic community which transformed fundamental rights into a vehicle for integration and a tool to create leverage in interactions with national and private actors seeking to contest the supremacy of the European courts. This increasingly nested linkage gave rise to new forms of supranational judicial diplomacy that went beyond traditional understandings of adjudication and that has had a deep impact on policy-making. This evolving relationship, marked by dialectics of competition and cooperation, became the essential vehicle for a mutual empowerment of supranational jurisprudence and therefore a significant vector of legitimacy for European institutions.

The remaining three chapters of the second part will focus more specifically on particular policy problems and closely examine the strategies adopted by specialised actors (European, governmental and interest groups), the institutional filters inhibiting or favouring the 'take up' of specific problem definitions, and the reformulation which takes place within European policy forums and arenas. Each chapter will seek to not only identify specific opportunity structures and constraints leading to the construction of particular problem definitions and proposed policy solutions, but will demonstrate how Europeanisation can be seen as a way to gain tactical advantages in other spaces of political action.

This prism of analysis is particularly well developed in Chapter 6, with Hélène Michel's study of the strategic Europeanisation of homeowners' associations. Interest groups are widely recognised as central actors of European governance and decision-making. However, the example of homeowners' associations demonstrates that the presence of interest groups at the European level doesn't simply depend on 'pull' factors created by new venues for action. The case demonstrates that the reason for action at the European level can also be found in national configurations. It is the competition with other national interest groups to gain access to the central state that initially drew the French interest group examined to Europe in the hopes of obtaining a strategic advantage. A national interest group 'went European' despite the fact that housing issues did not fall within the explicit competencies of the

EU. The drafting of the Charter of Fundamental Rights in 2000 and 2001 represented an opportunity to act at the European level because it enabled a redefinition of their interest (defence of property owners) into an wider interest that fitted with the framing of the Charter (defence of property rights). In seizing this opportunity it was necessary to 'denationalise' the cause through universal legal repertoires and the forging of a coalition affirming property rights against groups mobilised in the defence of a 'right to housing'. The sociological constructivism adopted in this chapter consists in analysing interest group action as the result of strategic action whose form is largely determined by the political and administrative space of interaction, but also the resources of its representatives. Europe constructs interest groups, or rather reconfigures resources, legitimate forms of action and group identities. This interpenetration of national and supranational logics contributes to the definition of institutional norms in Europe, while at the same time it transforms practice and identity in national spaces of policy formulation.

In Chapter 7, Andy Smith closely analyses the link between problem definitions, the institutionalisation of policy tools and legitimisation by studying Protected Geographical Indications (PGIs) in the food industry. Political impetus came from southern European countries and well-organised socio-professional groups relayed by regional and local elites. The European recognition of pre-existing national PGIs and the examination of new applications required the creation of a cognitive link between a geographical perimeter, the history of a product and the specifics of its production. Simultaneously framed as an issue of 'intellectual property', 'rural development' and 'agricultural development', by mobilised actors with often divergent interests, PGIs succeeded in obtaining a status of exception to the overarching competition imperative of the EU. However, the diversity in national implementation, tortuous initial negotiations, and mediatised legal appeals have sent conflicting political signals undermining their ultimate legitimacy. By analysing the shifting configurations of actors (the Commission, national governments, socio-economic groups) and the conflicting logics of the different arenas where institutionalisation took place, Andy Smith convincingly shows how contradictory frames and the recourse to technical criteria to depoliticise a potentially conflictual issue have resulted in the construction of a policy instrument with little legitimacy.

In the final chapter of the second part, Willy Beauvallet retraces the process leading to the rejection of the two port services directives in 2003 and 2006. Based on interviews, observation and discourse analysis, Beauvallet reconstructs the conditions leading to a rare, but significant, process of overt politicisation of European decision-making in which interactions between MEPs, the Commission, Eurogroups, labour unions and the media resulted in a political stand-off. Contrary to the usual pattern of decision-making, the case demonstrates how a process of politicisation of European problems can occur via transactions between MEPs and mobilised external actors such as trade unions. Recontextualising political oppositions within the framework of shifting alliances between strategic actors, the chapter shows how competition between left of centre Eurogroups and their connection with trade unions generated a political dynamic which shifted the dominant framing of the issue from a question of competition and economic liberalisation to a question of security. The chapter demonstrates forcefully how political conflicts can transform the position of actors in the internal games of the European institutions and how socialisation to European norms can provide marginalised actors with new resources and the expertise necessary to challenge dominant policy frames.

Taken as a whole, the second section provides four important insights. The first is that the careful mapping out of the diversity of the sociological and institutional configurations crystallised around particular policy fields and issues demonstrates the limits of over-generalised metatheories on the 'nature' of the European polity. As such, the four chapters demonstrate both the force of cooperative and mutually binding forms of interaction among close-knit epistemic communities and the more conflictual dynamics in other fields which are more open to group mobilisation and competition in defining legitimate policy frames. The second insight points to the close attention that needs to be paid to the sociological and institutional properties of significant actors in understanding shifting alliances and their differential ability to convert resources into action to further their interests. Third, the examples of protected geographical indications, trade union mobilisation and the Europeanisation of homeowner interest groups demonstrate the need to take into account national power configurations to understand that Europeanisation is often a means to further, at least initially, largely 'national' aims in a strategy of resource accumulation. Finally, the contributions of Willy Beauvallet and Hélène Michel point to the need to unravel the general concept of socialisation and the logics of appropriateness. Indeed, both show that if the ability to influence decisions depends on the ability to adjust to legitimate forms of argumentation, through adapted language and the mobilisation of accepted forms of knowledge (legal language and categories, economic arguments, security, etc.), the process of socialisation does not necessarily entail sharing common policy frames or causal stories.

Constructing reality through policy instruments
The partial transfer of sovereignty to European institutions has implied the creation of specific instruments to generate comparable knowledge for policy-making and to implement policy in a context of pooled and fragmented sovereignty. Much work has been done on the politics of regulation (Majone, 1996) and more generally on the question of fitting policy tools to political objectives (Hood, 1986; Peters and Van Nispen, 1998). Since the end of the 1990s and the introduction of benchmarking and the subsequent insti-

tutionalisation of the open method of coordination, a great deal of attention has been paid to the procedures, efficacy and underlying logics of these new policy tools (Arrowsmith, Sisson and Marginson, 2004). The emphasis in this section will not be put on the choice of instruments and political goals to be attained in an intentionalist perspective. It will rather be to understand specific instruments as both the result of institutional interactions and constraints and as a vehicle, or materialised support, for ideas and cognitive categories (Thévenot, 1985). Instruments will here be analysed as a 'missing link' between discourse-based constructivism and neo-institutionalism as they institutionalise and translate ideas into categories and numbers recognisable for decision-makers, thereby shaping problem definitions in a particular way and constraining the scope of choices to their resolution (Campana, Rowell and Henry, 2007).

Contrary to much of the literature on instruments centred on fitting means and ends, which portrays policy instruments as political neutral vehicles for policy delivery at the disposal of rational decision-makers, neither the choice of the instrument, nor the representations, categories or political and social hypotheses underlying them can be considered to be politically neutral (Lascoumes and Le Galès, 2004, 2007). Instruments are here considered to be a bone of contention and a bridge between 'soft' and 'hard' norms structuring interactions. As such, instruments can be seen as a way to empirically specify and amend theoretical claims made by social constructivists who have insisted on socialisation, group pressure and influence, but who have paid little attention to the ways in which ideas are institutionalised and become natural prerequisites of action through their reiteration and inscription in a variety of materialised texts, statistical categories and indicators, rules, regulations, benchmarks, etc. The approach developed here will link together a grounded sociological analysis of actors who manipulate a variety of instruments (cognitive instruments used to construct 'objective' representations of social problems, policy implementation instruments, instruments of evaluation and comparison, etc.) and the way in which their use frames policy problems. Cognitive categories inscribed in instruments are constraining by predefining the way in which problems are perceived, thereby excluding a series of possible alternatives, and can facilitate or hinder specific types of translation into delivery tools, procedures and discourse. At the same time, the process of inscription and 'extraction' of information throughout the multiple arenas also introduces opportunities for policy entrepreneurs.

More specifically, the four chapters gathered together in the last part will address two essential questions. In their respective chapters on the 'acclimatisation' of benchmarking to Europe and the construction and subsequent uses of the Eurobarometer in the Communications policy of the EU, Isabelle Bruno and Philippe Aldrin analyse the process of institutionalising new cognitive instruments through a double process of importation and integration of available instruments by specific groups of actors confronted with new policy problems (structuring the Lisbon strategy on competition; finding solutions to the 'democratic deficit'). Beyond the ideological and discursive construction of the competition imperative analysed by Isabelle Bruno in Chapter 9, the managerial technology of benchmarking can be analysed as a tool seeking to produce an 'indefinite discipline', to use Foucault's expression, directed towards politically defined objectives in policy areas where sovereignty has not been pooled and intergovernmental coordination represents the main institutional challenge. It lays the foundation for building a 'competitive Europe' which somewhat paradoxically creates union through competition. The second central question consists in studying the capacity of these instruments to construct, through reiteration and the power of numbers (Desrosières, 1993), collective beliefs as to the reality or the pertinence of performance indicators used in benchmarking procedures or the invention of a European public opinion (rather than the sum of national opinions) through the homogenising effects of the Eurobarometer. Philippe Aldrin, in Chapter 10, demonstrates how the Eurobarometer was progressively transformed from a 'pet project' cobbled together at the margins of the Commission into a central instrument in legitimising Community policies and more globally, the project of political unification of Europe confronted with recurrent criticisms on its 'democratic deficit'.

Romuald Normand and Jay Rowell pursue a similar line of enquiry around the use of statistical indicators to anchor and institutionalise shared problem definitions in fields of action that have progressively emerged over the last decade in European politics: lifelong learning and policies directed towards the social and economic integration of people with handicaps. 'Trust in numbers' (Porter, 1995) and their integration into discourse, policy frames and causal stories depends not only on their formal characteristics, but above all on the authority and institutional positions of those who use them as a basis for creating shared meanings in these two relatively open fields of public action.

In Chapter 11, Romuald Normand shows how the European harmonisation of education and training policies progressed unevenly, with failures and successes, but also with its compromises between states following different cycles of negotiation. But what is often overlooked by observers is that these procedures have been accompanied by often irreversible measurement instruments designed by international expert networks. It is this very articulation between instruments of measurement, European government, and international expertise networks that has formed the material fabric of an increasingly dense set of norms and institutions surrounding lifelong learning analysed by Romuald Normand.

Jay Rowell's chapter (Chapter 12) on the emergence of a European disability policy starts with an overview of national diversity embedded in history, thereby creating a challenge to promoters of a European policy which could neither identify nor 'upload' an available national model nor easily find common ground to define the problem, its magnitude and the adequate policy tools. Following the development of the European employment strategy and the Lisbon strategy, disability was tied into the more general goal of increasing activity rates and became linked to the overarching policy recommendations seeking to increase inflow into the workforce through active labour market policies. Numbers played an important role in identifying the problem at the national level, however, and the inability to produce uncontested indicators and evidence-based causal links at the European level caused disability to 'fall' into a space between the employment strategy and social inclusion. Both chapters demonstrate the importance of expert knowledge as a prerequisite for generating trust in numbers in a polity where 'evidence-based policy' has become a categorical imperative.

We have structured the chapters of this book around three logics of mutually reinforcing processes of institutionalisation of careers and policy fields, policy problems and policy instruments which construct the very fabric of Europe and help to explain its capacity to weather successive storms. European professions and careers are both the product of socialisation and a driving force of institutionalisation processes in which actors with specific 'European resources' forge, in their daily interactions, professional and political norms corresponding to their distinctive identities and resources. Structured European policy sectors have forged common definitions of policy problems and, in doing so, have contributed to legitimising Europe as the proper scale of action and most appropriate level of regulation in many policy areas. If the strategies of many actors and organisations are often driven by national or sub-national logics of action, the existence of European venues creates new opportunities, resources and configurations which subsequently irrigate a wide variety of social and political arenas with new norms and practices. Finally, instruments which are often reduced in the scientific literature to a question of utilitarian adjustments of means to ends, are both a construct of interactions and play an important role in institutionalising specific European scales of action, problem definitions and policy objectives.

Notes

1 A large part of the research, and preparatory workshops, for this book was financed by a research contract with the French ministry of research on the Europeanisation of public problems coordinated by Jay Rowell at the Centre for European Political Sociology (GSPE) in Strasburg.
2 This aspect of socialisation theory focused on the stabilisation of expectations and anticipations follows the initial insights of Berger and Luckmann for whom 'institutionalisation is applied by groups of individuals to maintain cognitive order' (Berger and Luckmann, 1966: 110–111).

3   This book builds on perspectives developed in a precedent volume which sought to examine the pertinence of applying sociological research methods and concepts normally applied to studying national politics to the European polity in order to span the gap between irreconcilable theoretical propositions structuring the field of European Studies (Campana, Henry and Rowell, 2007).

4   Such exercises are more often than not attempts to stake out theoretical ground and the proliferation of speculative theoretical propositions, which has led to a multiplication of hyphenated theoretical propositions, sometimes resulting in surprising combinations which often look good on paper, but have yet to prove their ability to solve empirical problems and generate new insights based on fieldwork. Rather than add to this cottage industry, the origins of this book emerged out of common questions faced by empirically orientated researchers looking for more satisfactory tools of interpretation than are available in much of the standard literature in European Studies.

Bibliography

Arrowsmith, J., Sisson, K. and Marginson P., 'What can "Benchmarking" Offer the Open Method of Co-ordination?', *Journal of European Public Policy*, 11 (2), 2004, 311–328.

Aspinwall, M. and Schneider, G., 'Same Menu, Separate Tables: the Institutionalist Turn in Political Science and the Study of the European Integration', *European Journal of Political Research*, 38, 2000, 1–36.

Bachrach, P. and Baratz, M., 'Two Faces of Power', *The American Political Science Review*, 56 (4), 1962, 947–952.

Berger, P. and Luckmann, T., *The Social Construction of Reality. A Treatise in the Sociology of Knowledge*, Garden City: Doubleday, 1966.

Bourdieu, P., *Practical Reason. On the Theory of Practice*, Cambridge: Polity Press, 1998.

Campana, A., Henry, E. and Rowell, J., (eds), *La construction des problèmes publics en Europe. L'état des savoirs*, Strasburg: Presses Universitaires de Strasburg, 2007.

Checkel, J., 'Social Construction and Integration', *Journal of European Public Policy*, 6 (4), 1999, 554–560.

Checkel, J., 'International Institutions and Socialization in Europe. *Introduction and Framework*', International Organization, 59 (4), 2005, 801–826.

Checkel, J. and Moravcsik, A., 'A Constructivist Research Program in EU Studies?', Forum debate, *European Union Politics*, II, 2001, 219–249.

Christiansen, T., Jorgensen, K. and Wiener A., *The Social Construction of Europe*, London: Sage, 2001.

Cini, M. and Bourne, A., *European Union Studies*, Basingstoke: Palgrave, 2006.

Cini, M. and McGowan, L., *Competition Policy in the European Union*, London: Macmillan, 1998.

Desrosières, A., *La politique des grands nombres: histoire de la raison statistique*, Paris: Éditions la découverte, 1993.

Diez, T., *Die EU Lesen: Diskursive Knotenpunkte in der britischen Europadebatte*, Opladen: Leske & Budrich, 2001

Fligstein, N., *Euroclash: The EU, European Identity and the Future of Europe*, Oxford: Oxford University Press, 2008.

Georgakakis D., 'The Historical and Political Sociology of the EU: What's New in France?', European Consortium of Political Research Workshop, Rennes: 2008.

Georgakakis, D. (ed.), *Les métiers de l'Europe politique. Acteurs et professionnalisations de l'Union européenne*, Strasburg: Presses Universitaires de Strasburg, 2002.

Giddens, A., *The Constitution of Society: Outline of the Theory of Structuration*, Cambridge: Polity Press, 1984.

Guiraudon, V., 'The Constitution of a European Immigration Policy Domain: A Political Sociology Approach', *Journal of European Public Policy*, 10 (2), 2003, 263–282.

Hacking, I., *The Social Construction of What?*, Cambridge: Harvard University Press, 2000.

Hassenteufel, P. and Surel, Y., 'Des politiques publiques comme les autres? Construction de l'objet et outils d'analyse des politiques européennes', *Politique Européenne*, 1, 2000, 9–24.

Hay, C. and Rosamond, B., 'Globalization, European Integration and the Discursive Construction of Economic Imperatives', *Journal of European Public Policy*, IX, 2002, 147–167.

Hood, C., The Tools of Government, Chatham: Chatham House, 1986.

Hooghe, L., *The European Commission and the Integration of Europe: Images of Governance*, Cambridge: Cambridge University Press, 2001.

Journal of European Public Policy, special issue on '*The Social Construction of Europe*', 6 (4), 1999.

Jupille, J., Caporaso, A. and Checkel J., 'Integrating Institutions: Rationalism, Constructivism, and the Study of the European Union', *Comparative Political Studies*, XXXVI, 2003, 7–41.

Kallestrup, M., 'Europeanisation as a Discourse: Domestic Policy Legitimization through the Articulation of a Need for Adaptation', *Public Policy and Administration*, XVII, 2002, 110–124.

Kauppi, N., *Democracy, Social Resources and Political Power in the European Union*, Manchester: Manchester University Press, 2005.

Lascoumes, P. and Le Galès P. (eds), *Gouverner par les instruments*, Paris: Presses de Sciences Po, 2004.

Lascoumes P. and Le Galès P., 'Understanding Public Policy Through its Instruments', *Governance*, 1, 2007, 1–21.

Majone, G., *La Communauté européenne: un état régulateur*, Paris: Montchrestien, 1996.

March, J. and Olsen, J., *Rediscovering Institutions: The Organizational Basis of Politics*, London and New York: Free Press, 1989.

Marcussen, M., *The Social Construction of Economic and Monetary Union*, Aalborg: Aalborg University Press, 2000.

Moravscik, A., *The Choice for Europe: Social Purpose and State Power from Messina to Maastricht*, Ithica: Cornell Univeristy Press, 1998.

Parsons, C., *A Certain Idea of Europe*, Ithaca: Cornell University Press, 2003.

Peters, G. and Van Nispen F., (eds), *Public Policy Instruments*, Cheltenham: Edward Elgar, 1998.

Petersen, J. and Bomberg, E., *Decision-Making in the European Union*, Basingstoke: Macmillan, 1999.

Peterson, J., 'The Choice for EU Theorists: Establishing a Common Framework for Analysis', *European Journal of Political Research*, 39, 2001, 289–318.

Pierson, P., 'The Path to European Integration: A Historical Institutionalist Analysis', *Comparative Political Studies*, XXIX, 1996, 123–163.

Porter, T.M., *Trust in Numbers. The pursuit of Objectivity in Science and Public Life*, Princeton: Princeton University Press, 1995.

Richardson, J. (ed.), *European Union: Power and Policy-Making*, London: Routledge, 2001.

Rumford C., *The European Union: A Political Sociology*, Malden, MA: Blackwell Publishers, 2002.

Scharpf, F., *Governing in Europe. Effective and Democratic?*, Oxford: Oxford University Press, 1999.

Schmidt, V. and Radaelli, C. (eds), *Policy Change and Discourse in Europe*, London: Routledge, 2004.

Smith, A., *Le gouvernement de l'Union Européenne. Une sociologie politique*, Paris: LGDJ, 2004.

Stone, D., 'Causal Stories and the Formation of Policy Agendas', *Political Science Quarterly*, 104 (2), 1988, 281–300.

Thévenot, L., 'Les investissements de forme', *Cahiers du centre d'études de l'emploi*, 29, 1985, 21–72.

Trondal, J., 'Beyond the EU Membership–Non-Membership Dichotomy? Supranational Identities among National EU Decision-makers', *Journal of European Public Policy*, IX, 2002, 468–487.

Vauchez, A., 'The Force of a Weak Field: Law and Lawyers in the Government of the European Union', *International Political Sociology*, 2 (2), 2008, 128–144.

White, J., 'Theory Guiding Practice: the Neofunctionalists and the Hallstein EEC Commission', *Journal of European Integration History*, 9 (1), 2003, 111–131.

PART I

The construction of European fields

Didier Georgakakis and Marine de Lassalle[*]

1

Making top civil servants: Europeanness as an identity and a resource

The theory of European integration was for a long time centred on elites. For Haas and Lindberg (Haas, 1958, 1964; Lindberg, 1963), bureaucratic elites constitute a key vector in the transfer of loyalties towards an emerging political centre. This general perspective explains for the most part why the literature on European officials has focused on their loyalty, deemed either 'national' or 'supranational'. While European officials have constituted an object of research for many years, authors have nevertheless drawn very different conclusions. For some, European officials remain very largely marked by national loyalties (Scheinman and Feld, 1972; Michelman, 1978). More recent research has pointed out that there is an ongoing process of integration (Trondal, 2004). Building on these various approaches centred largely on 'preferences', Lisbeth Hooghe developed a third path by refusing to choose between the socialisation to supranational institutions, which she considered to be rather superficial, and national allegiance. She focused instead on political preferences to explain the wide diversity of positions in relation to supranationalism (Hooghe, 1999, 2000).

The goal of this chapter is not to evaluate the pertinence of these diverging conclusions, but hopefully to shift the perspective and recast the question in another way. Our starting point is that choosing between national loyalty and European socialisation of officials is a vain endeavour if the historical processes of institutional construction are not taken into account. Indeed, what is at stake here, or at least in the institutional spaces populated by the most permanent agents, is a process of autonomisation operating under forms comparable to those of the autonomisation of other social fields (Bourdieu, 1996).

*Translated by Jean-Yves Bart

This perspective presents several advantages. The first is that it aims to open a black box by questioning the process of integration (or Europeanisation) of European elites. Though the creation of European positions and careers is certainly one of the most tangible expressions of the institutionalisation of the EU, it remains to be seen in what way these positions are 'European' and in what way high civil servants and the positions they hold are 'Europeanising' themselves. Work on permanent representatives, working group negotiators or senior officials of the Commission has demonstrated that agents holding posts closely linked to states were led to adopt completely different attitudes derived from the interplay between, on the one hand, their role representing their country of origin and, on the other, the set of interdependencies in the complex policy forums in which they interact (Hooghe, 1999; Trondal, 2004). In the absence of statistical studies, we however know very little about the structural dimensions of careers or socio-professional structures over time. Can we actually speak of a Europeanisation of political and administrative careers? If so, what does it consist in and what are the possible indicators? Is it a continuous process or a more punctuated and uncertain process? How do institutional positions, nationalities and the insertion in particular political sectors interact with this process?

Secondly, the framework proposed here allows for the integration of many diverging points of view existing in research on elite preferences and loyalties by embedding them in the complex structural realities which can explain the plurality of loyalties and preferences identified in other research traditions. We can understand the diverging conclusions by taking into consideration the historical period examined, methodology and the populations on which conclusions were reached. Our framework shows that there are identifiable dynamics of autonomisation which create interdependencies specific to the European political and administrative field. These dynamics are twofold. Top-ranking officials construct the institution in the same process that the institution constructs them. More than accumulating a practical experience of these institutions, they accumulate specific resources (experience in Commissioners' cabinets, institutional longevity, a more or less pronounced degree of sectoral transversality) as they collectively construct forms of credit that are linked to these resources (distance from national authorities, incarnation of Community interest, transversal vision, etc.). The unequal distribution of these resources and of this specific form of credit constitutes a major cleavage, both in terms of the institutional positions they are liable to attain and in terms of world visions and public interventions (Georgakakis and de Lassalle, 2007). On the other hand, this process is ongoing and limited in so far as nation-states represent a political form that is still strongly present in mental blueprints and that remains central for players in the process of EU decision-making. Thus, if states are no longer the single determining variable of the agents' career, they continue to weigh on representations and anticipations. National origins also affect career possibilities, i.e. the posts they can attain or the credit they have at their disposal in investing certain positions. By adopting such an analysis, we hope to leave behind issues of preferences and types of loyalties, which carry the risks of tautological explanations, and replace them in the framework of larger structural dependencies.

Getting a handle on these processes requires breaking with the empirical methods most often used, i.e. interviews or value or attitude surveys. While it has indisputable shortcomings, the prosopographical method (Charle, 2001) which we will use enables us to avoid certain pitfalls (the explanation of ideas by ideology, the passive recording of legitimisation discourses produced by officials, the bias of analysis linked to the multicultural and linguistic dimension) to shed light on the structure of careers and their historical evolution.[1] On the basis of our biographical database, we will analyse the paths of Europeanisation of these high-ranking officials and the variations and inflections of this process.[2]

The Directors-General's careers: between national and European dependencies

One might be surprised that a study aiming at explaining the Europeanisation of careers focuses on officials who are already reputed to be the most European. This would ignore the fact that the 'Europeanisation' of the Commission's Directors-General cannot be taken for granted from a sociopolitical point of view. The rare literature on very high-ranking European administrators shows that the attitudes of Directors-General are very heterogeneous and many do not reflect the Commission's presumed supranationalism (Page, 1997; Hooghe, 1999). Doubt can also arise when analysing the political features of the position. Located at the peak of the administrative pyramid, the post of Director-General is kept under tight national watch and has long been considered a target for national officials who are 'pitchforked' (Spence, 1997). These very particular features make the Directors-General and their deputies a privileged observation point from which to understand the logics of demarcation from national administrative paths and also to identify indicators of a Europeanisation of careers.

A double position
The Directors-General illustrate the fact that European construction goes hand-in-hand with the construction of particular positions. However, this particularity does not mean that the agents who hold these positions automatically give up ties with their country of origin. Their position is twofold: on the one hand, their remit requires that they remain interdependent from national allegiances; on the other hand, the structure of their careers remains

heavily influenced by their nationality and links to their state of origin.

Situated at the top of the administrative hierarchy, Directors-General hold the highest rank in the European Civil Service: A1 in the former nomenclature, A 15/16 following the Kinnock reform of 2004. Their mission is so central in the Commission's activity that it has been subjected to ever-greater codification, as the recent administrative reform of the Commission shows. In principle, Directors-General have to 'supervise' the activity of the Directorate-General (DG): legislative proposals or communications, implementation of European policies or programmes, assessment of policies. They are also the main 'transmission belt' between the Commissioners and the civil service: 'the *main tasks* of a Director-General are to train, inform and supervise their personnel in order to see to it that the political intentions of the Commission are carried out'.[3] Since the reform was implemented, their political and managerial responsibility has been reinforced and is now coupled with the legal responsibility for the nature and the funding of decisions.

Such responsibilities turn the Directors-General into 'managers' or 'supermanagers' – as it is said today inside the Commission. Directors-General have direct authority over the whole DG, beginning with the Directors and the Heads of Unit. The Directors-General are assisted in this task by a mini-cabinet composed of one assistant and counsellors and seconded by their deputies. This position in the hierarchy gives them great leverage on decision-making. It implies that they manage a number of political practices, such as (often delicate) relations with their Commissioner's cabinet, the distribution of positions of responsibility within the DG, the defence of the interests of their DG in cross-sectional negociations, and their ability to defend proposals of their DG outside the Commission, particularly before permanent representatives of member states. They can also set in motion profound reforms of the DGs. Therefore, it is often the case that Directors-General with great longevity (sometimes more than a decade in the same position) have contributed on a long-term basis to structuring the working habits or the 'administrative culture' of a DG, as has been demonstrated in the case of Agriculture, Development and Competition (Abelès, Bellier and Mac Donald, 1993; Cini, 1996a).

These features of the position make the Directors-General see themselves as members of an elite 'club'. This perception is a product of the homogeneity of their activity and their weekly meetings. It is also based on the relative convergence of their sociological and professional characteristics. During the first years of European construction, most Directors-General and deputy Directors-General were senior officials in their country of origin before coming to Brussels. Less than 5% of them had previous experience that did not pass through one civil service or the other. Even though they came from different countries, they shared traits which set them apart from their counterparts who remained in national administrations. For example, German

Directors-General were usually younger than their national counterparts. The British Directors-General, at least for the first generations, were less often 'fast-streamers' than their national counterparts, and more predisposed to transversal careers (Eymeri, 2001). The age and gender conditions of the Directors-General and their deputies who converged in the Commission were also quite similar (for further details, see Georgakakis and de Lassalle, 2004).

These converging properties must not hide the fact that differences between Directors-General do exist. Within this group, one can identify a series of cleavages or, at least, gradations that lead to varying authority within the Commission. Still, these gradations depend less on the presumed administrative culture inherited from their countries of origin than on the structure of the European political and administrative game. If each DG encompasses one policy sector, their relative importance creates a specific European hierarchy. This is typically the case with regard to differences in sectoral autonomy and competences, when high community competence sectors (Competition, Agriculture) are compared to lower-competence sectors (Social Affairs, Enterprise, etc.). It is also the case in the personnel sector: the Admin (personnel and administration) and Relex (external relations) DGs are respectively composed of 2,000 and 1,700 officials, whereas the JHA (Justice and Home Affairs) and DEV (development) Directorates-General respectively comprise 170 and 250 agents.[4] From this point of view, the influence of Directors-General is connected to their sectoral autonomy, or in other words, to their ability to implement policies that are specific to the EU. Adjustments in the scope of action can alter the pre-existing order, but here again, such changes most often operate in relation to changes in the European polity (enlargements, changes in the Commission's agenda, etc.). It is also the case that longevity in a position determines the 'European credit' their peers and partners accord Directors-General.

Assuming that these different elements support the hypothesis that the exercise of the function is above all the product of European constraints and interdependencies, the status of the post of Director-General and its consequences for the selection of post holders need to be questioned. Despite recent codification, the position of Director-General is still understood as a highly political assignment. Recruitment is a controlled process involving three institutional actors: the College, the Secretariat-General and national governments through their Permanent Representations. Their relative influence has changed over time. The authority of Emile Noël, Secretary-General from 1960 to 1985, has given way to more direct negotiations between the College and the Permanent Representations. The most recent Commissions have sought to make appointments in a highly 'managerialised' process.

Vacancies are published and candidates are evaluated by DG Admin on their 'management skills'. An Advisory Committee interviews the candidates and gives its opinion to a Commissioner who will make the final decision.[5]

Informally, however, the political skills required appear obvious to insiders as the result of the procedure is often known beforehand.[6] Although it maintains a strong collegial dimension, the Commission is thought of as a government (without being called so). This has strengthened the authority of Commissioners in the appointment of 'their' Director-General.

The political status of the position is consequently reflected in the two ambiguous dimensions of the adjective 'political' in Brussels. First, Directors-General are above all holders of political resources. These resources can be associated with political commitments, participation in networks or clubs, experience in cabinets of Ministers, especially those who later became Commissioners, etc. But above all – and this is often the primary meaning of the adjective 'political' in European circles – their country of origin is highly relevant. For many years, nationality represented a condition or a limit to the accession to particular positions. The logics of national representativeness remain an essential unwritten rule in appointments, resulting in a rough proportionality of nationalities. The most numerous are German and the fewest (leaving aside the 12 newest member states) are Finnish, Swedish and Austrian (see Table 1.1).

Table 1.1   Directors-General by nationality (1958–2005)

Nationality	Total	DG	Deputy DG
German	47	30	17
Italian	45	29	16
French	43	24	19
British	39	22	17
Dutch	21	12	9
Belgian	16	8	8
Spanish	16	10	6
Danish	9	5	4
Irish	7	5	2
Luxembourg	6	3	3
Portuguese	5	4	1
Greek	5	4	1
Swedish	4	2	2
Austrian	4	2	2
Finnish	4	2	2
Total	271	162	109

Source: GSPE database.

Note: All DGs of the Commission were considered; the positions held were taken into account, not the individuals (i.e. a deputy DG who subsequently became DG was counted in each category).

Nationality has also limited the ability of candidates to choose their sector of activity. As Tables 1.2 and 1.3 show, a non-French Director-General is unlikely to head the Agriculture DG, a Director-General who is not Italian has rarely been appointed to the Economic Affairs DG, and the Director-General for Competition has usually been German, etc. We can say the same about the deputy Directors-General, even if their appointments are related to the management of political balances which remain linked to the appointment of the Directors-General. Therefore, if the post of the Agriculture DG has been 'flagged' French, deputies have been German, British or Italian. The deputy Directors-General of the Economic Affairs DG are German, the Directors-General of the Development DG ('German flag') have usually been French or British, etc.

The results on pages 32 and 33 show that Europeanisation is not necessarily a linear process. In the case at hand, the national ties are definitely present, particularly in relation to conditions of accession to specific positions. Still, contrary to other international organisations, national ties exist here under an identity form rather than an assimilated one: they define career possibilities in a given sector, and play a role in the distribution of the political capital of very high-ranking posts. If you are French or Portuguese, you are likely to be treated differently under the presidency of Delors or Barroso. That remains one of the main characteristics of the Europeanisation process.

· Europeanisation paths

If nationality remains essential to accessing particular positions, Directors-General cannot be seen as completely national agents. The question remains how and in what way their careers at the Commission create 'European' properties or resources. From this point of view, the prosopographic analysis requires the definition of a set of indicators in order to understand what the 'Europeanisation' of careers means.

Before examining these indicators, it must be emphasised that the Europeanisation of careers means that they undergo a *modification in career development patterns*. Joining Europe means *de facto* entering a field in which recognition patterns are, at least in part, linked to the legitimate representations predominating in this circle. The explicit demarcation from member states, putting forward a European 'vocation', help top civil servants adjust their career record to the imperative of defending 'Community interest', which is essential to legitimacy within the Commission. These processes are all the more crucial as the analysis developed here is based on entries in Who's Who, based on the agents' own biographical presentation.[7] These biographical entries record 'objective' career elements as much as identity strategies (Collovald, 1988). Consequently, while analysing 'objective' career patterns,

Table 1.2 Number of years of DG's directorate by nationality

	Relex.	Ecfin.	Dom. Mk.	Comp	Emp.	Agri.	Trans.	Dev.	Admin.	Pres.	Rech.	Telec.	Regio.	Ener.	Budg.
Ger.	32	6	4	37	0	0	0	34	6	7	16	0	0	0	0
Brit.	11	0	10	3	3	0	23	3	7	4	0	14	3	10	
Bel.	5	0	0	0	27	0	0	0	13	0	8	0	0	8	8
Dan.	5	0	0	0	0	0	0	3	2						
Spa.	8	0	0	0	0	6	4	0				1	13	5	7
Fren.	3	0	10	0	6	44	6	0	8	12		10	5	1	26
Gre.	0	0	0	0	0	0	0	0		3	6			7	
Dut.	4	0	4	11	0	0	0	4	2				11		
Ita.	3	42	5	0	0	0	9	1	3	3	14	5	4		5
Luxb.	0	0	17	0	0	0	0	0		9			4		
Total	71	48	50	51	36	50	42	45	41	38	44	30	40	31	46

Source: GSPE database.
Notes: Only nationalities and Directorates-General with significant staff were taken into account.

Table 1.3 Number of years of the DDG's directorate by nationality

	Relex.	Ecfin.	Dom. Mk.	Comp	Emp.	Agri.	Trans.	Dev.	Admin.	Pres.	Rech.	Telec.	Regio.	Ener.	Budg.
Ger.	8	18	15	2	0	42	0	0	0	0	4	0	0	0	0
Brit.	4	0	3	5	7	31	0	25	6	3	0	15	0	0	8
Bel.	17	0	0	0	5	0	0	6	0	2	0	0	0	0	0
Dan.	5	0	0	2	3	1	5	0	0	0	0	0	0	0	0
Spa.	9	0	0	0	0	15	0	0	0	0	0	0	16	0	0
Fren.	21	6	0	20	0	6	0	19	1	0	1	0	0	4	5
Gre.	0	0	0	0	0	0	3	6	0	0	0	0	0	0	0
Dut.	18	0	13	0	0	10	3	0	0	0	0	15	0	0	7
Ita.	13	0	12	10	0	34	0	0	13	0	0	5	0	2	0
Luxb.	0	0	0	0	0	0	0	0	0	0	0	0	4	0	0

Source: GSPE database.
Note: Only nationalities and Directorates-General with significant staff were taken into account.

prosopography also brings in the historical transformation of biographical accounts, and the differing emphasis put on European or international credentials: membership of European associations, foreign diplomas, mastery of foreign languages, etc. Beyond the strategic dimensions of self-portrayal, these transformations are an indicator of the transformation of social and political resources required by these positions, and more indirectly, professional habits.

If these transformations are considerable, their empirical saliency is reinforced by the examination of a more structural process underlying the definition of *specific European careers*. These careers can be observed by mobilising the indicators of European longevity and experience. Among Directors-General, we can thus distinguish three groups. The first group includes agents (28%) whose whole career unfolded within European institutions. Conversely, the second group comprises those (30%) whose entire previous career was in national civil services before being directly appointed Director-General or Deputy Director-General. Finally, the third group pools agents with 'mixed' careers. Among the latter, we can distinguish between those who have more extensive professional experience in national administrations (47%) or Community institutions (53%). If there is an overall balance between the relative weight of European or national professional careers, the balance has shifted towards an increasingly preponderant European pattern over time.

For those who come directly from the states, professional reputations are built within their national administration or as European negotiators. For example, some participated in accession negotiations and/or represented their states before European institutions or in Permanent Representations, and/or held posts linked to the European institutions in their national civil service. For those whose career within the Commission is the longest, paths vary depending on whether agents had a sectoral or a more transversal career. In the first case, sectoral mobility is low and we find agents who demonstrated at the national level specialised skills which were later put to use at the European level. For example, Peter Pooley, born in 1936, graduate from Cambridge and civil servant at the UK Ministry of Agriculture from 1958 to 1978, participated in the first accession negotiations between 1961 and 1963. He then became a member of the Permanent Representation from 1979 to 1982, before being appointed Deputy Director-General of the Agriculture DG in 1982. This type of career is very frequent, particularly in the 'monosectoral' DGs which tend to import specialised officials from member states (Economic Affairs, Agriculture, Transport and Energy, among others). In the second case, we are confronted with more varied careers that include experience in Commissioners' cabinets (see below).[8]

The Europeanisation of political networks and resources is another dimension of the Europeanisation of careers. Accession to a post is often linked to national political resources, such as membership of a ministerial cabinet at the national level. It is not rare to see a former minister bring close colleagues with him when named Commissioner. But ressources dependent on links to European institutions predominate. For example, past member-ship of a Commissioner's cabinet has become an increasingly important resource. In the 1960s, 11% of the Directors-General and Deputy Directors-General were previously members of a Commission cabinet. This number rose to 17% in the 1970s, 21% in the 1980s, 30% in the 1990s and 45% at the beginning of the 2000s. In other words, working in a cabinet has become, if not quite a prerequisite, an increasingly sought-after form of professional experience.

Conversely, we can observe a process of 'euphemisation' or dilution of national political resources. The Directors-General with multisectoral profiles are a good example. It is common to begin a career as a cabinet member of a Commissioner of the same nationality, and then work in cabinets of Commissioners from other countries. Having been a member of a cabinet of a President of the Commission is also an excellent way to accumu-late institutional credit distinct from national resources.

This Europeanisation of political resources can also be identified in political or partisan activism. The information provided by the *Who's Who*s is not sufficient to fully grasp the importance of these forms of political engage-ment or their effects. Only a few Directors-General and Deputy Directors-General mention their links to a political movement, and then mainly refer to 'youth' organisations. These discreet statements of political affiliation are quite surprising considering the importance of political networks in the senior civil service. In countries like Germany, where there is no equivalent to the French *énarque* networks (graduates of the *Ecole Nationale d'Administration* – ENA), political affiliations are the cornerstones of structuring policy networks (Derlien, 1997). At first glance, this omission in the *Who's Who*s can be explained in part by euphemisation strategies of political affiliations that are the norm within senior national civil services. At the same time, there is also a more specific European dimension to this question linked to the structural weakness of the European party federations. As party ties remain largely national (SPD, CDU, Labour, etc.), making political affiliations public simultaneously nationalises their profile. As a result, explicit mentions of ties to European associations are more numerous, such as membership of the *European Movement.*[9]

Finally, the Europeanisation of the very high-ranking administrative personnel goes hand-in-hand with *processes of selection of agents already 'Europeanised' or who have a strong international profile.* Several indicators show this. The biographical indicators available in the database do not or hardly ever allow us precisely to know the social origins of the Directors-General. Among the 200 Directors-General and Deputy Directors-General, few have bi-national origins or parental paths marked by formative experi-ences abroad (sons of ambassadors, diplomats, private executives abroad, and even political refugees, etc.).[10] The selection processes of a more Europeanised personnel generally take other forms, especially through diplomas from foreign universities, which have become increasingly important. Academic and professional training testifies to an internationalisation of careers as much as a 'Europeanisation' *stricto sensu*. Thus, degrees obtained in the United States are among the most numerous (fifteen Directors-General and Deputy Directors-General). In Europe, several cities and universities predominate: Paris (foreign ENA, Sorbonne), London, Strasburg and Bruges (College of Europe). The possession of foreign diplomas is moreover very variable according to national origins and confirms national differences in elite training structures. More than half of the Greek Directors-General mention a degree course abroad. The British are well represented in the United States. The German case is interesting as they divide their studies between France and the USA. Sectional cleavages also appear as some sectors (Relex or Economic Affairs DGs, for example) have a much higher percentage of agents with foreign academic resources.

A differentiated process of Europeanisation

If we have demonstrated the general trend of Europeanised careers, this trend is far from a linear or homogeneous process across time and space. Indeed, the Europeanisation processes take different paths according to time, nationalities and policy sectors.

Variations in time

What did the Directors-General and their deputies do ten years before their appointment? This simple question is a good way to gauge the underlying influence of the national political and administrative ressources in comparison to the accumulation of European resources. It particularly allows us to identify clear cleavages between those who held national positions and those who were previously working in Community institutions.

   Using this indicator, the trend follows the same pattern as shown previously and indicates the increasing weight of careers in European institutions, but contrary to the idea of a linear trend, the data show a U-shaped curve: in the 1970s, the Directors-General came more clearly from European careers than in the 1980s, but the trend reversed again in the 1990s. For example, in 1971, three Directors-General out of the thirteen whose careers were known were in national administrations ten years earlier. Significantly, none was directly appointed to the post of Director-General from a national administration. R. Toulemon was Commissioner R. Marjolin's head of cabinet (Commission's VP) before being Director-General at DG External Relations, and Director-General of Industrial Affairs from 1968. H. Sigrist, a German diplomat, was Deputy Secretary-General of the Commission between 1965 and 1967 before becoming Director-General of External Relations in 1968. Other Directors-General either worked in institutions other than the Commission (F. Spaak, J. Cros or E. Albrecht for example), or were promoted internally after being head of unit or director (J. Van Gronsveld, P. Rho, J.-R. Rabier, L. Lambert, H.-B. Krohn, W. Schlieder), and finally one agent was member of a Commissioner's cabinet (E. Albrecht). These internal recruitments confirmed the orientations of Emile Noël concerning the importance of recruiting Directors-General with an 'in-house' culture.

In the 1980s, we can observe a clear shift. This change allows us in a certain way to assess the consequences of the first enlargement (UK, Ireland and Denmark). The consequence of the UK joining Europe, as it has been identified by top civil servants, is not only the sudden presence of British nationals, but a more global modification in the career paths to the position of Director-General. The data confirm a 'renationalisation' of the profiles that goes beyond the mere presence of the new personnel, who, by definition, did not have previous experience in Community institutions. Six Directors-General out of sixteen whose career trajectories we have been able to reconstruct, held posts in the national civil service ten years earlier and were mostly directly appointed Directors-General from national administrations. They are: R. Denman and E. Gallagher, diplomats holding positions in various British ministries and who became respectively Directors-General of External Relations in 1977 and Fisheries in 1978; O.B. Henriksen, a Danish official of the Ministry of Economy appointed to the Credit and Investment DG in 1977; P. Fasella, an Italian scholar appointed to the Research DG at the beginning of the 1980s; T. Padoa-Schioppa, who came directly from the Bank of Italy to become Director-General of Economic Affairs and C. Villain who went from the French economy and finance sector to the Agriculture DG.

During the 1990s, the trend progressively reverses. 13 Directors-General out of the 21 whose careers are known held a post in the European Civil Service ten years earlier, whereas only three held a post in a national civil service, and a fourth was a permanent representative. The remaining four had a more atypical career path with two Directors-General coming from the political sphere, one from the international civil service, and one from the private sector.

This trend was amplified in the following decade. Out of 22 Directors-General, 19 were members of the European Civil Service ten years earlier. At the same time we can identify the constitution of typical careers, in the sense that the circulation of personnel from one position to another becomes more stable and predictable. Four were already Directors-General ten years earlier (against only two who were in place for more than ten years a decade earlier). Directors-General increasingly move from one post to another, which reveals internal promotion channels, generally from sectoral channels to more functionally diverse DGs or to more 'powerful' DGs. For example E. Cioffi went from the Credit and Investment DG to the External Relations DG,

R. Coleman from the Transport to the Health and Consumer Protection DG, Guy Legras from Agriculture to the External Relations DG.[11]

Variable Europeanisation paths according to nationalities

If experience in community institutions has become an increasingly essential resource, paths of Europeanisation vary according to nationalities. It is not here a question of awarding 'good European' certificates or stigmatising those who were 'pitchforked' (Georgakakis and de Lassalle, 2004). On the other hand, we must integrate national career opportunities in assessing the structure of anticipation of the relative opportunities offered by European or national administrations. While many German, Belgian, Luxembourg or even French careers are predominantly European, in the case of British and Spanish officials, the move to Europe comes later and is considered rather as a 'secondary' career.

Table 1.4   Average types of career according to types of employer and nationality (in %)

	1	2	3	1+2+3	4	5	1+2+3+4+5	6	7	6+7	8	9	+9
German (n=39)	3	31	2	36	0.5	0.5	38	0	61	61	0	2	2
Austrian (n=3)	2	75	4	80	0	0	81	0	12	12	0	8	8
Belgian (n=15)	6	30	2	38	2	0	40	0	58	58	0	3	3
British (n=37)	13	49	0.5	62	4	0	66	0	33	33	1	01	1
Danish (n=7)	5	35	0	40	12	0	51	0	43.5	44	2	4	5.5
Spanish (n=15)	13	49	2	64	9.5	0	74	0	21.5	22	01	5	5
Finnish (n=3)	7	82	0	88	0	0	88	0	3.9	4	0	8	8
French (n=34)	2	25	0	28	0.5	2	30	0	68	68	1	1	2
Greek (n=4)	21	42	2.5	65	4	0	69	0	21	21	11	0	11
Irish (n=6)	14	37	0	50	0	0	51	0	47	47	3	0	3
Italian (n=40)	12	28	0	40	3.5	2	45	0	51	51	0.5	3.5	4
Luxembourg (n=4)	12	5	4	21	9.5	5	35.	17	47.5	65	0	0	0
Dutch (n= 18)	9	42	6	56	0	0	56.	0	41	41	3	1	3.5
Portuguese (n= 4)	10	21	4	35	0	0	35	0	50	50	5	15	15
Swedish (n= 3)	26	66	7	98	0	0	98	0	2.5	2.5	0	0	0
All (n= 230)	8	36	2	46	3	1	50	05	47	47	1	2	3

Source: GSPE database.

Key: 1: National private sector; 2: National public sector; 3: National political mandate; 4: Permanent Representations; 5: General Secretariat of the Council of Ministers; 6: MEP mandate; 7: European Commission; 8: International private sector, 9: International organisations.

Note: On the basis of 230 DG and DDG of whose prior career we have knowledge. On average, Germans have spent 2.9% of their career in the private sector before becoming DG or DDG; the results of some nationalities should be considered with caution due to a small number of cases.

A quick count shows that of the German-, the French- and the Luxembourg-appointed Directors-General and Deputy Directors-General, 61%, 68% and 65% had pursued their entire career or most of it in Community institutions. Taking the German case as an example, in the 1960s a majority were direct appointments, mainly from the diplomatic services. In the 1970s, more than two-thirds of the Germans appointed had pursued their entire career, or most of it, in Community institutions. In the 1980s and 1990s, only two Directors-General out of 20 German appointments were direct appointments, and after 2000 no more direct appointments were made. Thus, since the end of the 1970s, no German has more 'national' than 'European' experience. If one uses another indicator, one can see that the Germans and Belgians are the only top civil servants to practise clear 'denationalisation' strategies. If one takes the sub-population of the Directors-General and Deputies who have experience in a Commissioner's cabinet, only Germans and Belgians were numerous in cabinets of Commissioners of another nationality. Not surprisingly, the Commissioners most open to denationalising their cabinets are themselves predominantly from Belgium, Germany or Luxembourg.

In contrast, British and Spanish agents in our sample spent most of their career in national sectors. If these differences tend to polarise personnel coming from the original member states and the newer member states, there are nonetheless important differences among the Directors-General and their deputies originating from newer member states. If the Danes in the sample pursued a large part of their career in national civil service, half of them nonetheless had European experience before their appointment, while at the same time, far fewer British or Spanish had experienced previous socialisation to Europe. If many of them did participate in the accession negotiations or their Permanent Representation, this experience remains nonetheless marked by the national framework.

This group of nationals 'Europeanised' itself more slowly and later than others. Out of the 12 British-appointed Directors-General or Deputy DGs in the 1970s, only one had prior experience within a European institution: R. Appleyard first pursued an international career as a biologist in the United States and Canada and joined the UN before spending ten years as Euratom's director and being appointed Director-General of Information and Innovation in 1980. This pattern continued in the 1980s, even if 'Europeanisation' processes were at work. If half of the Directors-General or their deputies were directly appointed from a national civil service, they had worked more often than their predecessors in the British Permanent Representation. During the 1990s, there were no more 'direct appointments' of Directors-General through a Permanent Representation even if some Deputy DGs followed this path. Out of the ten Directors-General and their deputies appointed, eight had experience within Community institutions,[12] and half of those had spent a majority of their careers in Europe.[13] Spanish nationals have followed a relatively similar scenario.[14]

Variable Europeanisation paths according to the sectors

The Europeanisation process appears finally differentiated by sectors. DGs whose management is Europeanised, headed by Directors-General with experience in several sectors of the Commission as well as in cabinets, are structurally in conflict with the DGs whose management is more state-related and specialised. The most typical of the first group are the Competition DG and the Personnel DG, but other sectors can correspond to this type (Internal Market, Development, Press and Information, Telecommunications, Regional Policy, and all the most recent DGs). In this case the Directors-General and the Deputy Directors-General spent all their career or parts of it in Community institutions, but they circulated between sectors and alternated with positions in Commissioners' cabinets. For the other DGs with more specialised and more state-related managements, such as DGs of Industrial Affairs, Social Affairs, Agriculture, Transport, Environment, and Energy, the profiles are less 'Europeanised'. The most typical cases of these polarities will not be explored here (on this point, see Georgakakis and de Lassalle, 2004), but there has also been a trend of Europeanisation of the Directors-General's profiles in sectors reputed to be the most technical and 'national', even if the pace and depth follow differentiated patterns.

The way the Europeanisation of careers spreads, from the most political sectors to the most technical ones, is well reflected in the transformations experienced by the Transport and Energy DG. This DG stands out by a recruitment that has been both very national and specialised since its creation. Italian Railway Officials and British Senior civil servants who specialised in maritime, rail or air traffic issues occupied top positions in the early decades. They were followed by an Italian scholar specialised in the transportation economy who was Deputy Director-General before becoming Director-General until the end of the 1980s. The managers' prerogatives then changed, as the careers of the three last Directors-General or Deputy DGs appointed show. R. Coleman practised law in London at the beginning of his career. He then joined the Industrial Affairs DG as an administrator in 1971, became head of unit in 1983 and Director in 1988 before being appointed Director-General of the Transport DG in 1990, a post he held until 2000, when he was appointed Director-General of the Health and Consumer Protection DG. The case of R. Lamoureux is similar. After beginning his career as a scholar, he joined the Secretariat-General as an administrator in 1978 where he remained until 1980, before moving to the Commission's Legal Service from 1981–83. He then became an adviser (1985–88) and later deputy head (1989–92) in the cabinet of J. Delors. He was appointed Director of the Community Legal Service and then Director-General of DG Industry, where he remained from 1994–95. In 1996, he became Deputy Director-General at the External Relations DG, before being appointed Director-General of the Transport and Energy DG in 2000. Finally, the career of F. Esteban Alonso, a Spaniard born in 1947, is in itself a symbol of the sector's transformation. As an academic specialised in the transportation economy, he was initially an administrator at the European Conference of Ministers of Transport at the OECD in Paris from 1968 to 1981. He then became President of the Spanish regional railways, and later Director-General of the shipping enterprise Navinoe and of a state-owned agricultural enterprise, before joining the Commission as the Eurostat Director in 1989. He was then appointed Director at the Personnel DG before becoming Deputy Director-General of the Energy and Transport DG in 2001.

These three careers reflect several evolutions that can be spotted in the careers in other 'technical' DGs, suggesting a simultaneous process of Europeanisation and desectorisation. Europeanisation because it seems more and more difficult to appoint to these posts agents that are directly imported from the national administration; desectoralisation because careers seem structured around increasing mobility, even for representatives of the less 'Europeanised' nationalities. Therefore, whereas in a first period British civil servants were directly imported into highly specialised positions in Community institutions, the current British Directors-General have careers that are marked both by a longer stay in Community institutions and a greater cross-sectoral mobility. These two dimensions now exist in all sectors of the Commission where, in other words, they now structure professional norms in the political and administrative arena of the Commission.

This process of autonomisation is determined by characteristics specific to each DG, which should not be over-generalised or interpreted as a total and linear homogenisation of the properties of the Directors-General. Nonetheless, the neutralisation effects of the most salient properties of what has been described as a specific 'DG culture' (Abélès, Bellier and MacDonald, 1993) are at work. This relative homogenisation is for example reflected by career evolutions within the Employment and Social Affairs DG.

The Employment DG stands out insofar as its administrative leaders – at least in the first decades of the EC – did not seek to hide their political leanings. In a profession where law and economy are dominant, they had generally studied social sciences (J.D. Neirinck, first Director-General from 1963 to 1967 has a PhD in social sciences, R. Rifflet, second Director-General studied History and teaches at the Sociological Institute). They published articles or essays which specialised in the social policy area, or even social Europe (J. Neirinck published for example, *The Rome Treaty Social Policy and EEC Applied Labour Economics* in 1969 and *Social Policy of the EEC* in 1970, at a time when the 'social Europe' theme was not yet politically mobilised. F. Vinck wrote about the *Limites de l'action sociale de la Haute Autorité de la CECA* and R. Rifflet published several articles in the journal *Cahiers de Sociologie*). Finally, they were more 'politicised' in that they displayed their political leanings (Neirinck is a trade unionist, Rifflet is President of the European International Left and published in '*Socialisme*', etc.). In 1973 the British appointed W. Shanks to the Directorate-General of the Employment

DG. He was a former correspondent of the conservative *Financial Times,* and had spent several years in the private sector.

From the end of the 1970s, the 'Europeanisation' effect became visible at the top of the Employment DG with the appointment of J. Degimbe. He was a head of cabinet at the European Coal and Steel Community (ECSC) from 1958 to 1966 and an adviser in the cabinet of R. Barre and then of F.-X. Ortoli from 1967 to 1976, before becoming Director-General of the Employment DG (until 1992). This logic was extended by the subsequent appointments of H.C. Jones and, most of all, of O. Quintin,[15] who held extensive experience within the Directorate-General. The recent appointment of Karl-Johan Lonnröth, a Swede of Finnish origin, as Deputy Director-General also reflects this Europeanisation effect and the neutralisation of the most specific properties of the former leaders: Lonnröth has an ENA diploma (for foreign students) and had experience as an international expert as director of employment at the International Labour Organisation (ILO) before his appointment). He nonetheless incarnated the 'social' logic of the DG, as he holds a social sciences degree and is a specialist in employment, having worked for a long time at the Swedish Ministry of Labour.

Finally, the example of the Economic Affairs DG allows us to show that acculturation within Community institutions and desectoralisation are not the only possible paths of 'Europeanisation'. The DG remains specific and atypical insofar as the study of the DG's leaders' careers shows that they come from the economic sector of the state, that is to say their country's Department of Finance, but also and above all from national banks or international organisations (IMF, OECD, UN). Therefore another form of 'Europeanisation' is particularly 'internationalised' and in this sector, very close to the patterns of the elites of international banking analysed by F. Lebaron (2000: 208–211).

Several cases illustrate the point. The case of U. Mosca, Director-General from 1967 to 1979 is a good example. He was a diplomat who alternated posts in embassies and in the Ministry of Foreign Affairs before being directly appointed Director-General, which reflected typical patterns of the time. Thereafter, the specificity of the DG stands out. T. Padoa-Schioppa, an Italian, born in 1940, graduated in economics from the University Bocconi in Milan and obtained a Masters in economics at MIT. After experience in the private sector in a German firm (1966–68), he joined the research department of the Bank of Italy. He became Head of the Monetary Market Department of the bank in 1975 but left in 1980 to become Director-General of what was then DG2 (from 1980–85), before becoming Deputy Director-General until 1997. After a term as President of the Italian Stock Exchange Committee he returned to Community institutions as a member of the Executive Board of the European Central Bank (ECB) to the end of his career. H. Matthes, a German-appointed Deputy Director-General in 1983, began his career between positions in the national banking sector (he was Chief Executive at the Bundesbank for more than ten years) and the OECD. M. Russo, an Italian, was appointed Director-General just after obtaining a Masters degree from Yale. He had previously held positions at the OECD and the IMF over a period of nearly 15 years. A. Costa was the UN Secretariat-General's economic adviser for more than 10 years before becoming Deputy Secretary-General at the OECD and then Director-General of DG2.

Conclusion

In conclusion, we hope the research on which we have reported here has improved our understanding of the Europeanisation of careers. If this process emerged progressively and unevenly over time and space, it has nonetheless constructed quite solid structures and norms. In particular, what we could call a European institutional capital is defined less and less by the ability to transform national resources within 'flag-bearing DGs' and more by the accumulation of specifically European resources (in-house careers, cabinet positions, the control of internal political resources, etc.). We may need to specify and perhaps balance more precisely all the conditions (often very heterogeneous) that lead to the structuring of this process in both its common and differentiated trends. As our various cases show, the appointment logics simultaneously result from differentiated national and sectoral European habits, political opportunities offered by the power distribution within national political and administrative elites, enlargement circumstances, the power of national capitals in determining personnel decisions, and sectoral trajectories. All in all, the power distribution mechanisms between DGs, and therefore within European institutions, appear to progressively dominate and marginalise other competing logics, producing an increasingly autonomous field structured by its own polarities and criteria. From this point of view, the prosopographical analysis of European agents produces results which are similar to the historical analysis of state-building in Europe between the seventeenth and nineteenth centuries. It leads us to speculate, beyond what necessarily differentiates these trajectories, whether there is a more or less universal pattern, at least in Europe, for the building and structuring of political institutions (Descimon, Schaub and Vincent, 1997).

Notes

1   This study on the Directors-General and Deputy Directors-General of the European Commission is part of a research programme developed since 2001 by the Centre for European Political Sociology (GSPE, CNRS–University of Strasburg) on European elites. The database includes Commissioners, Directors-General, Deputy Directors-General and the General Secretariat of the European Commission, as well as the main

positions in the European Parliament (Presidents, Vice-Presidents, Quaestors, Presidents of committees and groups). This database now constitutes more than 600 entries including 'bio-social' data (age, gender, place of birth, nationality, marital status, etc.), information on careers (positions successively held), diplomas and universities of training, engagements in political or European associations, publications and awards. We currently have 198 biographies on Directors-General.

2   This chapter builds on an *EU consent working paper* 'Who are the DG? Trajectories and Careers of the Directors-general of the Commission'. Both authors are grateful to Andrea Birdsall, Jay Rowell and Jean-Yves Bart for their comments and assistance.

3   www.europa.eu.int/comm/reform/2002/selection/chapter1_fr.html (accessed November 2004; emphasis in original).

4   Report DG Admin, October 2002.

5   www.europa.eu.int/comm/reform/2002/selection/chapter1_fr.html (accessed November 2004).

6   The 'Renouveau et Démocratie' Commission staff trade union, which opposed the Kinnock reforms, sometimes reveals the name of the chosen candidate before the end of the procedure to expose the lack of transparency (Georgakakis, 2002).

7   Such as: *The European Companion*, Ed DPR (from 1991 to 1994) or more recently *Eurosources, Ed Dod's* and *le Trombinoscope* since 1999.

8   On the political status of cabinets at the Commission, see Joanna and Smith (2002).

9   This is the case for French DG's Riflet and Toulemon or Dutch DGs, such as Wissels and Van Rijhn.

10 Some exceptions are: Christopher Audland, son of a British brigadier born in Germany, Eneko Landaburu Llaramendi, a Spaniard born in Paris, and Daniel Strasser, a Belgian also born in Paris.

11 The enlargement to 27 countries is obviously going to transform this evolution.

12 The two exceptions are: J.F. Mogg, an official of Trade and Industry who held positions in the Permanent Representation before becoming successively Deputy Director-General and Director-General of Internal Market and Industrial Affairs and then Director-General of the Industrial Market DG in 1993. D. Roberts, official at the Ministry of Agriculture since the 1970s, joined the British Permanent Representation in 1988 and became Deputy Director-General of the Agriculture DG in 1991.

13 This is the case for Coleman, Jones, Richardson and Lowe.

14 Four direct nominations were made in the 1980s. In the 1990s we found nominations of agents who had pursued the major part of their career (2/7) or a considerable part of it (4/7) in community institutions. There again, in 1990 and 2000, direct nominations become exceptional.

15 Head of unit in DG Agriculture in 1971, she moved to DG External Relations in 1974 where she remained until 1981 before becoming head of unit in DG5 (Social Policy; 1982-93); her career accelerated thereafter as she became Director from 1994 to 1999 before being appointed Deputy Director-General in 1999 and Director-General in 2000.

Bibliography

Abéles, M., Bellier, I. and MacDonald, M., *Approche anthropologique de la Commission européenne*, Bruxelles: Commission Européenne, 1993.

Bourdieu, P., *Rules of Art: Genesis and Structure of the Literary Field*, Stanford: Stanford University Press, 1996.

Charle, C., 'Prosopography (Collective Biography)', *International Encyclopedia of the Social and Behavioral Sciences*, 18, Oxford: Elsevier, 2001, 12236–12241.

Cini, M., 'La Commission européenne: lieu d'émergence de cultures administratives. L'exemple de la DG IV et de la DG XI', *Revue française de science politique*, 46 (3), 1996a, 457–472.

Cini, M., *The European Commission. Leadership, Organisation and Culture in the EU Administration*, Manchester: Manchester University Press, 1996b.

Collovald, A., 'Identité(s) stratégique(s)', *Actes de la recherche en sciences sociales*, 73, 1988, 29–40.

Derlien, H.-U., 'Historical Legacy and Recent Developments in the German Higher Civil Service', International Review of Administrative Sciences, 63 (4), 1997.

Descimon, R., Schaub, J.-F. and Vincent B., *Les figures de l'administrateur. Institutions, réseaux, pouvoirs en Espagne, en France et au Portugal, 16ème–18ème siècles*, Paris: EHESS, 1997.

Eymeri, J.-M., *Pouvoir politique et haute administration. Une comparaison européenne*, Maastricht: IEAP, 2001.

Georgakakis, D. (ed.), *Les métiers de l'Europe politique. Acteurs et professionalisations de la construction européenne*, Strasburg: Presses Universitaires de Strasburg, 2002.

Georgakakis, D. and de Lassalle, M., 'Les directeurs généraux de la Commission européenne: premiers éléments d'une enquête prosoppographique', *Regards Sociologiques*, 27–28, 2004, 6–69.

Georgakakis, D. and de Lassalle, M., 'Les très hauts fonctionnaires de la Commission européenne: genèse et structure d'un capital institutionnel européen', *Actes de la Recherche en Sciences Sociales*, 166–167, 2007, 39–53.

Haas, E., *Beyond the Nation-State*, Stanford: Stanford University Press, 1958.

Haas, E., 'Technocracy, Pluralism, and the New Europe', in R. Stephen (ed.), *A New Europe?*, Cambridge: Harvard University Press, 1964, 62–88.

Hooghe, L., 'Supranational Activists or Intergovernmental Agents? Explaining the Orientations of Senior Commission officials', *Comparative Political Studies*, 32, (4), 1999, 435–463.

Hooghe, L., 'Euro-socialists or Euro-marketers? EU Top Officials on Capitalism', *Journal of Politics*, 62 (2), 2000, 430–454.

Joanna, J. and Smith A., *Les Commissaires européens. Technocrates, diplomates ou politiques?*, Paris: Presses de Sciences Po, 2002.

Lebaron, F., *La croyance économique, les économistes entre science et politique*, Paris: Seuil, 2000.

Lindberg, L., *The Political Dynamics of European Economic Integration*, Stanford: Stanford University Press, 1963.

Michelmann, H., 'Multinational Staffing and Organisational Functioning in the Commission of the EEC', *International Organisation*, 32 (2), 1978, 477–496.

Page, E.-C., *People Who Run Europe*, Oxford: Clarendon Press, 1997.

Scheinman, L. and Feld, W., 'The European Economic Community and National Civil Servants of The Member States', *International Organization*, 26 (1), 1972, 121–135.

Smith, A. (ed.), *Politics and the European Commission: Actors, Interdependence, Legitimacy*, London: Routledge, ECPR, 2004.

Smith, K., 'The European Economic Community and National Civil Servants of the Member States – A Comment', *International Organization*, 27 (4), 1973, 563–568.

Spence, D., '*Structure, Functions and Procedures in the Commission*', in G. Edwards, and D. Spence (eds), *The European Commission*, 2nd edn, London: Catermill, 1997.

Trondal, J., 'Political Dynamics of the "Parallel Administration" of the European Commission', in Smith, A. (ed.), *Politics and the European Commission: Actors, Interdependence, Legitimacy*, London: Routledge, ECPR, 2004, 67–82.

Trondal, J., 'An Institutional Perspective on Representation. Ambiguous Representation in the European Commission', *Working Papers Eiop*, 2006.

*Michel Mangenot**

2

The invention and transformation of a governmental body: the Council Secretariat

European construction has been, and still is, a testing ground for institutional innovations, as is evidenced by the reform processes of the Maastricht, Amsterdam, Nice or Lisbon treaties or the constitutional treaty project. Research in political science on institutional change has followed a certain institutional division depending on the topics studied. Analysis of the European bureaucracy revolves around the Commission; a formal or legal approach is centred on the European Court of Justice; and a study of the issue of political representation is likely to focus on the Parliament. Falling somewhere between these academic divisions, one institution at the core of the European decision-making process, the Council of the European Union, falls somewhere in between and appears to be a blind spot in European studies. Its permanent body, the General Secretariat, is the subject of this chapter.

The General Secretariat of the Council sheds light on the ambivalent nature of the Council: it is intrinsically an expression of state interests but it is simultaneously a Community institution. Its composition is purely national, but it is nonetheless European. The ambivalence of such an institution, constituting an arena of aggregation of national interests and nonetheless an important locus of Europeanisation, can be explained by the role played by the General Secretariat. Whereas the Council is often presented as simply intergovernmental, and the Secretariat as a traditional international organisation, I would like to show that on the contrary, it has been the place where a shared government culture has developed – in fact more than within the Commission, which is generally thought to embody the European ideal as 'guardian of the Treaties'. Made up of European officials, the Secretariat

* Translated by Jean-Yves Bart.

exercises its role at all levels of the European decision-making process, from the lowest (working groups) to the highest (European Councils), and it is the European Union's main government structure.

The General Secretariat was not mentioned in the Paris (1951) or Rome (1957) treaties and only received legal recognition in the Maastricht Treaty, article 151: 'The Council shall be assisted by a General Secretariat, under the direction of a Secretary-General. The Secretary-General shall be appointed by the Council acting unanimously. The Council shall decide on the organization of the General Secretariat.' The role of the institution has been more widely acknowledged since the Amsterdam Treaty, which made of its publicly anonymous Secretary-General the High Representative for the Common Foreign and Security Policy (CFSP).

The Secretariat, however, was created as early as 1952 – its 55th anniversary was celebrated on September 9, 2007, and it developed after 1958. The Maastricht Treaty only granted official recognition to an old institution. The Council's weak public notoriety is explained by the fact that since it does not have 'institution' status, it remained outside the gaze of jurists who for a long time dominated the study of European institutions. Moreover, the low profile kept by the Secretariat fed the idea of an absence of power, a choice which has become a genuine strategic resource for an organisation claiming to be harmless and devoid of any formal power.

In the context of unceasing transformations of European institutions since 1952, the General Secretariat also represents a rather unique element of continuity. Unlike the Commission, with its more or less direct roots within the ECSC's High Authority, and the Parliament, which was originally a non-elected residual assembly without legislative power, or the Court, which after being marginal in the ECSC, created a space for itself through the sheer force of its jurisprudence, the Council has remained remarkably untouched by these general shifts in the balance of power.

The General Secretariat of the Council is derived from the initial choices of European construction. But in line with historical neo-institutionalist approaches, these choices were for the most part tentative and the result of expediency; they did not emanate from a strategic or planned reflection. In other words, this 'second' European bureaucracy, quite different from the Commission, was a contingent product of bargaining. In this sense, it is fundamental to go back to the earliest stages in order to understand the organisation's path.

Even though the Council Secretariat was at first conceived as a mere representative of the states and as a guardian of their sovereignty, it managed to have its competences recognised by the emerging power – the Presidency of the Council – by taking advantage of the latter's increasing role and frequent rotations. Supported by several member states, the Secretariat, which started by assuming the role of a 'clerk', became an assistant, an adviser and then a mediator. The Secretariat also progressively became the main actor

– entrepreneur – of the Common Foreign and Security Policy, and of the Justice and Home Affairs policies, even before this leadership role became official in 1999 with the appointment of its chief as High Representative for the CFSP.

Since my first study (Mangenot, 2003), the Secretariat has not drawn much attention from intergovernmentalists or neo-functionalists. Despite their deep disagreements, both currents have cast the Council as a 'temple of the states' where diplomatic negotiations prevail, but they ignore the Council for opposite reasons. Intergovernmentalists consider that compromises take place between (and within) member states and favour the analysis of government preferences materialised by votes. Neo-functionalists assume that since the 'supranational entrepreneurs' are either in the Commission or the Court, there is no need to study the Council, despite the intuition of their founding father, Ernst Haas, who early on saw in the ECSC's council elements 'of symbiosis of interministerial and federal procedures' (Haas, 1958: 526). Finding 'supranational entrepreneurs' in the Council would embarrass intergovernmentalists who do not acknowledge their existence, and certainly not in the Council, as much as the neo-functionalists who locate them in the Commission. The story of the blind men and the elephant, used by Donald Puchala in 1972 to describe European studies, still appears relevant today.

This is why historical or sociological neo-institutionalists such as Derek Beach, Jeffrey Lewis and Thomas Christiansen have been more interested in the Secretariat. Derek Beach integrated these approaches into his study on 'the supranational construction of the Council', while Lewis and Christiansen included them within the framework of a broader understanding of IGC actors, treaty reform and institutional rivalries. These studies focus on a set of norms and practices but do not venture into the question of the profiles, careers and practices of the actors who embody the institution. More recently, Thomas Christiansen and Sophie Vanhoonacker have re-placed the institution within its historical path by applying the concept of 'critical juncture' central to historical institutionalism (Christiansen and Vanhoonacker, 2008).

In the first section, I would like to focus on the conditions of creation of the Secretariat and outline the social and political conditions of its institutionalisation. Then, as a counterpoint to Thomas Christiansen and Sophie Vanhoonacker, I will attempt to interpret the recent transformations undergone by the Secretariat. Indeed, if it is clear that since 1999, when the function of High Representative was introduced, and especially after 2000 and the apparition of the Security and Defence Policy (ESDP) structures, the Secretariat has gone through significant transformations and a process of institutional fragmentation, can we claim that the 1999 institutional innovations represented a 'critical juncture' in the history of the Secretariat? This amounts to presenting a rather linear path from 1952 to 1999, which, as we will show, does not correspond to the socio-historical reality of the organisation. The moment of genesis is certainly at the origin of a certain institutional inertia, but it is possible to observe a series of earlier inflexions. In other words, the major transformations of 1999 should be replaced within a longer history, marked by a series of successive adaptations. It is precisely this capacity to adapt and to adjust that explains the success of the Council Secretariat.

I am not so much interested in knowing if there was a change of institutional path (and a new path), or if that has been good or bad for the institution (with the underlying idea of 'putting the Secretariat back on the right path'). I will rather focus in the causes and the conditions of these inflexions. The 1999 shift engaged the organisation in a broad movement of reform and self-reflection, but why was that choice made in 1999? The answer comes from a reasoned use of the 'path dependency' concept – the past evolution of the Secretariat determines the ensuing possibilities for change and choices. Nonetheless, the capacity of institutional adjustment to changing European configurations has led it to maintain its central role in the choices considered by negotiators. We find here this resource that consists in almost imperceptibly occupying the institutional 'centre of gravity' of the Community. If European institutions can be considered as the centre of the European politico-institutional space, the General Secretariat of the Council can then be described as the 'centre of the centre'.

In the perspective of a sociology of institutions (Lacroix and Lagroye, 1992), I aim to observe the progressive construction and adjustment of this European institutional role. It is through the combination of multiple social processes (professionalisation), the succession of contexts and configurations (e.g. the negotiation of treaties), crises and competitions (with the Commission) that the institutionalisation of this European role can be understood. I will show how this organisation progressively took on, in specific configurations, a pivotal role between member states and European Communities, the Commission and the Presidency (of the Council) and then the European Council. The Secretariat is at the heart of a twofold compromise that is deep-rooted in the European decision-making system: compromise between the states themselves, and between the states and the Commission. This is not a linear process: between moments of very strong institutional affirmation, there have been moments of decline, such as between 1973 and 1980, or of differential consolidation, between 1994 and 1999.

Origins of a power of coordination

Let us begin with the birth of this organisation that officially had 'no position to defend', according to a Secretariat member (Vignes, 1969: 80): neither national interests, nor the 'Community interest'. Supported by several states, the institution constructed itself largely through its opposition to the High Authority, and then to the Commission.

The Council is absent in Schuman's declaration of May 9, 1950, which mentioned only the High Authority. Dutch negotiators imposed it during the treaty negotiations. When Jean Monnet expressed reservations, the diplomat Dirk Spierenburg, head of the Dutch delegation, reportedly warned: 'Either the Council of Ministers or the Benelux leaves the negotiating table' (Spierenburg and Poidevin, 1993: 19). It appears in the Paris Treaty of April 18, 1951 under the name of Special Council of Ministers of the ECSC.[1]

This Council of Ministers had its first meeting in Luxembourg on September 8–10, 1952. During this inaugural session, certain states, represented by their Minister of Foreign Affairs and a technical minister, generally of Economy or Industry, wanted to play up the importance of the event. Adenauer even referred to the Council as 'the federative organ of the Community'. On September 9, the Council adopted provisional rules of procedure and created a Secretariat, headed by Christian Calmes, a 39-year-old German-speaking diplomat from Luxembourg, trained as a lawyer, who had caught Adenauer's attention during the negotiations.

Originally appointed for six months, but with his appointment consistently extended, Calmes started the organisation's conflict with the High Authority. There was at the time no definition of the Secretary's responsibilities: procedural rules only mentioned that the 'Secretary manages, under the responsibility of the President and according to his directives, the funds that are placed at its disposal'. Faced with this legal vagueness, Calmes wanted to affirm his independence vis-à-vis the High Authority. By December 1952, a violent conflict had already opposed him to Jean Monnet over the control of the drafting and diffusion of the minutes from the sessions – the Council Secretary wanted ministers to perform the task (Spierenburg and Poidevin, 1993: 75). This initial conflict was fundamental for the positioning of the young Secretary, who remained in place for twenty years, whereas Monnet resigned less than two years later.

As the Secretariat was imposed by certain member states, it was seen to be their representative in Luxembourg, as there were no Permanent Representations there yet. Monnet had indeed opposed the idea of national representations in Luxembourg. The Council did create a non-permanent Commission of Coordination in Luxembourg on February 7, 1953, soon referred to as COCOR, composed of two senior officials from each state in charge of ECSC in their respective capitals. The decision set forth that the Secretary would summon this Commission at the President's initiative.

In 1954, the position of Secretary was replaced by that of Secretary-General at the request of Adenauer in conformity with the dominant administrative terminology. Limited to the role of an administrative organiser of an institution with little power – the image of Calmes duplicating documents himself remained – the Secretariat nevertheless grew to be the permanent representative of an emerging power: the Presidency. Indeed, arguing in favour of the need for continuity in an institution where the presidencies rotated every three months, it became, as of June 1954, the obligatory addressee of any correspondence addressed to the Presidency.[2]

This did not initially represent an important increase in workload. But the Secretariat soon benefited from the opportunity of the post-Messine boost in European construction. Carles was chosen by the national delegations for his role as a mediator to be secretary of the Intergovernmental Conference on the Common Market and Euratom. This recognition marked the second birth of the Secretariat. Calmes subsequently became Secretary-General of the Interim Committee for the Rome treaties and in March 1958, was appointed as head of the General Secretariat shared by the Councils of the three European Communities. The second-generation Secretariat was set up in Brussels, with a section remaining in Luxembourg for ECSC activities until July 1967, when the merger treaty came into force.

This centralisation of the activities of the three Councils in a single service contributed to the indispensable coordination between the three Communities in an otherwise confrontational environment leading up to the difficult merger into a single Commission in 1967. The General Secretariat thus played an essential pre-emptive role in unifying the European Communities.

The Rome treaties in particular led to an increasing diversification of the Secretariat's tasks, notably with the appearance of the Committee of Permanent Representatives (COREPER) in 1958. Far from being a hindrance to the Secretariat, it reinforced its role as organiser by multiplying the number of negotiation arenas. In 1959, for instance, the Secretariat prepared, monitored and recorded more than 400 meetings. Since then it has provided technical and legal assistance to the Council and its subdivisions and the COREPER, as well as numerous working groups. It now handles the entire legal process, from sending the Commission's initial proposal to publication in the Official Journal.

There are striking similarities with the General Secretariat of the French government, created in 1935 at the same time as the Presidency of the Council of Ministers (Bonini, 1986). This national historical comparison seems much more heuristic than more frequently used parallels with General Secretariats of international organisations (UN, NATO or OECD). Indeed, in the latter cases, the secretariats cover the entire institution, unlike the Council Secretariat, which is not the secretariat of the Community, but only that of one of its institutions. Importantly, the function of the General Secretariat of the French government as a 'memory' of the institution (Massot, 1979: 33) is analogous to that of the Secretariat of the EU council: monitoring legal procedures, coordinating governmental work, advising and arbitrating, as well as preparing Councils of Ministers.

The description of the French General Secretariat of the Government by one of its former Secretaries-General could easily be applied to the Council Secretariat: 'a light and flexible tool of coordination and continuity, both at the service of the head of government' (here the Presidency) 'and of the entire

government' (here other member states).[3] As with its historical French coun-
terpart, it was also able to take advantage of the absence of legal codification
of its tasks,[4] and the longevity of Secretaries-General is exceptional (5 for the
Council Secretariat; 7 for the General Secretariat of the French Government
since 1946).

Constructing an autonomous administration

Before its role as assistant for the Presidency was recognised in 1980, the
Council Secretariat had developed as a strong administration with 'espirit de
corps', and it did so, quite strangely, without any intervention from member
states. With the expansion of its tasks, the Secretariat, which employed 30
officials in 1953, had 3,000 fifty-five years later. This administration, derived
from a small and provisional organisation with a handful of officials working
with the Secretary, developed impressively, so much so that the Commission
once feared that it would dwarf its own services.

Although the Council itself had originally stated its intention to limit the
Secretariat's staff to the strict minimum (a maximum number of 20 was even
mentioned), the staff doubled in 1954, even though the very small number of
'A' level officials remained stable – around six. The first senior officials
expressed the will 'that the Secretariat constitutes itself as an *avisé* administrative body at the service of the Council'.[5] The same note mentions the need
to recruit senior officials with experience in international negotiations: the
author cites statistics on the structure of the League of Nations' staff. Another
note from a senior official (December 12, 1952) insists that 'it is unacceptable
that the Council Secretariat should be discriminated in comparison to other
Community institutions as far as functions [ranks] go'. The document,
entitled 'Organisation plan, thesis to defend', goes on to say that 'it is
essential' that 'the officials of the Council Secretariat are equal to those of
other institutions. Similarly, it is necessary that in relationships with national
administrations, Secretariat agents are not placed in a state of inferiority.
These two principles are a condition of the Council's very credit.' Another
official who would be one of the first heads of division, F. de Schacht,
recruited on November 11, 1952, focused on the issue of administrative
organisation and proposed a structure in a note dated February 1953.

The first organisation chart of 1954 was based on his proposal with three
divisions: General Affairs, Commercial Affairs, and Economic Issues. In
another note (December 3, 1953), the same Belgian official, reacting to demands
from the High Authority and member states for information on the Secretariat
staff, proposed to increase staff numbers at the rate of four per month.[6]

Unlike the Commission, built in 1958 following a pre-established model
conceived by its first president Walter Hallstein, it seems that senior officials
had a lot of freedom in shaping the Secretariat. 'There were one or two indi-

viduals who were much more important than Calmes, who all told, was a lovely man, but had a bit of a dull personality,' a former senior official recalls (interview, Brussels, February 19, 2002). The Secretariat's form was initially similar to a French mission administration (Pisani, 1956) structured around a precise goal, transversal in its organisation, light, without any management functions, flexible, and built around small clusters.

The structure was fleshed out in 1958, with the creation of the positions of Head of Cabinet for the Secretary-General and Press Officer, as well as the creation of a Legal Service, and five divisions. An A1 official (the highest rank in Community public service) was put in charge of each division, with the title of 'director' (Houben, 1964: 152). The fact that this title, corresponding to the title of Director-General in the Commission, was not used or 'claimed' by the Council can be seen as a sign of a certain institutional 'modesty'. Some were indeed already alarmed about the rapid development of this administration. Far from being recent, as is too often assumed today, the competition with the Commission in fact goes back to the earliest stages of the Secretariat. The European Parliament (before which the Commission is accountable) explicitly expressed the concern that the Secretariat might overtake the Commission's services (Mégret, 1969: 253). Indeed, the staff grew quickly in 1958–59, with the inclusion of the temporary staff recruited during the negotiations for the Rome treaties.

Table 2.1   Development of Secretariat staff (administrative data)

	Council Secretariat total	Rank A (except linguists)
1953	30	5
1954	61	6
1957	69	24
1959	264	68
1962	315	76
1967	520	92
1970	603	94
1975	1475	161
1980	1593	183
1985	1790	188
1990	2183	217
1995	2290	248
1997	2415	285
2001	2560	343
2007	3036	1332[a]

[a] Including translators.

The rapid increase of the Secretariat's tasks – with the multiplication of marathon councils, in particular for Agriculture – then legitimised staff enlargements for COREPER. In 1962, for instance, following a report by the Secretariat's doctor, which reported several serious illnesses as well as several cases of overwork,[7] Calmes used the argument of 'general exhaustion' to ask COREPER for the creation of new positions for 1963. Calmes also spoke of two 'serious alerts on the social front', and he obtained most of the positions he had requested, despite limitations imposed by the French delegation for each category.[8] The conference for negotiating British membership also required 70 additional agents in 1961 and 1962. The working conditions had drastically changed over the space of a few years.

Indeed, unlike in the Commission of EEC or Euratom, where entire sectors had no actual activity because of the lack of development of common policies in their fields, the whole Council Secretariat staff was (overly) used. Apart from legitimising the growth of staff, this overactivity also gave internal cohesion to the organisation. It led to the creation of a Staff Committee, constituted between 1961 and 1964, to represent staff vis-à-vis the Secretary-General and member states.[9]

Progressively, large Directorates-General, independent and hierarchical (like the Commission's), took shape. The Secretariat had progressively abandoned its initial form as a mission administration and was progressively segmented around seven DGs. This shift can be analysed in terms of institutional isomorphism (Powell and Dimaggio, 1991).

If the first enlargement saw the staff again doubling in size, the Secretariat's functioning and size nonetheless remained very different from the Commission's and followed what Jean-Louis Quermonne (1991) called a 'administration d'état major'. The gap between the size of its staff and that of the Commission, which developed according to a ministerial pattern, widened, especially for A-ranked officials.

Table 2.2   'A' rank officials in the Commission and Council Secretariat (administrative data)

	Commission	SG Council
1954	55	6
1957	188	24
1959	903	68
1962	1066	76
1970	1415	94
1975	1554	161
1980	2800	183
1990	3450	187
1997	6593	285
2001	7068	343
2007	11850[a]	1332[a]

[a] Including translators.

Positions of responsibility in the Secretariat were proportionally greater than in the commission. Access to the hierarchy for an A-ranked official was therefore easier in the Secretariat, especially as internal promotion was more frequent than in the Commission where, early on, national pitchforking often occurred. In the 1970s–1980s, several key officials from the Secretariat were promoted to the rank of Director-General. The administration of the Secretariat, through the Staff Committee, succeeded in asserting itself during the 1970s, faced with a 'weak' Secretary-General (Nicolas Hommel). The end of Hommel's term was marked by social conflicts, and Niels Ersboll's arrival by the great strike of 1981. Subsequently, vigilance was applied: indeed, when Greece, Portugal and Spain joined the EU, the Committee managed to ensure that the Council would be the only institution not to adopt derogatory regulations for the recruitment of officials from these countries.

Power based on trust: the 1980–82 inflexion

The Secretariat thus benefited from the progressive increase of the Presidency's weight (also not mentioned in the Rome Treaty) in the decision-making process. The importance of the Secretariat's role consequently depended on the quality of its relationship with the Presidency's team and the Presidency's trust in its expertise. While the French Gaullist Presidency (Edwards and Wallace, 1977: 26) and the British one were initially reluctant, the recourse to the Secretariat became a constant, from the frequent German demands to the osmosis with Luxembourg (O'Nuallain and Hoscheit, 1985), maintained after Nicolas Hommel's departure in 1980. In October 1979, a report from the Committee of Three admitted that 'the Council Secretariat holds resources which all member states could in their interest use more frequently and more thoroughly. Its knowledge of procedures, general overview of the mechanism, and its ability to objectively assess the attitude of other member States are unparalleled, even in the most powerful of national administrations.'

Within this context, the Secretariat saw its function of 'assistance to the Council in general and to the Presidency in particular in carrying out their tasks' officially recognised in September 1980.[10] Originally, the idea proposed by Klaus von Dohnanyi was even to have the Secretary-General be the President of the Council's alter ego, his closest collaborator for Council affairs, who would have been able to represent him in his absence, for instance in contacts with the representatives of third countries. Some states thought this went too far, and the final decision only stated that 'in order to implement the necessary improvements, the function of Secretary-General is of great importance'.

This decision appointed Niels Ersboll for a five-year term (renewable once), and defined the function's mandate for the first time. Ersboll, 54 years old and the first Danish permanent representative to the EEC, had been since 1977 the State Secretary in charge of economic affairs in the Foreign Affairs ministry in Copenhagen, a position that he had created for himself.

It is largely thanks to its increased role in preparing European Councils that the Secretariat was considerably strengthened in the 1980s, developing as an 'administration d'état major'. How did the Secretariat take advantage of the creation of these meetings of Heads of State and governments at the top of the European institutional structure which diminished the Council of Ministers' influence (Taulègne, 1993: 144–157)? How was the Secretariat able to have more power even when the institution for which it worked was weakened? Although an article on the decision-making process within the European Council already raised this point fifteen years ago (Bonvicini and Regelsberger, 1987: 164), it is necessary to closely examine the precise conditions of the conquest of this new role.

The transformation actually dates back to 1982. From the creation of the European Council in 1974, the management of negotiations (i.e. the drafting of conclusions) was in the hands of the permanent representatives, after the idea of an ad hoc Secretariat had been envisioned.[11]

At the end of the November 1981 London Council, whose summary of conclusions, prepared by the Permanent Representatives and described as a 'monster' by Margaret Thatcher, would eventually not be adopted, Ersboll, assisted by his cabinet, began to assist the President of the European Council, whom he had only advised until then. Whereas in the past, the Presidency's initiative would be 'fed' to the Council and then handled by the Permanent Representatives, the Secretary of the Council, with no legal text to follow, entirely directed his activity towards the preparation of a summary of conclusions, imagining and testing the delegations' positions in order to anticipate the result of the final deliberation, in close collaboration with the Presidency and the Commission. This activity was in particular reinforced in the 1984 Fontainebleau Council, during which Ersboll took part in the coordination meetings in Paris.

He was assisted by the same small team for almost fifteen years – his head of cabinet, Poul Skytte Christoffersen, a 'young genius' of Danish diplomacy; Frenchman Max Keller-Noellet, Secretariat official since 1969 in the Agriculture DG, and the British Merrick Bryan-Kinns, who had joined the cabinet in 1975. Avoiding the press above all, he discretely perfected his methods, such as the preliminary determination of instruments and negotiation scenarios, especially decisive during Councils on financial questions. Following the 'shock' of the London Council – the text prepared by the Permanent Representatives being politically useless as such – the Secretariat displaced the Permanent Representatives. During the Councils, the role of the Secretary-General, sitting next to the President, became official: he facilitated compromise, in particular during the meeting of the first evening where the final conclusions were hammered out.

It seems that Ersboll's unusual personality played a key role in establishing this new working method and having it accepted. Whereas Calmes was a diplomat with socialite tendencies – his wife was Lady of Honour to the Grand Duchess of Luxembourg[12] – and Hommel was a 'classic' diplomat and former ambassador, Ersboll was above all a technician of Community affairs.[13] Francophile and with socialist sensibilities, he was soon held in high esteem by Jacques Delors as well as Helmut Kohl. As he represented a 'small' country, he won the sympathy of the Benelux states. Delors and Ersboll – they both left their positions in late 1994 – formed a tandem on the eve of European Council (European Commission, 1999: 243). The title of a tribute book released when he left office is revealing: *L'équilibre européen* (Ludlow, 1995).

This role put the Secretary-General in a new position in relation to the Commission, as there was not only a connection with the General Secretariat (in charge of the relations with the Council), but increasingly direct ties with the Presidency. The Secretariat found itself placed at the vortex of the complex institutional configuration derived from the development of the European Council. Some in the Commission feared that the Secretariat would have too much power in this new configuration, and even thought that it was playing against them, which it however could not really do, due to its relative lack of resources. The 'pragmatic' line of action of the Secretariat worked to its advantage, especially as the Commission remained stuck on unrealisable 'maximalist' positions that it could not back away from. As the Secretariat knew well, ultimate responsibility remains in the hands of the Presidency.

This role in the organisation of European Councils from 1982 onwards, maintained in September 1994 by Ersboll's successor – German diplomat Jürgen Trumpf – and even since then proceduralised, had the effect of strengthening the entire Secretariat and permanently transforming the professional identity of its higher agents. Indeed, the work of these Community officials increasingly consisted in giving political advice and compromise solutions to inferior levels (ministerial meetings, COREPER, groups) moving beyond the mere drafting of reports, even though in that field, as one of the officials noted early on, 'being faithful doesn't mean you can't write skilfully' (Vignes, 1969: 79). Ersboll ended up lifting the 'taboo' of a substantial intervention of the Secretariat.

Politicisation through the management of the pillars (1994–99)

While it was legally recognised, the Secretariat had to find its place after November 1993 at the core of the new institutional architecture of the Union built around three pillars. A journalist summed up the problem in this way:

> The rotating presidency of the Council of Ministers is in charge of the new policies on external relations, security, immigration and justice [...] The

permanent Secretariat of the Council is responsible for carrying out these policies. An organisation of services gathering stenographers and officials who keep their eye on the clock, the Council Secretariat will immediately become the European Union's second executive. (Buchan, 1993: 60)

But if it was entrusted with these two new pillars, it was precisely because of the transformations of its role which we have explored – the journalist chose to retain the image of a merely logistical Secretariat and not take into account these transformations which would have discredited this choice. The General Secretariat also gained this position thanks to the role it played in intergovernmental conferences. Acting in a context of great institutional instability, it became the Secretariat of the IGCs, and its Legal Service became the Legal Service of the negotiations. Moreover, Ersboll's strong role in the drafting of the Maastricht Treaty was criticised in the Commission (Cini, 1996: 87). In these two fields, the Secretariat thus became a real 'actor' of European policy-making (Wallace and Wallace, 2000: 18).

In 1995, the Secretariat moved into the Justus Lipsius, a building which was for the first time owned by the Council, and which gathered together all of its services and hosted all meetings. The Secretariat found itself in the same location where the meetings organised under its auspices took place. The organisation's spatiality seems important as this building, overlooking the Schuman roundabout and the rue de la Loi, redefined Brussels' European geography. The Secretariat was also now located in front of Berlaymont, symbol of the Commission's almightiness since the late 1960s, but which was at the time being treated for asbestos, forcing the Commission to scatter its services. To some extent, this move could be seen as a handover to the Council. Ironically, the Secretariat was originally meant to move into Berlaymont, but because of lack of space, difficult negotiations led to a commitment by the Belgian State to have the Council building erected in front of the rue de la Loi.

The new responsibilities of the Secretariat came at a time when the institution it assisted, the Council, lost its status as the single Community legislator, as the new treaty made the European Parliament a co-legislator in several fields. This institutional innovation of co-decision led to a new confrontation between the Council and the Parliament. The Secretariat, which had monitored parliamentary commissions since 1958, as well as the participation of Council members in the Assembly and the preparation of answers to the written and oral questions of MEPs, was put in charge of organising tighter contacts with the new legislator: it had to follow the various readings in order to inform the Council and advise the Presidency, and if needed, organise conciliation committees. This new task was entrusted to a 'co-decision legislative procedure' created in July 1995. The Council Secretary and senior officials were also entrusted with a new power that increased their politicisation: the right to represent the Council in parliamentary commissions.[14]

The politicisation of the Secretariat was at its strongest in the management of the new pillars. Let us take a look at Justice and Home Affairs, which gives us an opportunity to show the leeway of the Secretariat in the elaboration of a public policy. Before Justice and Home Affairs, originally a mere task-force of the Commission, was transformed into a genuine DG in 1999 with its own commissioner, the Secretariat had already had a DG (DG H) at its disposal since 1994. Unlike the Commission, it was composed of experts on legal cooperation. DG H defended numerous projects of the third pillar, the high point being the preparation of the Tampere European Council in October 1999. The Schengen Secretariat was included at the same time.

If managing the third pillar gave the Secretariat an opportunity to considerably develop its role, the CFSP was the main factor that imperceptibly endowed it with a new political dimension. In 1999, two French diplomats recognised that 'the Council Secretariat has acquired an irreplaceable role' and that 'this evolution has taken place without any modification of the texts and without any consideration from outside observers'. They went on to explain:

> Today, we are far removed from the theological debates on whether it is sensible to recognise the autonomy or to give the right of initiative to the General Secretariat of the Council. Through its increasing importance in the concrete elaboration of the common foreign policy, it has already acquired this right of initiative in practice. (Dumond and Setton, 1999: 42)

There is a process of informal importation in the second pillar of the Community method and an almost mimetic reproduction of the role played by the Commission in the first pillar, which the Commission refuses to play in the second pillar, disapproving of its 'intergovernmental' structure.

Constituted as a pole of expertise of European procedures and then as political adviser of the Presidency, the Secretariat naturally assumed a role as initiator of public policy. This shift happened almost imperceptibly through the power of the pen. The 'adjusted' character of its propositions explains their usefulness to the Presidency. The Secretariat benefited from the incorporation of the former secretariat of the European Political Cooperation (EPC), housed in the same building since 1986 but operating autonomously until then: it was integrated into DG External Relations (DG E) as well as external, economic and political relations. The Secretariat, in order to face these new responsibilities, opened a second office to the United Nations in New York in 1994 (after the office to the GATT in Geneva set up in 1968).

The period of implementation of the Maastricht Treaty until the Amsterdam Treaty was a time of adaptation and transition. Trumpf, who had arrived in 1994, taking over Ersboll's difficult succession, had to deal with the new pillar organisation and the new enlargement. More restrained and less political, focusing on the Secretariat's functioning, he had to manage a new conflict and the awakening of the unions during the integration of the Schengen Secretariat: following a resolution of the general meeting of the staff in April 1999, a strike was declared in May. Like Hommel, the end of his mandate was marked by a climate of internal turmoil.

With the increased leeway in the context of the pillars, these years can be seen as a growth crisis or transition. But this did not prevent the Secretariat from playing an increasing role in IGCs, for example in Amsterdam, so much so that some have referred to the Secretariat as 'an unseen hand' in the negotiations to reform the treaty (Beach, 2004). Trumpf, who in May 1999 inaugurated his function as High Representative, launched, with the March 1999 report cosigned with Jean-Claude Piris, the political reflection on the reform of the Council.[15] The report's proposals appear in the conclusions of the Helsinki European Council in December 1999, which explicitly called for the strengthening of 'the Secretariat's supporting role as adviser to the Council and the Presidency [...] by being continually and closely associated in programming, coordinating and ensuring the coherence of the Council's work'. They also encouraged it 'to play a more active role, under the Presidency's responsibility and guidance, in assisting it in its "good offices" function and searching for compromise solutions.' The term 'adviser' is officially used for the first time, bringing the texts closer to actual practice.

Leadership and diarchy (1999–2008)

In the meantime, the Cologne European Council of June 1999 appointed a new duo at the head of the General Secretariat, implementing the Amsterdam dispositions. On October 18, 1999, the Secretariat seemed to 'win', in particular in its competition with the Commission, in the conquest of the CFSP, with the appointment of its Secretary-General as High Representative; the other solution envisioned consisted in entrusting the Commissioner in charge of external relations with this function. The creation of this new position, proposed by France on June 6, 1996 (Buchet de Neuilly, 2002), reinforced the Council Secretariat. This recognition can be analysed in terms of organisational leadership (Selznick, 1957), the Secretariat being, for the first time, recognised in its own right.

Since then, there has been a renewed sense of competition with the Commission, similar to the 1958–59 years, with external relations often being the cause of disagreements. But the General Secretariat had accumulated much greater authority. While it has become the informal initiator of the CFSP, it is integrated in a logic of representation of the European Union, with the October 1999 appointment of a 'politician' as Secretary-General of the Council and High Representative for the CFSP: Javier Solana, member of the Spanish Socialist Party, MEP and several times minister before becoming Secretary-General of NATO in 1995. The position of Secretary-General was then supplemented with the appointment of a Deputy Secretary-General in charge of the internal management of the Council Secretariat. This position was entrusted to Pierre de Boissieu, Permanent Representative of France in Brussels since 1993, in keeping with the tradition of diplomatic recruitment. De Boisseau, although he had worked in the Commission,[16] had notably been, as French negotiator in Maastricht, one of the inventors of the pillar structure.

What were the effects of this diarchy? The first transformation engaged was a differentiation between the General Secretariat (GS) and the position of High Representative (HR), whose holder also became, on November 25, 1999, Secretary-General of the Western European Union (WEU). The debate on the opportunity to endow the High Representative with its own services quickly ensued. The negotiations on the localisation of the Policy Planning and Early Warning Unit (PPEWU), programmed by a declaration appended to the Amsterdam treaty, were related to this issue. The decision to place the PPEWU directly under the responsibility of the High Representative can be interpreted as the desire to give autonomy to the position. The high point of this process was the attribution of a specific building in 2000 – the Cortenberg. The mode of recruitment of the staff, largely renationalised, turned it into a service that was very different from the culture of the General Secretariat. Indeed, out of 20 'A' level officials working there, fifteen came from member states and only three from the General Secretariat.

A double structure was thereby constituted on foreign policy issues: on the one hand, the Policy Unit, on the other, DG E, perceived as more 'bureaucratic'. The function of coordination coexisted with the function of representation. The activity of the Policy Unit consists in directly assisting the High Representative through policy papers, drafting speeches, ensuring the liaison with Special Envoys attached to Solana and preparing his numerous trips.

Despite this differentiation of the function of the High Representative, elements of unification appeared. The setting up of the Political and Security Committee (PSC) in 2000 brought the Policy Unit closer to DG E, in charge of preparing its work. In January 2001, the constitution within DG E of the new administration of the European Security and Defence Policy (ESDP), made up of specialists in civilian crisis management or force planning, reaffirmed the usefulness of the General Secretariat's institutional structure for the High Representative. The management of the ESDP, with the first military operation in March 2003 in Macedonia, following a police mission in Bosnia, indeed involved considerable logistics for the preparation and the monitoring of operations. The progressive replacement of the detached national diplomats by internal staff or the creation of positions of common directors between the Policy Unit and DG E can also be mentioned.

But these elements remained linked to the DG E and 'loyalty' tensions could still flare up. This happened in April 2001 when the Military Staff was set up, directly attached to the HR (like the Policy Unit). There were sometimes fierce confrontations of professional cultures between the ESDP structure of the DG E and the Military Staff who failed to take into account the framework or the constraints of the treaty in their propositions.

The GS/HR coupling and this new leadership have had strong repercussions on the entire Secretariat, especially in that they 'liberated' the expression of many members (especially in the DG E) and increased mobility. But the diarchy was also a source of confusion. The synergy that had been envisioned, or more precisely the ability of the General Secretariat to combine both functions, did not meet expectations. If the developments of the CFSP and the subsequent ones with the ESDP were probably underestimated during the negotiation of the Amsterdam Treaty, it turned out that the two functions have contradictory goals and logics. Whereas the General Secretariat requires a certain discretion in order to exert its influence, the HR needs media exposure for its activities, and if the HR has to travel, the GS must be present in Brussels. On a more fundamental level, whereas the CFSP is essentially 'declaratory', the rest of the Community's activities are a matter of rules and procedures. The function of High Representative has become more autonomous and the position of Secretary-General was taken up almost naturally by the Deputy Secretary-General, Pierre de Boissieu.

One of the diarchy's effects was to 'externalise' the activity related to the preparation of European Councils out of the cabinet, with the 1999 creation of the Directorate for General Political Questions, entrusted to M. Keller-Noellet and upgraded to the rank of Deputy Director-General in March 2003. This directorate was put in charge of following-up European Council conclusions, of the agenda of COREPER and the General Affairs Council, but also of the coordination and general planning, as well as reflection on specific strategic issues. With this directorate, methods have undergone adjustments and the use of instruments of negotiation such as the 'negotiating box' have been systematised. This was in particular displayed during the Seville European Council,[17] which for the first time allowed the Secretariat itself to preside over certain working groups: once again, a taboo was lifted. Seville concentrated the Council configurations, whose multiplicity constituted a risk for the Secretariat's influence. It also replaced COREPER at the core of the preparation of European Councils: but far from a return to the situation prior to London (1982), it perfected the method invented in the Secretariat and entrusted to the Directorate for General Political Questions.

One of the DSG's key tasks was organisation. While Ersboll had expressed little or no interest in this, de Boissieu made it a priority. On the basis of the 'mandate' given by the Helsinki European Council, this policy took the shape on April 18, 2001 of a long 'programmatic' note to permanent representatives on the process of adaptation of the Secretariat.

Whereas the General Secretariat used to be mainly focused on the inside of the European political system and was only meant for 'customers' such as national delegates and ministers, especially those in charge of the Presidency, these transformations led it to consider completely new issues, such as the management of relations with the general public, with the adoption of a code of good administrative behaviour on June 25, 2001.

One might say that for the first time, the Secretariat became self-reflexive, it acquired the 'care of the self' – to paraphrase Michel Foucault's phrase 'the State's care of the self'. This process of reflexivity took place much earlier in the Commission: a first study was ordered from a consultant as early as November 1958. As it only progressively became aware of its role, the Secretariat paid attention to its organisation, its machinery and the need to reform only much later.

Conclusion

All in all, the progressive development of the Council Secretariat appears to reflect the success of a flexible and non-codified organisation. Benefiting from the support of several member states, taking advantage of the successive opportunities linked to the indetermination of the European process, of a relatively small size – unlike the Commission – which attracted less (hostile) attention, of a remarkable absence of external intervention on its structure, the General Secretariat illustrates the institutionalisation of Europe that has yet to be fully explored. At the heart of the tension between a Commission under the pressure of interest groups, and member states and their 'national interests', this development also shows the necessity for the European political system to have an organ of central coordination at its disposal. If elements of codification have occurred, they are limited by the specific structure of the organisation, which leaves its role as *conseiller du Prince* or a *magistrature d'influence* to the Presidency intact. From this point of view, the more operational character of certain activities (in the ESDP structure for instance) presents the risk of diluting this specific role by transforming it into a classical management administration.

While some recent transformations of the Community's decision-making system hurt its influence – i.e. for instance the Open Method of Coordination put the control of new committees in the hands of the Commission – the Secretariat is now caught in a web of tensions that will determine its future evolution. While its organisation remains heavily influenced by its origins (flexibility, team-work), the adaptation and reform process seems to have favoured a certain 'bureaucratisation' following the pattern of the Commission in the 1970s. A second tension concerns the officialisation of its very real powers within the context of increasing the transparency of the Council's proceedings. As the success of the Secretariat relies to a great extent on its discretion, opening up or having greater media exposure represents a risk of dilution or questioning of its expertise. Finally, the 'parliamentarisa-tion' of the Council (from a diplomatic negotiating table to a set-up close to an assembly in which every delegation wants to 'exist') since the 2004 enlargement will force the Secretariat to come up with new procedural innovations.

Future evolutions will depend on the Lisbon Treaty. Its implementation will have two immediate and important effects on the Secretariat.

A new High Representative for Foreign Affairs and Security Policy was created and the holder is simultaneously Vice-President of the Commission. This new architecture, which had been rejected during negotiations on the Amsterdam Treaty, will profoundly impact the organisation of the Commission. One can make the hypothesis that this institutional change will result in a progressive transfer of responsibility for these policy areas from the Council to the Commission. The compromise on the European External Action Service (comprised of members of the Council, the Commission and member states) will probably not reverse this movement, given the density of the network of Commission delegations compared to the Secretariat's delegations (123 to only 2). Politically responsible before the Parliament, the High Representative will tend to construct his role as that of a member of the Commission. Without competence on trade policy, development or enlargement, the High Representative will likely use his footing in the Commission to overcome his institutional 'schizophrenia', thereby creating conflicts of loyalty with DG RELEX. In any case the diarchy within the Secretariat will disappear, and tensions within the Secretariat, between the traditional 'legislative adviser' function and the 'executive agency' function, will tend to diminish.

With the retreat of foreign and security policy from the Secretariat, the 'normalization' of its activities will bring it to refocus on its 'Community' orientations, including foreign economic relations, development and enlargement. A new General Secretary (Pierre de Boissieu) was named and his function will likely be defined in similar terms to those before 1999. But this 'return to tradition', or more precisely to the situation between 1982 and 1998, is marked by two important differences: the treaty officialises the role of the Secretariat-General in assisting the European Council and above all, the President of the Council will be elected and remain in place over time. This double modification will undoubtedly reinforce the position of the Secretariat and more than counterbalance the 'loss' of High Representative. When the President convenes, presides over, and prepares the European Council (Article 9.B, TEU modified), he or she will necessarily rely on the Secretariat-General as no national administration will be available. How will this relationship, determined until now by the intermittent nature of the function, be transformed with the establishment of routine work relations over a period of years? One could imagine a stronger politicisation of the function, following the model of the European Parliament. In this context the Secretariat may risk losing a part of its political neutrality, so central to its identity.

A second evolution involves the mechanisms of coordination with and within member states. Presently, the system relies on the coherence between the hierarchical chain of command at the national level and the decision-making circuit in Brussels: the President of the European Council acts as head of government and the Presidents of the Council act as his ministers. This distribution of functions is overhauled in two areas: the President of the Council on Foreign Affairs (and its administrative underpinnings) and at the level of the President of the European Council. This discontinuity complicates the mechanisms of national coordination as a Prime Minister will be confronted with a situation in which ministers can chair European Councils whilst being but one of 27 members of the European Council. Although the Ministers of Foreign Affairs are not able to preside over the Council on Foreign Affairs, they will nonetheless continue to chair the General Affairs Council (GAC). This configuration can only be beneficial to the Secretariat-General: the President of the European Council will necessarily need to maintain a direct link to the President of the GAC as this council prepares the work of the European Council. As the close relationship and hierarchical relationship between the President of the Council and his minister will no longer exist, it will be the role of the Secretariat-General to ensure the coordination of the entire process and circulate information between the European Council, the Council of General Affairs and the other sectoral councils. This reinforcement of working relations to the European Council strengthens its hand in dealings with member states presiding over sectoral councils. This configuration will again place the Secretariat-General at the heart of European institutions and decision-making processes.

Notes

1   The original French text read 'Conseil *de* ministres', which seems to reveal a will to differentiate it from the 'Conseil *des* ministres' used for governmental councils, probably to diminish its importance. This terminological distinction is also found in the institutions of Benelux, where the 'Comité *de* ministres' is the supreme organ.
2   Council archives, 'Centralisation du courrier de la présidence du Conseil au secrétariat du Conseil', CM1/1954, no. 240.
3   In the words of a former Secretary-General of the government, Marceau Long (*Institut français des sciences administratives*, 1986, p. 26).
4   The French 1958 Constitution does not mention the General Secretariat of the government.
5   'Note relative à un certain nombre d'arguments qui pourraient être invoqués pour la défense du Projet d'Organisation du Secrétariat', 26 September, 1952, Archives du Conseil, CM1/1952, carton 38.
6   Archives du Conseil, CM1/1952, carton 38.
7   Confidential note from the medical service to Mr Calmes, May 25, 1962, CM2/1962, carton 346.
8   CM2/1962, carton 346.
9   An interim Staff Committee had been elected in Luxembourg in 1955, following a General Meeting.

10 Council Decision of 26 September 1980 appointing the Secretary-General of the Council of the European Communities (80/918/EEC, Euratom, ECSC), *Official Journal of the European Communities*, October 4, 1980.

11 The debate was only settled by the Single Act, which created a new Secretariat solely in charge of the European Cooperation Policy.

12 When he resigned as Secretary-General in 1973, he was appointed as Chamberlain to the Grand Duke, and in 1981 Marshal of the Court.

13 Originally working in economic diplomacy, he worked in 1960 at the Secretariat of the European Free Trade Association (EFTA) in Geneva.

14 Council Rules of Procedure from 1993.

15 The report of the working group presided over by the Secretary-General (the Vice-President being J.-C. Piris, Director-General of the Legal Service), was presented on March 10, 1999 within a context marked by the 'crisis' of the Commission.

16 As head of cabinet of François-Xavier Ortoli, Vice-President of the Commission from 1977 to 1985.

17 'Measures concerning the structure and functioning of the Council', Annex II, Presidency Conclusions, Seville, June 21–22, 2002, p. 23.

Bibliography

Beach, D., 'The Unseen Hand in Treaty Reform Negotiations: The Role and Influence of the Council Secretariat', *Journal of European Public Policy*, 3, 2004, 408–439.

Bonini, F., *Histoire d'une institution coutumière: le secrétariat général du gouvernement de la République française*, PhD thesis, IEP de Paris, 1986.

Bonvicini, G. and Regelsberger, E., 'The Decisionmaking Process in the EC's European Coucil', *International Spectator*, 22 (3), 1987, 152–175.

Buchan, D., *Europe: l'étrange superpuissance*, Rennes: Éditions Apogée, 1993.

Buchet de Neuilly, Y., 'L'irrésistible ascension du Haut représentant pour la PESC. Une solution institutionnelle dans une pluralité d'espaces d'action européens', *Politique européenne*, 8, 2002, 13–31.

Christiansen, T., 'Out of the Shadows: The General Secretariat of the Council of Ministers', *The Journal of Legislative Studies*, 8 (4), 2002, 80–97.

Christiansen, T. and Vanhoonacker, S., 'At a Critical Juncture? Change and Continuity in the Institutional Development of the Council Secretariat', *West European Politics*, 31 (4), 2008, 751–770.

Cini, M., *The European Commission. Leadership, Organisation and Culture in the EU Administration*, Manchester: Manchester University Press, 1996.

Dumond, J.-M. and Setton, P., *La politique étrangère et de sécurité commune (PESC)*, Paris: La Documentation française, 1999.

Edwards, G. and Wallace, H., *The Council of Ministers of the European Community and the President in Office*, London: Federal Trust for Education and Research, 1977.

European Commission, *Quarante ans des traités de Rome 1957–1997*, Bruxelles: Bruylant, 1999.

Haas, E., *The Uniting of Europe: Political, Social and Economic Forces, 1950–1957*, Stanford: Stanford University Press, 1958.

Houben, P.-H.J.M., *Les conseils des ministres des Communautés européennes*, Leyden: A.W. Sythoff, 1964.

Lacroix, B. and Lagroye, J. (eds), *Le Président de la République. Usages et genèses d'une institution*, Paris: Presses de Sciences Po, 1992.

Lewis, J., 'Informal Integration and the Supranational Construction of the Council', *Journal of European Public Policy*, 10 (6), 2003, 996–1019.

Ludlow, P. (ed.), *L'équilibre européen. Etudes rassemblées en hommage à Niels Ersboll*, Brussels: General Secretariat of the Council, 1995.

Mangenot, M., 'Une "Chancellerie du Prince". Le Secrétariat général du Conseil dans le processus de décision bruxellois', *Politique européenne*, 11, 2003, 123–142.

Massot, J., *Le Chef du gouvernement en France*, Paris: La Documentation française, 1979.

Mégret, J., 'Le Secrétariat général des Conseils', in W. J. Ganshof Van Der Meersch (ed.), *Les Nouvelles. Le droit des Communautés européennes*, Brussels: Larcier, 1969.

O'Nuallain, C. and Hoscheit, J.-M. (eds), *The Presidency of the European Council of Ministers. Impacts and Implications for National Governments*, London: Croom Helm, 1985.

Pisani, E., 'Administration de gestion, administration de mission', *Revue française de science politique*, 16 (2), 1956, 315–331.

Powell, W.W. and Dimaggio, P.J., *The New Institutionalism in Organisational Analysis*, Chicago: University of Chicago Press, 1991.

Quermonne, J.-L., *L'appareil administratif de l'Etat*, Paris: Seuil, 1991.

Selznick, P., *Leadership in Administration. A Sociological Interpretation*, New York: Peterson, 1957.

Spierenburg, D. and Poidevin, R., *Histoire de la Haute Autorité de la Communauté européenne du charbon et de l'acier. Une expérience supranationale*, Brussels: Bruylant, 1993.

Taulègne, B., *Le Conseil européen*, Paris: Presses Universitaires de France, 1993.

Vignes, D., 'Le rôle du Secrétariat des Conseils', in P. Gerbet and D. Pepy (eds), *La décision dans les Communautés européennes*, Bruxelles: Presses Universitaires de Bruxelles, 1969, 13–32.

Wallace H. and Wallace W., *Policy-Making in the European Union*, 4th edn, Oxford: Oxford University Press, 2000.

CHRISTELE MARCHAND AND ANTOINE VAUCHEZ

3

Lawyers as Europe's middlemen: a sociology of litigants pleading to the European Court of Justice

Whether it has dealt with treaty-making dynamics, sector-specific policy-making or the actual functioning of EC institutions, European integration research has mainly focused on decision-making processes. Although it has taken various guises, the paradigmatic problematique addressed by EU studies has been, for the most part, 'who counts the most', or, put differently, the study of inter-institutional struggles over the level and the scope of EC regulation. It is around this particular question that the long-lasting divide between liberal intergovernmentalists and neo-functionalists was organised, the latter emphasising 'national preference formation' whereas the former are mostly interested in 'supranational' dynamics. Over the past fifteen years, new theoretical propositions have provided a more complex picture. Constructivists have started paying attention to new sorts of influential actors (Secretariat General, cabinets, etc.) deemed critical in shaping the cognitive and normative frames in which decisions are actually taken (Christiansen et al., 1999). The literature on governance and public policies has emphasised the growing inter-connections between private and public actors (Héritier, 1999). Last but not least, political economists have strongly insisted on the role played by non-state actors such as multinational firms and transnational corporate advocacy coalitions (Van Appeldorn, 2002). These contributions have proved crucial in enlarging the picture beyond the 'official' centres of political and diplomatic command and including new dimensions to Europeanisation processes (private sector, EC bureaucratic politics, transna-tional coalitions, etc).

However, even if most of the 'false dichotomies' (private/public, national/European, bureaucratic/political, legal/political) that initially struc-tured European studies' research have now been questioned (Green Cowles,

2006), what lies in between these lines, i.e. the cross-sector activities within the fragmented and multi-level EU polity, has remained largely under-investigated. While European studies have generally been very meticulous in accounting for changes within EC-implicated groups and institutions and analysing their interactions and reciprocal influences, they have tended to overlook both arenas and professionals of intermediation. Studying such activities becomes essential if one considers EU government not only in a classical institutionalist sense (the institutions in charge of making EU decisions). A wider definition, taking into consideration a wider and often conflictual set of social activities appears necessary to understand the overall hierarchy of EU institutions, the rules that govern their relations and the credentials considered critical to take part in the debates over their possible reform (Smith, 2004). In this framework, cross-sector arenas and professions are a critical locus of EU government as they are integral to the formation of principles of unity of this fragmented polity, and as they often stand out as mediators between the dense array of sector-specific policy networks.[1]

Although it is too often reduced to its institutional actor (the European Court of Justice – ECJ), the Euro-litigation arena is certainly one of these specific fora where a variety of social and professional groups interact. Strangely however, while there now seems to be a general agreement on the fact that litigation has been central in Europeanisation processes (Cichowski, 2007), the literature has remained strikingly oblivious of its specific experts. Most of the time, lawyers appear in the literature as neutral and almost invisible defenders of the different 'heavy' interests (companies, states, EU institutions, interest groups, associations, etc.) that confront each other before the Court.[2] In line with the general debates of European studies, most of the statistical accounts of the ECJ[3] have addressed the 'who-counts-more?' issue (states, 'civil society' or EC institutions?), thus denying any specific role to the lawyers who represent these various contending institutions and groups (Harding, 1992; Stone Sweet and Brunell, 1998). Contradicting such a trend, we submit that lawyers can be regarded as Europe's 'middlemen' (Scheingold, 1971) deploying their activities essentially in between member states, firms, EC institutions or individuals. It is our hypothesis that EC-implicated lawyers can not be considered as peripheral for they constitute a specific group of brokers at the heart of the EC polity serving a variety of clients while at the same time furthering the position of law as *the* common language and credential of all EC-implicated actors (Vauchez, 2008a; 2008c).

The present chapter tests this general assumption by looking at the lawyers who became recognised as the first specialists of litigation before the ECJ. Two empirical tests derive from this general assumption. The first one questions the formation of a specific group of Euro-lawyers: these are not just a group of lawyers that have been randomly 'thrown' into the European judicial scene by the various sorts of clienteles that commissioned their services. Rather, they polarised around a small group of recognised experts of the field characterised by specific profiles, professional interests and world-views. In other words, the existence of 'Europeanised lawyers' generally taken for granted as a logical or necessary consequence of the development of economic exchanges and EC regulation is here turned into the very object of inquiry. If this is true, we would expect, for example, that the Euro-litigation arena would not just mirror general hierarchies among EC member states, such as that of intra-community commerce or of EC power politics, but would possess its own specific internal logic. In other words, the Euro-lawyers' group would be partly autonomous from economic, political, and professional logics that shape the other sectors of EC polity. The second empirical test deriving from the 'middlemen' hypothesis is that success within the EC litigation arena lies less (or not only) in their legal skills but in their ability to attract clients across national and sectoral boundaries. We would then expect that the most integrated segment of ECJ litigants is the one that accumulated a portfolio of resources that enabled them to circumvent the dichotomies of EU polity.

In order to test those hypotheses, we have built a comprehensive database of all jurists (n=607) who intervened in a case before the European Court of Justice between 1954 (first case) until 1978, regardless of the parties they were defending (for example the European Commission, member states, firms, EC civil servants). The data were collected from the ECJ and the Eur-lex websites,[4] and a database was formed listing all the jurists, including both plaintiffs and defendants. However, the database does not include preliminary rulings before the ECJ (art. 177). As they primarily depend on decisions in national jurisdictions, these art. 177 procedures would introduce an important bias in ascertaining the role of lawyers.[5] As for the chronology, 1978 was chosen as a chronological limit as the first EC Service directive was the first significant step towards establishing a unified legal market through the freedom of establishment of lawyers.[6] On the whole, the database comprises 857 cases *lodged and judged* between 1953 and the end of 1978 (including 'orders' of the Court but excluding cases that have been removed from the register before a judgment was actually reached).

Table 3.1   Actors of the Euro-litigation arena (1953–1978)

EC Legal advisers (n=106)	In-house legal counsels (n=148)	
National jurisconsults (n=42)		
Legal practitioners (n=413)		Jurists (n=608)
	Litigants (n=460)	
Law professors (n=47)		

The information available on the websites is succinct yet valuable. Basic bio-graphical data (place of birth, nationality, age, training, diplomas, as well as the father's profession) and other professional information (seniority, previous positions, structure of the law firm, position in the elected organs of the bar, etc.) usually deemed essential to assess legal practice have thus not been collected. However, the data are well adjusted to the hypothesis of the brokerage role of jurists in the EU polity tested here. We were able to gather a complete record of each jurist's activity before the Court and, notably, the 'clients' defended and the 'legal domains' covered over the years. In addition, the database was enriched with further biographical details in order to estimate legal and professional capital.[7] On this empirical basis, the chapter argues that the first group of jurists with recognised expertise in EC law (hereafter: 'Euro-lawyers') had a specific set of resources (connections with the European Commission, geographical proximity to EC institutions, transnational social capital, etc.). Their importance is related to the fact that they possessed resources allowing them to act as go-betweens between different sectors and nations. As these forerunners of Europeanised legal practice pleaded the most important cases (both financially and symbolically) brought before the ECJ, they strongly contributed to define the specific position of laywers *at the intersection* of the variegated set of groups and insti-tutions that constituted the EC polity. In the first part of this chapter, we chart this Euro-litigation arena as an 'UnCommon Market' (Holland, 1980). Given its limited size, its segmentation along national lines and the structural domi-nation of the Legal Service of the European Commission, lawyers could hardly build a strong and lasting expertise in the field. The second part of the chapter indicates how, despite these limitations, a small group of lawyers was able to capture an important share of cases. The various factors favouring such a successful integration in this nascent area of practice are then identi-fied.

UnCommon Market: charting the nascent Euro-litigation arena

When looking at the aggregate picture provided by the data-set, it is evident that the Euro-litigation arena was too limited to provide a lasting and prof-itable livelihood for private practitioners. Although it developed more rapidly than other international venues (Alter, 2006), the ECJ remained a venue of very secondary importance. Over the 25 years considered here, 857 cases were handled by the Court via direct legal action. While there was a general increase in the caseload, the numbers followed a rather irregular trend with ups (72 cases in 1963) and downs (10 in 1967). Figure 3.1 displays the annual number of *standings* (participation in one case = one standing) that jurists (defined as all of those who pleaded before the Court) had at the ECJ.

However, these raw numbers do not reveal much about the importance

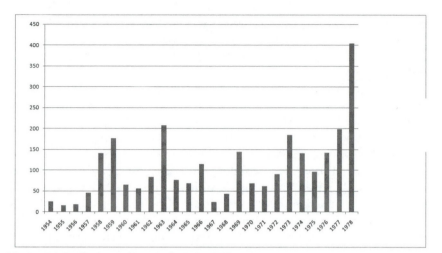

Figure 3.1 Jurists' standings before the ECJ

of the cases (financial and economic stakes, the number of firms involved, the legal principles under scrutiny, political and institutional issues, etc.). It is well known that this initial period offered many good opportunities to launch test-cases. Lawyers such as Ter Kuile in *Van Gend en Loos*, Flaminio Costa and his 1,700 lira bill in *Costa V. ENEL* (Vauchez, 2008c), Gert Meier in *Cassis de Dijon* (Alter and Meunier, 1994) or Eliane Vogel-Polsky in the *Defrenne* cases successfully took advantage of the Court as a pulpit for pushing consolidation and widening of EC law agendas. Similarly, during the 1970s, one can observe the emergence of the first Euro-wide litigation strategies of corporative interests. For instance, the suit lodged in 1973 against the Commission regulation on the sugar market brought together 17 firms from the six countries and no less than 28 Euro-litigants.[8] A growing number of cases involved important financial and commercial interests as the domains of EC regulation expanded. Out of the 30 legal suits that mobilised the largest number of Eurolitigants – arguably a proxy for the economic importance of the case – 24 were lodged between 1973 and 1978. Despite the general increase in the number of cases, the figures show that this trend remained relatively limited (with the exception of 1978). It is thus quite safe to say that there was probably no lawyer for whom ECJ cases were the exclusive area of specialisation. Within the most active quartile of the Euro-litigants (n=75) none went before the Court more than an average of 2.5 times per year.

Beyond its limited size, this nascent field of practice has two other major features. First, it was segmented along national lines, which made it difficult for jurists to attract clients across borders. Secondly, it was under the domination of one actor, the European Commission, which held the largest share of the standings before the Court. These elements created an asymmetric judicial arena in which public entities (member states, EC institutions) dominated through their experience and expertise.

A judicial arena of its own

Most scholars of European Studies writing about the ECJ identify the period studied here as the establishment and consolidation of the Court as a 'real' jurisdiction through its landmark cases. The literature insists on the fact that with cases like *Van Gend en Loos* or *Costa V. ENEL*, the ECJ deviated from the trajectory of other international courts and increasingly resembled national standards of justice. Two major elements however qualify such a thesis. First of all, the ECJ was hardly accessible to individuals. Given its very restrictive jurisprudence on individual legal standing, the Court was exclusively mobilised by a restricted set of actors, namely member states, the Commission, economic actors directly affected by the Community's regulatory machine and EC civil servants involved in disputes with their employers. Secondly, among them, there was only one real repeat player (the European Commission) with an overwhelming presence in the Euro-litigation arena.

An arena segmented along national lines
In these early years of the EC, the ECJ caseload was far from constituting an open and unified legal market where internationalised lawyers would compete for equally internationalised clients. With national legal professions keeping a jealous hold on statutory regulations, the national legal markets remained highly protected from foreign competition. Although the Commission had early on set up committees on the issue of free establishment of professionals, the Rome Treaties hardly had any effect on legal practitioners, whose regulation remained an exclusively national and often local issue. Bar admissions in particular differed significantly from one country, or even one region, to another. Although economic exchanges increased, lawyers had few opportunities to gain clients from other regions, let alone from other countries. It was not until the March 1977 Directive 'facilitating the effective exercise by lawyers of freedoms to provide services' that this monopoly of national bars was first questioned.

The respect for national regulations of legal markets was an integral part of the Court's functioning, as demonstrated by the use of languages. As the member states had initially refused to choose *one* language for the ECJ's proceedings, a multilinguistic language policy was adopted. In the eyes of the first judges, this was the only way to find acceptance with legal elites in the different member states (Vauchez, 2008c). The rule according to which 'the procedural language [was] the national language of the defence' meant that equal access of the various national bars before the ECJ was paramount to the Court's *modus operandi*. As a consequence, it soon became customary for the different protagonists of a case (lawyers, EC legal advisers, national jurisconsults and even the Advocate-General) to share the same nationality or, at least, the same mother tongue. Strikingly, even the most supranational actors of this ensemble (the European Commission or the High Authority) tended to obey this unwritten rule and, within the pool of its legal advisers, picked agents from the plaintiff's nationality. When support of an exterior legal counsel was needed, a fellow countryman would be chosen most of the time. In the *Barbara Erzbau AG and other companies versus the High Authority* case judged on May 10, 1960, for example, all 14 jurists involved were Germans, including the Commission's legal adviser, its two external legal counsels and the Court's Advocate-General, as well as the pool of six legal practitioners and six law professors defending German steel companies and the *Länder* that had joined in the complaint. Everything occurred as if all European legal disputes had to operate through some sort of national delegation putting the resolution of the cases in the hands of fellow countrymen. The collected data confirms this pattern of national segmentation for even among the most active quartile of Euro-litigants, only a very limited number (n=10) had defended a firm from a different nationality. Most of them did so on very specific and rare occasions when defending a large group of firms coming from numerous member states.

A unique repeat player: the European commission

Beyond its segmentation along national lines, this nascent Euro-litigation arena was strikingly asymmetric in its structure. On the one hand, one actor, the European Commission, was called to Luxembourg on a very frequent basis; on the other hand, hundreds of parties appeared before the Court only once or twice. In fact, the European Commission alone commissioned 40% of the 2,710 legal standings during the examined period, whereas the remaining 1,216 ECJ standings involved 700 individuals, firms and member states.

Table 3.2   The 10 major actors before the ECJ

Actor	No. of legal standings commissioned
European Commission	1082
European Council	113
Italy	56
European Parliament	40
Germany	18
France	18
Meroni & Co.	17
The Netherlands	19
United Kingdom	16
Lemmerz-Werke GmbH	10

Among these actors, almost none had recurring judicial disputes with the Commission that would have enabled them to build up systematic legal strategies, except for a few firms such as Meroni & Co. or Lemmerz-Werke. Not even the major member states have even a remotely equivalent slice of the Euro-litigation market. Even considered altogether, the most active states – Italy, Germany and France – only represented a tenth of the Commission's share. The Commission was thus the only actor qualifying as a repeat player according to Mark Galanter's definition of the concept: 'a unit which has had and anticipates repeated litigation, which has low stakes in the outcome of any one case, and which has resources to pursue its long-run interests' (Galanter, 1974: 102).

Unfair competition? The dominance of public institutions (and its consequences)

As EC institutions (45%) and member states (6%) accounted for more than half of this nascent legal market, public institutions – whether national or European – had a strong hold on this emerging Euro-litigation arena. This asymmetry produced a proportionally unequal distribution of the emerging expertise (defined here as encompassing both legal knowledge but also the practical mastery of the Court, including its written and unwritten rules). As a matter of fact, these public institutions were able to specialise early on. Unsurprisingly, the Legal Service of the European Commission stood out, as it had progressively accumulated an unequaled collective experience before the Court. The quite remarkable stability of the Legal Service and of its personnel – beyond the many institutional changes of the EC during the timeframe – played a role in this respect. From 1958 to 1969, it was actually the only administrative department that was common to the three Communities; and together with the Secretariat-General, it remained one of the few cross-sector departments within the Commission. Structured in a classic hierarchical manner, the Legal Service kept the same director, Michel Gaudet, a very influential figure with a pro-active pan-European legal agenda for more than 17 years, from 1952 to 1969 (Vauchez, 2008b).

By contrast, specialisation processes remained embryonic for law firms whose EC-related cases remained occasional and limited to their usual national clienteles. While only 106 EC legal advisers stood 925 times before the Court over the period (an average of 8.8 standings per legal adviser), 460 Euro-litigants appeared 1,452 times before the Court (an average of 3.1). More often than not, Euro-litigants were brought to the Court by one sort of clientele (firms, individuals, member states, EC institutions) in one specific legal domain. In other words, it seems that their appearance before the Court was more dictated by their previously acquired portfolio of clients than by a general specialisation in EC law. One good example of this is Italian lawyer Arturo Cottrau, one of the most active lawyers before the ECJ (61 standings) who worked exclusively on 'ECSC prices' cases for a handful of Italian coal and steel companies. Thereby, not only did the immense majority of the 460 Euro-litigants qualify as 'one-shotters' as three-quarters of them pleaded only once or twice before the ECJ, but they were also more often than not individual practitioners working in small firms, thereby limiting the possibility of any sort of collective accumulation of experience. Last but not least, the legal profession was dominated at the time by small firms organised around one or two well-established partners and a few associates. Just as the many national barriers impeded the emergence of a unified market for legal service in Europe, there were no pan-European law firms built on the model of the large US law firms having a 'critical mass' sufficient to counter-balance the expertise of the Commission.

This limited capacity of the private realm of legal practice to accumulate experience and expertise in EC law is confirmed by career paths. Most of the career moves within the Euro-litigation arena were centred on a circulation between the ECJ (*référendaires*, judges) and public entities (EC legal advisers, national jurisconsults), largely bypassing private legal practitioners. Until 1978, at least three *référendaires* left the Court for the Legal Service of the Commission;[9] reciprocally, two national jurisconsults and two EC legal advisers moved from their Legal units to become judges at the Court.[10] By contrast, there was no circulation between private legal practice and the Court with the unique exception of Jossé Mertens de Wilmar, a lawyer and president of the Belgian section of the *Mouvement européen*. There is no record of a EC legal adviser or *référendaire* leaving the Court for private legal practice at the time.

As they were unable to build collective expertise within private firms, legal practitioners of this early Euro-litigation arena could hardly counterbalance the strong in-house legal units of the EC Commission or member states. On the contrary, as the Legal Service of the Commission accumulated experience, it relied less and less on external legal expertise. While it had frequently appointed private legal practitioners as external advisers in the first decade (213 times from 1954 to 1963), the Legal Service did so on only 101 occasions during the following 15 years. This 'internalisation' process both at the Commission and legal units of national bureaucracies deprived private Euro-litigants of an important share of the legal market, even if in some countries like Belgium or England the recourse to external expertise remained important (Granger, 2006). But the Legal Service of the *Quai d'Orsay* in France (essentially composed of *Conseillers d'Etat*) or the *Avvocatura dello Stato* in Italy retained a quasi-monopoly over the legal defence of their states.[11] For instance, Italian jurisconsults such as Piero Pieronaci or Mario Braguglia spent most of their careers defending Italy before the ECJ, thus becoming renowned specialists of Euro-law.

In sum, private legal practitioners did not manage to impose themselves as the unique, nor as the major players in that emerging litigation arena. This asymmetry between private and public institutions would remain until the legal 'big bang' of the late 1980s when large European law firms were created and national resistances to the free establishment of lawyers were partly overcome. These structural constraints that hindered the development of a private market of European litigation did not prevent the emergence of a small number of early specialists in EC litigation. However, it is argued in the second part of this chapter that the specific structure of the arena – segmented along national lines and dominated by EC institutions – was essential in determining what sort of social and professional norms would emerge.

Paths of European legal glory

A variety of indicators can be chosen to measure jurists' successful integration into the Euro-litigation arena. The most obvious one is the total number of cases pleaded. The 20 most active Euro-litigants (out of a total number of 460) were involved in more than a quarter of the total ECJ standings, a total equivalent to the activity of the 392 least active litigants. The raw number is however an insufficient indicator. The 'number of years of practice' indicator brings about a slightly different image of Euro-lawyers. Similarly, the 'diversity of clientele' as well as that of 'the span of legal domains covered' are also indicative of successful integration. Although the variety of clientele generally remained very limited, some legal practitioners (27 out of 413) managed to accumulate two, three, and up to four types of clientele (private or public, individual or corpor-ate, national or supranational clients and interests). Diversification might not *per se* be correlated with an increased level of activity before the Court; however it is positively correlated to the duration of litigation activity. Indeed, with an average of 11 years of presence before the ECJ, this particular group remained 2.5 years longer than the quartile of most active Euro-litigants. Our aim here is not to quibble about the most relevant yardstick for measuring successful integration, each one of them being one possible criteria of measurement. Rather we intend to single out what sort of social or professional resources were critical to become a legitimate player in Euro-litigation.

'Founding fathers': a field of practice pre-empted by its founders
The number of years of practice before the Court is correlated to early entry in the Euro-litigation arena (38% correlation). The fact that the early entrants secured a strong position in this new field of practice is not surprising *per se*. However, the phenomenon is particularly pronounced here for at least two reasons. First of all, Euro-litigation did not attract many new litigants after the initial founding period when both the Treaty of Paris and the Treaties of Rome started producing their first effects (1954–63). As a matter of fact, the 1964–72 period is marked by a sharp reduction in the number of incoming litigants. Figure 3.2 compares the average number of newcomers in the Euro-

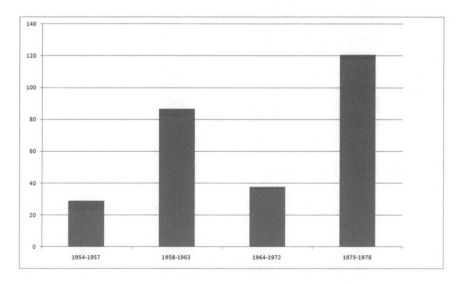

Figure 3.2   Newcomers in the Euro-litigatic arena (yearly average; n=75)

litigation arena (defined as Euro-litigants having their first legal standing before the ECJ) over four periods of time.

This relative closure of the Euro-litigation arena is all the more striking as the average number of standings before the Court simultaneously increased from 56 annually between 1954 and 1963 to an average of 71 between 1964 and 1978. In other words, in the early 1970s the Euro-litigation arena was still dominated by jurists present at the inception as the early entrants accumulated enough experience and expertise to secure a long-lasting hold on the arena. However, early entry is by itself not a sufficient explanation. Not all of these 'founding fathers' managed to diversify their clientele or the type of legal issues they pleaded. A number of early players actually progressively left the scene during the 1964–72 period as the caseload on particular issues dried up. This is the case for example of two previously mentioned lawyers – Arturo Cottrau and Roger Coutard – who were among the most active Euro-litigants before the Court (more than 60 legal standings in the initial years) but intervened just once after 1963. In order to understand how some others remained highly active, one has to take into account the role of the European Commission in securing a lawyer's reputation and hence, new clients.

'Associated rivals': when the European Commission co-opted its legal opponents

One essential element that made these early years so crucial in structuring the Euro-litigation arena is the role played by *public* institutions – essentially the European Commission – in securing the notoriety and credit of *private* practitioners. This role was all the more important as there were initially no clear standards of excellence in this new field of litigation. At the time, the Commission's legal service appointed external private counsels for every fourth legal standing in order to second its own legal advisers. This recourse to external legal resources was particularly pronounced in the first period (1954–63). Early on, EC legal advisers had little authority compared to that of the well-established lawyers or law professors they faced at the ECJ. Indeed, the positions within the Legal Service were not as prestigious as they would later become – most of its jurists were young and rather inexperienced. Most – including the director himself, Michel Gaudet – were in their late thirties at the time of their recruitment. EC legal advisers could hardly match the legal and professional authority of their opponents, for they faced high-profile figures such as renowned and extremely influential international law professors Henri Rolin (case no. 9–55), Paul Reuter (case no. 1–54), Riccardo Monaco (case no. 2–54), J.H.M. Verzilj (case no. 6–54).

As it tried to strengthen its position, the Legal Service of the Commission looked for external support from equally influential national law practitioners. A sizeable share of the Euro-litigants group worked at least once for EC institutions (1 out of 6). This percentage is even stronger among the most active quartile of Euro-litigants (n=75) for which 1 out of 4 had the Commission as their *principal* client. Ironically, this early effort to heighten its authority within the Euro-litigation arena through external consultants resulted in the *de facto* selection and accreditation of its future opponents. In this nascent arena in search of standards of excellence, being selected by the major player of this field of practice had strong reputational effects. Regularly appointed by the Commission to second its defence, lawyers like Jean Coutard (France; 1955; ECSC Prices), Wijckerheld Bisdom (Netherlands; 1957; Competition) or Alex Bonn (Luxembourg; 1956; EC Civil Service), and law professors such as Hans Peter Ipsen (Germany; 1958; Transportation), George Van Hecke (Belgium; 1955; Competition) secured solid reputations. Co-opted by the EC as relevant and competent actors, these legal practitioners and law professors were subsequently perceived as central legal players by firms, individuals or even member states, who would hire their services in legal suits that often involved the Commission itself. Euro-litigants having worked for the Commission tended to have a greater variety of clients than those who had not (an average of 2 instead of 1.5). In other words, the position of the European Commission was strong enough to chose not only its defendants through its important Legal Service but also, indirectly, those who would later become its opponents.

Euro-lawyers par excellence

If one sorts the data by 'legal domains', a more complex picture appears. Agriculture, EC staff regulation, competition and 'ECSC prices', which represented 82% of the ECJ caseload, had specialists with different profiles. The national origin of the litigants involved in Agriculture and 'ECSC prices' cases reflected the general hierarchy of member states in terms of economic weight: French, German and Italian jurists together represented respectively 85% and 83% of the standings in these two legal domains. By contrast, in the case of competition law and of EC staff regulation, the hierarchy was reversed, for lawyers from Belgium and Luxembourg were highly over-represented. This was certainly not because plaintiffs were more frequently from Belgium or Luxembourg, but rather because Euro-litigants from those two countries had managed to capitalise on a comparative advantage. Two elements seem to have played a role: the proximity to EC institutions and the possession of transnational social capital.

National paths to European legal practice: the Belgian and Luxembourg comparative advantage

Physically present at the site of the legal battle, Belgian and Luxembourg jurists managed to capture the most internationalised segment of this emerging market. At a time when the ECJ was just an occasional venue for most French, German or Italian lawyers, lawyers of these two countries engaged in early specialisation, turning their intimate knowledge of the functioning and personnel of EC institutions into an important professional resource going beyond the theoretical mastery of EC law. Taken as a whole, Belgian (in fact, Brussels) lawyers were thereby the second most represented national contingent among the most active Euro-litigants (n=75) with 17 practitioners, just after Germany

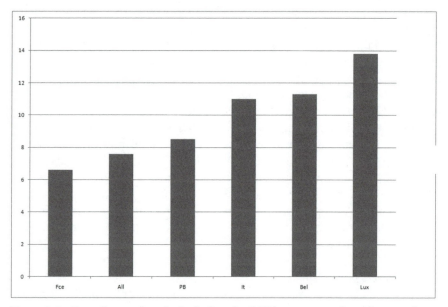

Figure 3.3   Euro-lawyers' seniority before the ECJ (average number of years of practice)

but before France. The Luxembourg bar also appears to have adapted very efficiently to this new market with five lawyers being among the most active – more than the Netherlands. Even more striking is the fact that Belgian and Luxembourg lawyers were more often *permanent* players, with an average seniority much greater than other nationalities.[12]

This comparative advantage was even more pronounced if one considers only 'EC staff regulation' and 'competition' branches of litigation. The former was arguably the first authentically supranational branch of litigation. Data indicate that the plaintiffs – EC employees – preferred to appoint local lawyers than jurists from their own country: Belgian and Luxembourg jurists account for 70% of the total standings in this domain (respectively 43% and 27%). This privileged position did not only concern such cases with limited economic opportunities but also involved competition law, a field where firms could provide much more substantial sources of remuneration than individual EC employees. In this area, Belgian lawyers acquired a central position, as they were involved in more than a third of the standings. This placed them ahead of German lawyers. Renowned Belgian anti-trust lawyers launched their careers at that time: Michel Waelbroeck, Walter van Gerven and Jean-François Bellis, one of two Microsoft's leading lawyers in the recent Microsoft ECJ case.

Among the various factors that help explain these patterns, geographical proximity to the institutions was vital, as procedural rules required parties in a case to pick a legal residence in Luxembourg for the duration of the litigation, so that documents could be easily exchanged. This explains in part why Luxembourg lawyers were often chosen as 'hosts' for many law suits. From this unique position, they could become acquainted with most Euro-litigants that came to plead before the ECJ. This immediately located them at the crossroads of various otherwise unconnected national legal networks. It is therefore not coincidental that the most active Luxembourg lawyers before the ECJ (Ernst Arendt, Tony Biever, Alex Bonn, André Elvinger and Jacques Loesch) also 'hosted' the largest number of suits (between 20 and 50 each) in their law firms. As a result of this privileged position, Belgian and Luxembourg lawyers were the first to found specialised law firms, further establishing their competitive advantage. The most emblematic example in this regard is the foundation in 1969 of the 'de Bandt-Van Hecke-Lagae & Van Bael' law firm gathering Belgian corporate lawyers with strong international credentials (three of the four founding partners had studied for at least a year in the United States) and expertise in the field of EC law.

From Cosmo- to Euro-lawyers: the case of EC competition law

While EC staff cases remained a limited market with little competition, Belgian and Luxembourg jurists specialising in the much more lucrative field of competition litigation had to face an embryonic form of global competition. In fact, while firms from the various member states tended to look for lawyers from their own nationality, the extra-EC clientele (particularly English, American and, in the 1970s, Japanese) was in search of lawyers capable of defending their interest in the EC. Belgium's main competitors in this emerging market were actually North American. US law firms in particular showed an early interest in the potential of this market and opened small offices in Brussels. Observers noted as early as the 1960s that 'foreign law firms [read: US law firms] have already installed their own boutiques and are thereby paradoxically (becoming) the first European lawyers by the extension of their activity' (Goldsmith, 1968: 74). Although the American presence in Brussels is difficult to assess, various accounts enable us to reconstitute the basic chronology of their establishment, for example Baker, McKenzie and Hightower in 1957, Cleary Gottlieb and Steen Hamilton in 1960, and Coudert Brothers in 1965. US lawyers could not however directly compete with European lawyers within the Euro-litigation arena as ECJ regulations established that only bar members from one of the EC states could actually plead before the Court. Although this prevented US lawyers from appearing before the ECJ,[13] they nonetheless became serious rivals in providing legal counsel. The threat was perceived by European lawyers to be acute enough to incite the Brussels bar to lobby the Ministry of Justice for extremely strict rules governing foreign jurists.[14] However, the continuous informal presence of many US lawyers as simple *agents d'affaires* circumventing Belgian regulations is acknowledged in various accounts.[15] Building a reputation in the more competitive legal domain of EC competition law therefore required a different portfolio of resources from the one necessary for excelling in EC staff regulation cases. As they faced international and European challengers, competition lawyers needed to develop contacts in *both* international and European legal circles in order to connect with EC institutions as well as with multinational firms. Not only did they have to maintain a strong presence in international networks where cosmopolitan lawyers traditionally gathered but they now also had to simultaneously invest in academic publications on EC law (many of them were actually professors) and participate in pan-European legal conferences and congresses.

Table 3.3   International and European legal capital
(A comparison by legal branch of litigation)

	The 20 most active EC competition lawyers	The 20 most active EC staff lawyers
National academic position	8/20	3/20
EC law academic capital	10/20	3/20
Pan-European legal capital	8/20	1/20
Cosmopolitan legal capital[16]	7/20	0/20

It is quite safe to consider that being at the crossroads of various international *and* European networks played a crucial role in helping these Euro-litigants secure a privileged position in the emerging EC competition law market. These Euro-lawyers had a 'special' relationship with the Commission, as 6 out the 20 competition lawyers considered in Table 3.3 had worked directly for that institution. They were also able to cross national borders (8 out 20 had clients from a country other than their own) and cross sectors by cumulating various types of clientele (6 out of the 20). To be introduced in both international and European settings may explain their relative success vis-à-vis the first American or British law firms established in Brussels who had a hard time making Brussels a profitable venue.[17] As one leading Belgian anti-trust lawyer recalls: 'expectations were high, but for some they soon crashed. Dewey Ballantine left after a couple of years, White & Case closed down about five years' (Van Bael, quoted in *International Financial Law Review*, 1988: 8). With few exceptions,[18] they lacked the contacts and the practical knowledge of EC institutions that European – particularly Belgian – lawyers had managed to secure.[19]

In many ways, Belgian lawyer George Van Hecke, a regular player before the ECJ (23 legal standings during the period), is the quintessential example of this blending of both European and international credentials and resources. Born in 1915 in Cambridge, he married Marie-Emilie Rolin-Jaequemyns, a member of a family of prominent and internationally known Belgian jurists. He soon secured both international and national credentials. Graduating from the Universities of Louvain and Harvard with a speciality in international business law (his Phd deals with *The Legal Stakes of International Loans*, 1955), he became professor at the Catholic University of Louvain in 1949. He taught anti-trust law in many renowned universities and academies on both sides of the Atlantic: Amsterdam (1955), Oxford (1957), Luxembourg (1958), Columbia (1960), Nancy (1960) and the Academy of International Law of The Hague (1962 and 1969) (Van Hecke, 1962). Able to speak and write in four languages, he was an early member of the International Law Association and never missed a bi-annual congress. As a lawyer since 1942, he was repeatedly called upon by the Belgian government to give his expertise and represent his country in various international settings where international private law issues were at stake.[20] Called upon by the European Commission as an outside legal counsel as early as 1954, he soon became one of the leading specialists of EC competition law and would later be frequently called upon by international firms in their legal actions against the Commission.

The example might be extreme as it aggregates in one person the various critical resources that we have identified. It is however indicative of the progressive emergence of specific canons of professional excellence in the Euro-litigation field where Euro-lawyers are not just people with legal skills remaining outside the social and political contexts in which they intervene.

They rather represent a specific type of European elite deeply embedded in the set of networks and professional groups that constituted this EU polity.

Conclusion

Just as there was no 'immaculate conception' of the ECJ's position in EU polity, there is no *ex-nihilo* creation of a transnational legal elite naturally and spontaneously engendered by the development of exchanges or EC regulation. Europe, we have also argued on the basis of our data-set, is not just one unique and open judicial scene or legal market equally appealing and equally accessible to the thousands of lawyers practising in the member states. Looking at some of the social and professional features of those first jurists who made it to the Court has helped us identify which resources proved critical at this nascent stage of the Euro-litigation arena. We have demonstrated that what defined this early Euro-lawyers' group was not just legal skills but also extra-legal credentials such as contacts with the European Commission and international social capital, etc. As they stepped across the borders and dividing lines that shaped European polity (notably the divides between national/European/international levels or between the public and the private realm), they also contributed to define law's specific position at the crossroads of this fragmented and weakly institutionalised polity.

Notes

1 For two recent examples, see the various empirical investigations in Cohen and Vauchez (2007) and in Georgakakis and de Lassalle (2007).
2 Sources such as *Who's Who* seem to confirm this invisibility of lawyers – and more generally of private professionals who locate most of their practice at the informal or, at least, unofficial level, thereby very rarely appearing in *Who's Who* volumes which tend to over-represent bureaucratic and political positions.
3 For a detailed account of this stream of research see Conant (2007).
4 www.curia.europa.eu/en/content/juris/index.htm; www.europa.eu.int/eur-lex
5 Moreover, preliminary rulings were only opened with the Rome Treaties and only started to develop in the 1970s.
6 Directive 77/249 of March 22, 1977 gave lawyers the freedom to provide occasional services.
7 For more details on the coding and on the sources, see www.ssrn.com /author=894536.
8 Judgment of 16 December 1975. Coöperatieve Vereniging 'Suiker Unie' UA and others *v* Commission of the European Communities. Joined cases 40 to 48, 50, 54 to 56, 111, 113 and 114–173.
9 Pierre Mathijsen, former *référendaire* of judge Peter Serrarens from 1952 to 1958, stood four times before the ECJ between 1963 and 1966 as a legal adviser to Euratom; Jean-Pierre Delahousse who helped Advocate-General Maurice Lagrange moved to the Commission in 1958, where he intervened five times before the ECJ between 1963 and 1974; Heinrich Matthies, former assistant of Walter Hallstein at the University of

Frankfurt and law clerk of Karl Roemer from 1954 to 1959 intervened ten times before the ECJ between 1959 and 1974, as a legal adviser for the High Authority and for the Commission.

10 Pierre Pescatore had pleaded twice as former jurisconsult for Luxembourg Foreign Ministry before his nomination to the Court in 1967; Riccardo Monaco, the head of the Italian Legal Unit, had represented Italy six times before his nomination in 1962. Nicola Catalano had worked for the Legal Unit of the High Authority and was a representative of the Italian State during the negotiations of the Treaty of Rome before his nomination in 1958. Last but not least, Alberto Trabucchi, while not being a civil servant of EC institutions, had pleaded for them 11 times between 1956 and 1960 before his nomination to the Court in 1962.

11 Germany and the Netherlands alternatively relied on in-house counsels or on external advisers.

12 Measured by the time elapsed between the first and the last ECJ case between 1954 and 1978.

13 Besides the legal barrier, it should be noted that no US firm or individual was in any way concerned by a lawsuit before the ECJ during that period.

14 The 1963 and 1964 directives of Brussels' *bâtonnier* provided that Belgian lawyers were forbidden to engage in any sort of collaboration with foreign lawyers based in Brussels without his explicit permission. Less than than ten authorisations were actually delivered to foreign lawyers (*International Lawyer*, 1968–69: 639).

15 The presence of US lawyers would remain a heated and recurrently debated issue within the Brussels bar until a specific status was granted to foreign lawyers in the early 1980s. In April 1967, the Brussels' *bâtonnier* was 'bitterly lamenting the fact that US lawyers did not seem to respect neither the spirit nor the letter of the authorisations that have been granted to them' (*Bulletin de l'Ordre des avocats du barreau de Bruxelles*, 1967).

16 These various forms of capital are measured through proxies. National academic position is measured by their being (1) or not (0) law professors. Their contribution to EC law doctrine is evaluated by their publication record (1/0). Pan-European legal capital is quantified through their participation in two important congresses organised in 1963 by the *Fédération internationale pour le droit européen* (FIDE) and by the Köln Institute for European Law. Their membership of the International Law Association or in the Institute for International Law (0/1) measures their 'cosmopolitan' legal capital.

17 According to Judy Slinn, 'the growth of the Cleary Gottlieb Brussels office [opened in 1969] was slow, even after Britain joined the EEC in January 1973' (Slinn, 1993: 165). Similarly, the office opened by the American Coudert Brothers in 1965 was hardly profitable (Veenswijk, 1994).

18 Some US lawyers did have special relationships with top figures of the EC, such as former Under-Secretary of State George Ball, a partner of Cleary Gottlieb and a close friend of Jean Monnet.

19 At least until the 'legal big bang' of the mid-1980s that occurred with the Single European Market (Whelan and McBarnet, 1992). Important changes occurred at the time, ranging from the blossoming of big law firms' offices in Brussels, to the numerous mergers between national middle-sized law firms – which transformed them into multi-jurisdictional and multi-national law firms – or to the loosening of statutory regulations governing legal professions in most EC countries.

20 Member of the Belgian delegation during the 7th (1951), 8th (1956) and 9th (1960) Conferences of The Hague on the Codification of Private International Law; member of the Belgian delegation to the Inter-allied Reparations Agency (1947), member of the Permanent Commission of the Belgian government for the examination of questions of private international law (from 1965), etc.

Bibliography

Alter, K., 'Private Litigants and the New International Courts', *Comparative Political Studies*, 39 (1), 2006.

Alter, K. and Meunier, S., 'Judicial Politics in the European Community. European Integration and the Pathbreaking Cassis de Dijon', *Comparative Political Studies*, 26 (1), 1994.

Bulletin de l'Ordre des avocats du barreau de Bruxelles, 'Juristes américains établis à Bruxelles', April 1967.

Christiansen, T. et al., 'The Social Construction of Europe', *Journal of European Public Policy* 6 (4), 1999, 528–544.

Cichowski, R., *The European Court and Civil Society. Litigation, Mobilization and Governance*, Cambridge: Cambridge University Press, 2007.

Cohen, A. and Vauchez, A. (eds), *La Constitution européenne. Elites, mobilisations, votes*, Bruxelles: Presses de l'Université libre de Bruxelles, 2007.

Conant, L., 'Review Article: The Politics of Legal Integration', *Journal of Common Market Studies*, 45 (1), 2007, 45–66.

Galanter, M., 'Why the "Haves" Come Out Ahead: Speculations on the Limits of Legal Change', *Law and Society Review*, 95, 1974–75, 95–160.

Georgakakis, D. and de Lassalle, M., La 'nouvelle gouvenance européenne'. Genèses et usages politiques d'un livre blanc, Strasburg: Presses Universitaires de Strasburg, 2007.

Goldsmith, J.-C., 'Le barreau français et la liberté d'établissement des avocats dans la CEE', in *Barreau et médecin face au droit d'établissement*, Louvain: Librairie Universitaire, 1968.

Granger, M.-P., 'States as Success, Litigants Before the European Court of Justice', *Croatian Yearbook of European Law*, 2, 2006.

Green Cowles, M., 'Non-State Actors and False Dichotomies. Reviewing IR/IPE Approaches to European Integration', in M. Cini and A. Bourne (eds), *Palgrave Advances in European Union Studies*, Basingstoke: Palgrave, 2006, 25–38.

Harding, C., 'Who Goes to Court in Europe? An Analysis of Litigation Against the European Community', *European Law Review*, 17, 1992.

Héritier, A., *Policy-making and Diversity in Europe. Escaping Deadlock*, Cambridge: Cambridge University Press, 1999.

Holland, S., *UnCommon Market: Capital, Class and Power in the European Community*, Basingstoke: Macmillan, 1980.

International Financial Law Review, '1992: too soon to be European', 7, 1988.

International Lawyer, 'Practice of Law by US lawyers Abroad', 3 (3), 1968–69.

Scheingold, S., *The Rule of Law in European Integration*, Westport: Greenwood Press, 1965.

Scheingold, S., 'The Law in Political Integration', Working Paper, Centre for International Affairs, Harvard University, 1971.

Slinn, J., *Clifford Chance. Its Origin and Development*, Clifford Chance, 1993.

Smith, A., *Le gouvernement de l'Union européenne. Une sociologie politique*, Paris: LGDJ, 2004.

Stone, A., *The Judicial Construction of Europe*, Oxford: Oxford University Press, 2004.

Stone Sweet, A. and Brunell, T., 'The European Court and the National Courts: A Statistical Analysis of Preliminary References, 1961–1995', *Journal of European Public Policy*, 5 (1), 1998.

Van Apeldoorn, B., *Transnational Capitalism and the Struggle Over European Integration*, London: Routledge, 2002.

Van Hecke, G., 'Le droit anti-trust: aspects comparatifs et internationaux', *Recueil de cours de l'Académie de la Haye*, 1962.

Vauchez, A., 'The Force of a Weak Field. Law and Lawyers in the Government of Europe (for a Renewed Research Agenda)', *International Political Sociology*, 2008a, 128–144.

Vauchez, A., 'How to Become a Transnational Elite. Lawyers and Legal Elites at the Outset of the European Communities (1950–1970)', in H. Petersen, H. Krunke, A.-L. Kjær and M. Rask Madsen (eds), *Paradoxes of European Legal Integration*, London: Ashgate, 2008b, 129–148.

Vauchez, A., 'Review Article: Democratic Empowerment through Euro-law?', *European Political Science*, 7, 2008c, 444–455.

Veenswijk, V., *Coudert Brothers, a Legacy in Law: The History of America's First Global Law Firm, 1853–1993*, New York: Truman Talley Books/Dutton, 1994.

Whelan, C. and McBarnet, D., 'Lawyers in the Market: Delivering Legal Services in Europe', *Journal of Law and Society*, 19, 1992.

*MARINE DE LASSALLE**

4

The emergence of 'European' careers in subnational French administrations

Despite the increasing interest in Europeanisation as a social and political process in which the traditional top down approaches are now widely recognised as insufficient, there has been as yet little empirical research done to understand specific dynamics of Europeanisation at the sub-national level. This chapter will seek to understand the way in which the European dynamic interacts with other political and administrative logics to construct an emerging group of European professionals in local and regional administrations.

The creation of new institutional and political spaces, public policies and procedures in Europe has stimulated the production of new scientific concepts. Multi-level governance (henceforth referred to as MLG) is one of the most influential of these new concepts.[1] It was defined for the first time by Gary Marx, who in a 1993 paper describes the EU as a 'polity creating process in which authority and policy-making influence are shared across multiple levels of government – subnational, national and supra national, as the result of broad processes of institution creation and decisional re-allocation' (Marx, 1993).

Following this initial definition, many authors have used the term which was more of a 'notion' open to many uses than a firm conceptual construction (Jordan, 2001). MLG was for instance used in European studies to criticise intergovernmentalism, by emphasising the existence of processes other than the confrontation of member states and European institutions by including subnational actors. Thereby, MLG also became the scientific theory that accompanied the political advent of a 'Europe of regions' (Hooghe and Keating, 1994; Jeffrey, 1997; Christiansen, 1999). In more recent studies, Marx and Hoogue add that the multi-level analysis framework takes into account less institutionalised territorial constructions such as networks,

* Translated by Jean-Yves Bart

programmes, territories of public action: in short, actors and arenas whose degree of institutionalisation is less than that of actors usually included in studies on European integration.

Numerous criticisms have been levelled against MLG, which has been accused of being a science too close to politics, and especially of being a somewhat soft science (Benz and Eberlein, 1999; Jordan, 2001).[2] There would thus not be a lot to add if MLG was not one of the only available tools in the field of European studies to deal with issues of articulation or adjustment between levels of government (Benz and Eberlein, 1999). Before going on to my analysis of the emergence of European careers in French sub-national administrations, I will briefly develop a few additional points of criticism of MLG-inspired studies that differ slightly from those that have already been formulated.

The first lies in the overly normative character of the multi-level governance concept, which seeks first and foremost to provide general models of articulation between 'levels' that account for the weakening or the hollowing-out of the central state (Hooghe and Marx, 2003). While the state has undergone transformations, the notion of a 'hollow state' is not necessarily pertinent. On the contrary, the state and the public policies developed in its name continue to give credit – material and symbolic (in Bourdieu's sense)[3] – to national public action undertaken officially for European compliance (Brenner, 2000).[4] In addition, the urge to modelise and typify leads to an overly one-sided emphasis on institutional variables, by homogenising and simplifying sub-national actors, reducing their relationships to legal prescriptions or advocating an approach focused on institutional design, thereby neglecting ever-changing dynamics of competition within member states between sub-national territories on the one hand, and between the centre and the periphery on the other (for a more exhaustive critique, see Carter and Smith, 2008). It bears noting that all the authors who have worked in a more empirical perspective have shown that the EC level has contributed to strengthen horizontal logics of action and competition (Smith, 1995; Pasquier, 2004). In other words, there are strong internal differences within member states which invalidate overly generalising models. Empirical research has clearly shown to what extent thinking in terms of levels has led to homogenising particular levels (regions, the central state, Europe), when fieldwork uncovers evolving alliances, exchanges and competition between institutions embedded in differentiated contexts and power relations and endowed with variable degrees of agency (Smyrl, 1997; Nay, 2002; Pasquier, 2004). If 'institutional design' is indeed a factor in the determination of the resources and agency of local institutions and the structure of the relationships between sub-national actors, it is an indicator of the structure of political power relations, more than an explicative variable; it does not in itself account for theoretical agency, as Romain Pasquier's comparisons between French and Spanish regions shows (Pasquier, 2004).

The second criticism concerns the very notion of 'level' (or tier). The use of this term implies a hierarchy between levels and therefore presupposes specific types of relations between them. As long as research on Europeanisation starts with the EC 'initiative' of regional policies, the European level (conceived as the 'top' level) determines the reactions of the 'bottom' (sub-national) levels, which in return produce effects on the 'top' level. This is merely an update of the 'top down' and 'bottom up' approach, translated in the MLG prism by the concepts of 'downloading' and 'uploading' Europeanisation (Börzel, 2000; Marshall, 2005). In some studies, Europeanisation becomes the product of the progressive but mechanical assimilation of local levels to the rules and categories issued by the EC level (Marshall, 2005). Other papers consider the interactivity of Europeanisation more critically, and often insist on the essentially domestic character of the transformations attributed to the EC (Benz and Eberlein, 1999). However, even this approach, generally centred on legal transpositions and institutional perspectives, leaves aside the actors who set these processes into motion.

It should be emphasised that these 'inter-level' relationships, this permeability and circulation, have been presupposed, but not empirically verified. Indeed, if there is a circulation, its forms of existence and conditions of possibility need to be studied – which MLG literature never does. Therein lies the third – and most important – weakness. The MLG framework posits the general hypothesis of a 'fit' (or a Europeanisation)[5] of sub-national levels to EC policies (and broadly speaking, to the recommendations, principles, modes of action, norms, etc. issued by the EU) without actually questioning the politico-administrative processes or enterprises (Offerlé, 2002) which make this Europeanisation possible and effective. While Hooghe and Marx stress the role played by weakly institutionalised networks or institutions, they never really describe them, nor do they propose an analysis of the processes of articulation that they enable (for a description of these networks, see Heinelt and Niederhafner, 2008). MLG is unable to do so because it only perceives these actors as they are constructed by political and administrative practices, and fails to locate them in socially and institutionally structured spaces. This has the effect – describing these actors as they present themselves – of conferring on them legitimacy and credit. This also contributes to naturalising Europeanisation processes and perceiving them as inevitable, leaving little room to understand their possible differentiated forms (beyond often rather crude generalities on national or administrative cultures rarely informed by empirical research), nor to comprehend their conditions of possibility. Recommendations, principles, modes of action and norms of the EU circulate, but this process does not take place in a sociological vacuum. Thus, we need to uncover processes of circulation, appropriation and translation operated by social actors with variable dispositions and interests and inscribe these actors in socially, politically and institutionally structured spaces that confer a sociologically relevant meaning to their uses of Europe (Desage and Godard, 2005).

In contrast with the hypothesis of a mechanical adaptation, our investigation will seek to closely observe the dynamics that determine the constraints and resources which transform modes of institutional structuring, such as the modes of action and organisation of sub-national levels, and posit that these dynamics have effects on Europeanisation processes.

Among these dynamics, I will focus on the actors, and especially those to whom I will refer as 'local professionals of Europe'. The recruitment of staff specialised in European matters has been used as an indicator of the 'Europeanisation' of sub-national levels (Marshall, 2005). However, we do not know much about the defining features of this population and what precisely confers on them their 'European' character. It thus appears that the emergence, the development, strengthening and transformations of professional markets specialised in Europe in local institutional spaces, can lead to more realistic and sociologically insightful descriptions of Europeanisation processes, all while testing the multi-level hypothesis empirically.

Following other scholars (Smith, 2004), I will argue in favour of using traditional tools of political sociology. Thus, I will rely on the sociology of institutions and their relationships, institutions defined here as a set of norms and representations objectivated and observable in practice (Lagroye, 1997). I will show that the dynamics which contribute to structuring the market of professional positions needs to be situated in their context of competitive alliances. However, the analysis of the relationships between institutionalised spaces turns out to be limited as soon as the emphasis is laid on the circulation and the multipositionality of actors. Thus, I have also studied capital, resources and their circulation between levels. Like other research on the sociology of the professionals of Europe (*Regards sociologiques*, 2004), I will examine the hypothesis of the existence of a specific *sectoral* capital (Georgakakis and de Lassalle in this volume). This idea of capital (Bourdieu, 1984) cannot be separated from the existence of fields, or structured spaces, which determine both the pertinence and the distribution of this capital.

Applied to the local professionals of Europe, the efficient forms of capital hypothetically consist of 'Community' resources (linguistic capital, social capital, specialised knowledge, know-how related to the EC, symbolic credit) and 'local' resources (knowledge of the local fields, specialised knowledge, know-how adapted to territorial spaces, symbolic credit) and can be transposed to different spaces of implementation of regional policies (EC, national, local). If its structure (i.e. the relative weight of the resources that constitute it) obviously depends on the institutional context where it is accumulated and invested, it is assumed that it is likely to allow its possessor to 'circulate' in 'multi-level' institutional networks of the EC regional policy.[6] By refining this first general hypothesis, one can hypothesise that each political-administrative space produces specific professionals endowed with specialised resources, but whose capacity of circulation remains limited, thereby creating a rather segmented market for local professionals of Europe.

I would therefore like to insist on the fact that the unbridled 'circulation' posited by the MLG approach is here not a given – it depends on a set of morphological, political and institutional processes which will be analysed. This circulation is institutionally organised in Germany (Lozac'h, 2007), but as we will see, much less organised and frequent in France. Rather than assuming the existence of multiple and interdependent levels, I will discuss the factors hindering or favouring circulation between spaces, which vary according to the degree of segmentation of professional markets. The second hypothesis is that this capital is unequally distributed in the local space. By studying the specific forms of accumulation, and the poles where it is accumulated (or not), we can grasp the structuring of the local European sector and thereby contribute to an empirically grounded understanding of the dynamics of Europeanisation.

I will present the results of an ongoing survey. A first set of questionnaires has enabled the processing of about a hundred replies by local French professionals of Europe (35 in prefectures and external state services, 65 in local authorities). These first findings, to be further explored in the ongoing research project, do not allow for a statistical analysis but provide valuable, if indicative information on professional status, educational resources and professional paths, the services in which the respondents work, career prospects, etc. A series of in-depth interviews provided for more qualitative empirical material allowing us to present the first results and to formulate a series of hypotheses.

I will first outline the processes that have led local authorities to set up specialised services, showing that the EC 'offer' in terms of regional policy does not alone account for the pace of this emergence and consolidation. In line with these processes, I will then show how these institutional structures determine the forms of production and circulation of this sectoral capital, demonstrating the limits of the latter's multi-level character before concluding with a series of tentative findings and hypotheses on the structuring of the job market.

The emergence of 'local' markets of professionals of Europe

The emergence of services, specialised staff in municipalities, departments, regions and decentralised central state administrations in France progressed at different speeds and with variable intensity. This suggests that, far from being a 'product' of Europe and the funds it distributes, the organisation of specialised services on European matters was determined by dynamics of institutional competition and cooperation that characterised the field of political power in France, opposing – schematically – local authorities and bureaucratic segments of the central and decentralised state administrations on the one hand, and local authorities among themselves on the other. In the same way, the EC has not led to a standardisation in the organisational shape of the services dedicated to Europe. They remain linked to the institutional competences – partly the product of internal competitions – which define the general framework of the 'European services' of local authorities and state bureaucracies. They also depend upon the forms of political and symbolic investment in European and/or international issues by politicians, as well as each local authority's own institutional history.[7]

The emergence of services seen through the prism of the centre/periphery competition

Regional policy was originally controlled by central state networks and their territorial services (Smith, 1995). Not only did the national level contribute to negotiations that enabled it to determine the size and the distribution of European Structural Funds, it was also prevalent in the management and the use of these funds. This prevalence was inscribed in law in France by the 1992 ATR law,[8] which reasserted the decentralised state's authority on two levels. The regional prefects were in charge of preparing and implementing European programmes. The law entitled them to coordinate the relevant local partners, from the elaboration of the programmes to their evaluation. The decentralised directions of ministries in charge of the management of structural funds were responsible for the processing of European funding applications (Nay, 2001). At the central state level, the central regional development agency DIACT (which replaced the regional planning agency DATAR) held a pre-eminent position, due to the credit held by its officials, recognised as uncontested specialists in negotiation with Brussels, and their knowledge of the territories and their configurations which enabled them to provide partners with the benefits of their experience (Duran, 1998). This particular position has been underlined in numerous studies in many policy areas. For instance, representatives of the DIACT took part in the framework regulations of structural funds, negotiated in the Council of Ministers, which provided them with important informational resources. They were in contact with officials in the relevant DGs and were also able to have access to parallel information sources through permanent national representations in Brussels or the information networks set up between the Commission and the decentralised services. This reinforced their capacities of mediation and they were the first 'enablers' who allowed other territorial actors to appropriate structural funds and turn them into localised public policies (Nay, 2002/3).

Our study confirms the prevalence of decentralised state services in the sector of European programmes in the 1980s and 1990s, as the 'Europe' services in prefectures (SGAR) were created or developed long before those of local authorities: a quarter were created before 1983, half between 1984 and 1999, and the rest after 1999. These are often relatively large services, with up to 15 members. The professionals in specialised services of prefectures mention two main types of mission: processing and controlling applications, and ensuring the activity and the development of territories, which is consistent with their role of coordination between political actors (regional, departmental and intercommunal executives) and the representatives of economic and social interests (*caisses des dépôts*, chambers of commerce, agriculture, associations, employment agencies, development agencies, unions, corporations or developers).

In the 1990s, however, this institutional role was challenged by services specialised in European issues within regional and local authorities. This development was partly due to the increase in financial flows linked to structural funds, but it can also be analysed as a consequence of the structure of political power in France and institutional competition.

Multi-level governance analysts have proposed several general hypotheses to account for the Europeanisation of local authorities. The forms of institutional recognition of local authorities through treaties post-Maastricht (creation of the Committee of the Regions, recognition of regions with legislative competences within federal states), the increasing development of structural funds and the partnership principle (1988) said to be the 'cornerstone' of EC intervention in the second planning phase of the reformed regional policy (1994–99), were thought to have contributed to a direct dialogue between the Commission and local authorities, bypassing the central state (Jeffrey, 1997). The development of new positions dedicated to the local management of Europe, as well as the development of regional offices in Brussels (Costa, 2002) can be seen as indicators of the increasingly direct links between the Commission and sub-national actors.

The increase in credits related to the development of regional policy and structural funds (SF) led to the development of services in local authorities (Duran, 1998). This increase indeed represented an important source of funding for some local authorities, notably after 1988. Between 1975 and 1986, French regions received 1.95 billion ECUS (of which 20% went to Corsica and overseas regions). During the 1989–93 period, they received 3.42 billion ECUS (about 6% of the entire SF); for 1994–99, 15.17 billion ECUS (over 8% of the entire SF) and 16.3 billion Euros for the 2000–6 period. Respondents to our questionnaire often cite the local authority's eligibility for structural funds or European programmes as a reason for the creation of services. More concretely, the credits for technical assistance linked to Community initiative programmes (Interreg, Urban, etc.) have favoured the creation of administrative positions to ensure their implementation and control (Mathiot, 1998). These positions are more recent, often externalised to public interest groups and often hold fewer statutory guarantees than 'European' positions of the decentralised state apparatus. Although the financial dimension linked to Community opportunity cannot be overlooked, the emergence or the consolidation of specialised services derives just as much from institutional competition in the French political field.

First, as Patrice Duran pointed out, Europe did not initiate the principle

of partnership which is 'closely tied to the nature of the institutional arrangements specific to the French State' (Duran, 1998: 115) and had already been
used in state–region plan contracts (CPER). Duran explains that the negative
experiences of the first-generation CPERs led local authorities to better
prepare themselves for future negotiations, thereby acclimatising them to the
logics of negotiation of European structural funds. Subsequently, whereas the
level of funding from Brussels increased (in a context of national budget
constraints), the experience of regional planning by the decentralised state
services between 1994 and 1999 was marked by the under-utilisation of
European credits, for which the prefecture service was partly responsible
(short deadlines for the elaboration of programming documents, political
pork barrelling, terms of payment delayed by more than 18 months, etc.). As
a result, 20% of credits programmed during this period were not spent, which
amounted to a loss of 1.7 billion, and placed France at the bottom of the list
of the 'good users' of European credits. Local political leaders (notably those
who were also senators, thanks to the possibility in France of holding multiple
elected offices) mobilised against the complexity of the funding circuits and
contributed to the framing of the role of the decentralised state administrations as a 'problem'. In the name of a simplification of procedures, local
officials asked for direct responsibility for managing funds. The organisation
of specialised services developed within this context of competition over the
most adequate level to manage funds. This is at least what the first results of
our questionnaires reflect – they show that there were no creations of
specialised services in regional and departmental councils before 1989. They
developed after 1989, but remained very limited until the 1994–99 period
(when 40% of departmental councils and 35% of regional councils had
dedicated services) and especially the 2000–6 programming period (65% in
regional councils, 50% in departmental councils), despite a stagnation or
even a decline in European funds.[9]

The context was also marked by the return of the decentralisation issue
on the government agenda, which can be analysed through the prism of the
political competition where the socialist government sought to reform the
Senate and its institutionally more or less guaranteed conservative majority.
This led to a counter-mobilisation of representatives from local authorities
who were often also Senators, support from the conservative President
Chirac, the setting up of competing commissions (the Mauroy Commission
for the government and a senatorial mission on decentralisation) and the
adoption of the decentralisation law in June 2001. This project, initially
meant to reinforce the regional level, led to the mobilisation of regions and
was partly motivated by the desire to directly manage structural funds
(Pasquier, 2006). The developments in the loosening of state regulations on
Community policy during Prime Minister Raffarin's right of centre government (2002–5) (right to experimentation, block grants) and the adoption of
the August 2004 law, which gave a legal basis to the delegation of management

of European funds to local authorities, should also be seen within this context. A few regions were able to experiment as early as 2003, and the extension to other regions was already planned. However, the political change which occurred during the 2004 regional elections, with the majority of regions shifting to the left, temporarily stopped the process. A bill neverthe-less programmed the continuation of these experiments for 2007–13 as part of the 'territorial cooperation' objective with the extension of the experiment carried out in Alsace over that period. Local authorities have prepared for this extension, and this anticipation as well as the block grant procedure (2000–6) have also contributed to the development and consolidation of services specialised in the management of structural funds.

Finally, Act 2 of devolution produced new compentence transfers and increased financial pressure on local authorities. Even if European funds decrease, they remain a possible source of financing in a context of shortage. Thus, the creation of specialised services can be analysed as the product of multiple attempts to maximise benefits, rather than as an effect of the Europeanisation of local authorities. This interpretation is supported by the fact that many specialists of Europe were previously specialists of other kinds of funding methods and grants.

If the state retained most of the responsibility in the management of funds, the increase in credits and more or less direct forms of management favoured the development of specialised positions in local authorities, thereby creating new career opportunities. This emerging professional market developed thanks to the shifting centre/periphery relationship, but was also driven by horizontal alliances and competitions.

Competition between local institutions

The development of services in local authorities is also a consequence of struggles between sub-national authorities, notably between regions and departments. These relationships are regulated by the centre under the influence of interests of local officials, due in particular to the ability of elected officials to hold both local and national political mandates. While the debate on the conservation of two intermediate administrative and political levels is recurrent in French politics, successive governments have adopted reforms that confer resources to both alternately. Indeed, if the 1995 land planning law was favourable to departments (Gaxie, 1997), the 1999 law was favourable to regions and brought back a balance in the power relations. The 2003 decentralisation project was meant to ensure the regionalisation of local public action in France by reinforcing the strategic dimension of the regional level, but the Parliament – where many representatives of department interests sit – ended up preserving the *status quo ante* (Le Lidec, 2005).

Shared competence in the implementation of EC public policies is a good illustration of this institutional competition. Formally, the regional level is endowed with the competence over Community policies. Inherited from the role of planning and programming of the regional public planning units set up in the 1960s (Duran, 1998), the strategic dimension of the region was reinforced by the 1992 ATR law, and reasserted by the 1999 land planning law, which defines a link between the Community level, the regional level and metropolitan areas. The periodicity of four-year state–region funding contracts now overlaps with European structural funds and regional executives are given more leeway in how funds are to be spent.

These institutional competences have however not systematically given a determining role to the regional councils, whose influence on the coordination of Community policies varies according to political configurations in each region. First, it depends on the relationships between regional councils and decentralised state services in regions. In other cases, there are strong ties between decentralised services in regions and regional councils in their opposition to the historically dominant departmental level. Furthermore, and this is particularly relevant here, it generally depends on the political and institutional power relations between regions and departments. In Rhône Alpes, for instance, the regional council is in competition with the Drôme and Ardèche departments, and the dynamics are all the more complex due to the political weight of departmental councillors within the regional council (Nay, 2002/3). While the law reorganised the management of structural funds at the regional level, in some regions the negotiation and the administration of European credits paradoxically favoured the reinforcement of the departmental level (see Smyrl (1997) for the PACA region, Pasquier (2004) for the Centre region), elsewhere even more perceptible regarding the management of certain funds destined for rural areas (FEDER and FEOGA, Balme and Jouve, 1995). This explains one of the first results of our study, which shows that departments developed specialised services at the same time as regional councils, or sometimes before. In the department councils, half of the positions held by respondents were created before the 2000s, compared to only a third in the regions.

This competition does imply an institutional homogeneity in the definition of the missions of sub-national levels actors. Indeed, the 'Europe' services in regions developed most frequently as offshoots of 'international relations' services (59%), whereas in departments 'land planning' (52%) and 'local development' (45%) were the dominant administrative matrix of development. Moreover, the missions of departmental services – except in specific cases such as cross-border programmes – consist less often in direct management or project supervision than in forms of active monitoring, assistance and coordination of other actors (land planning and local development, application assistance). This explains why services are bigger in the regions – as they manage bigger global grants, structural funds and a higher number of sectoral programmes – than in the departments where they are often reduced to a single policy officer, and are nearly always smaller than their regional counterparts. This also explains why officials or contract workers who work in departmental councils want to switch posts more frequently and move to another institution. They are relatively isolated, in charge, sometimes on their own, of the institution's entire European policy, which implies a great deal of dispersion of their daily activities. Career prospects within the institution also appear very limited in most cases.

One of the indicators of this last point is the low number of potential applicants for posts specialised in European affairs in department councils. Recruitments come more often from unsolicited applications, press or official announcements than in regional councils, where the recruitment paths more often involve 'networks' and internal promotion procedures. Nevertheless, as soon as services attain a certain size and perimeter of action, the similarities outweigh the differences between the two administrations, both in terms of working conditions and career anticipations.

I have shown that 'European' services depend more on domestic institutional configurations than on pull factors linked to European policies. While the configuration I have described is based on the French case, forms of institutional competition exist in all member states and comparative research on the institutional origins of 'professional markets' in other EU countries will be necessary to generalise these findings. I will now show that this institutional structuring also has effects on the structuring and segmentation in the job market.

Structuring and segmentation of the professional market: the limits to multi-level circulation

Our research points to the existence of a local job market specialised in European affairs. Local authorities have felt the need to consolidate their Europe services in order to improve the monitoring of Brussels imperatives, the management of structural funds, the quality of applications and the identification of local partners as well as partners in other member states. As I will show, the statutory competence devoted to state services and the local authorities' demands to manage these competences have led the latter to recruit specialised staff, coinciding with (and reinforcing) the growth in specialised Masters programmes seeking to train these professionals. This Europeanisation of local authority employees has also changed the patterns of recruitment in prefectures, which increasingly follow this pattern of 'specialisation'. However, the Europeanisation of these professionals does not imply a predisposition to multi-level circulation. Their career profiles precisely meet the needs of local authorities – which in turn consolidates the specialisation and segmentation of the market.

Polarisation and the field effect

Local professionals of Europe hold specific but very unequally distributed resources that make them 'specialists of Europe' and separate them from other personnel in their administrations, with whom they otherwise share common characteristics. I will first explain how their social origins, the structure of their educational resources or their career paths are close to those of other staffers in local authorities or decentralised services, even if they hold specific sectoral resources. I will then proceed to show how this market is polarised, despite a recent trend of homogenisation of the types of competences of local and prefecture services.

Franck Bachelet's study on the highest-ranking officials in local authorities (Bachelet, 2006) enables us to initiate a comparison with other professionals working in local authorities. The structure of the social and educational resources of both populations is relatively similar. Their social origins are often from the middle and upper classes of the intellectual pole of the social space, and they often hold degrees in law, economics or political science from a major provincial university (most with a Masters degree) or an Institute of Political Science. Their professional paths are generally embedded in the public sector, even if some, like senior officials in territorial authorities, have had experience in a specific private sector close to local authorities such as consultancy, or bureaus of local development. They distinguish themselves essentially through their sectoral specialisation. This 'sectoral competence on Europe' is mainly acquired through education. They have a general training in law, economy/management, or political science, but often also hold a Masters degree on European affairs and/or have written a Masters thesis on a European subject. When they have another form of specialisation, for instance in economic development and planning, they acquire a specialised training on Europe through continuing education. They have frequently studied in foreign universities, which provides them with linguistic capital, especially in English, and sometimes in a second or even a third foreign language. Those who hold the most European resources have also completed an internship in European institutions in Brussels, notably the Commission. This has favoured the development of a personal European network, along with their investments in European institutional networks (regional associations, networks of cities, associations of local authorities, etc.). Occasionally they are also personally involved in Europe and have been members or even leaders of a pro-European association. Beyond these institutionalised forms of investment, some also insist that they see their work as a personal contribution to Europe and its values ('Europe is an integral part of me', 'I'm addicted to Europe', 'I deliberately chose this position, it did not happen by accident or opportunity', etc.), and some were active in recent political mobilisations such as the defence of the European Constitutional Treaty (ECT). This specialisation is marked by the mastery of the jargon of the sector. Last but not least, they frequently go on to hold several successive positions with a European dimension during their careers, which proves that it is possible to have a career in the local European sector, and some agents obtain civil service status.

At the same time, the market for local professionals of Europe is also highly polarised. Indeed, there is on the one hand a pole specialised in European affairs predominantly located in local authorities, and on the other hand a more generalist administrative pole located within prefecture services. In local authorities, around two-thirds of the agents occupying a position labelled 'Europe' are specialised in European affairs, while one in ten are in prefectures, where the 'generalists' prevail.

All indications converge to attest to this differentiation, starting with university training. The highest degree held is discriminatory: only 10% of respondents in prefectures hold a specialised European degree compared with 50% in local authorities. On the contrary, one-third of respondents in prefectures hold a degree linked to administration (law, public administration, etc.). The respondents holding a Masters degree on Europe are most present in local authorities (around 40%) and much more rarely in prefectures (7%). Among respondents who completed a Masters thesis during their studies (three-quarters of the total), 45% of those working in local authorities wrote on a 'Community' issue – 30% in prefectures. Specialised continued education on Europe is also less frequent in prefectures (33%) than in local authorities (65%).

Having studied in another EU country is rarer in prefectures (about 10%) than in local authorities (about a third), as is work experience in another EU country. Correlatively, the mastery of foreign languages is one of the competences explicitly highlighted by half of the respondents to justify their access to their positions in local authorities, with only one in ten respondents from the prefectures making the same argument.

Similarly, if 'theoretical knowledge' (law, economy, management) constitutes the first type of competence thought to have favoured the access to the post held (82% in councils, 72% in prefectures), knowledge of European institutions is mentioned by most professionals in local authorities (86%) and seems less necessary to those in prefectures (32%). Specific forms of know-how on the management of Community programmes are also thought to have been important in recruitement. This is always the case in services in charge of European programmes (mainly management of structural funds and project applications), almost always in departmental or regional councils (project applications, management of structural funds and public relations) and more rarely in prefectures where in seven cases out of ten, no such specific competence is mentioned. Those whose career evolution predominantly involved the European sector are consequently much less numerous in prefectures (11%) than in local authorities (about half). Similarly, internship experiences in Brussels are more frequent in regional and departmental councils (about half), than in prefectures (one in four), producing a differentiation in the density of personal European social capital.

These distributions obviously have much to do with the activities specific to each institution. However, one can also suppose that, to rebalance the statutory asymmetry with state services, local authorities have recruited far more 'Europeanised' collaborators than prefecture services, sometimes even hiring away the most 'European' staff from prefectures. The strictly technical competence is found more often in local authorities than in prefecture services, which raises the issue of the continued pre-eminence of state services. It seems however that prefecture services are reacting to the challenge by progressively following the pattern set by local authorities through the recruitment of staff with greater European capital.

One of the explanations for this polarisation is a 'generation effect'. Indeed, European positions in prefectures are much more frequently held by men (six in ten) than in local authorities, where the proportion is reversed. Similarly, agents are much older in prefectures (37% born after 1970) than in local authorities (63% in regional and departmental councils). In addition to this generation-related cleavage, a second cleavage is related to the types of degrees held. In prefectures, the 'professionals of Europe' have more frequently completed a *licence-maîtrise* or the *Baccalauréat* alone, even if some are highly trained engineers, and much more rarely, holders of a Masters degrees or graduates from Institutes of Political Science. There is an important difference in terms of generation, which has consequences on gender, age and the type of degree held but also on career paths. Prefecture agents often hold a position labelled as 'European' after a long and multisectoral career, and reach these positions through internal circuits in two-thirds of the cases.

If we disregard this generation effect to focus on the youngest recruits in prefectures (those born after 1970), the profiles of 'young' recruits in prefectures are closer to those of their counterparts in local authorities. They have not necessarily spent their entire careers in prefectures, but have often held Europe-related positions in local authorities. They have more frequently received training or specialised continued education on Europe, sometimes with internships in Brussels, or are professionally specialised in European issues. They are likely to know several languages, be contract workers and envision switching posts a bit more frequently, but not necessarily within the same institution. Pending further research, we can posit that profiles in prefectures increasingly follow the pattern of those in local authorities. This could be explained by morphological market transformations and – this has yet to be proved – in an explicit recruitment policy of prefectures.

A segmented market: the limits of multi-level circulation

The professionals of Europe take part in the contractualisation of the relationships between Europe and their 'territories' and put together projects associating a variety of partners to be funded by the Commission. They monitor European programmes, assist project contractors, and represent their authority in the decision-making process (in various monitoring or evaluation committees) as well as occasionally performing the first-level control when the local authority manages programmes or structural funds directly.

They have a function of translation and mediation between the institution (political representatives, officials of the other operational directions), the field (associations, businesses or other partners), Europe, or even state institutions. They have technical know-how which enables them to comply with European regulations, a good command of foreign languages, knowledge of the field and a capacity for mediation. But outside those specialised resources, they mostly lack the social capital related to the accumulation of experience in Community milieus and the circulation in 'European' networks which is an essential part of the multi-level dynamic theorised by the MLG approach. This creates a rather segmented professional market of European positions in France.

This reading is supported by the extremely marginal presence of degrees from 'European schools' (ENA, Bruges or Natolin, LSE) amongst the respondents. Some initial and continuing training programmes favour the access to positions in local authorities (PAPE Strasburg, MAPROC Montpellier, *Centre d'Etudes Européennes* in Nancy, etc.), but they emphasise the territorial or regional dimension (Nancy, MAPROC, etc). If careers are rarely exclusively limited to the same local authority and tend to be characterised by institutional and/or territorial mobility, they have several features which demonstrate the limits of multi-level circulation. They unfold either in moves between local authorities, or within the prefecture networks; crossing from one career corridor to another is the exception rather than the rule. They also very seldom go from Europe to the local level and back, or between the national (European) and the local (European) level. The perception of the future is another confirmation of the degree of market segmentation. If 40% of respondents envision a change of position, they more often express the wish to move to a different region and/or institution in their own region, and much more rarely (18% of those who envision a change of position) to work in a European institution. Local positions specialised in Europe are therefore not a springboard to work in multi-level Europe – within national administrations, in another member state or in Brussels – other than in locally formed networks. As a result, European specialisation at the local levels opens only a limited number of doors. Due to the limited size of the potential market, positions of responsibility in European affairs are few and far between; local European careers therefore remain limited and agents have to change activity to progress in their careers.

This market is however marked by forms of heterogeneity that make the affirmation of a shared 'professional competence' difficult. This is visible in the questionnaires and interviews but needs to be systematised. A few avenues of thought on the structure of the professional space and positions that are associated with it can nonetheless be tentatively explored.

First, there is a differentiation according to the programmes and structural funds which vary according to the variable level of funding. Indeed, if Objective 1 funds are rare in metropolitan France, their management is concentrated in the Nord–Pas de Calais region. Within the framework of the 2000–6 programming, the programmes under the banner of Objective 2, financially more substantial, have received more attention from political representatives than Interreg-related programmes, for instance. With the 2007–13 programming, Interreg becomes more attractive again thanks to its promotion as a structural objective and the increased funding accorded to this new status – and all the more so as local authorities manage them directly. Beyond those European Regional Development Fund-related funds, the other two main funds, the European Social Fund (ESF) and the European Agricultural Guidance and Guarantee Fund (EAGGF), mobilise specific competences and types of networks (Duran, 1998; Nay, 2003). Finally, sectoral programmes (such as Comenius, Leonardo, etc.) became more attractive as the funding for more global structural funds dried up following enlargement. Unlike the latter, funding depends on the capacity to put together convincing and efficient programmes, thereby putting local authorities in competition with one another.

In addition, there are also status-related forms of differentiation. The statutory fragility of jobs linked to the management of Community initiative programmes (for example Urban) contrasts with the institutionalisation of services that implement programmes related to structural funds. The professionals in regional and departmental councils are thus more often civil servants, whereas professionals in municipal services and in development agencies and agglomerations who manage sectoral programmes tend to be contract workers. This probably explains why 80% of respondents in development agencies with a limited existence contemplated changing jobs in the near future, compared to 40% in regional councils, departmental councils and prefectures.

It is not surprising – even if these results have yet to be systematised – that the social background, professional experience or even perceptions of the future of those in charge of sectoral EU programmes (often contract workers), are more related to the private sector (22% of respondents in councils or prefectures have experience in the private sector – 50% in municipal or agglomeration services) than their counterparts working to implement programmes linked to structural funds. European sectoral capital, notably personal social capital enabling multi-level circulation, is also more often associated with these positions.

Conclusion

Beyond the potential use of this type of approach, allowing for a more socio-logical description of Europeanisation processes, I would argue that it raises the question of the relevance of the ceaseless search for new concepts in European studies. Indeed, we are confronted with a vicious circle where even those who voice criticisms on the concept of MLG use it, because it suppos-edly favours transnational comparisons and discussions and allows them to position themselves against the supposed provincialism of national academic traditions. However, the price to pay in terms of analytical and empirical precision is high. Neither the specificity of Europe nor the epistemological conditions of international discussions always justify this permanent race for new concepts. While this study is based on tentative results which need to be systematised, I wish to plead for the usefulness of a European comparison – based on empirical data and produced with the tools of the sociology of insti-tutions and public action – of local professional markets in Europe. Such an endeavour would allow for a better understanding of the capacity of circula-tion of these actors, who, at the intersection of various institutional spaces, participate in and produce the multi-level of 'governance'.

Notes

1 Rather than presenting a critique of the governance aspect of the question, which has already been done (Georgakakis and de Lassalle, 2007), I aim to focus on the multi-level aspect in this chapter.
2 Jordan (2001) provides a synthesis of the recurrent criticisms: the lack of a fresh perspective; the deficit in terms of causal explanation; the confusion between mobil-isation and influence of subnational actors; the overly 'top down' approach; the underestimation or absence of the 'international level' and a focus on local 'authori-ties' to the detriment of others.
3 See for instance Swartz and Zolberg (2004).
4 See among other examples the competitive cluster strategy, implemented from 2004, or the transformation of the name of the DATAR (*Délégation à l'Aménagement du territoire et à l'action régionale*) into DIACT (*Délégation interministérielle à l'aménagement et à la compétitivité des territoires*) in 2005.
5 There are several possible definitions – here is one adapted to the 'local' object: 'Europeanisation is a process whereby European ideas and practice transfer to the core of local decision-making as well as from local policy-making arenas to the supra-national level. The European function is a means whereby public authorities can innovate and initiate policies and programmes in the context of trans-national coop-eration and European policy-making' (John, 2001: 73).
6 In the case of France: local authorities or decentralised services, networks of cities or regions, national administrations and organisations specialised in regional planning and development, regional offices in Brussels, Permanent Representation, *Comité des Régions*, or even EC administration.
7 I will not elaborate on this dimension due to lack of space.

8   Loi relative à l'administration territoriale de la République.
9   Considering that the programming period was extended from six to seven years.

Bibliography

Bachelet, F., 'Sociologie, formation et carrière des hauts fonctionnaires territoriaux', *Annuaire 2006 des collectivités territoriales*, Paris: CNRS Éditions, 2006, 99–113.

Balme, R. and Jouve, B., 'L'Europe en région. Les fonds structurels et la régionalisation de l'action publique en France métropolitaine', *Politique et Management Public*, 13 (2), 1995, 35–58.

Benz, A. and Eberlein, B., 'The Europeanization of Regional Policies: Pattern of Multi-level Governance', *Journal of European Public Policy*, 6 (2), 1999, 329–348.

Börzel, T., 'Europeanization and Territorial Institutional Change – Towards Cooperative Regionalism?', in J. Caporaso, M. Green Cowles and T. Risse (eds), *Transforming Europe – Europeanization and Domestic Change*, Ithaca: Cornell University Press, 2000, 137–158.

Bourdieu, P., 'Espace social et Genèse des "classes"', *Actes de la Recherche en Sciences sociales*, 52, 1984, 3–14.

Brenner, N., Building '"Euro-regions" – Locational Politics and the Political Geography of Neoliberalism in Post-unification Germany', *European Urban and Regional Studies*, 7 (4), 2000, 319–345.

Carter, C. and Smith, A., 'Revitalizing Public Policy Approaches to the EU: "Territorial Institutionalism", Fisheries and Wine', *Journal of European Public Policy*, 15 (2), 2008, 281–283.

Christiansen, T., 'Territorial Politics in the European Union', *Journal of European Public Policy*, 6 (2), 1999, 349–357.

Costa, O., 'Les représentants des entités infra-étatiques auprès de l'Union. Processus de professionnalisation diversifiés et intérêts communs', in D. Georgakakis (ed.), *Les métiers de l'Europe politique Acteurs et professionnalisations de l'Union européenne*, Strasburg: Presses Universitaires de Strasburg, 2002, 147–168.

Desage, F. and Godard, J., 'Désenchantement idéologique et réenchantement mythique des politiques locales. *Retour* critique sur le rôle des idées dans l'action publique', *Revue française de science politique*, 55 (4), 2005, 633–661.

Duran, P., 'Le partenariat dans la gestion des fonds structurels: la situation française', *Pôle sud*, 8, 1998, 114–139.

Gaxie, D. (ed.), *Luttes d'institutions. Enjeux et contradictions de l'administration territoriale*, Paris: L'Harmattan, 1997.

Georgakakis, D. and de Lassalle M. (eds), *La nouvelle gouvernance européenne, genèses et usages d'un Livre Blanc*, Strasburg: Presses Universitaires de Strasburg, 2007.

Heinelt, H. and Niederhafner, S., 'Cities and Organized Interest Intermediation in the EU Multilevel System', *European Urban and Regional Studies*, 15 (2), 2008.

Hooghe, L. and Keating, M., 'The Politics of European Regional Policy', *Journal of European Public Policy*, 1 (3), 1994, 53–78.

Hooghe, L. and Marx, G., *Multi Level Governance and European Integration*, Lanham, MD: Rowman and Littlefield, 2001.

Hooghe, L. and Marx, G., 'Unraveling the Central State, But How? Types of Multi-Level Governance', *The American Political Science Review*, 97 (2), 2003, 233–243.

Jeffery, C., 'Sub-national Mobilisation and European Integration', *Journal of Common Market Studies*, 38 (1), 2000, 1–23.

Jeffery, C. (ed.), *The Regional Dimension of the European Union – Towards a Third Level in Europe*, London: Frank Cass, 1997.

John, P., *Local Governance in Western Europe*, London: Sage, 2001.

Jordan A., 'The European Union: An Evolving System of Multi-level Governance ... or Government', *Policy and Politics*, 29 (23), 2001, 193–208.

Lagroye, J., *Sociologie politique*, 3rd edn, Paris: Presses de Sciences Po, 1997.

Le Lidec, P., 'Pourquoi une nouvelle étape de la décentralisation? Modernisation politique et compétition politique', in G. Marcou and H. Wollmann (eds), *Annuaire 2004 des collectivités locales*, Paris: CNRS Éditions, 2004.

Le Lidec, P., 'La relance de la décentralisation en France: de la rhétorique managériale aux réalités politiques', *Politiques et management public*, 3 Sept. 2005, 101–125.

Lozac'h, V., 'Les communes allemandes face à la gouvernance européenne: entre logique de transposition et stratégies de repositionnement', in D. Georgakakis and M. de Lassalle (eds), *La nouvelle gouvernance européenne, genèses et usages d'un Livre Blanc*, Strasburg: Presses Universitaires de Strasburg, 2007, 255–286.

Marshall, A., 'Europeanization at the Urban Level: Local Actors, Institutions and the Dynamics of Multi-level Interaction', *Journal of European Public Policy*, 12 (4), 2005, 668–686.

Marx, G., 'Structural Policy and Multigovernance in the EC', in A. Cafruny and G. Rosenthal (eds), *The State of the European Community*, London: Longman, 1993, 391–410.

Mathiot, P., 'Les effets de la gestion de dispositifs communautaires sur les acteurs et les systèmes d'action nationaux – L'exemple de l'Objectif 3 du FSE', *Politix*, 43, 1998, 79–91.

Nay, O., 'Négocier le partenariat – Jeux et conflits dans la mise en œuvre de la politique communautaire en France', *Revue française de science politique*, 51 (3), 2001, 4459–4481.

Nay, O., 'La négociation en régime d'incertitude. Une comparaison des partenariats publics régionaux dans la mise en œuvre de la politique européenne (I)', *Revue internationale de politique comparée*, 9, 2002/3, 409–425.

Offerlé, M., *Les partis politiques*, 4th edn, Paris: PUF, 2002.

Pasquier, R., *La capacité politique des régions: une comparaison France – Espagne*, Rennes: Presses Universitaires de Rennes, 2004.

Pasquier, R., 'Quel avenir pour les régions françaises? Un scénario de moyenne portée?', *Pouvoirs locaux*, 70, 2006, 139–142.

Regards sociologiques, 'Sur l'Europe', 27–28, 2004.

Smith, A., *L'Europe politique au miroir du local*, Paris: L'Harmattan, 1995.

Smith, A., *Le gouvernement de l'Union européenne. Une sociologie politique*, Paris: LGDJ, 2004.

Smith, A. and Négrier, E., 'Echanges politiques territorialisés et action publique européenne: le cas du Languedoc Roussillon', in E. Négrier and B. Jouve, *Que gouvernent les régions d'Europe?*, Paris: L'Harmattan, 1998, 85–104.

Smyrl, M., 'Does European Community Regional Policy Empower the Regions?', *Governance*, 10 (3), 1997, 287–309.

Swartz, D. and Zolberg, V. (eds), *After Bourdieu, Influence, Critique, Elaboration*, Boston: Klewer Academic Publishers, 2004.

PART II

The social construction of European problems

LAURENT SCHEECK

5
Constitutional activism and fundamental rights in Europe: common interests through transnational socialisation

Interests defended by political actors are deeply embedded in social, histori-cal, normative and institutional contexts. But when analysing why political motives emerge and how political agendas are being shaped, one cannot merely acknowledge the importance of norms, discourses, identities, and institutions without taking into account the concrete demands and concerns that underpin the behaviour of political entrepreneurs and the socio-historic context in which they evolve and relate to each other.

Human rights in Europe exemplify a situation where the strategic social-isation of legal elites has led to the emergence of a common transnational culture of rights that has become tightly knotted to the mobilisation of a shared view of the EU's political and institutional architecture. This border-less socialisation of European judges, entrenched into a complex set of intertwined jurisprudence and upheld by supranational judicial institutions, has contributed to set up a sophisticated mechanism of supranational human rights supervision which had not been planned at the beginning of the construction of Europe. The European Court of Justice (ECJ) and the European Court of Human Rights (ECHR) are at the core of this mechanism.

Similarly, the European Union's judge-made human rights system was developed long before member states agreed on including it into the treaties – the European Constitution and the Lisbon Treaty,[1] which then proved to be hard to ratify, while the judges keep the existing jurisprudential system up and running. Beyond the idea of protecting people from the actions of European institutions and member states implementing EU politics – this is what the question of human rights at the EU level of governance is concretely about – fundamental norms have been given a deeper political meaning over time. Human rights at the EU level have indeed become an instrument for a federalist cause driven by lawyers in or around the ECJ (see Vauchez and

Marchand in this volume). Their constitutional discourse has not been limited to judicial politics. For more than forty years, Europe's lawyers have been calling for a rights-based supranational constitutionalism in their dialogue with policy-makers and have argued for the incremental constitutionalisation of the European political order.

This chapter aims to empirically trace back the mutually reinforcing relationship between both European courts resulting from the mobilisation of some leaders in both courts who opted in favour of a high-profile, diplomatic socialisation after years of indirect jurisprudential interactions. The objective is to provide explanations for the emergence of common interests between judicial actors through transnational socialisation.

On the one hand, this research is a case study of inter-institutional socialisation where institutions are not seen as mere arenas for the convergence of national representatives but as supranational platforms of an emerging multi-level system of government. On the other hand, it studies how 'normative entrepreneurs' seek to be continually present in specific judicial and political environments in order to spread shared ideas gained through previous inter-institutional socialisation.

Firstly, I will address the particularities of transnational socialisation in a supranational setting. Secondly, I will study the mobilisations of a transnational legal elite focusing on the judges of the two European Courts, who, against strong internal and external political and judicial resistance, engaged in a cooperative dialogue at a supranational level. Thirdly, I will analyse the overall political effects of the socialisation between Europe's lawyers on European politics, institutions and treaty-making. A most striking feature that appears when studying the socialisation of these transnational elites is that their multifaceted interactions tend to reduce 'intergovernmental choice' – i.e. the decisions taken jointly by member states in intergovernmental conferences, in the European Council and in the Council of the EU – when it comes to agenda-setting, institutional design and shaping policy outcomes.

The European courts as supranational platforms for inter-institutional socialisation

This research focuses on how supranational lawyers have engaged in processes of transnational socialisation since the end of the 1990s. Tracing back these processes can help explain why and how evolving political, institutional, social, public and private interests contribute to construct and shape a political space. Because socialisation highlights the nexus between institutions, policy processes and political entrepreneurs, a contextual socio-historical study of their motives and the modalities of their mobilisation is an important factor in explaining the emergence of shared ideas and 'common sense'.

In this particular case, we address the issue of the emergence of a

European political space as the result of intensive socialisation between legal entrepreneurs that use courts as supranational platforms for policy- and treaty-making and the expansion of EU rules, as well as a for transnational mobilisations on constitutional issues in political, judicial and academic fora all over Europe that effectively contribute to the institutionalisation of supra-national governance.

Inter-institutional and cross-organisational interaction at the level of European supranational governance is a rather neglected but particularly significant variable of the European process of integration. Tracing the emergence of new policy agendas also implies looking at the strategic mobil-isation of stakeholders acting in often unexpected configurations, beyond the borders of institutions they formally belong to. In this vein, this article aims to study the relationship between the ECJ and the ECHR. The ECJ's funda-mental role in the process of European integration has been studied extensively by political scientists (Burely and Mattli, 1993; Dehousse, 1998; Alter, 2001; Stone Sweet, 2004; Vauchez 2008). The ECHR's role in this regard has not been as fully investigated in political science (for two excep-tions, see Madsen, 2007 and Anagnostou, 2008). Legal scholars have of course always had a keen interest in fundamental rights at the EU level and in the EU–ECHR relationship (for a recent contribution, see Krisch, 2008). While they generally address the competition and conflicts of the ECJ and the ECHR, this chapter also addresses the cooperative nature of the fundamental rights dialogue of supranational judges and the unexpected mutually empow-ering relationship of the two European courts. Moreover, the ECJ has played an important role in the making of the European constitution – not only from a judicial point of view, but as Marie-Pierre Granger has demonstrated, also through the activism of the European judges in political arenas (Granger, 2005). Yet the relationship between fundamental rights and the judicial constitutionalism of the ECJ and the ECHR remains largely unexplored.

Historically, the study of socialisation in Europe has been a way to explain how elites from different member states get together in order to construct Europe (Haas, 1958). More recent studies also have emphasised the role of elite socialisation in the emergence of a 'common European identity' and tried to explain how national actors are being transformed into European-minded agents through regular cooperation in highly institution-alised settings (Checkel, 2005). While these studies have shown *how* institutions matter as 'promoters of socialisation in public arenas' (Checkel, 2001), the conceptualisation of international or, in this case, European insti-tutions as mere *receptacles* of processes of socialisation, also has several limits.

In this chapter the phenomenon of elite socialisation in Europe is approached from a different, non-cognitive angle. Socialisation is defined in a symbolic interactionist sense (Becker, 1963), as a set of socially rooted, continuous, not necessarily voluntary or successful transmission of practices, know-how and knowledge that is highly dependent on a permanently (re-)negotiated and changing order. While socialisation can lead to a broad range of not necessarily compatible or expected outcomes, it produces particular behaviour and normative outcomes that are specific to a particular social sphere, leading to reflexive effects on the set of institutions in which actors socialise.

When it comes to assessing effects and outcomes, as Norbert Elias argued, the obligations, rights and forms of reciprocal empowerment that derive from socialisation have to be taken into account (Elias, 1987). While neo-functionalist accounts of judicial integration have shed light on the macro-processes of integration (Stone Sweet, 2004), the socialisation of judicial actors might also help to give us a better understanding of the practices of individuals working inside and around European courts who shape European law in their daily activities, as well as the complex web of social relations in which they evolve (Cohen, 2007; Vauchez, 2008). Contrary to most neo-institutional studies, which study the role of institutions in an often monolithical way, our emphasis is on the 'sociological study of the European political space' (Georgakakis, 2008) and the sociability of normative entrepreneurs in inter-institutional contexts.

When linkage matters more than institutions

By approaching this phenomenon from a different angle and in a more contextual way, we seek to link the phenomena of socialisation, interest formation and inter-institutional relations in the European configuration. This also means that Europe is not limited to the organisational boundaries of the EU and shows, more generally, that political spaces cannot be reduced to a purely institutional vision. The following four methodological propositions might help to put studies on socialisation in Europe on a more firm footing.

1) This chapter does not address the psychological, identity-related side of socialisation: rather than speculating on the transformation of individual preferences, socialisation is studied as a historically embedded political process. European institutions are not seen as arenas for intergovernmental socialisation, but rather as *supranational platforms* allowing for the socialisation of actors that are *relatively* autonomous from governmental influence. By focusing on tangible qualitative and quantitative evidence (i.e. interviews, discourse analysis, official documents on the one hand, and statistical data on the evolution of the jurisprudence on the other), we study the emergence and political impact of shared ideas as a result of inter-institutional socialisation. In order to trace back the relationship between all actors involved and to reconstruct their subjective points of view, this research is based on more than 80 interviews with European judges, legal secretaries, law clerks, civil servants, trial lawyers, NGO representatives, and law professors in Strasburg,

Luxembourg, Paris and Brussels from April 2002 to November 2007 at the ECJ, the Court of First Instance (CFI), the ECHR, the European Commission, the Permanent Representation of the Council of Europe to the EU, several Permanent Representations to the EU (France, Germany, Luxembourg, Sweden), the Secretariat and Committee of Ministers of the Council of Europe and the French and Belgian Councils of State.

2) We also take into account contextual elements, like the socio-historical evolution of European politics, institutions and case law, as well as reactions to jurisprudence. The evolution of the jurisprudence of the European courts has been traced back through a qualitative and quantitative case law analysis. This allows us to highlight the changing politics of the courts. Legal change is seen as a process of normative empowerment and autonomisation, by which courts tend to initially build up case law based on (inter)governmentally designed conventions and law, the latter becoming progressively less significant as judges infuse their own interpretations into their judgments, hence producing more autonomous laws and, sometimes, a noticeable political impact as policy-makers adapt treaties and laws to jurisprudence. This socio-historic approach demonstrates the limits of intergovernmental accounts of human rights in Europe (Moravcsik, 1995). Actors from member states have certainly played an important role in the creation of the human rights system of the Council of Europe, but intergovernmental approaches fail to explain why and how rights that were initially absent from the European Communities were invented in the first place, as the ECJ did in the 1960s in conjunction with national courts and a multitude of private, supranational and academic actors. Nor do intergovernmental approaches take into account the fact that human rights in the EU are a mostly judicial product or the crucial role of the European Court of Human Rights in this process.

3) Shared ideas among European judges belonging to different institutions are seen as the result of transnational mobilisations based on jointly constructed interests and systemic pressure resulting from previous 'reciprocal actions', as Georg Simmel would have put it (Simmel, 1908), rather than stable pre-existing identities. Far from being rational outputs of individuals able to efficiently translate their preferences into political action, new policy agendas appear to be the product of social mobilisations by directly concerned and often highly mobilised groups interacting in a context of uncertainty and unexpected normative interdependence.

4) Interests are not given and they evolve constantly as normative entrepreneurs shape them. But there is no socialisation without an incentive to do so either. The case of the relationship between the two European courts shows that the leaders of both European courts have found a fundamental shared interest to cooperate and to minimise their rivalry. More cooperation potentially means more autonomy and power over public and private judicial entrepreneurs; more competition or even conflict means a higher exposure for each court to the resistance of public and private actors to EU

and human rights law. Despite occasional clashes and disagreements, the formation of an inter-institutional 'common interest' between the European courts turns out to be the direct result of the *strategic socialisation* between the leaders of these courts and their subsequent common mobilisation in political, judicial and academic circles – a multifaceted diplomacy of the European courts which then led to an institutional policy shift in both institutions where inter-institutional linkage began to matter more than institutional egoisms.

From fundamental rights to judicial constitutionalism

Moving the protection of human rights to the European level was a highly political act. Unlike in the context of the Council of Europe, protecting rights *from* the level of the European Union could imply a much stronger and autonomous control of European but also national actors implementing EU policies and law. For this reason, most debates and concrete advances have been about protection rights *at* the EU level of governance (i.e. protecting persons with regard to the working of the European institutions, as opposed to an EU supervision of purely national politics).

But at this particular level, there has been a lot of controversy about human rights because these norms have become instruments for the judicial constitutionalisation of the EU, and for the deepening of integration (Scheeck, 2005a). The evolution of jurisprudence as well as discourses of judges and politicians show that human rights have indeed been used, quite often successfully, to uphold the legal foundations of the EU, to improve the implementation of EU law at the national level and to extend the scope of EU competences. Many federalists have tried to create a human rights catalogue similar to the German *Grundgesetz*. All these activities have of course met with strong resistance, less by human rights opponents than by those seeking to protect spheres of national sovereignty and those fearing that the discourse of a European federal state could become reality with the creation of a rights-based constitution (Weiler, 2000; Von Bogdandy, 2000).

The EU's constitutional failure in 2005 was a turning point. As we are moving away from the possibility of a state-like entity at the European level, we are also reminded that the constitutional discourse of many European actors has always been questionable when describing and qualifying the nature (or the future) of the EU political regime. Now that Europe's 'constitutional fever' has passed, it is still possible to argue that the EU has some aspects of a federal structure, but it lacks a constitutive moment which would enable the Union to present itself as a federation and be identified as such. Yet the emergence of rights at the EU level is so tightly linked to the idea of a federal Europe that the constitutional activism of the protagonists of this configuration needs to be taken into account.

Historically, the origins of EU rights lie in the courts. Member states only took up this matter decades after the courts started to deal with it.[2] The link with European constitutionalism was created parallel to this evolution. It can be synthesised as follows.

As of the 1970s, the ECJ started to eagerly protect human rights, most of all because some national constitutional courts did not accept the primacy of European law, arguing that rights were not sufficiently protected in the European Communities. By the end of the 1970s, we witnessed the emergence of a constitutional fundamental rights-based jurisprudence in the European courts, when the ECJ started to be confronted with many human rights cases and when its judges increasingly relied on the ECHR. Since the late 1980s, there has been an increasing interaction between jurisprudence and treaties. The human rights provisions of the Maastricht and subsequent EU treaties as well as the Charter of Fundamental Rights, are strongly inspired by the ECJ jurisprudence, itself derived from the ECHR. Subsequently, there has been an increasing mobilisation of European judges, by positioning themselves as constitutional judicial actors, through the development of inter-institutional socialisation and more direct interaction with the masters of the treaties by the end of the 1990s.

The question of human rights protection at the European level only appeared gradually when private actors started to mobilise this repertoire before the ECJ,[3] when some judges and law professors (Waelbroeck, 1965; Pescatore, 1969) started to write about this problem and when national constitutional courts bound the fate of the European Communities to their ability to protect rights.[4] In the 1950s, the drafters of the European treaties did not plan for any kind of protection of citizens with regard to the action of Community institutions. It also appeared that the Council of Europe's European Convention of Human Rights and its human rights court were hardly competent to provide external control on the European Communities. Since national constitutional courts bound their acceptance of the primacy of European law to the existence of appropriate human rights control mechanisms at the European Community level in the 1970s, protecting rights became important, even if EU treaties did not focus on this issue. ECJ judges therefore felt compelled to invent their own competencies and expertise in this area. In parallel, the Strasburg-based human rights court somewhat unexpectedly provided for an incremental external control of EU institutions, including the ECJ, and EU member states implementing EU law.[5]

As the ECJ became a second European court dealing with human rights issues at a supranational level and the relationship between the EU and the Council of Europe became increasingly nested in the 1990s, the judges of the two European courts were giving increasing attention to their relationship. Despite a history of tensions between these two jurisdictions, linked to very different organisations holding a historically competitive, but now converging position (Brosig, 2006), judges of the European courts have chosen to proceed in a cooperative manner.

Their common mobilisation can be explained as a means to regulate bilateral conflicts and inter-institutional competition, but also by their joint exposure to (new) political and judicial forms of resistance to supranational adjudication (Weiler, 2007). In addition, the setting of a new context has been facilitating the relationship between the two institutions due to two main legal elements: first, the drafting of the Charter of Fundamental Rights, and the agreement, after decades of dissention, to make it legally binding in the next treaty; second, the agreement reached to include the necessary provisions to make the EU accede to the European Convention of Human Rights, controlled by the European Court of Human Rights.

Entangled courts

Beyond the institutional context, cooperation between the ECJ and the ECHR has been favoured for two further reasons. On the one hand, each court has hung a sword of Damocles over the head of the other. The Strasburg court has very carefully positioned itself in a way to be able to sanction EU law and ECJ decisions – yet a bad human rights record might trigger more national resistance with regard to the primacy of EU law (Scheeck, 2005b). A withdrawal of the jurisprudential and symbolic support for the ECHR by the very powerful EU court might also considerably weaken the Strasburg court. On the other hand, the growing awareness of this risk has led both courts to uphold their respective work in practice.

Until now, the European Court of Human Rights has never sanctioned an ECJ decision as such, as doing so would qualify the ECJ as a transgressor of human rights and bring into question the supremacy of EU law, a principle which does not appear in the treaties and only holds in constitutional courts as long as fundamental rights are respected. The more the ECJ aligns itself with Strasburg, the more it reduces the risk of being disavowed by the European Court of Human Rights (Scheeck, 2008).

Conversely, the less the European Court of Human Rights puts the ECJ under pressure, the more it reduces the risk of being sidelined by the ECJ. Just as the ECJ's supranational authority is not carved in stone, the European Court of Human Rights has also been increasingly put under pressure by national courts and institutions. This might not be surprising, as Strasburg spends its time assessing whether or not national institutions have violated the Convention. Here, the ECJ could exert pressure by intentionally or unintentionally encouraging national actors to make diverging interpretations from Strasburg case law by issuing preliminary rulings that diverge from established ECHR jurisprudence.

If Strasburg, for its part, started to sanction EU acts before the EU's formal accession to the Convention, it would run the risk of reprisals from ECJ judges. As the EU grows larger, the ECJ would, in theory, have the institutional power and political resources to sideline the ECHR and its court, especially since some governments would have no objections to a less prominent human rights court. The ECJ could, for example, stop aligning its case law or exclusively rely on the Charter of Fundamental Rights, which provides a slightly higher level of protection than the ECHR for EU citizens.

Apart from reciprocal intrusions, there can also be direct conflict between the European courts. The *Senator Lines* case at the European Court of Human Rights (10.03.2004), which was directed against all EU member states, is a recent illustration of inter-institutional conflict and an example of how a private actor, marching into both supranational arenas at the same time with the help of lawyers, strategically and successfully managed to bring unwelcome turbulence into the relationship between the two courts at the very moment when judges tried to insist on the positive side of their linkage (Scheeck, 2005b).

So there has been a concern in Strasburg about the ECJ's power to undermine its case law in the absence of a formal accession to the Convention, which could put the ECHR into a hierarchically more comfortable position with regard to the ECJ and the Charter of Fundamental Rights. In Luxembourg, many fear that one day Strasburg could declare an ECJ decision void, opening up the Pandora's box of a potential national judicial refusal to respect the primacy of EU law in the absence of sufficient human rights observance.

The balance between the two courts remains very delicate. By confronting each other, the courts run the risk of reciprocally untying the authority of their increasingly overlapping legal orders to the benefit of those actors that are generally suspicious of independent judicial institutions, especially when they perform an external control with regard to human rights. Yet by respecting and referring to each other's work, the European courts uphold their own position and, incidentally, the other court's. The latter scenario is now clearly favoured in Strasburg and in Luxembourg given their common supranational specificity, their comparable exposure to sovereignist actors, and their comparable objective of upholding supranational institutions and legal orders.

Their discreet solidarity has translated into strong dynamics of 'cross-fertilisation'. This cooperation allows them to prevent public and private actors from increasing the fragmentation of EU and European human rights law and, hence, increases their autonomy within their basic organisational units. The European judges would themselves be the first victims of a war of European judges. Although they don't always trust each other – thus the need to keep all channels of dialogue open – ostentatious references to Strasburg's case law in Luxembourg and Strasburg's occasional support of the supremacy of EU law have an appeasing effect.

Mutual judicial assistance

These dynamics of cross-fertilisation have not only led to an enrichment of both courts' ability to protect human rights. They also increased both courts' autonomy with regard to the EU and Council of Europe member states and private actors.

Intentionally or not, Strasburg has been promoting the supremacy of European law invented by the ECJ in the 1960s, but which has sometimes been difficult to enforce at the national level. For example, in the *Dangeville* and *Cabinet Diot et SA Gras* cases against France (16.04.2002 and 22.07.2003), the European Court of Human Rights condemned France for failing to align French law with EU law, thus promoting the implementation and coherence of European law.

The European Court of Human Rights judges also have made use of the EU treaties and they have increasingly been referring to Luxembourg's case law in order to fortify their decisions (Spielmann, 2004). Similarly, the ECJ has radically aligned itself on Strasburg's jurisprudence and increasingly refers to its decisions. Whereas Luxembourg sometimes gave the impression of avoiding a submission to the ECHR (see opinion 2/94 in 1996, where the ECJ ruled against an EU submission to the ECHR), its current approach is less defiant. By using the ECHR the Court of Justice has filled its own void of human rights instruments and it has 'charmed' the ECHR by using the Convention without being formally obliged to. Given its authority over national courts, the ECJ's recent approach has a legitimising effect on Strasburg's activities. References to the ECHR have indeed increased dramatically over the last ten years.

As shown in Figure 5.1 the references to the ECHR by ECJ and CFI judges and Advocates-General have been increasing constantly since 1998. It also shows that the use of the ECHR has, by far, become the main human rights instrument of the ECJ,[6] despite the fact that the EU has not acceded to the ECHR and that there is no legal obligation for the ECJ to refer to the Convention.

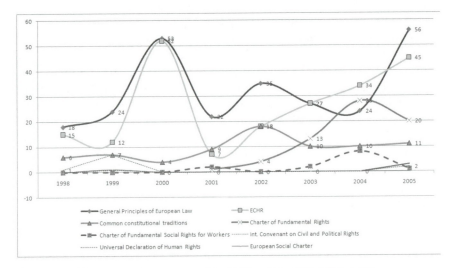

Figure 5.1   The normative sources of the ECJ and the CFI, 1998–2005

From a qualitative point of view, ECJ references to Strasburg's case law are a way to streamline case law in the rather fragmented European normative space and reduce the gaps that enable resistance to EU and human rights law. The *Schmidberger, Internationale Transporte und Planzüge* case (12.06.2003) is a good example where the Luxembourg court put human rights before fundamental freedoms, *de facto* favouring rights protected by the ECHR – more specifically freedom of expression – over economic rights – freedom of movement of goods – granted by the EU treaties (Alemanno, 2004; Morijn, 2006).

In this vein, the ECJ has helped to put an end to the debate on the clash between the 'Europe of human rights' and the 'Europe of trade' by relying on the ECHR and its case law. By referring to each other's case law, the web of 'judicial law', as opposed to 'political law', which emerged from the interactions of the two courts, has had a reinforcing effect on both judicial institutions. Whereas the Strasburg court has found an ally in protecting human rights in EU member states, the inclusion of the ECHR in ECJ case law increases the legitimacy of its judgments and its impact on the national level. Human rights and the primacy of European law have thus become inextricably linked in the EU – they are not only about protecting individuals or groups against governments but about protecting and constitutionalising the institutional and legal architecture of the EU.

This might appear paradoxical in the sense that human rights usually tend to diminish the power of public actors, whereas in the European case, human rights empower supranational public actors. Upholding rights is a means for the ECJ to protect the EU's constitutional system and to become more autonomous; the active protection of rights at the supranational level has even become a way to deepen integration and, if not to erode national sovereignty, at least to circumvent the resistance of national judicial systems to European politics and to anchor supranational norms at the national level. As they relate to each other in order to prevail over national and private actors in supranational courts, the European courts have thus brought up a common supranational 'jurisprudential screen' to protect their institutional interests. However, these various forms of mutual assistance, which uphold and strengthen each court, would not have emerged without the continuous socialisation of the European judges.

A supranational judicial diplomacy
Since the ECHR became a permanent and more independent institution in 1998, the judges and court officials of the ECJ and the Strasburg court have been meeting on a regular, but not formally institutionalised, basis. After having communicated with each other for many years through their respective case law, their direct encounters take many different forms: the judges have been holding regular bilateral meetings since the ECHR became permanent in 1998;[7] they have been inviting each other to make speeches at

the other court (Rodriguez Iglesias, 2002) and, according to an ECJ judge, some have regular contact by phone or email and even meet privately.[8] The dialogue of European judges finds a broader audience in political institutions,[9] legal fora,[10] when they meet at conferences on European issues[11] or even at colloquia.[12] In the same vein, they jointly give interviews on their courts' relationships[13] and they actively contribute to the body of literature on the subject.[14] As the judges contribute to shape the image of their relationship (toward more cooperation), it appears that the objective of these new judicial politics, no longer restricted to courtrooms, is to shape wider political and judicial processes on European as well as national levels of governance.

Some of these legal entrepreneurs emphasise the courts' inter-jurisdictional 'cross-fertilisation' (Jacobs, 2003). It is also asserted that the impression of mutual defiance between the two courts is 'in fact the opposite of what happens in reality' (Puissochet and Costa, 2001: 164 – ECJ judge Puissochet speaking). For ECJ judge Allan Rosas,

> the thesis, often put forward in the legal literature, that there is a tension or even conflict between Luxembourg and Strasburg case-law is somewhat exaggerated, to put it mildly. Harmony, rather than conflict, is a much more likely scenario. (Rosas, 2005)

According to some judges and court officials,[15] the presidents of the two courts, Luzius Wildhaber (ECHR) and G.C. Rodriguez Iglesias (ECJ) played the most important role in the effective rapprochement between the two institutions. Advocate-General Francis Jacobs (now retired), who regularly went to Strasburg when working for the ECJ, also played a pivotal role in this respect. He had argued in favour of a rapprochement between the two courts in the early 1990s and many see him as the driving force behind their reinforced relationship.

Speculation on the contents of the more confidential regular discussions between judges is proportional to the culture of secrecy that surrounds their gatherings. According to interviewed judges in Strasburg and in Luxembourg,[16] the European judges' bilateral meetings, alternately held in Luxembourg and in Strasburg on an annual basis, are relatively informal. Not all judges participate in these gatherings. The delegations that are sent to the other court usually comprise the president and the judges who are most familiar with the EU–ECHR relationship.

According to the judges interviewed, these discussions tend to avoid direct confrontation on institutional issues and their encounters do not take the form of direct bilateral conflict resolution. Instead, presentations and debates on the evolution of their respective case law are central, allowing judges to compare their approach to similar judicial problems. Comparisons of recent case law are not only useful for reciprocal inspiration, but also help to prevent divergent case law on similar cases, and hence lessen the risks of inter-institutional conflict.

The judges' meetings have played an important role in streamlining case law as they produce a trust-building effect. Whereas the judges of the ECHR, and above all its president, have pleaded in favour of the EU accession to the Convention on a regular basis, the ECJ judges increasingly welcome it as well (see Wathelet, 2002; interview with a judge at the ECJ, June 2004). For ECJ judge Allan Rosas, the EU's accession would 'remove an outdated anomaly in today's European human rights system' (Rosas, 2005). Taking good care of the courts' relationship is both a way to protect their institutions' respective position within their respective organisations and to consolidate the supranational protection of human rights in Europe.[17] Since both courts' case law simultaneously contains the seeds of possible convergence or conflict, the judges' direct dialogue has taken the form of high-profile diplomatic consultations. While norms and institutions proliferate and increasingly overlap, the linkage between institutions has not only become a way to overcome a highly fragmented process of regional integration, but also provides a means for coherence without uniformity.

In Luxembourg it is now commonly considered that formal accession to the ECHR would not change the current state of affairs and the judges appear to be aware of their joint influence on European politics. According to an ECJ judge, 'by citing other courts we keep the member states together. If a member state does not comply with a certain interpretation, it is important that all international courts have the same analysis'.[18]

The European judges have indeed learned to prefer a mutual reinforcement of the two supranational courts, rather than run the risk of weakening both institutions by asserting a claim to be the 'highest court' in Europe. As the courts are entangled in a web of constraining relations, it now seems that a formal accession would have more advantages than disadvantages – even for member states that have traditionally opposed the EU's accession to the Convention.

The European courts have played a decisive legal and political role with regard to the planned EU accession to the European Convention on Human Rights, which we have understood as a mainly unintended effect of the ECJ's and ECHR's simultaneously competitive, conflicting and cooperative position in the general institutional and organisational configuration leading to the progressive emergence of a relation of strategic interdependence. In other words, in the absence of EU member state agreement on human rights, the European governments have been pushed to proceed to such an accession to the Convention as a result of the somewhat turbulent interaction between European courts. Of course, while the European courts remain agents for the politicisation of the EU and while each court *individually* increases its domination over national and private actors by engaging into a networked relationship with the other European court, the political agreement between member states to create a legal basis for accession to the ECHR does not mean that there will be such an accession any time soon, as the UK and Poland opt-out of the Charter of Fundamental Rights or the difficult ratification of the Council of Europe's Protocol 14 amply demonstrates. From this perspective, the strategic interdependence of the ECJ and the ECHR is all the more essential to guarantee the protection of rights in Europe.

The reasons why many actors of this inter-jurisdictional configuration take a positive stand with regard to the EU's accession to the Convention are closely linked to the effects of both courts' previous reciprocal arrangements and the mobilisation of the leaders of both courts. The socialisation of a small group of judges, Advocates-General and law clerks, worried about the possibly damaging jurisprudential conflicts of the European courts and the continuing political pressures on their courts, is indeed the main explanatory factor for the overall convergence of the two courts and not simply – as one might spontaneously assume – the fact that some judges who used to work in Strasburg became judges in Luxembourg.

In 2005, 23.5% of the ECJ's main actors (judges, Advocate-General and clerks) had a previous working experience in the Council of Europe. This relatively high percentage certainly contributes to maintain the ECHR's momentum in Luxembourg.[19] Yet the circulation of judges has been slow in previous years and was only counterbalanced after 2004 when four Strasburg judges of new member states were transferred to the ECJ. These were the only four judges who were directly transferred. All the other lawyers from the ECHR who continued their career in Luxembourg either had non-decision-making positions or served in another Council of Europe body than the court. Whereas Advocate-General Jacobs briefly worked in the Strasburg Court in the 1980s, no other leader of the ECJ–ECHR relationship previously held a position in Strasburg. Regarding the four judges mentioned, their transfer to Luxembourg is easily explained by their proximity to political power and by their high-profile national positions as former Supreme Court judges in their member states. Jerzy Makarczyk, the Polish judge at the ECHR from 1992–2002 became an EJC judge in 2004, after having been a special counsellor to the Polish president for two years from 2002 to 2004. Pranas Kūris worked simultaneously at the European Court of Human Rights and at the Lithuanian Supreme Court from 1994 to 1998 (when the ECHR became independent). He immediately went to Luxembourg when his country joined the EU in 2004. The Estonian judge, Uno Lõhmus has a similar professional trajectory. He joined the ECJ in May 2004 after having been a judge at the European Court of Human Rights from 1994–98 and the president of the Estonian Supreme Court from 1998 to 2004. Egils Levits, who has shown interest in the dialogue of European judges, was a judge at the Strasburg court from 1995 onwards, before becoming the Latvian judge at the ECJ in 2004. While these judges sometimes participate in the dialogue between the two European courts, their role does not help to explain, however, why the ECJ became interested in the ECHR's work in the first place – this relationship indeed emerged well before their transfer.

This also shows that the reciprocal influences and the direct cooperation between the courts cannot be reduced to inter-institutional exchanges of judicial actors. The ECHR experience of many ECJ lawyers might help to stabilise the relationship between the two courts. Yet the creation of a cooperative link pre-dates the rise of the number of lawyers transferred from Strasburg to Luxembourg. This link is much more an effect of an inter-institutional socialisation of a minority of powerful judicial actors, reacting to the dangers of the jurisprudential overlap of the two courts. These leaders very often have personal and professional paths that show a special interest in public and human rights law. But their interest for the 'other' court hardly stems from cross-organisational multiple loyalties but rather from their multi-positioned professional profile and their political and institutional interests to drive human rights and constitution-making in an inter-dependent European polity that is in many ways larger than the EU itself.

Conclusion

The European courts' nested linkage has given rise to new forms of supranational judicial diplomacy between judicial actors of the ECJ and the ECHR that go beyond traditional understandings of adjudication and have had a deep impact on law- as well as policy-making. The strategic interactions of judges fostered a common discursive and jurisprudential 'thread', allowing each of the two European institutions to increase their domination of those public and private actors who march into judicial arenas. The judges and lawyers of both courts have strategically engaged in these networks because the upholding and reinforcing of the institutional architecture and the policies of the European Union have become intrinsically linked to the protection of human rights. Since the end of the 1990s, the convergent case law of these courts (which no one had expected), the annual high-profile meetings between European judges, a joint discourse on jurisprudential cross-fertilisation between their courts, the positive complementarity of the Charter and the ECHR, as well as similar positions regarding the future of human rights in Europe and their own courts' relationship in political, judicial and academic fora, are indicators of what can be qualified as the emergence of a 'common supranational diplomacy' of European judges. Entirely based on fundamental rights, this transnational normative and discursive web tends to encompass European politics and to change the direction of integration itself. This linkage did not evolve in a linear way, nor are the European courts monolithic institutions.[20] However, through their jurisprudential and face-to-face dialogue and their multifaceted investment in emerging transnational networks, Europe's supranational judges have produced path-making and path-breaking effects on the process of European integration.

Notes

1 See for instance article 6.2. of the new Treaty of Lisbon and the Treaty Establishing the European Community signed by the EU member states (13 December 2007).

2 The first references to human rights and the ECHR only appeared in the preamble of the Single European Act and later in article 6 of the Maastricht Treaty. The ECJ effectively started to protect human rights in 1969 (*Stauder*, 12.11.1969).

3 *Stork v. ECSC* (4.02.1959)

4 See the German Constitutional Court's *Solange* decision (29.05.1974, BVerfGE 37, 271) and the Italian Constitutional Court's *Frontini Pozzani* decision of 27.12.1973.

5 For an analysis on how both courts 'intruded' into each other's legal order, see Scheeck, 2005.

6 The general principles of European law have been included because they are sometimes used in human rights-related cases, but they are frequently used in all areas of EC law, hence the high number of occurrences in this graph.

7 Interview at the ECJ (June 2004). Statement confirmed in Strasburg (February 2005).

8 Interview at the ECJ (June 2004).

9 Among many examples, see the joint appearance of ECHR judge Tulkens and ECJ judge Levits at the EP LIBE Commission Public Seminar 'Judges and legislators, for a multi-level protection of fundamental rights in Europe' of 8 October 2007.

10 See Wildhaber's speech at the 3rd Convention of European Lawyers in Geneva (8 September 2005), where he dealt with the EU–ECHR relationship in depth (Wildhaber, 2005).

11 Workshop with J.-P. Costa (ECHR judge) and Ph. Léger (Advocate-General at the ECJ), *Constitution européenne, démocratie et droits de l'homme* colloquium at the Sorbonne, 13-14 March 2003 (Cohen-Jonathan and Dutheil de la Rochère, 2003, pp. 270-277).

12 For example, the Luxembourg symposium on the relationship between the Council of Europe Human Rights and the Convention and EU Fundamental Rights Charter, Schengen, 16 September 2002 or; the conference 'Europe of the Courts' at the Institute for European Studies of the Université Libre de Bruxelles (21 September 2007). With the notable exception of French judges, European judges are often academics which also explains why so much has been written on the two courts' relationship.

13 Puissochet (the French judge at the ECJ) and Costa (the French judge at the ECHR), 2001.

14 We counted more than a hundred written contributions by judges on these issues. See for example: Costa (President of the ECHR), 2004, Lenaerts (ECJ judge) and De Smijter, 2001, Jacobs (at that time Advocate-General at the ECJ), 2003, Pescatore 2003 (former ECJ judge), Tulkens (ECHR judge) and Callewaert, 2002, Rosas (ECJ judge), 2005, Wildhaber (at that time president of the ECHR) and Callewaert (legal and executive assistant to the Pesident of the ECHR), 2003, Spielmann (an ECHR judge) 2004.

15 Interviews at the ECJ (June 2004 and June 2005) and at the ECHR (February 2005).

16 Interviews at the ECJ (June 2004) and at the ECHR (February 2005).

17 Interviews at the ECHR (February 2005).

18 Interview at the ECJ (June 2005).

19 It appears that there has never been a judge, Advocate-General or law clerk who went from Luxembourg to Strasburg.

20 On the contrary, as shown by dissenting opinions in the ECHR as well as increasing internal tensions in the ECJ after the recent EU enlargements and new political turbulences in the EU (Rasmussen, 2007).

Bibliography

Alemanno, A., 'À la recherche d'un juste équilibre entre libertés fondamentales et droits fondamentaux dans le cadre du marché intérieur. Quelques réflexions à propos des arrêts "Schmidberger et 'Omega'", *Revue du droit de l'Union européenne*, 4, 2004, 709–751.

Alter, K.-J., *Establishing the Supremacy of European Law. The Making of an International Rule of Law in Europe*, Oxford: Oxford University Press, 2001.

Anagnostou, D., 'L'incorporation de la Cour européenne des droits de l'homme. Une analyse politique de l'impact des normes juridiques supranationales sur le plan national', in E. Bribosia, L. Scheeck and A. Ubeda (eds), *L'Europe des Cours: résistances et loyautés, penser le droit*, Bruxelles: Bruylant, 2008.

Becker, H., *Outsiders: Studies in the Sociology of Deviance*, New York: The Free Press, 1963.

Bribosia, E., 'Le dilemme du juge national face à des obligations contradictoires en matière de protection des droits fondamentaux issus des deux orders juridiques européens', in M. Dony and E. Bribosia (eds), *L'avenir du système juridictionnel de l'Union européenne*, Brussels: Éditions de l'Université de Bruxelles, 2002, 265–277.

Brosig, M. (ed.), *Human Rights in Europe. A Fragmented Regime?*, Frankfurt/Main: Peter Lang, 2006.

Burley, A.-M. and Mattli, W., 'Europe Before the Court: A Political Theory of Legal Integration', *International Organization*, 47 (1), 1993, 41–76.

Checkel, J., 'International Institutions and Socialization in the New Europe', ARENA Working Papers, WP 01/11, 2001.

Checkel, J., 'International Institutions and Socialization in Europe: Introduction and Framework', *International Organization*, 59, 2005, 801–826.

Cohen, A., 'Constitutionalism without Constitution. Transnational Elites between Political Mobilization and Legal Expertise (1940s-1960s)', *Law & Social Inquiry*, 23 (1), 2007, 109–135.

Cohen-Jonathan, G. and Dutheil De La Rochère, J. (eds), *Constitution européenne, démocratie et droits de l'homme*, Brussels: Bruylant, 2003.

Costa, J.-P., 'La Convention européenne des droits de l'homme, la Charte des droits fondamentaux de l'Union européenne et la problématique de l'adhésion de l'Union européenne à la Convention', *EUI Working Paper*, no. 2004/5.

Dehousse, R., *The European Court of Justice. The Politics of Judicial Integration*, London: Macmillan, 1998.

Elias, N., *Engagement und Distanzierung. Arbeiten zur Wissenssoziologie*, Frankfurt/Main: Suhrkamp, 1987.

Georgakakis, D., 'La sociologie historique et politique de l'Union européenne: un point de vue d'ensemble et quelques contre points', *Politique européenne*, 25, 2008, 53–85.

Granger, M.-P., 'The Future of Europe: Judicial Interference and Preferences', *Comparative European Politics*, 3, 2005, 155–179.

Haas, E., *The Uniting of Europe. Political, Social and Economic Forces, 1950–1957*, Stanford: Stanford University Press, 1958.

Jacobs, F.G., 'Judicial Dialogue and the Cross-Fertilization of Legal Systems: The European Court of Justice', *Texas International Law Journal*, 38, 2003, 547–556.

Krisch, N., 'The Open Architecture of European Human Rights Law', *Modern Law Review*, 71 (2), 2008, 183–216.

Lenaerts, K. and De Smijter, E., 'The Charter and the Role of the European Courts', *The Maastricht Journal of European and Comparative Law*, 8, 2001, 90–101.

Madsen, M., 'From Cold War Instrument to Supreme European Court: The European Court of Human Rights at the Crossroads of International and National Law and Politics', *Law and Social Inquiry*, 23 (1), 2007, 137–159.

Moravcsik, A., 'Explaining International Human Rights Regimes: Liberal Theory and Western Europe', *European Journal of International Relations* 1 (2), 1995, 157–199.

Morijn, J., 'Balancing Fundamental Rights and Common Market Freedoms in Union Law: Schmidberger and Omega in the Light of the European Constitution', *European Law Journal*, 12 (1), 2006, 15–40.

Pescatore, P., 'Die Menschenrechte und die Europäische Integration', *Integration*, 1969, 103–136.

Pescatore, P., 'La coopération entre la Cour communautaire, les juridictions nationales et la Cour européenne des droits de l'homme dans la protection des droits fondamentaux. Enquête sur un problème virtuel', *Revue du Marché Commun et de l'Union européenne*, 466, 2003, 151–159.

Puissochet, J.-P. and Costa, J.-P., 'Entretien croisé des juges français', *Pouvoirs*, 96, 2001.

Rasmussen, H., 'Present and Future European Judicial Problems after Enlargement and the Post-2005 Ideological Revolt', *Common Market Law Review*, 44, 2007, 1661–1687.

Rodriguez Iglesias, G.-C., 'Discours à l'occasion de l'audience solennelle de la Cour européenne des Droits de l'Homme', *Council of Europe*, Strasburg, Janurary 31, 2002.

Rosas, A., 'Fundamental Rights in the Luxembourg and Strasburg Courts', in C. Baudenbacher et al. (eds), *The EFTA Court: Ten Years On*, Oxford: Hart Publishing, 2005.

Scheeck, L., 'Solving Europe's Binary Human Rights Puzzle. The Interaction Between Supranational Courts as a New Parameter of European Governance', *Questions de Recherche – Research in Question*, no. 15, Paris: CERI, Sciences Po, 2005a.

Scheeck, L., 'The Relationship Between the European Courts and Integration Through Human Rights', *Zeitschrift für ausländisches öffentliches Recht und Völkerrecht*, 65(4), 2005b, 837–885.

Scheeck, L., 'La diplomatie des juges européens et la crise constitutionnelle de l'Union européenne', in P. Poirier, R. Leboutte and S. Devaux (eds), *Le Traité de Rome: histoires pluridisciplinaires. L'apport du Traité de Rome instituant la Communauté économique européenne*, Frankfurt/Main: Peter Lang, 2008.

Simmel, G., *Soziologie Untersuchungen über die Formen der Vergesellschaftung*, Berlin: Duncker & Humblot, 1908.

Spielmann D., 'Un autre regard: la Cour de Strasbourg et le droit de la Communauté européenne', in *Libertés, justice, tolérance. Mélanges en hommage au Doyen Gérard Cohen-Jonathan*, Brussels: Bruylant, 2004, II, 1447–1466.

Stone Sweet, A., *The Judicial Construction of Europe*, Oxford: Oxford University Press, 2004.

Tulkens, F. and Callewaert, J., 'La Cour de justice des Communautés européennes, la Cour européenne des droits de l'homme et la protection des droits fondamentaux', in M. Dony and E. Bribosia (eds), *L'avenir du système juridictionnel de l'Union européenne*, Brussels: Éditions de l'Université de Bruxelles, 2002, 177–205.

Vauchez, A., 'The Force of a Weak Field: Law and Lawyers in the Government of the European Union (For a Renewed Research Agenda)', *International Political Sociology*, 2 (2), 2008, 128–144.

Von Bogdandy, A., 'The Europan Union as a Human Rights Organization? Human Rights and the Core of the European Union', *Common Market Law Review*, 37, 2000, 1307–1338.

Waelbroeck, M., 'La Convention européenne des droits de l'homme lie-t-elle les Communautés européennes?', *Droit communautaire et droit national*, Bruges: De Tempel, 1965, 305–318.

Wathelet, M., 'Le point de vue d'un juge à la Cour de justice des Communautés européennes', in J.-Y. Carlier and O. de Schutter (eds), *La Charte des droits fondamentaux de l'Union européenne. Son apport à la protection des droits de l'homme en*

Europe, Brussels: Bruylant, 2002, 241–252.

Weiler, J.H.H., 'Editorial: Does the European Union Truly Need a Charter of Rights?', *European Law Journal*, 6 (2), 2000, 95–97.

Weiler, J.H.H., 'The Essential (and Would-Be Essential) Jurisprudence of the European Court of Justice: Lights and Shadows Too', in *The Future of the European Judicial System in a Comparative Perspective*, European Constitutional Law Network Series, 6, 2007, 117–127.

Wildhaber L., 'The Coordination of the Protection of Fundamental Rights in Europe', 3rd Convention of European Lawyers, Geneva, 8 September 2005.

Wildhaber, L. and Callewaert, J., 'Espace constitutionnel européen et droits fondamentaux. Une vision globale pour une pluralité de droits et de juges', in N. Colneric, D. Edward, J.-P. Puissochet and D.R. Colomer (eds), *Une Communauté de droit. Festschrift für Gil Carlos Rodriguez*, Berlin: Berliner Wissenschafts Verlag, 2003, 61–85.

*Hélène Michel**

6

The construction of a European interest through legal expertise: property owners' associations and the Charter of Fundamental Rights

Interest groups have held a prominent place in EU studies. Functionalist scholars were quick to identify them as essential vectors of the European integration process (Haas, 1958; Lindberg, 1963). Currently, they are perceived as useful or even indispensable contributors to the efficient and democratic functioning of European institutions. Partaking in the decision-making process, they are thought to help the Commission to be better connected with socio-economic realities and improve the quality of decision-making through the consultation of a broad range of interest groups. As a result, interest groups are central in studies that seek to highlight their contribution to the setting of the European policy agenda (Peters, 1994) as well as research more centred on decision-making (Fouilleux, 2004). For both research traditions, the development of interest groups is presented both as a direct consequence of European integration and as the key to understanding the process of European decision-making. The study of the structure and action of interest groups at the European level therefore provides an essential element to understand how Europe works and the forces of change (Kohler-Koch, 1997).

However, this way of studying European interest groups raises several problems, mainly linked to the underlying normative conception of the EU and the resulting heavy reliance on institutional and legal research perspectives. The importance of regulation policies in the EU (Majone, 1996) further amplifies the tendency to consider public policies as essentially legal processes and outcomes. Legal expertise is consequently favoured in the decision-making process, which in turn benefits actors most capable of making their claims in legal terms (public officials with legal training, private law profes-

* Translated by Jean-Yves Bart

sionals and interest representatives). Law acts as a gateway to the European political system, an essential element in being taken seriously as a partner in the elaboration of public policies. The legal bias of European institutions is well understood both by actors who intervene on the European level and influence decisions, and by analysts looking for an explanation to a particular policy outcome. If all observers and participants in the European polity agree that law is the language, resource and strategy of influence, they very rarely reflect on the fact that 'the force of law' (Bourdieu, 1986) derives less from the intrinsic qualities of the tool and the specific framing of reality it engenders, than from the social and political position of the actors who wield it. Although they rarely explicitly analyse the relationship between what is assumed to be the legal *nature* of Europe and the recourse to legal modes of action, studies on the contributions of interest groups to public policies nonetheless implicitly contribute to the promotion of a technical and legal conception of Europe, considered to be incompatible with the articulation of political and politicised interests and issues. While the depoliticising effects of such a legal-technical conception of public action have rightfully been emphasised (Smith, 2006), as have the strategies of circumventing political action through the mobilisation of seemingly apolitical expertise (Robert, 2004), there has perhaps been too little attention paid to the construction and legitimisation of this legal conception of Europe as such (Vauchez, 2008). Seen in this light, legal repertoires can be conceptualised, alongside economic expertise (Bruno, 2007) as a political, if euphemised, mode of action in the Europe institutional game. In this perspective, the legal framing of claims by interest representatives is not only a means of influence. It is simultaneously a way to be recognised as a legitimate political actor of European governance. The recourse to legal formulations of collective interests should therefore go beyond the study of the factors which allow certain ideas or interests to prevail. More importantly perhaps, they allow us to explore the social and political processes that strengthen collective beliefs in the efficiency of legal repertoires in European arenas.

It is the domination of a functionalist vision of the goals, role and successes of interest groups central to decisionist approaches of Europe which has stymied the advent of a genuine political sociology of EU governance (Smith, 2004). Interest groups are most commonly defined by the pressure they apply and their European character is determined by the institutions they seek to influence. Consequently, not only is the presence of interest groups in Brussels explained by the development of the European institutions themselves, but the analysis of their action is limited within this framework to their relationships with European institutions. This institutional Eurocentric definition of interest groups used in most studies constitutes a 'readymade theory' (Courty, 2006) that focuses on the bias of interest representation in favour of economic interests, the difficult structuring of interests on the European level and the unequal access to institutions of the organisations. By focusing on the financial incentive strategies of the Commission, the promotion of consultancy or the granting of prerogatives or institutional roles to interest groups, many studies have of course rightly identified the important role played by the Commission in the development of a pluralistic system of interest groups (Mazey and Richardson, 1993). Yet, through this focus on the Commission and more generally on the European level of governance, these studies overemphasise the 'top down' structuring of interest groups, and therefore have overlooked the presence of interest groups in Brussels who are not concerned by any specific public policy – unless they confer spontaneous reality effects to the promotion of the 'participation of civil society' derived from the White Paper on European governance (de Lassalle and Georgakakis, 2008). They also struggle to explain the logics behind these organisations' activities when they do not follow the institutional agenda and when their scope of action falls outside policy sectors for which there is explicit EU competence.

This is precisely the case of the configuration of GEFI (*Groupement Européen des Fédérations intervenants dans l'Immobilier*).[1] This organisation, which presents itself as a representative body of real estate owners and managers, has its headquarters in Brussels, near the European Parliament, in the building of the European Landowners' Organization (ELO), presented as a 'sister organisation'. Whereas the ELO is primarily focused on the agricultural and environmental sectors, GEFI's objective is to 'promote the central role of private property in the housing sector, as well as the implementation of environmental policies in the private housing sector'.[2] This is why it took part in the Urban Housing Parliament intergroup created in 2005 to 'promote urban and housing policies in a transversal and integrated way'.[3] The presence of GEFI in this European intergroup thus seems self-evident. Even if housing is not an EU competence, an approach in terms of long-term agenda-building (Cobb and Elder, 1972) could explain GEFI's contribution to the emergence and a definition of the 'housing problem' that is different from the one which emerged in the field of the fight against social exclusion.

This initial reading does not however suffice to explain the presence of the organisation in Brussels, and suffers from several shortcomings. First, by starting from the successful inscription of the organisation into the institutional game, this interpretation fails to take into account the contingency of an uncertain process and creates an assumption that the outcome was determined by the original intention. Secondly, it recycles the discourse of GEFI's spokesman, according to whom housing should be a sector for European public intervention. The confusion between intentions, official discourse and outcomes is all the more problematic, as GEFI was created in 2000 through the initiative of French housing federations in order to defend property rights during the elaboration of the EU Charter of Fundamental Rights, a position quite far from subsequent developments in the building of an EU agenda on housing policy. Since its creation, it has continued to promote the inclusion of private property as a fundamental right in the Charter as well as in the development of the EU Agency for Fundamental Rights.[4] The story of the genesis of this interest group does not solve the question of the existence of this organisation on the European level, but it shifts the focus to the field of fundamental rights and invites us to examine more closely the conversion of national organisations to Europe. These successive shifts should be analysed as a contingent process constructing a *European* interest group integrated into the European political space. If, in retrospect, the constitution of GEFI as a European interest group seems self-evident, looking back to the beginning of this process raises a challenging question: why would an organisation initially created to defend property as a fundamental right on the European level choose housing as its central battleground despite the fact that it is not a sector of European intervention?

This chapter seeks to show how a constructivist approach of interest groups can resolve this enigma by explaining what generally remains unexplained: the very existence of groups and the process of definition of the interests they seek to defend; in this case, the somewhat surprising creation at the European level of an organisation defending property ownership mobilised around the housing sector. The constructivist approach considers that the shape of the organisation and the form of the interests defended is the result of political work performed by the members of a group, which depends on the resources they possess and their perceptions of the situation. This approach seeks to render the co-construction of the group and the definition of its interest (Offerlé, 1998). This perspective avoids the pitfalls of reducing the study of interest groups to its public stances, as often happens when the interest group is only analysed in relationship to a specific decision. By examining the evolution of the group over a longer time period and focusing on the activities and resources of those who represent the group, the approach developed here implies a sociology of interest representatives necessarily contextualised in the political and social spaces that shape their behaviour. Indeed, if agents constantly create the world that creates them, they are nevertheless bound by established social forms (Berger and Luckmann, 1966). Interest groups are the result of a confluence between agents who struggle to make their interests visible and be recognised, and structures – political and social, national or transnational – that make this continuous work possible, define possibilities and contribute to its institutionalisation.

Explaining the presence of interest groups on the European level therefore involves the identification of the conditions which make mobilisation in European arenas possible and how the available 'interest group form' enables the organisation and defence of these interests. This boils down to treating interest groups as a form of collective action among others (Balme, Chabanet and Wright, 2002), which appears to social actors as the most efficient institutional form to define interests and access to European institutions. While the role of the Commission in the invention of European interest groups is incontestable, I also want to point out the conditions under which these institutional incentives, entailing a redeployment of existing groups and a reformulation of the interests they defend, can be efficient.

Applied to the case of GEFI, we will first show how this organisation is the European extension of a French interest group representing house owners, resulting not so much from the desire of its leaders to become active on the European level but more from the anticipation that such a position would consolidate their position in France. This will allow us to analyse the conditions of possibility of a mobilisation for the Charter of Fundamental Rights and to show that this campaign goes beyond a simple strategy seeking the formal recognition of a right. What is at stake in this mobilisation and those that would follow is the Europeanisation of private ownership through the constitution of a Eurogroup, the redefinition of owner interests (defence of property rights) and the inclusion of this interest group in a political space of discussion and representation (housing).

The genesis of a European interest group: the national origins of the transition to Europe

The study of GEFI's genesis starts at the national level and requires the study of the members of the UNPI (*Union nationale de la propriété immobilière*),[5] who were the 'prime movers' (Becker, 1963) of this association. The long-term sociological perspective enables us to show that, contrary to a Eurocentric perspective, incentives from the EU played a minor role compared to the transformations of the national field of interest representation. While this organisation of the defence of private ownership is structured at the national level and based in a sector (housing) with which the EU is not directly concerned, the UNPI found itself confronted with the necessity of taking Europe into account in order to keep the upper hand on competing interest groups in its relationship to the central state.

The national structuring of an interest and of an organisation

The UNPI was created in the late nineteenth century to defend urban property interests. The history of the defence and representation of real estate ownership (Michel, 2006) can be read as a recurring failure to endow this group with a social existence, represent its interests and have the state actively promote the development of real estate ownership. Whereas the interests of rural ownership had been integrated in the agricultural field, institutionalised since the late nineteenth century, and the interests of the ownership of means of production merged with those of employers and became institutionalised in industrial relations, only much later did the interests of real estate ownership become integrated into a policy sector.

Only in the late 1970s when the government liberalised and reorganised the housing market (Bourdieu and Christin, 1990) and, in the 1980s, when the promotion of housing ownership was considered by the state as an objective, was the UNPI associated to the process of elaboration and implementation of public policies. This specialisation in housing enabled the UNPI to be recognised in the real estate sector, even if the interest around which the organisation was structured escaped administrative classifications: the UNPI can neither be assimilated with real estate professionals (owners are not considered as professionals even though some derive their entire income from their properties) nor with consumer associations. In the housing sector, successive UNPI representatives have turned this unusual position into a resource: it enables them to be present in several policy arenas related to the use, sale or management of private housing (consumer protection, loans, fiscal provisions, construction norms, estate planning, etc.). Present throughout the territory, they have become indispensable mediators for the elaboration and implementation of public policies. In the housing sector, the UNPI enjoys a monopoly of the interest representation of real estate owners.

The UNPI thus has a strong presence on the national level, not only because its representatives work closely with the state in several policy sectors, but because the current form of the organisation is the result of a differentiation and structuring process related both to France's socio-economic evolutions and to the transformations of the modes of organisation and action of political power. It is therefore anchored in a national configuration of interest representation in a sector structured by historically rooted relations to the state and problem definitions.

Europe as a resource for getting access to the state

Europe has therefore nothing to do with the UNPI's action and the interest it defends is only very marginally affected by 'what happens in Brussels'. Housing is not a EU competence, and therefore remains an object of national public intervention. Despite this, representatives of UNPI nonetheless perceived strong incentives to integrate a European dimension into their activity.

It was initially at the margins of the housing issue that UNPI leaders were encouraged to become involved in Europe. Because of their multisectoral status, representatives of owners participated in a wide variety of commissions set up by the administrations in charge of consumer protection, the environment, or housing loans. This participation brought the UNPI into contact with several problems linked to the EU's legal production (sales contracts, rent-to-own, time sharing, etc.). The actual origins of the legal norm were of little importance. Like the other members of these commissions, UNPI representatives worked essentially to interpret directives and 'bend' the legal implications of actual or proposed rule changes in their favour. In this exercise, legal competence is essential, and the UNPI held a certain advantage over consumer protection advocates, who are, for reasons related to financial resources and recruitment methods, generally at a disadvantage. On the other hand, the mobilisation of examples taken from other European countries confronted with the same European legislation became an important resource in negotiations. In this respect, organisations belonging to a European network providing this valuable information hold an advantage. Insertion into a European structure therefore provides important resources first and foremost in the national arenas of negotiation. As the UNPI does not however represent real estate professionals or users, it finds itself excluded from existing European networks of real estate agents, property managers, developer-builders,[6] consumer protection groups or family associations. As other groups present in the various national commissions could access these European interest groups, it risked losing influence at the national level.

Furthermore, interest representatives are often confronted with strategic uses of Europe in their exchanges with ministers or state agents. Even in a sector that is not directly concerned by EC intervention, the reference to Europe by ministerial representatives is frequent, either to justify certain policy options or to shift responsibility for controversial policies to Europe. Confronted with these tactics, UNPI representatives saw the importance of integrating a European dimension in their own argumentation. Present in policy forums that contributed to normalising the reference to Europe, interest representatives can no longer afford to ignore Europe. Europe therefore becomes a resource for additional access or for maintaining access to the state. In order to mobilise this European register, an organisation must have representatives who, without necessarily having direct experience in European affairs, are able to perceive and interpret national issues in European terms. This requires the development of new ways of expressing and defining problems and claims. This transformation in the perceptions of the configurations and efficient resources of the policy game leads to a change in the players' relative positions and as a result, in a transformation of the game itself (Bailey, 1969).

In the housing sector, the European dimension was introduced progressively. This transformation was not directly induced by European norms but rather through the presence and actions of actors who at some point in their political or administrative careers had worked with or within European institutions and who, once back in France, sought to use this European experience to their advantage. This is the case of Marie-Noëlle Lienemann, former member of the European parliament (MEP) and French minister of housing, who was appointed president of the National Housing Council (CNH) in 1999. This is also the case of civil servants detached to Commission services or French representatives of organisations from the social sector who have worked with European federations, such as the FEANTSA (European Federation of National Organisations working with the Homeless). These actors have not only learned to 'think European', as they say, but they have also developed ties with actors working in Brussels. They encouraged the creation of a 'Europe' group in the National Housing Council in order to monitor European evolutions and thereby echo the May 1977 European Parliament resolution on the social dimensions of housing. This initial introduction of the European dimension of housing in French administration was framed as a social issue focused on the 'problem' of access to housing for the underprivileged.

Faced with this European and social definition of the housing issue, the UNPI, which defends a conception of housing based on private property and the market, saw its position weakened. In this configuration, UNPI leaders, seeking to maintain their organisation as a representative and a valid partner of the state, tried to adapt to Europe, in other words followed the example of their national allies and opponents in the sector. Clearly in this case, the path leading to Brussels did not derive from the objective of applying pressure on European institutions or even national institutions through a 'domestication' of European mobilisation (Imig and Tarrow, 2001). However, in order to justify their presence in Brussels, it was necessary to identify a cause to defend if the form of European integration did not take the form of inclusion in an existing European network. UNPI leaders were directly confronted with the problem of Europeanising their national organisation and the very specific interest they defend. Paradoxically, the same elements that had made the UNPI's inclusion in a national space of representation possible was an obstacle in its transition to Europe. The transition to Europe does not consist in a mere transposition of a group and of an interest from the national level towards the European level. It implies a redefinition of the interest and the group represented which, in contradiction with a purely strategic vision of interest representation, is doubly limited: on the one hand by the modes of aggregation of diverse interests which are contingent upon its resources and its network of allies and, on the other hand, by the structure and the functioning of the European space.

The Charter of Fundamental Rights: an opportunity for the transition to Europe

According to the UNPI members interviewed, as soon as the Cologne European Council (June 3–4, 1999) announced the Charter of Fundamental Rights project 'in order to make their overriding importance and relevance more visible to the Union's citizens',[7] they decided to intervene in order to have the right to property declared a fundamental right and see to its proper definition. The Charter seemed like an opportunity to act on the European level and include the interests of real estate ownership. However, contrary to a spontaneous vision of 'civil society' reacting to an institutional agenda, intervening at this level was not self-evident for an organisation that had never ventured outside the national space and had defended the interests of a very specific socio-economic group. Yet, for UNPI representatives, the drafting of the Charter of Fundamental Rights came at a time when they were already engaged in a reflection on representation of real estate ownership on the European level. It became possible to transpose to the European level one of the forms of action well tested in the national space: the definition and defence of rights.

How to make a European group

In the late 1990s, the obligation to 'go to Brussels' required the creation of a structure allowing them to act efficiently and, in particular, to be recognised as a viable European actor. This widely shared conclusion adopted by leaders of the UNPI was confirmed by the observation of other organisations and various lobbying manuals. In theory, they had the choice between several modes of representation (Greenwood, 2007) such as the European federation of national organisations, direct representation or the recourse to consultants, or the association to an existing network. The exploration of these various strategies was carried out pragmatically and the final choice depended on the available resources, as well as the weight and position of federation members.

One might think that the constitution of a Euro-federation would not be a problem for the UNPI as it is a founding member of IUPO (International Union of Property Owners).[8] Despite the heterogeneity of the national contexts, the various types of interest aggregation of real estate property (for instance there are obligatory groups and voluntary ones) and the different kinds of objectives pursued by these groups (some, like in the Netherlands, fulfil a real public function such as authenticating deeds), this Internationale of owners tried to achieve recognition as an international organisation by UNESCO or the UN. Within this federation, UNPI representatives have tried in vain to develop a European branch of the UIPO. But neither the objectives of the International Union, turned towards Central and Eastern Europe seeking to 'help them make a democratic transition of private property', nor its status as 'lead culture', in the words of a UNPI representative, have allowed the creation of a structure liable to intervene in the EU. After three years of fruitless negotiations, UNPI leaders decided to invest in more 'modern' structures, better reflecting their perception of Brussels as a 'stronghold of lobbying'.

They explored another possibility of action in this line of reasoning. For members of the UNPI's board, hiring a professional lobbyist is a 'modern' and 'dynamic' mode of action and representation. It would therefore suit the image they want to promote, as the public image of the UNPI suffered from stigmatisation of large property owners as archaic 'fat cats'. This appealing idea was nonetheless not pursued for two essential reasons: the financial costs and the absence of particular claims to be defended. Nothing justified a defence of real estate ownership, as it was not attacked or targeted by European public action. They were therefore forced to stick to a 'small-scale' mode of defence and representation. Some found solace in the fact that 'consultancy is not a French tradition'. Others came to the vague realisation that the recourse to lobbyists was not adapted to the representation of a group built around the identity of a social group (Boltanski, 1982). Mandated by those he is supposed to defend, the representative makes the group exist by speaking in its collective name and making it act (Bourdieu, 1981). In the process, the individual representing the group often lends it his image. The option of resorting to a professional lobbyist was therefore not chosen, to the great dismay of some who considered that lobbying at the European level necessarily involved a consultant (Michel, 2005).

Little by little, the possibility of becoming active in an existing network took shape. This meant less financial costs and this would allow national representatives to learn at little expense about the unfamiliar and somewhat intimidating European space. Indeed, if they knew French institutions and administrative and political networks well, they had very few European references. The oldest representatives, who are often lawyers, notaries, real estate agents or businessmen, had never dealt with these questions in their professional contexts. As for the younger representatives, who know 'people with European careers', they remain a minority in the UNPI. But they knew that their counterparts in other sectors, such as the FNPA (National Federation of Farmland Owners) or the federation of forest owners, are members of a European organisation: the ELO. The UNPI is objectively not concerned by rural issues, but it has the defence of ownership and owners in common with the ELO. Representatives therefore contacted the ELO and their permanent representative in Brussels was introduced into the board of the UNPI in 1998. There was no formal alliance, but their relationships now enabled them to envision common action if the need should arise.

When the representative of the ELO announced the Charter of Fundamental Rights project, UNPI representatives thought it was a good opportunity to consolidate the relationships that had been established. At the same time, they wanted to intervene as real estate owners. During the summer of 1999, UNPI leaders forged contacts with twelve other French real estate federations (mainly professional federations) and created GEFI. According to them, it was an 'ad hoc coalition', 'an empty shell only formally constituted by the UNPI and ELO', but that allowed them to 'become European'. While retaining its identity and autonomy of action, the ELO placed its European network and their representative at the UNPI's disposal – during the mobilisation, the ELO also became GEFI's representative. Once redefined, the owners' group was now represented in Brussels.

Reusing a winning strategy: the legal repertoire of action

Being present in Brussels was however not enough to participate in the drafting of the Charter. One had to be able to defend the specific interest of the organisation by reframing it as a 'universal' fundamental right. But this transition from defence of a group interest to the defence of rights is not automatic. For instance, an organisation such as UNICE, speaking for European employers and private ownership of the means of production, never specifically defends ownership rights, even when it challenges labour laws. Similarly, ownership rights are not systematically defended as a human right, as is attested by the absence of this issue in claims made by the League of Human Rights. The link between the defence of owner interests and the defence of ownership as a fundamental right thus results from a process of legal formalisation of group interests. In the UNPI's case, this legal translation of the real estate ownership interest started in the 1990s in France and was pursued during the mobilisation around the Charter.

Only in 1989 did ownership rights become one of the group's explicit objectives. They were defined as 'fundamental' as they were 'guaranteed by Article 17 of the Declaration of the Rights of Man and the Citizen (August 26, 1789), by the Universal Declaration of Human Rights (1948), the Constitution of the French Republic and the European Convention (November 4, 1950)'.[9] This transformation was visible in the UNPI's publications which gave increasing attention to the defence of ownership *rights* in addition to the defence of owners' *interests*. This legal shift was also noticeable in the action of the organisation. In the name of the respect of ownership rights, the UNPI appealed to the Constitutional Court, through a referral to the Parliament, after the vote of the July 29, 1998 law on the fight against social exclusion.[10] The law, among other things, enabled the possibility of requisitioning and levying surtaxes on unoccupied housing in order to force owners to rent or sell their properties. This legal mobilisation demonstrates both a judiciarisation of the political space and a politicisation of so-called technical aspects of public policies. Within this context, the formulation in legal terms of claims from the owners' group drew attention away from specific economic interests by recasting them as elements of fundamental and universal rights. It also enabled the transformation of a special interest group into a group constituted around a consensual 'cause' (Gusfield, 1981) which, by definition, is shared by all – as a UNPI representative stated in good faith: 'You cannot be against ownership rights!'

By 1999, UNPI representatives had therefore already reframed their 'cause' in universalistic legal terms. Even if the members interviewed on their role around the Charter never explicitly mentioned the appeal to the Constitutional Court won in July 1998, this episode left traces in advocacy practices and strategies to define interests.

The role of the Charter in constructing a European agenda on housing

The stage was set for the UNPI to be able to intervene on the European level in the name of the defence of fundamental rights; especially as the consulting process with representatives from civil society, which prefigured the conventional method adopted for the Convention on the Future of Europe, favoured the participation of new organisations such as GEFI. But the UNPI's objective was not just limited to the inscription of property rights in the Charter. It is also likely that the drafters of the Charter had included it in the initial list of fundamental rights before the ELO and GEFI requested it, following the recommendations of the expert group on fundamental rights.[11] In other words, GEFI did not so much intervene to obtain a decision that was already more or less a given, as work to make the issue of real estate ownership more visible on the European level. This objective, which cannot be seen if we limit ourselves to GEFI's contributions to the elaboration of the Charter, leads us to observe the mobilisation as a process which makes the existence of the issue of housing ownership possible. The mobilisation involves a threefold process.

A process of legal formalisation

Legally formalising owner interests involves moving claims from the economic and social field to the legal field and de-nationalising claims. For a national organisation such as the UNPI, specialised in real estate, this is an important objective. By defending property rights, they can break their isolation and find allies in other fields. This is also the case for the ELO, as the defence of property rights in general allows them to find allies outside of the field of agricultural policy.

Indeed, the first substantial text drafted jointly by the leaders of GEFI and the ELO in order to have property rights recognised as a fundamental right attests to the attempt to universalise property rights. The argument is based on an initial ELO document, 'Property Rights within European Law',[12] published at the beginning of 1999 on their website. It borrows from various elements from the report written by a constitutional law professor commissioned by the UNPI in 1998, such as the examination of case law in European courts and of the constitutions of member states regarding property rights.[13] While the Charter's aim was to synthesise the rights contained in national and European constitutional texts, the ELO proposed its own synthesis granting property rights a universal dimension.

Once the principle of the recognition of property rights was agreed upon, there was still work to be done regarding the content of the article on property rights. There was no consensus on the definition and its concrete implications. The ELO representative tried to reach a consensus among his members. National situations are very heterogeneous and the conceptions of the respect of this right diverge, which did not facilitate the writing of the article on compensation in case of the non-respecting of ownership rights. But by conceiving ownership as a fundamental right, or even as a future European constitutional right, they placed themselves on the level of fundamental norms while ensuring that member states retained their power of regulation on property in national frameworks, within the framework of common principles. The debate could thus be organised around the search for common ground not necessarily reduced to the lowest common denominator. It became possible to go beyond the legal 'race to the bottom' and garner the support of those who hoped that a strongly worded article would reinforce rights at the national level.

UNPI representatives had no previous experience in this type of concensus building. But they shared a strong legal competence with other representatives and were therefore able to find a common ground, despite the existence of fundamental oppositions, for instance between Roman law and common law, or between the reference to contracts and law. This legal know-how was an advantage for UNPI representatives who were new to Europe. Being involved in this legal work acclimatised them progressively to European affairs in a system of legal references they mastered well. The setting-up of a public consultation process encouraged this conception of European affairs centred on legally formulated contributions and proposals. The legal analysis and the drafting of the articles enabled them to get acquainted with practices of defence and representation they came to perceive as typically European, thereby reinforcing the belief in the legal functioning of Europe and the necessity to translate economic and social issues into legal terms. This necessity also results from the fact that members of a group 'do what they know how to do' (Agrikoliansky, 2002) and transpose this know-how from one context to another.

A Europeanisation process

This judiciarisation process of owners' interests was accompanied by a Europeanisation process, both of this legal claim and of the group that defended it. Indeed, the interests defended by the UNPI progressively became European interests. Thanks to the ELO's action, the various representatives of rural and urban owners agreed on several points that provided a specified content to European property rights. They were thus able to formulate common claims for the drafting of the article on property rights.[14] At the end of the process, the ELO representative joined UNPI representatives in celebrating the fact that property had become a European object:

> Property is not an object of subsidiarity, despite what we were always told. When I started, I was always told 'Why are you talking about property? Property is an object tackled through subsidiarity' [...] But today, European leaders have understood that when they deal with property, there are effects and the problems are not solved by subsidiarity. That is a change of philosophy right there, a very important change of orientation.[15]

This European dimension of interest is complemented by the recognition of GEFI as a European interest group, as part of two series of relationships. The first is the relationship with representatives of European institutions. GEFI took part in Internet consultations organised by the Convention and in the hearings.[16] By participating in these different systems meant to 'ensure communication with civil society', the organisation acquired a European institutional existence. The second consists of relationships with other organisations in Brussels. Whereas in the early stages of the mobilisation the UNPI was isolated and forced to team up with the ELO to set up GEFI, its members progressively saw other organisations join the consultation and take position on property rights. These contributions seemed to validate the position of UNPI representatives as to the relevance of their action and their analysis of the salience of property rights. The French federations of GEFI remained in the background but provided moral and financial support; the Spanish and Portuguese owner federations joined the UNPI. Other interest representatives such as the European Union of Developers and House Builders (UEPC) and the European Society of Chartered Surveyors also defended property rights and shared GEFI's central claims.[17]

The Europeanisation of the owner group entailed not only the adoption of a European form of representation (GEFI), but also the European definition of the interest and the recognition of its actions and of its existence on the European level.

A process of sectorisation

By defending property rights, the owners' representatives went beyond the sectoral framework of housing that confined them to the national level. But during the mobilisation, a process of re-sectorisation of the GEFI unfolded, notably through its opposition to those defending the right to housing.

UNPI representatives had already mobilised against actions in favour of the right to housing in France. If the movement for the right to housing has a long existence in France (Péchu, 2006), it grew in the 1990s. Ever since it was recognised by the Constitutional Court as a right 'of constitutional value',[18] the right to housing was perceived as a threat to property owners who used property rights to oppose it. During the elaboration of the Charter, this opposition between supporters of the right to housing and supporters of property rights crystallised, even though these rights were not relevant to the same articles and the same issues. If UNPI members had little doubt about the inclusion of property rights in the Charter, they were nevertheless worried by the mobilisation in favour of the inscription of the right to housing as a fundamental right. To them, this right is not a 'genuine right', as they tried to explain to Convention members. The measure of GEFI's success thus has less to do with the recognition of property rights as fundamental rights than to the non-inscription of the right to housing. The latter, despite being recognised in a European Parliament report on Social Rights in Europe,[19] was not included as such in the Charter. Even though it was defended by the French government's representative Guy Braibant, article 34 of the Charter mentions only the 'right to ... housing assistance'.

This opposition between property rights and the right to housing contributed to reposition GEFI with respect to housing issues, in opposition to the European Housing Forum (EHF), regrouping organisations working in the field of social housing. Two opposing conceptions of housing policies were confronted. On the one hand, GEFI, joined by other real estate federations, defended a market-centred conception of housing policies. Based on the affirmation of property rights, various arguments were elaborated[20] in order to support 'another housing policy' as it was developed by the UNPI.[21] The role of real estate property in housing policy was no longer defined as a part of a wider policy aiming to ensure universal access to housing, but as the contribution of private and public actors to ensure the smooth functioning of one or several 'housing service' markets. As a UNPI representative explained: 'I think property rights remain the key element of a good housing policy.' On the other hand, various federations in the EHF defended the existence of social housing and of public intervention to find 'solutions' to the 'housing problem'. For this coalition, GEFI's intervention in the name of the defence of property rights was an attempt to redefine the 'problem' and the legitimate actors of the housing sector. Even though a 'European space of real estate property'[22] could not be created, this redefinition of a European space of housing policy enabled GEFI to use the theme and get recognition as a central actor in that field.

Conclusion

This constructivist approach of interest groups demonstrates the importance of studying actors who constitute them and who then contribute to defining the political spaces in which they exist (Guiraudon, 1998; Favell and Guiraudon, 2009). The analysis of their practices allows us to show how the shaping, expression and public staging of interests and of the social group can function at the European level. The mobilisation around the EU Charter of Fundamental Rights is an excellent example for two reasons. First, it shows how the Europeanisation of an interest group takes shape – the transition to Europe of a national group initially seeking resources to weigh at the national level, the adoption of a mode of interest representation on this level and the process of definition of a European interest. It also shows the extent to which the European political space is the result of diverse investments. The recourse to law as the dominant language of exchange can play an important part if interest groups are only considered according to their relationships with European institutions and their contributions to public policies. If we disregard this conception of the EU, which is the result of the joint work of

EU institutions' civil servants and interest group representatives, we can study interest groups as real European political protagonists.

Notes

1 European Association of Real Estate Private Owners.
2 Position paper (12.17.2004), GEFI's remarks on the project for a European Fundamental Rights Agency.
3 www.urban-logement.eu/spip.php?rubrique24.
4 On the June 30, 2005, the Commission proposed the creation of the independent Agency to replace the Observatory on racism and xenophobia (COM (2005) 280 final).
5 National Union of Property Owners.
6 For instance EPAG: European Property Agency; CEAB: European Confederation of Property Managers, *Confédération européenne des administrateurs de biens*; UEPC: European Union of Developers and House Builders.
7 Annex IV to the conclusions of the presidency, Cologne European Council, June 3-4, 1999.
8 Founded in 1923 by the Frenchman Jean Larmeroux, IUPO gathers the national organisations of real estate ownership and claims to represent 'directly or indirectly, dozens of millions of citizens who own a property which often is the fruit of their savings'.
9 UNPI statement, 1989.
10 Framework law no. 98-657, July 29, 1998 on the fight against exclusions and Decision no. 98-403, July 29, 1998, Constitutional Court.
11 European Commission, DG Employment, Industrial Relations and Social Affairs: *Affirming Fundamental Rights in the European Union – Time to Act*, Report of the Expert Group on Fundamental Rights, Brussels, February 1999 (group of 8 academic experts presided over by Spiros Simitis).
12 First published in their online newsletter (*Countryside*, February 1999), this document was addressed to Convention members as 'Property Rights within European Law'. Report by the ELO, Draft Charter of Fundamental Rights of the European Union, CHARTER 4110/00, January 21, 2000, CONTRIB8.
13 Contribution by GEFI, Project of EU Charter of Fundamental Rights, CHARTER 4168/00, March 16, 2000, CONTRIB52.
14 Contribution by GEFI and the ELO, *Article 16: Right to Ownership*, CHARTER 4190/00, March 27, 2000, CONTRIB73.
15 Ibid.
16 ELO, *Presentation by Johan Nordenfalk at the Public Hearing Regarding the Charter of Fundamental Human Rights*, April 27, 2000.
17 Contribution by UEPC, EU Charter of Fundamental Rights project, CHARTER 4485/00, September 26, 2000, CONTRIB336.
18 For example the so-called 'Besson law', no. 90–449, May 31, 1990, on the implementation of the right to housing. Constitutional decision of January 19, 1995: 'the possibility for each person to benefit from decent housing is an objective of constitutional value'.
19 European Parliament, DG Research, *Fundamental Social Rights in Europe*, working paper, social affairs series, November 1999.
20 Contribution by GEFI, EU Charter of Fundamental Rights project, CHARTER 4168/00, March 16, 2000, CONTRIB52.

21   See UNPI, *Le logement en 2100. Rêves et réalités,* Actes de la Journée de la Propriété Immobilière, Paris, CNIT La Défense, May 17, 2000, multigr.
22   Contribution by GEFI, EU Charter of Fundamental Rights project, CHARTER 4168/00, March 16, 2000, CONTRIB52, p. 5.

Bibliography

Agrikoliansky, E., *La Ligue française des droits de l'homme et du citoyen depuis 1945: sociologie d'un engagement civique,* Paris: L'Harmattan, 2002.

Bailey, F., *Stratagems and Spoils: A Social Anthropology of Politics,* Oxford, Blackwell, 1969.

Balme, R., Chabanet D. and Wright V. (eds), *L'action collective en Europe,* Paris: Presses de Sciences Po, 2002.

Becker, H., *Outsiders: Studies in the Sociology of Deviance,* New York: The Free Press of Glencoe, 1963.

Berger, P. and Luckmann, T., *The Social Construction of Reality, A Treatise in the Sociology of Knowledge,* Garden City: Doubleday, 1966.

Boltanski, L., *Les cadres: la formation d'un groupe social,* Paris: Éditions de Minuit, 1982.

Bourdieu, P., 'La représentation politique. Eléments pour une théorie du champ politique', *Actes de la recherche en sciences sociales,* 36–37, 1981, 3–17.

Bourdieu, P., 'La force du droit. Eléments pour une sociologie du champ juridique', *Actes de la recherche en sciences sociales,* 64, 1986, 3–19.

Bourdieu, P. and Christin, R. 'La construction du marché. Le champ administratif et la production de la "politique du logement"', *Actes de la recherche en sciences sociales,* 81–82, 1990, 65–85.

Bruno, I., *A vos marques, prêt, cherchez!,* Bellecombes-en-Bauges: Éditions du Croquant, 2007.

Cobb, R. and Elder, C., *Participation in American Politics: The Dynamics of Agenda-building,* Boston: Allyn and Bacon, 1972.

Courty, G., *Les groupes d'intérêt,* Paris: La Découverte, 2006.

de Lassalle, M. and Georgakakis D. (eds), *La nouvelle gouvernance européenne: genèse et usages politiques d'un livre blanc,* Strasburg: Presses Universitaires de Strasburg, 2008.

Favell, A. and Guiraudon, V., 'The Sociology of European Union: An Agenda', *European Union Politics,* 2009, 550–576.

Fouilleux, E., 'Policy Change and Discourse in Europe', *West European Politics,* 27 (2), 2004, 183–379.

Greenwood, J., *Interest Representation in the European Union,* 2nd edn, Basingstoke, New York: Palgrave Macmillan, 2007.

Guiraudon, V., 'L'espace sociopolitique européen, un champ encore en friche?', *Cultures et conflits,* 38–39, 1998, 7–37.

Gusfield, J., *The Culture of Public Problems: Drinking-driving and Symbolic Order,* Chicago: Chicago University Press, 1981.

Haas, E., *The Uniting of Europe: Political, Social and Economical Forces, 1950–1957,* Stanford: Stanford University Press, 1958.

Imig, D. and Tarrow, S. (eds), *Contentious Europeans: Protest and Politics in an Integrating Europe,* Boulder: Rowman and Littlefield, 2001.

Kohler-Koch, B., 'The Evolution of Organized Interests in the EC: Driving Forces, Coevolution or New Type of Governance?', in H. Wallace and A. R. Young (eds), *Participation and Policy Making in the European Union,* Oxford: Oxford University Press, 1997, 42–68.

Lindberg, L.N., *The Political Dynamics of European Economic Integration,* Stanford: Stanford University Press, 1963.

Majone, G., *Regulating Europe*, London: Routledge, 1996.

Mazey, S. and Richardson J. (eds), *Lobbying in the European Community*, Oxford: Oxford University Press, 1993.

Michel, H., 'Former au public affaires. Défense et illustration d'une profession', in H. Michel (ed.), *Lobbyistes et lobbying de l'union européenne. Trajectoires, formations et pratiques des représentants d'intérêts*, Strasburg: Presses Universitaires de Strasburg, 2005, 169–194.

Michel, H., *La cause des propriétaires. Etat et propriété en France, XIXe- XXe siècles*, Paris: Belin, 2006.

Offerlé, M., *Sociologie des groupes d'intérêt*, Paris: Montchrestien, 1998.

Péchu, C., *Droit au logement, genèse et sociologie d'une mobilisation*, Paris: Dalloz, 2006.

Peters, G., 'Agenda-setting in the European Community', *Journal of European Public Policy*, 1 (1), 1994, 9–24.

Robert, C., 'Doing Politics and Pretending Not To: The Commission's Role in Distributing Aid to Eastern Europe', in A. Smith (ed.), *Politics and the European Commission. Actors, Interdependence, Legitimacy*, Andover: Routledge, 2004, 17–29.

Smith, A., *Le gouvernement de l'Union européenne, une sociologie politique*, Paris: LGDJ, 2004.

Smith, A., 'The Government of the European Union and a Changing France', in P. Culpepper, P. Hall and B. Palier (eds), *Changing France: The Politics That Markets Make*, Basingstoke: Palgrave Macmillan, 2006, 179–197.

Vauchez, A., 'The Force of a Weak Field: Law and Lawyers in the Government of the European Union (For a Renewal Research Agenda)', *International Political Sociology*, 2 (2), 2008, 128–144.

Andy Smith

7

A constructivist–institutionalist approach to EU politics: the case of Protected Geographical Indications for food

This chapter examines how Europe constructs public problems. In so doing an approach will first be developed which draws upon constructivists and institutionalists whose work has been structured by the sociological method.[1] Then reasons will be presented for choosing a case study of EU food labelling as the empirical 'test' for this approach throughout the remainder of the chapter.

In order to firmly link constructivist theory and methods when studying the definition, institutionalisation and legitimisation of European public problems, three concepts need clarifying from the outset: institutionalisation, problematisation and legitimisation.

At the basis of sociology is the thesis that social life is structured by rules and norms that have been institutionalised, i.e. stabilised guidelines which structure accepted and acceptable behaviour within social spaces (Elias, 1978: 75–76). Within the study of politics, the 'new institutionalism' of the last three decades has of course attempted to reassert this claim. To some extent this collective endeavour has largely succeeded, particularly within studies of the EU (Pierson, 1996; Sandholtz and Stone Sweet, 1998). However, over the last ten years or so, and particularly since Hall and Taylor's review essay (1996), far too much energy has been devoted to increasingly sterile reflection about 'institutionalisms', their similarities and their differences. Meanwhile, far too little attention has been devoted to developing operational approaches to the making and unmaking of institutions – institutionalisation and deinstitutionalisation – and allying this aim to that of the constructivist project.

As our current work on the politics of various industries underlines (Jullien and Smith, 2008), bridging this ontological gap is crucial because even if the sustainability of the institutions which structure daily conduct within firms and industries is inevitably linked to functional issues (i.e. designing, producing and selling goods), their durability is above all a political construction. It follows that the critical condition for the stable regulation of an industry is the capacity of certain actors to impose and maintain a division of authority that rests upon justifications which are generally accepted by the practitioners concerned. Consequently, we define the regulation of industries as a set of stabilised rules which, within any industry, transform production, marketing and competition into durable and 'secure' processes: institutions structure and liberate individual action by reducing uncertainties via collective action without which industries would be paralysed. Institutions are therefore constraints upon commercial action but also provide the very conditions for such action. Taken together as an Institutional Order, institutions thus provide a framework for activity within an industry which, far from determining precisely what each individual actor will do, allows them to situate and position themselves within a broader set of considerations.

When attempting to grasp the decision-making processes through which the construction of institutions takes place, the second concept which needs defining is that of 'public problem' shaping. As numerous authors have underlined for some time now, the problems that are debated and regulated within any social space are representations of reality which different protagonists have sought to 'make social', i.e. that are made to possess intersubjective meaning (Rochefort and Cobb, 1994; Muller, 1995; Campana, Henry and Rowell, 2007).

Again, our work on industry highlights the deeply constructivist and institutionalising character of this process. Contrary to functionalist theory, 'industrial difficulties' do not arise spontaneously from social conflict or technological innovation and then automatically or mechanically become objects of collective or public intervention. In reality, an industrial difficulty only engenders such action through undergoing a process of *problematisation*. In order to study this process, it is useful to distinguish between different stages of a form of the 'political work' which defines, institutionalises and legitimises industrial controversies. On a day-to-day basis, companies work within sets of 'conditions' which include transport costs, health and safety law, employment and tax law etc. As long as representatives of these companies do not seek to change these conditions they remain 'flat' and unproblematised (Kingdon, 1984). Within an industry for example, in such circumstances, production, finance, purchasing and commerce are subjects which actors within companies engage with by adopting a logic of action that is essentially mono-organisational and market transaction-centred. However, as soon as such actors seek to modify these conditions, they attempt to transform them into 'problems' of two types:

- *collective problems* emerge whenever their definition is shared by an inter-organisational grouping of actors who can claim to be representative of their industry and/or their profession. Indeed, much of the regulation of industry takes place around struggles to define problems which actors consider merit collective action;

- *public problems* develop when the process of definition widens to include politicians and civil servants who, at least in theory, work for the public interest. Indeed, the formulation of public problems constitutes an indispensable step in both agenda-setting (Rochefort and Cobb, 1994) and the creation of policy instruments (Lascoumes and Le Galès, 2007).

Focusing upon the institutionalisation of public problems thus provides a means of systematically combining constructivist and institutionalist tools, thereby underlining that neither approach should be reduced to vague reflection about 'norms'. Instead, it is question of studying the 'problems' around which the instruments of public action have been set in order to better understand 'how allocating rights contributes to establish a historically contingent order whose genesis always results more from struggles of power than from quests for efficiency' (Jullien, 2004: 4).

In order to fully grasp these struggles, research therefore needs to equip itself with a third and final concept: legitimisation. Defined by Lagroye (1985: 405) as a political activity designed to acquire 'durable legitimacy', i.e. a form of recognition founded both on 'rational' argumentation ('our power is necessary and functional') and moral imputation ('our power is right, our power is founded on common values'), legitimisation is a means of simultaneously studying the making of public problems and the 'assignment' of power to be involved in the process (Carter and Smith, 2008). Indeed, such an approach is particularly salutary when studying European decision-making where struggles to legitimise both EU policies and the EU as a political system are so obviously omnipresent.

It is for this very reason that in a previous publication I made a distinction between 'European' and 'Community' problems (Smith, 2004a: 77). This analytical dichotomy was proposed in order to distinguish between public problems which are written in EU law but have not been politicised (Community problems) and those which have gained some social legitimacy (European problems). The first advantage of considering that Europe constructs problems which range in their degree of institutionalisation from 'Community' to 'European' is that research is forced to examine not only EU decision-making *per se*, but also the legitimising mechanisms typical of the EU's government, their specific characteristics and effects. The second advantage is to generate knowledge about the causes and effects of the conversion or the non-conversion of a Community problem into a European problem. In short, the overall aim of a constructivist–institutionalist approach founded upon the sociological method is to focus attention upon the EU's particular relationship to politics (Smith, 2004b) and how this matters within specific Institutional Orders and their respective negotiating sites.

In order to illustrate the approach set out above, the remainder of this chapter mobilises empirical material taken from a case study of the introduction into EU law and practice of a policy instrument which codifies a wide range of European food names: Protected Geographical Indications (PGIs). This instrument has allowed the EU to register the names of more than 600 foodstuffs as being specific to a particular area (e.g. Parma Ham, *Foie Gras du Sud-Ouest*). More precisely, our research has sought to grasp the emergence and consolidation of the pluri-territorial institutional order within which PGIs have evolved as a 'problem' for collective and public authorities (Smith, 2008). Our perspective on this problem highlights the legitimising arguments used within the EU to justify, and even reinforce, the institutionalisation of these instruments. In this way our research has sought to grasp the political meanings given to the Regulation concerning PGIs (2081/92) in the European Union. As will be highlighted, even if this Regulation is no longer openly disputed within the different member states, the problematisation which underpins this legislation has certainly not become entirely legitimate in the eyes of actors from all EU states working in agricultural matters, intellectual property or competition law. We also show that PGIs' contested legitimacy is not simply the result of 'poor communication' between protagonists coming from different 'national cultures'.

In order to grasp why PGIs remain a Community problem and not a European one, we first show that this is due to processes of construction around how the founding Regulation was originally negotiated. We next examine how each national institutional order has implemented the Regulation and the effects this has caused. Finally, we address more directly the legitimisations PGIs have inspired.

A regulation 'Frenchifying' European single market law

The negotiation of European law is a long process and that of Regulation 2081/92 on PGIs was no exception. A proposal to create this policy instrument emerged at the end of the 1980s, a process wherein French socio-professional and public actors played a central role widely supported by their Italian, Spanish, Portuguese and Greek counterparts. For once, Southern European countries succeeded in uniting and imposing their point of view on other Member States. However, it would be simplistic to consider that during the largely technicised negotiations which took place between 1986 and 1992 in and around the Commission and the Council, a collective learning process changed the prevailing approaches to indications of quality and origin, and more generally to intellectual property, in all the member states. Indeed, since the initial adoption of Regulation 2081/92, the implementation of this policy instrument has sparked considerable politicisation of a range of issues concerning PGIs which, in turn, has revealed how incomplete and non-linear their institutionalisation has proved to be. In order to grasp and explain the incomplete character of this institutionalisation over time, we will borrow Carter's (2008) distinction between 'framing' and 'operationalising' institutions. More precisely, our aim here is to 'enable the relational character of institutional change to be investigated by placing attention on the connections between active processes of framing and operationalising in institution building' (Carter, 2008: 348).

Problematisation as 'framing': adopting the PGI Regulation

This regulation's normative and cognitive foundations first emerged in the law and practice of designations of origin for wines and spirits in France which go back to the first decade of the twentieth century (Smith, de Maillard and Costa, 2007). In France as well at the Community level, regulation of the wine industry was thus a fundamental precondition for the genesis of the EU's PGIs. More particularly, French law concerning *Appellations d'origine contrôlée* (AOC) had already become a standardised model throughout Southern Europe well before the 1990s. By creating legal instruments to fight against the fraudulent use of geographical names, but also by creating an object around which deeply institutionalised professional and inter-professional relationships were built,[2] French laws from 1905, 1919 and 1935 contributed to structuring an institutional order that many actors from the food industry came to envy. Many of the French wine industry's regulating instruments were translated into Community law as early as 1970.[3] However, from the perspective of framing in a precise manner a projected EU indication of origin for all foodstuffs, the model of wine products only began to take on increased importance when two more general debates crystallised and began to overlap at the end of the 1980s.

The first concerned the completion of the internal market. The Single European Act and the '1992 project' reactivated a Community competition policy that forced both Commission services and national administrations to justify every exemption from EU law concerning competition (Dumez and Jeunemaître, 1991). Supported by a heterogeneous group of company representatives and neo-liberal public actors, 'competition' and 'the internal market' came to constitute a horizontal European cognitive and normative frame. From then onwards, every sector, and even every instrument of European policy, has had either to be made to fit within this over-arching frame or, alternatively, to justify its derogatory status. Simultaneously a network of Commission, national government and regulatory agency officials has developed with its own agenda of spreading the norms of competition policy and ensuring they are implemented in certain ways throughout the EU (McGowan, 2007). Thus one of the key motivations for the emergence of networks of collective and public actors in favour of GIs (commonly called 'GI Friends')[4] was to counter the power of an emerging network of competition policy advocates.

The second debate within the Community, which strongly affected the introduction of PGIs, concerned the Common Agricultural Policy (CAP) and rural development. From the beginning of the 1980s, the CAP had increasingly been criticised for its surpluses and cost. Whilst the main solution proposed by CAP opponents was a change of the instruments regulating agricultural markets, some also emphasised the importance of establishing in their stead a European rural development policy. Synthesised in 1988 by European Commission officials in a Communication to the Council entitled *L'avenir du monde rural*,[5] this proposal included sections about the desirable connections between the designation of food origins, the future of European agriculture and rural economic development.[6] Without overestimating the attention paid by politicians to this question at the time, it is important to note that this discursive link between food quality, indications of origin and the future of rural areas was legitimised using a strategy of politicisation during an informal meeting of Ministers of Agriculture held at the end of 1989 in Beaune.[7] Indeed, inserting this discursive link into the conclusions of this meeting constituted a significant achievement for the then emerging network of 'GI Friends' which, in turn, helped it to consolidate and grow.

In short, as of 1989, the conclusions of this meeting, as well as the more detailed proposals expressed in *L'avenir du monde rural*, became part of a draft Regulation put forward by the Commission to the Council. Representatives of the governments of some member states, such as Denmark, were hostile to this initiative because of its 'protectionist' character. Others, for instance civil servants from the British Ministry of Agriculture,[8] were sceptical about its economic validity. Nevertheless, in the end the Commission's initial draft was accepted as a piece of legislation which largely mirrored the original proposal.

Problematisation as 'operationalising': implementing the PGI Regulation

Once published in the Official Journal, the Regulation had to be made to 'live' and take effect through its implementation within the member states. As will be shown, however, conceptualised as 'operationalisation', this controversy-racked process has participated much more fully in the institutionalisation of PGIs than positivists or rationalists would predict. This is because the interplay between framing and operationalising institutions lies at the heart of how actors deal with the 'dilemmas' (Carter, 2008: 347) to which regulatory instruments such as PGIs invariably give rise.

On the scale of the EU as a whole, operationalisation of the Regulation was formally led by a unit of the DG Agriculture and through a regulatory committee that assembled the representatives of every national ministry of agriculture. Two phases marked the work of this committee to register each PGI. During an initial period (1992–96), it mainly registered indications of origin already sanctioned by the national certification systems. Subsequently, the committee's second phase began: the consideration of PGI projects became more exacting and evaluation criteria more discriminating. Criteria now had to be developed in order to implement the Regulation in full by reviewing then registering applications from new PGI candidates. The size of the protected geographical areas, for instance, was a criterion that gave rise to heated debates. For instance, interviewed about the geographical boundaries of 'South-West' France, an INAO representative admitted:

> We aren't at all sure this would have been accepted by the Commission after 1996 ... PGIs all want to have the largest area possible – however, the wider the area is, the more necessary it is to expand the characteristics of the specification, and the more the products will drop in quality. But neither can we reserve a very large geographical area for an elite. (Interview, January 2004)

In contrast to the South-West of France or Scotland, every attempt to register an 'English' PGI has failed. According to many of our interviewees, the issue here has not been the size of England's geographical area *per se* (after all, the area where Parma Ham is produced is almost as big as England). Rather they highlight the inability of English socio-professional actors to prove a link between geographical area, the history of a product and the specifics of its production methods. This example thus reveals the importance of how quite precise aspects of policy operationalisation often have wider consequences for their institutionalisation as a whole.

Simultaneously to this EU registration of PGIs, a process of legal argumentation through court cases also occurred in the mid to late 1990s and fed into the institutionalisation of this regulatory instrument. In particular, two cases brought before the European Court of Justice need highlighting.

This first concerned the specific or generic character of 'Feta' cheese. Subsequent to the introduction of the PGI Regulation, the Greek government applied to register this foodstuff. The Commission initially supported this proposal which posited the existence of a very close link between Feta and Greece, in particular by lauding the results of a Eurobarometer survey carried out in 1996. However, this construction of Feta as a fundamentally Greek cheese was contested by four member states where this name had come to be used on the labels of locally produced cheeses: Denmark (since 1963), Germany (1985), France (by the producers of Roquefort) and the Netherlands (1981). The first three countries appealed to the Court of Justice of the European Communities (ECJ) to dispute the methods used to establish the generic nature of Feta. After lengthy deliberation, this appeal was upheld, thus annulling the registration of Feta as a PGI, since it considered that the Commission had not sufficiently taken into account existing uses of the term. Nevertheless, after a second appeal in 1999,[9] the Court decided that the term Feta was not generic and that the product specification was sufficiently discriminating as regards production methods as well as geographical areas in order to justify its registration.

Without going into the detail of a complicated legal case, it is important to emphasise to what extent the stance of the governments that disputed the registration of Feta as a PGI – especially the French – sowed confusion over the economic and political meaning given to PGIs in general. The French government participated in the legal attack on the decision to register Feta as a PGI largely to protect the interests of Roquefort cheese producers who used an association with the term Feta in order to market their surplus production. However, according to a consultant then working for Parma Ham, 'Roquefort producers weren't consistent because they themselves created the link between their product and Greece by calling it "Slakis". They played against their own side' (Interview, December 2003). Shared by numerous interviewees,[10] the 'inconsistency' of the French government's and Roquefort producers' stance therefore did nothing to enhance the legitimacy of the PGI Regulation amongst specialised policy-makers, let alone in the eyes of the consumer.

The legal, social and political meaning of PGIs was also put to test through a second appeal to the ECJ concerning Parma Ham's PGI. Urged on by many cases of fraud concerning their product, the representatives of its producers (*Consorzio del Prosciutto di Parma*) were among the first actors to back the introduction of the Community Regulation on PGIs and to obtain their own protection in 1996 (Thual, 2003). Contrary to the Feta case, this appeal did not concern the geographical origin of a product, nor its generic nature. Rather, the question put to the Court consisted of deciding whether the protection of the designation also applied to products sliced and packaged in regions different from where they had been produced and processed.[11] The Court concluded in favour of Parma Ham producers by accepting their stance: the slicing and the packaging on site were essential to the preservation of its specific characteristics. Even if this analysis 'resulted from a detailed study on ham quality and risks of deterioration during slicing and packaging' (Chaltiel, 2003: 457), it is important to stress that this technical reasoning was supplemented by a political argument made by Parma Ham's representatives over the 'disastrous consequences' that a negative judgment would have on the location of the ham processing industry. In other words, the precedents set by this ECJ decision, and that made in a similar case concerning Grana Padano cheese, inscribed in Community law 'a renewed reconciliation between the principle of the free movement of goods and the protection of industrial property' (Chaltiel, 2003: 455). If, from the point of view of PGI advocates, these judgments 'clarified' the law concerning PGIs, it is less certain that the public debate around these judgments necessarily contributed to reinforcing the political and European meaning of the geographical indication concept.

All things considered, these episodes of legal action, as well as the small importance attached to public communication about the meaning of this certification system, leads our analysis to qualify the conclusion frequently heard in France that the 1992 Regulation constituted a 'victory' for a 'French' approach to the legal and political protection of indications of origin. Certainly, there are now 650 PGIs throughout the member states. Some national ministries of agriculture (for instance the UK's), have increasingly become supporters of PGIs. In the same way, the governments of some new member states – especially Hungary – are supporters of the PGI approach (Ansaloni et al., 2007). But it is far less certain that this eagerness has been shared by ministries of trade and industry. Similarly, as will be shown below, if the Commission's defence of PGIs within the WTO seems to suggest that officials from DG Agriculture, DG Market and DG Trade are in full agreement over this policy instrument, it would still be an exaggeration to conclude that the Commission as a whole has constituted the mainspring for political advocacy of PGIs. In fact, the absence of a European-wide shared cognitive frame has not facilitated the international promotion of PGIs. Instead this has only been tackled using technocratic channels and tools (Smith, 2008). Indeed, considered essential for the adoption of the 1992 Regulation, the technical arguments used during the initial problematisation of PGIs have subsequently come to hinder the legitimisation of these instruments both within the EU and beyond its borders. In short, Europe constructed a Community problem, not a European one.

National interpretations of the regulation

Indeed, this absence of shared representations within the European Union about the political meaning ascribed to PGIs has also been noticeable in the way in which each member state has implemented Regulation 2081/92. If the regulatory committee has registered PGIs through a single 'EU' set of procedures, national administrations have nonetheless participated in the 'operationalisation' of the Regulation in divergent ways. More precisely, every national institutional order has decoded this law through the prism of their respective institutional orders, before recoding it into examination and validation procedures. Often euphemised by invoking the principle of subsidiarity, this variety of implementing methods needs explaining in more detail by examining how PGI legislation has been integrated into pre-existing laws and, more fundamentally still, into national or local Institutional Orders.

The French system implementing PGIs provides a striking illustration of this phenomenon. Between 1992 and 2007, this national case was unique because of the link it established between PGIs as an indication of origin and labels for designating product quality (Product Conformity Certification (CCP) and *Label rouge*). Putting to one side the national debate this linkage frequently provoked,[12] within European arenas this interpretation of the Regulation transformed the French delegation to the regulatory committee into advocates for using PGIs as restrictive instruments for structuring food sectors by effectively delegating regulatory power to the collective organisations which dominate these sectors.[13] Indeed, from 1999 onwards, this trend has intensified as INAO took responsibility for PGI management[14] and members of this body began to attend meetings of the EU regulatory committee. More specifically, steeped in the cognitive and normative frame of the AOC, INAO representatives embodied the argument in favour of a strong link between the origin of a product and its quality.

It is important to underline that in some other member states, criteria for selecting PGIs have been just as exacting as those applied in France. This is clearly the case, for instance, in the United Kingdom, where not only has the British administration applied the Regulation 'to the letter', but it has also encouraged the progressive tightening of some PGI specifications. In 2000, for instance, the organisation in charge of the PGI Scotch Beef, *Quality Meat Scotland*, chose to move in this direction.[15] Supported by the UK and Scottish administrations, this demand for a 'more demanding' specification was welcomed by Commission officials.

However, contrary to these restrictive national approaches to PGIs, other national Institutional Orders have implemented less exacting registration procedures. Here our British, French, Danish and Commission interviewees cited the Italian procedure in particular. According to these actors, as in France or Britain, the Italian Ministry of Agriculture received applications for new PGIs that had been developed within regions. Rather than review and assess these applications though, they simply sent them on to DG Agriculture. This meant that the national administration merely acted as a 'letterbox' thereby giving subnational actors great autonomy. In cases represented by Commission and other national officials as 'the worst', this practice led to 'administrative negligence' that paved the way for political patronage. As two interviewees emphasised:

> There's a risk of increase in the number of PGIs because of subsidiarity. In Italy, there's a tendency to want to make a PGI for anything. There are very unequal applications ... such a system of examining applications is too much under local councillor influence. Because a PGI can be a political asset at the local level.[16]

> We have the feeling that there are regions that, for instance, began to produce lemons and are trying to register them as PGIs. We can't see the historical link. We ask questions about criteria in the specification too. But, in a general way, we must accept that if an application has been examined by a national administration, then by the Commission, and that we had the chance to comment upon it, we can't do more.[17]

According to some specialists, the 'inflationary' increase in PGIs potentially constitutes a two-sided 'threat' to the EU's approach. Firstly, it is considered that divergences in the examination methods of PGI applications will, sooner or later, end up unravelling the whole system, and engender a massive increase in legal appeals and a further loss of the political meaning for Regulation 2081/92. Secondly, such critics have highlighted that a law which gives rise to such varied applications is necessarily more difficult to defend at the WTO.

To summarise this analysis of issues triggered by the implementation of Regulation 2081/92, when studied through the prism of 'subsidiarity in action' (Faure, 1997), we clearly see that PGIs are far from being problematised in the same way in each member state. These differences are often explained using functional and essentialist terms which underline 'the heterogeneous nature' of European agriculture, food processing industries and consumption patterns. However, as our constructivist-institutionalist approach has sought to show, explaining what Europe has constructed here means grasping change within the institutionalised configurations of socio-professional and public actors that the implementation of PGIs has entailed.

Competing and conflicting legitimising strategies

With little homogeneous implementation, tortuous initial negotiation, mediatised legal appeals and very discreet political communication, it is hardly surprising that the political meaning of PGIs and their very legitimacy are still contested. More fundamentally still, our approach leads us to claim that the deep-set cause of the incomplete institutionalisation of this EU policy lies in the uneasy coexistence of three arguments used to legitimise PGIs: 'intellectual property', 'rural development' and 'agricultural development'.

At first glance, the argument that PGIs allow food products to be protected against fraud and 'passing off' seems to pose the fewest problems. In terms of values, all the European socio-professional and public actors involved are against fraudulent use of geographical designations and in favour of using them to maintain the profitability of exports. At closer inspection, however, one discovers that this policy goal has frequently not been reflected in strategies of collective and private commercial activity. Firstly, the court cases concerning Feta and Parma Ham remind us that some large companies and national governments (e.g. Denmark) do not support Community doctrine. Secondly, at the WTO, officials from the ministries of Trade of certain other member countries (e.g. the UK), agents from Commission DGs (e.g. Market and Competition), and even those working in the PGI unit within DG Agriculture, are ready to make concessions concerning PGIs in order to obtain a wider multilateral agreement on agriculture. Some of these actors even prefer the intellectual property protection defended in the WTO by American and Australian negotiators: private brands. Other European actors want to relinquish PGIs because they think that the farms involved are on the fringe of EU agriculture. For instance, as a top French civil servant talking about the WTO agriculture debate underlined:

> traditional agriculture still carries much weight in Europe. [In the Doha round] we won't concede something significant about agriculture, in order to obtain something for PGIs. The DG Agriculture has a personnel of 1,000 officials, and only a handful of them work directly on PGIs. They are not necessarily the future of agriculture.[18]

In short, there is no doubting that 'GI Friends' have consolidated their argumentations and interdependencies over the last ten years. The creation of the worldwide network of producer organisations, ORIGIN, and that of the *Association des régions européennes pour les produits d'origine* (AREPO) provide clear evidence of this. However, because these bodies remain outside the policy networks through which mainstream agriculture and trade policies are regulated, the future of the approach to agricultural intellectual property they claim to embody remains uncertain.

Even greater uncertainty and debate surround a second series of arguments in favour of PGIs presented by advocates of an EU rural development policy. Since 1988, actors within the Commission, French representatives and numerous socio-professionals have continually emphasised a strong link between indications of origin and the economic development of rural areas, especially the less-favoured of these. Indeed, in many regions EU structural funds financially and politically support indications of origin, such as Bayonne Ham. The fact remains that this involvement in favour of particular PGIs has not given rise to a consistent policy that clearly establishes the connection between indications of origin and rural development. The first explanation we can give is the absence of rigorous economic research on this connection. This lack of data concerning PGIs' impact on local development in rural areas is considered by certain 'GI Friends' to be a great hindrance.[19] The second explanation for imprecision over the linkage between PGIs and rural development results from the fragmentation of the Commission. The following point of view was evoked in several interviews:

> DG Agriculture has a regulatory perspective. They aren't concerned by rural development. When they talk of rural development, they talk of programmes financed by the structural funds. So does DG Trade, except when it authorises 'exporting' the PGI model abroad.[20]

The third explanation we can give to the weak link between PGIs and rural development refers to the observation that rural development is far from being defined and considered in the same way in every member state. For instance, according to a civil servant of the British Department of Food and Agriculture:

> We don't have any problem in proving our food products' history. We are less good at giving enough details about the link between production methods and regions without using this history. It's because we are not familiar with things like 'terroir'. We learn from other states. We need to be a little more 'romantic' in our arguments because we tend to be a little too logical. We need to enhance the characteristics of our products.[21]

In short, rural development remains a vague policy concept that generates little reflection and discussion between representatives of the Commission and the member states. Indeed, no stabilised forums exist within which to engage such reflection, let alone negotiating arenas that might generate a PGI–rural development actor alliance. Consequently, and more fundamentally, it is difficult for PGI advocates to know what arguments to deploy about economic development and public intervention, especially given the prevalence of constructions of 'the internal market' and 'globalisation' which are largely neo-liberal in character.[22]

This deeply ideological question is even more salient in the case of the third argument used to defend PGIs: that they encourage 'agricultural development' through the explicit structuring of sectors. Studying the effects of PGIs on these sectors shows that producers and processors' involvement in PGIs corresponds most often to a perspective of expansion of a sector which, in most cases, actually intensifies production. Certainly, and contrary to the products supported by the CAP between 1960 and 1990, this agricultural development does not rely on considerable public subsidies. Here the political support to economic growth is different since it is based more on regulating modes of production and processing than on redistributing sums of money. But with no cognitive, normative and symbolic EU frame with which to legitimise such an approach to the economy, most 'GI Friends' are sceptical of their chances of defending this type of public intervention in European and international negotiating sites.

Far from being theoretical or abstract, these confusions in the arguments used to defend and promote PGIs tend to be magnified when translated into the arguments adopted to defend them by French and Commission officials. Moreover, in the case of the former it is important to underline the complex division of competences that exists between the Ministry of Agriculture and INAO. According to a representative of the latter, for example, his organisation:

> is at a crossroads: a public institution under the patronage of the Ministry of Agriculture with a role of adviser and also a mission of asserting professionals' points of view, especially during international negotiations. All this can sometimes make things a little complex because the INAO plays the role of both advocate of PGIs and of adviser to the Ministry.[23]

Nevertheless, as far as this Ministry is concerned, PGIs are not necessarily approved of unanimously. Instead, they often arouse disagreements between the representatives of a type of agriculture which uses PGIs and other such labels (especially from South-West France), and those who consider that such indications are an obstacle to the expansion of their respective sectors (e.g. *foie gras* producers in the Vendée and Brittany). Ultimately, as in EU and international negotiating sites, the central issue raised by PGIs within France crystallises around the challenge of articulating a set of rules which gives products of origin special treatment on the one hand and, on the other, respects universalist competition law. If one is a representative of Dordogne *foie gras* producers, the INAO president or a civil servant in the PGI service of DG Agriculture, legitimising PGIs by emphasising their contribution to agricultural development is constructed as a 'self-evident' political strategy.

Whereas if one is the president of the Vendéen Chamber of Agriculture, the French Minister of Agriculture or a civil servant in DG Competition, it is also 'obvious' that the argument PGIs = agricultural development is at best extremely tenuous, and at worst completely heretical.

In summary, justifications used to argue for and against PGIs are constructions that actors from either side of this debate have sought to insti-tutionalise. Here 'Europe' has therefore constructed a policy instrument but, at least thus far, partisans of this institution have singularly failed to legitimise it.

Conclusion

Based on our analysis of the introduction, implementation and legitimisation of a European PGI system, this chapter raises questions about the coherence and consistency of the EU's policy on indications of origin. More fundamen-tally, it has questioned the very existence of a 'European problem' in this domain. Indeed, and to return to the distinction made at the end of the firstsection, the non-conversion of this Community problem into a European one has considerable effects upon other parts of 'what Europe constructs'. Firstly, the uncertainties which surround PGIs as a policy instrument weaken the hand of its partisans when they seek to participate in reforming the EU's Common Agricultural Policy. Secondly, within debates at the WTO, incon-sistencies within the problematisation of PGIs are currently making their 'global' defence extremely difficult. Indeed, some argue that intra-EU discord is now favouring the interests of governments and private firms (especially American ones), which try to depoliticise the quality food issue by technicis-ing the rules of intellectual property in this domain and, more broadly, the question of 'a right to food differences' (Noiville, 2003).

As a case study on how industries are regulated in Europe, more generally the PGI example brings to light many characteristics of the government of the EU's relationship to politics. Far from being absent from the construction and the regulating of markets at European level, politics is omnipresent but rela-tively 'silent'. It is omnipresent because, as we have shown, governing an industry such as agriculture constantly implies debates about the aims of collective and public action on one hand, and about the competitive construction of alliances seeking to take decisions on policy on the other (Jullien and Smith, 2008). However, this form of politics is generally discreet and little-publicised due to characteristics typical of the EU's overall institu-tional order, such as the centrality of a Commission which lacks political legitimacy or national ministers and ministries (who frequently undermine EU legislation both to make short-term gains for 'their' producers and, more fundamentally, because they question its very legitimacy) (Smith, 2004a and b). Put succinctly, these structural traits of 'the government of the EU' have either caused or reinforced more specific challenges experienced by actors seeking to institutionalise PGIs such as covering the whole range of negotiating arenas involved, maintaining actor alliances and evaluating this policy instrument's socio-economic impact.

Finally, the chapter as a whole illustrates the heuristic 'promise' of a constructivist–institutionalist approach. First, it has eliminated the functionalist hypothesis that instruments regulating the EU's economy, such as PGIs, are intrinsically 'technical' and consequently difficult to legitimise through politicisation. No social issue is necessarily technical. Its politicisation or technicisation depends instead upon how the actors concerned problematise and transform controversies into collective or public problems. PGIs could have become European rather than Community problems but they have not. Moreover, our approach also argues against rational choice theory by showing that it is only through thoroughly analysing the construction of actor perceptions, preferences, strategies and interactions that this 'non-problematisation' can be fully understood. Second, and perhaps above all, the approach's focus upon both the making of precise rules and the arguments used to legitimise them lends support to those who seek to analyse 'what Europe constructs' using rigorous institutionalist concepts and sociological methods of enquiry.

Notes

1 The standpoint defended here draws heavily upon two sources of reflexion about constructivism. The first concerns research on The Politics of Industry conducted over last five years with a number of colleagues and Bernard Jullien, an economist, in particular (Jullien and Smith, 2008). The second is my research centre SPIRIT's 2008 seminar series on 'Constructivisme(s) et analyse politique' (see www.spirit. sciencespobordeaux.fr).

2 Note in particular the creation of a regulatory authority in 1935 which established a permanent linkage between socio-professional actors and representatives of the state: the *Institut national des appellations d'origine* (INAO – National Institute of Designations of Origin). Indeed, to use Jobert's terminology (1995), INAO has since become both the key French 'forum' for reflection about geographical indications and the principal 'arena' within which decision-making in this domain takes place. In the first instance, INAO's office-holders and permanent staff are in constant contact with a community of GI-friendly economists, sociologists, geographers and agronomists. As a decision-making arena INAO brings together representatives of individual GIs as well as key officials from the Ministry of Agriculture and other ministerial bodies.

3 When the *Common Market Organisation* for wine was set up, a distinction was instituted between quality wines produced in a specific region (including all the French AOCs) and table wines whose origin is not specified. In 1999 this distinction was recodified by Regulation 1493/1999, but still remains in place (de Maillard, 2001).

4 Early leaders within an entity which then lay somewhere between a network of collective action and a social movement included representatives of specific products (Parma Ham) and agricultural regions where GIs were already strongly present (the South-West of France: *foie gras*, labelled chicken, *Jambon de Bayonne*, Agen Prunes).

5 COM (88) 501 final, Brussels, EC, July 29, 1988.

6 The report stated for instance that 'the rural population, which is made up mainly of farmers and farm workers, is maintained by full exploitation of extensive quality farming and by incentives to farmers to use these techniques' (p. 8). One aspect of the work would be 'the development of a policy relating to the quality of products: in this context, the Commission will be submitting in the near future appropriate proposals … to implement at Community level a coherent policy on labels, descriptions and designations of origin' (p. 9). An outline of these proposals is presented further on (pp. 44–46) where it specified in particular that this 'quality policy' 'ought to be integrated into a more general Community framework in this domain, and to take account of policy on industrial and commercial ownership' (p.44).

7 Ph. Tabary goes as far as to say that 'the French position consisted of giving a little poetic licence to economic reality and reminding other national delegations that 80% of AOCs are produced in less-favoured areas' (1995: 172).

8 According to a top civil servant from the British Department of Agriculture, 'we were not enthusiastic. In a general way, ministers and civil servants of that time considered that PGIs would not be very relevant for the United Kingdom. Moreover, they thought that the system had been conceived in a protectionist way that would penalise our producers' (interview, May 2004).

9 The judgments about the cases C 289/96, C 293/96 and C 299/96 were announced on March 16, 1999.

10 For example, an official from one of the international authorities in charge of regulating GIs went a stage further by declaring that: 'Producers informed the French government about the economic problems that the ECJ's decision would pose. It was a political question. On the other hand, when we look at the negotiation between the EU and South Africa on a free trade agreement, what we see is the contrary. In this case, the EU had made a draft: it was planned that the names Port and Sherry should no longer be used in South Africa. The Spanish and the Portuguese encouraged this view. Afterwards, the Italians and the Greeks said 'but grappa and ouzo' must also be protected. Ouzo was not produced in South Africa, but they said that it was a question of principle. Why did the French government not react in the same way for the French case? It's politics' (interview in Geneva, May 2004).

11 ECJ decision, May 20, 2003: case C-108/01, Consorzio del Prosciutto di Parma, Salumificio S. Rita SpA and Asda Stores, Hygrade Foods Ltd. For a stimulating analysis, see Chaltiel (2003).

12 This debate was particularly marked by discussions which led to the Law of January 1994 on the recognition of the quality of agricultural foodstuffs (the 'quality law') and the Agricultural Orientation Law of July 9, 1999. For an analysis, see the French Economic and Social Committee report, Qualité et origine des produits agricoles et alimentaires presented by Gilbert Louis in 2001 (Éditions Les Journaux officiels).

13 These groups of actors are mainly made up of representatives of foodstuff producers and processors. Their main negotiation arenas and socialisation places are interprofessional organisations such as the Bayonne Ham Consortium.

14 The INAO Committee 4 deliberates over every application for registration of a PGI. The committee, composed of 39 members, votes by secret ballot. Each application must obtain two-thirds of the votes.

15 In order to incorporate a 'traditional' agricultural practice (a part of 'Scottish' bovine animals were initially reared in Northern England), the first specification for the Scotch Beef PGI simply required that cattle spend at least 90 days in Scotland. Subsequent to very embarrassing and mediatised criticism (encouraged by newspaper headlines such as 'Scotch beef is English'), and because differentiating Scotch from English beef was seen as a means of profiting from the fact that the former was little

affected by BSE, a proposal emerged to limit the label Scotch Beef to the meat of animals reared entirely in Scotland.

16 Interview, a specialised consultant, Brussels, December 2003.

17 Interview, a British civil servant, DEFRA, May 2004.

18 Interview, January 2004.

19 Certainly, DG Trade's website cites analyses showing that PGIs 'give our producers added value'. It underlines, for instance, that 'the price of French cheeses enjoying a geographical indication is increased by 2 euros. The Italian olive oil "Toscano" has sold 20% more [product] since the registration of this geographical indication in 1998'. However, these analyses are based on highly questionable correlations rather than on rigorous demonstration of causal relations.

20 Interview, French Ministry of Agriculture, January 2004. In addition, it should be recalled that the structural funds are managed not only by other services within DG Agriculture, but also by those of yet another DG: DG Region.

21 Interview, May 2004.

22 For a more general analysis of this phenomenon, see Borraz (2007).

23 Interview, January 2004.

Bibliography

Ansaloni, M., Fouilleux, E., Allaire, G. and Cheynis E., 'Européanisation, changements et permanences de l'action publique à l'Est : l'exemple des Indications Géographiques de produits agricoles de Hongrie', *Politique européenne*, 2, 2007, 133–151.

Borraz, O.,'Governing Standards: The Rise of Standardization Processes in France and in the EU', *Governance*, 20 (1), 2007, 57–84.

Campana, A., Henry, E. and Rowell, J. (eds), *La construction des problèmes publics en Europe*, Strasburg: Presses Universitaires de Strasburg, 2007.

Carter, C., 'Identifying Causality in Public Institutional Change: The Adaptation of the National Assembly for Wales to the European Union', *Public Administration*, 86 (2), 2008, 345–361.

Carter, C. and Smith, A., 'Revitalizing Public Policy Approaches to the EU: Territorial Institutionalism, Fisheries and Wine', *Journal of European Public Policy*, 15(2), 2008, 263–281.

Chaltiel, F., 'Les appellations protégées en Europe: renforcement de l'identité des produits et la transparence de l'information', *Revue du marché commun*, 470, July–August, 2003.

de Maillard, J., 'La Commission, le vin et la réforme', *Politique européenne*, 5, 2001, 70–86.

Dumez, H. and Jeunemaître, A., *La concurrence en Europe*, Paris: Le Seuil, 1991.

Elias, N., *What is Sociology?*, New York: Columbia University Press, 1978.

Faure, A. (ed.), *Territoires et subsidiarité. L'action publique locale à la lumière d'un principe controversé*, Paris: L'Harmattan, 1997.

Hall, P. and Taylor, R., 'Political Science and the Three New Institutionalisms', *Political Studies*, XLIV, 5, 1996.

Jobert, B., 'Rhétorique politique, controverses scientifiques et construction des norms institutionnelles', in A. Faure, G. Pollet and P. Warin (eds), *La construction du sens dans les politiques publiques*, Paris: L'Harmattan, 1995.

Jullien, B., *Pour une méso-économie politique-Eléments d'une approche institutionnaliste du changement dans les industries, rapport pour l'HDR*, Roneo: University of Bordeaux IV, 2004.

Jullien, B. and Smith, A., *Organisation industrielle et politique des Indications géographiques protégées*, report commissioned by the Aquitaine Regional Council, July 2004.

Jullien, B. and Smith, A. (eds), *Industries and Globalization: The Political Causality of*

Difference, Basingstoke: Palgrave, 2008.

Kingdon, J., *Agendas, Alternatives and Public Policies*, New York: Longman, 1984.

Lagroye, J., 'La légitimation', in M. Grawitz and J. Leca (eds), *Traité de science politique*, Paris: Presses Universitaires de France, 1985.

Lascoumes, P. and Le Galès P., 'Introduction: Understanding Public Policy Through its Instruments', *Governance*, 20 (1), 2007, 1–21.

McGowan, L., 'Theorizing European Integration: Revisiting Neo-functionalism and Testing its Suitability for Explaining the Development of EC Competition Policy?', *European Integration Online Papers*, 27 May 2007.

Muller, P., 'Les politiques publiques comme construction d'un rapport au monde', in A. Faure, G. Pollet and P. Warin (eds), *La construction du sens dans les politiques publiques*, Paris: L'Harmattan, 1995.

Noiville, C., 'Brèves réflexions sur la reconnaissance d'un "droit à la différence alimentaire" dans le commerce international', *Sociologie du travail*, 45 (1), 2003, 63–76.

Pierson, P., 'The Path to European Integration. A Historical Institutionalist approach', *Comparative Political Studies*, 29 (2), 1996, 123–163.

Rochefort, D. and Cobb, R., *The Politics of Problem Definition*, Lawrence: University Press of Kansas, 1994.

Sandholtz, W. and Stone Sweet, A. (eds), *European Integration and Supranational Governance*, Oxford: Oxford University Press, 1998.

Smith, A., *Le gouvernement de l'Union européenne. Une sociologie politique*, Paris: LGDJ, 2004a.

Smith, A., *Politics and the European Commission*, London: Routledge, 2004b.

Smith, A., 'The Politics of Food Labelling: "Europe", "The New World" and the WTO', in W. Genieys and M. Smyrl (eds), *Elites, Ideas and the Evolution of Public Policy*, London: Palgrave, 2008, 67–84.

Smith, A., de Maillard, J. and Costa, O., *Vin et politique. Bordeaux, la France et la mondialisation*, Paris: Presses de Sciences Po, 2007.

Tarbray, P., 'Astérix et l'Europe', *Autrement*, 154, 1995.

Thual, D., 'Sui Generis Protection vs. Trademark Registrations. The Parma Ham experience', Paper presented at conference of the WTO-China programme, Beijing, December 2003.

*Willy Beauvallet**

8

The European Parliament and the politicisation of the European space – the case of the two port packages

Research on the modes of government of the European Union often place emphasis on the depoliticisation of issues and internal interactions, perceived to be a response to the weak political and democratic legitimacy of its institutions, particularly the European Commission. 'Technicisation' of European issues and depoliticisation refer to institutional practices based on the mobilisation of expertise as alternatives to insufficient political resources required to make 'social choices'. In an institutional space that was historically built on unity rather than conflict, it is also a form of 'denationalisation' enabling a permanent, if sometimes precarious, compromise in internal political exchanges. According to the literature, this depoliticisation is linked to the sectorised nature of the European space, its weak cognitive unification, its multi-level and multi-polar structure, the resulting dilution of power relations and the weakness of intersectoral arenas (Hooghe and Marks, 2001; Smith, 2004) as well as its elitist nature (Costa and Magnette, 2007). Finally, this depoliticisation affects specialised knowledge, practices and representations (Abélès and Bellier, 1996) which pervade institutional roles and marks a common feature of European careers (Georgakakis, 2002).

However, these generally admitted characteristics of EU governance are not completely satisfactory. Indeed, it is not so much depoliticisation that characterises the European space as the constant tensions between politicisation and depoliticisation, between 'technical' sequences and more political ones, between compromise and conflict. These tensions are linked to the structures of the institutional space, the competing forms of legitimacy on which it is based, the various interests involved and the different types of

* Translated by Jean-Yves Bart

resources mobilised. Focusing the analysis of the EU solely on depoliticisation processes, as much of the literature does, raises several important practical and epistemological issues. It could lead us to take at face value the actors' discourse on their practices and to forget that discourse and practice emphasising depoliticisation are part and parcel of political strategies, in a permanent quest for power (Robert, 2001). We might also neglect one of the key features of this space: the intense inter-institutional competition that characterises it and the importance of conflicts of legitimacy. From this point of view, the strengthening of the European Parliament and the increasing integration of parliamentary actors in European policy-making constitute one of the essential transformations in recent years (Costa, 2001; Judge and Earnshaw, 2003) given that the professionalisation of parliamentarians integrates new political resources into the European space (Beauvallet, 2007). Finally, while the importance of experts and expertise are essential, one should not underestimate the weight and the effects of the mobilisation – whether by institutional actors or others – of more directly political registers of action (Michel, 2006). In other words, not only are there increasingly diverse actors who influence decision-making, but there are also new repertoires of action: Euro-demonstrations, strikes and coordinated boycotts of companies, etc. In return, these transformations also influence institutional practice and roles. Thus, it seems difficult to continue to assume that MEPs can be considered more as 'technocrats' than 'politicians' (Wessels, 1998)

Europe therefore does not only produce 'consensus' and 'compromise'. It also generates conflict and is constructed through conflict. Although some research explicitly focuses on this dimension (Marks and Steenbergen, 2004), it nonetheless remains marginal in European Studies. Actor-centred political sociology could provide some tools for re-examining the conflicting aspects of European processes and their effects. Within this framework, the EU is perceived less as a 'system' (Hix, 1999) than as a partially autonomous space shaped by particular forms of interaction (Kauppi, 2005) within which actors compete to acquire more or less specific resources in order to preserve or to transform existing balances of power. Although unequally endowed with resources, they nevertheless gravitate around the same stakes and share a common belief in the importance of the specific issues of this field (Bourdieu, 1979). In this regard, conflict is seen less as the manifestation of a problematic externality (resistances to Europe as a problem to be resolved) than an integral part of the internal dynamics of the entire European political space.[1] Those tensions define the properties as well as the characteristics of the unification processes.

Although explicit and visible political and social conflicts remain the exception in the dynamics of the EU, their very existence can shed new light on the entire process. This chapter will focus on politicisation and sequences of mobilisation through the analysis of two successive directives on the liberalisation of port services, referred to as 'Port Package' (1 and 2) rejected respectively in November 2003 (third reading) and January 2006 (first reading) following strong trade union mobilisation and a series of parliamentary 'battles'. This institutional outcome (negative vote and political mobilisations) is quite exceptional but reveals to a large extent the structural consequences of the transformations mentioned above.

The rejection of these directives followed the alliance between trade unions and some MEPs against the Commission, the Council and the initial parliamentary majority that gradually emerged in a specific political and media context. This led to a new round of negotiations in which trade unions, which were originally marginalised, became more involved. Under the influence of various mobilisations, the politicisation of port directives thus helped to transform the existing balance of power and transformed not only the definition of the political 'problem' in question but also the institutional agenda (Cobb and Elder, 1972; Kingdon, 1984) and, at least partially, the cognitive frames used to treat this 'problem' (Berger and Luckmann, 1966). While this problematique was initially constructed by the Commission within the classic perspective of liberalisation and the 'necessary' competition in port services, the final and massive rejection of the directive reflects, on the contrary, the increasing salience of competing narratives. At the end of the sequence, issues such as the fight against social dumping and security occupied a more central place in the definition of the 'problem' than was initially the case.

The outcome of the port directives shows first and foremost how non-institutional and non-economic actors, who are generally considered as 'losers' in European processes, were able to acquire specific political resources (those required for European politics) to such an extent that they were able to change, at least temporarily, their position in the political game. This case also illustrates the internal logics of the European Parliament itself. Far from being a unified actor, it must on the contrary be considered as an arena from which attempts to change the inherent balance of power in the entire European space originate. It appears as a 'resonance chamber' of sorts, amplifying conflicts which criss-cross European government, where rival visions and 'narratives' of social, economic and political reality clash more openly than in other institutional arenas (Sabatier and Schlager, 2000: 222). Finally, although this situation is less about rendering the routine functioning of Europe than brief but politicised 'moments', the increasing number of such events feed a sedimentation processes which affect both the definition of institutional roles and the general functioning of the EU, i.e. its characteristic field structures and rules.[2]

After presenting the directives and their provisions in the first section, we shall proceed to study the way in which the framework on which they were based was redefined by political mobilisation in a propitious context, before finally studying the shift of the parliamentary debates and internal logics.

The origin of the port directives: liberalisation and competition as 'ideological matrixes'

Nothing in terms of procedure or content of the two port packages predisposed them to their strange fate. In 1997, the European Commission issued a Green Paper on port infrastructures seeking to 'launch a debate on the efficiency of ports and maritime infrastructure, their integration into the multimodal trans-European network and the application of competition rules to this sector'. The Commission underscored the fact that competition between European ports was heightened as a result of the liberalisation of the internal market, technological advances and the development of trans-European transport networks. Henceforth, 'a Community framework is needed to ensure the principle of free and fair competition'. Although ports had long been considered mainly as services of general interest, 'the trend has now moved towards considering ports as commercial entities which must recover their costs from port users who benefit directly from their infrastructures'. Thus, as far as port services were concerned,

> ... treaty rules, notably in the area of competition, should therefore be applied more systematically. This is consistent with ... the modernisation and efficiency of the sector, given structural developments in world-wide competition.[3]

These orientations were confirmed by the 'Lisbon Strategy' adopted by the European Council in 2000. The latter has widely been interpreted as an incentive for accelerated liberalisation, especially in the area of transportation. Thus, the White Paper on transport issued in 2001 underlined the need for a European policy on sea and river transportation, where the EC identified a certain number of structural bottlenecks.[4] Given that ports are subject to multiple types of regulation, it emphasised the need 'to make new and clearer rules in the areas of piloting, handling, stevedoring, etc.'.

The European Parliament received a set of documents entitled 'the Port Package' in 2001. The central document was the directive on the liberalisation of port services,[5] based on the conclusions of the Green Paper and the results of consultations that the Commission held with actors of the sector in 1999 and 2000. The main goal of this text was 'to establish a Community framework ensuring ... access to the port services market in application of the Treaty rules ...'.[6] The essential principles of the directive were therefore based on the obligation for states to ensure unrestricted access to port services (piloting, mooring, handling, warehousing, etc.) In this framework, the liberalisation of these services involved the recognition of the 'self-assistance' principle, i.e. giving ship-owners the option to exercise themselves, through either ground or onboard crews, some of the activities which had until then been carried out in many ports by professionals holding a monopoly on their services, such as pilots, coasting-pilots, stevedores, etc.

As far as the European Commission was concerned, the directive submitted to the European Parliament in early 2001 stigmatised the lack of competitiveness as a problem to be solved: the inadequate development of the port sector compared to other modes of transport despite the clear advantages of sea transport (such as low pollution emissions and energy inputs per ton); the low levels of private investments; the unfavourable position of the sector in terms of inter-modal competition and the internal market; regional imbalances at the European level (concentration of activity in Northern ports to the detriment of Southern ports); the fragmentation and complexity of the regulations on European ports (private ports, public ports, etc.); and the lack of transparency in terms of billing services and public finance management, which contributed to distort competition *between* ports. In addition to this definition of the problem, the texts proposed a series of solutions to resolve these shortcomings. The principle of a 'necessary' liberalisation and competition of port services was thus firmly asserted. Most port services were therefore reclassified as 'commercial' services, as competition was deemed necessary to ensure the development of the sector (by encouraging investments), regional rebalancing (to the benefit of Southern ports), increased competitiveness of European ports and sea transport in general.

Supported by ship-owners and port authorities, the directive was therefore based on a process that is characteristic of the politico-administrative activity of the EC, summed up by Nicolas Jabko: the market as a 'normative ideal' (Jabko, 2001). This directive is a typical example of the linking of a sectoral system of reference to a general cognitive framework. This case illustrates how the market, liberalisation and competition constitute both ideological matrixes and practical resources for action: they are substitutes to the absence of financial resources and thus authorise political action and also help actors to decode and explain complex and diverse social and economic realities.[7]

When first presented to the European Parliament in February 2001, the Commission's proposal did not attract the kind of opposition that would later emerge. Within the Regional Politics and Transport Committee of the European Parliament, the report on the directive proposal was attributed to G. Jarzembowski, a German member of the European People's Party–European Democrats (EPP–ED) and expert on the processes of liberalisation in transport in Europe. Another German, W. Piecyk (European Socialist Party – ESP) was appointed shadow-rapporteur. Although he would later spearhead opposition to the second port package, he initially supported the amendment to the directive proposed by the rapporteur during the first reading. Without calling into question the ideological matrix of the text, the amendment nevertheless introduced significant safeguards, namely the right of states to restrict access to the port services market (to ensure security and economic efficiency), the exclusion of piloting services from the scope of the directive, and the right given to states to limit the benefits of self-assistance to ships under the flag of a member state. Although proposals made by the major party groups differed considerably from the initial proposals, they remained within the ideological matrix defined in the directive, which was based on open competition, especially through the recognition of self-handling. The ESP however seemed to be divided along a north–south line, owing to the different situations of European ports. While the rapporteur and shadow-rapporteur, both German, were in favour of a compromise between the EPP–DE and ESP based on the rapporteur's proposal, a majority within the Greek, Spanish, Italian and French delegations opposed the idea, thus taking the same position as the European United Left (EUL). The text was adopted with a slim majority at the Committee level but managed to secure a large majority in the plenary session (292–223 with 32 abstentions) on November 14, 2001.

During the second reading, there were fewer internal divisions within the ranks of the ESP thanks to a more political approach (stronger condemnation of the breach of public services or security) leading to fewer differences at the national level between Northern and Southern delegations.[8] The Socialists agreed upon very firm positions aimed at limiting the liberalisation of port services (the exclusion of pilots, coasting-pilots and freight handlers from the scope of the directive).[9] The ESP supported the compromise amendments: a significant reduction in the scope of self-assistance (limited recourse to seagoing personnel, exclusion of piloting). In the final committee vote, 39 voted in favour of the directive while 10 voted against. This reflects both the narrowing cleavages within the ESP and the reconstruction of a EPP–ESP compromise on a more critical stance towards the text proposed by the Commission.

If this modified version of the text was adopted by a large majority during the second reading, it was at the cost of greater inter-institutional distortions between the European Parliament, on one side, and the Commission and Council, on the other. More directly, it reflects the opposition between the rapporteur (who both had to keep compromising with an increasingly combative shadow-rapporteur and to maintain the newfound unity of his group on this issue), part of the EPP group (advocating a strong liberalisation), and the Commissioner in charge of the case. From November 2002, the reciprocal stances and perceptions of the issue began consequently to change as result of a set of factors whose combined effects we shall now analyse, and which heralded the rejections that were to follow in November 2003 and January 2006.

The conditions of the redefinition of the 'port services' problem

The politicisation of the 'port services' problem – i.e. the redefinition of the framework and political game on related issues, entailed the (inter)action of several categories of actors from different arenas. The mobilisation of dockers' unions gradually merged with the initial mobilisation of a fraction of MEPs (the EUL MEPs and some from the ESP). This merging process coincided with a relatively open political climate linked to the increasing visibility of anti-liberal movements, and the environmental crisis caused by the sinking of two oil tankers, the *Erika* and *Prestige*, the rejection of the European Constitutional Treaty and the debate around the Bolkestein directive. This provided a window of opportunity which trade union and political actors would fully exploit in order to obtain substantial changes in the balance of power in their respective arenas.

Opening of the political and media context

It is in a somewhat particular context that the trade union mobilisation on one hand and the mobilisation of some left-wing MEPs on the other conspired to cause a shift in the ESP's position, the politicisation of the 'port services' problem and the final rejection of the two texts (in November 2003 and January 2006). Several factors provided significant media visibility to the issues raised both by trade unions and political actors, thereby giving them considerable credit.

First, one can cite the increasing visibility of the alter-globalisation movements in various national spaces. The 1999 Seattle protests announced the emergence of themes which would become ever more important. This mobilisation reached its peak in May 2005 with the rejection of the ECT. While summits were accompanied by counter-summits, alter-globalists had new accesses to the parliamentary arena, such as the newly created 'Capital tax, fiscal systems and globalisation' (Tobin Tax) intergroup and other mobilisations around these issues. It was also in this context that national politicians and journalists became increasingly sensitive to European issues. In some countries, particularly in France, debates on the ratification of the ECT were superimposed on debates over the 'Bolkestein' directive and EU enlargement to the East.

The influence of this sociopolitical and media context would be enormous in terms of the attention given to trade union mobilisation and the gradual re-qualification of the 'port services' problem, which became the rallying point for protests from fringe political parties in the European Parliament. They aggressively reinvested 'anti-liberal' themes in the directives on port services among others. Sustained by the smaller groups, the rhetoric inspired by new anti-liberal postures would also lead to frequent internal quarrels within the ESP, whose dominant political orientations depended mainly on the joint management agreements with the EPP–ED and on their support to Socialist commissioners.

Following the *Erika* catastrophe (December 12, 1999) and especially the sinking of the *Prestige* (which occurred during a parliamentary debate on November 13, 2002), the second contextual element surrounding the 'port package' case was the increased visibility of maritime security. The port services directives would gradually be redefined as being in contradiction with this new emphasis on safety. Records of parliamentary debates clearly show the superposition of two forms of risk associated with the liberalisation process (security and social), representing structuring principles of European and national public spaces. As a result, the number of references associated with these risks clearly increased between the first and the second reading, and even more during the third reading and the discussion on the second port package starting in 2005.

Of course, this context did not in itself mechanically produce a redefinition of the problems placed on the European agenda. Nevertheless, there was an opening of the intra- and inter-institutional political games which a group of political and trade union actors used to capitalise resources, transform the balances of power, and integrate institutional arenas where these actors had been until then marginal.

Reactions and trade union strategies

Faced with the Commission project, trade unions opposed to the port directive found themselves in a relatively classic position of inferiority within the EU as early as 1997 (Gobin, 1998). Although they were consulted, they could neither thwart the Commission's projects – the latter benefited from the support of shipping and logistics companies – nor turn them to their advantage. It was therefore entirely in their interest to resort to the new institutional arena represented by the European Parliament in order to reassert themselves in the negotiations on relevant legislative measures (Mazey and Richardson, 2002).

It was only after 2002, during the second reading by the parliamentary Committee, that trade union organisations actually started mobilising, to a large extent on a national basis (Belgium, Netherlands and Germany in particular). By playing on several registers, these organisations gradually led various actions both at the local level (with local and national authorities and actors) and at the European level, by trying to highlight the multinational nature of the mobilisations (common days of action in Brussels during parliamentary debates, European coordination of local and national actions, campaigns aimed towards the Commission, etc). The European Transport Workers' Federation (ETF) played an essential coordinating role.

The actions aimed at MEPs between 2002 and 2006 were first and foremost based on the mobilisation of expertise which, in the European Parliament and elsewhere, is the most legitimate form of participation. The trade unions thus insisted on the professionalism of port workers ('Leave it to the professionals, it's our work'),[10] questioned the technical knowledge of the Commission by denouncing its ideological bend ('this approach is marked by the seal of dogmatism (...) which shows a lack of adequate knowledge of the port industry') and supplied alternative assessments of the situation and problem definitions. The dockers' unions and the ETF fuelled a controversy centred on numbers, arguing that the estimates of the International Transport Workers' Federation demonstrated, contrary to the discourse of the Commission, that European ports were the most competitive in the world and that economic performance would be compromised rather than furthered if the Commission proposals succeeded. This type of register matched the usual modes of action used by interest groups in their interactions with European institutions: it is based on the mobilisation of qualified staff well integrated into the Brussels microcosm. But the repertoires of action mobilised by trade unions were multiple and included means which are relatively unusual at the European level, such as petitions, strikes, street demonstrations, coordinated blockages of port facilities and confrontations with police, etc. Thus both at the European and national levels, trade union action reactivated classic practices which were progressively redefined as European. These mobilisations reached a climax in 2006 during the big dockworkers' demonstration in Strasburg. However, parliamentary records show that right from the second reading, exchanges among MEPs were directly influenced by highly publicised demonstrations. They made frequent references to the demonstrations, either to condemn the 'violence' or, on the contrary, to support the protesters.[11] Similarly, the petitions submitted by trade unions with great pomp were relayed in the European Parliament by the opponents of the directive.[12]

The trade union action towards MEPs combined expertise, militancy and political marketing[13] through the development and maintenance of informal contacts with MEPs or their parliamentary assistants, participation in hearings, the fostering of territorial links through localised action, or the organisation of demonstrations and European rallies during parliamentary debates. These actions took place over relatively long periods of time and by trial and error, which enabled these relative newcomers to the European arena to learn the ropes of effective advocacy. This entailed understanding how the institutions work concretely in terms of spotting key players, identifying potential allies; being able to speak to representatives from different countries, conceiving 'admissible' arguments in this space; ensuring integration of the issue into the pertinent spatial and temporal coordinates; being able to generalise (or Europeanise) the perspectives of workers in national frameworks, etc. They therefore had to acquire a 'practical sense' of European games and accumulate the necessary resources to gain influence. Only gradually were these organisations able to place themselves at the centre of exchanges, thus compelling MEPs to position themselves in relation to them – to oblige them to some extent to 'choose their side'. Unions were thus able to partially redefine the terms of the debate in terms of their own understanding of the problem.

Nevertheless, trade union practices are not uniform. Each organisation follows a specific path, depending on its initial resources, capacity for mobilisation, strategies or degree of integration in European circles. From nothing, some unions such as those of coaster-pilots had a real 'on the job' learning experience of the means and conditions of access to the European Parliament, thus gradually acquiring the resources required to influence negotiations at this level.[14] The example of coaster-pilots thus shows how representatives of a minor profession 'learned Europe' through the mobilisations that followed the port directives. Inversely, other organisations, such as the dockworkers, show how existing resources and the practical mastery of European games were mobilised and developed in the framework of a large-scale mobilisation. Although the unions' own strength is essential to understand the success of their mobilisation, the ETF's role is equally important, not only for the mobilisations but also for the coordination of various organisations, as well as the neutralisation of national divergences. It is thus the specific European resources of the European federation that were the key element.

National divergences were glossed over by emphasising a strong sectoral identity and politicisation displayed in street demonstrations, for example. The ETF was able to mobilise and deploy a real 'international coordination of intelligence' on which its representative insisted during the interview.[15] ETF members (especially the 'ports and docks' section) mobilised technical know-how and accumulated experience, as well as the practical know-how of the organisation including the organisation's 'contacts' and collective 'address book', especially with MEPs,[16] the harnessing of technical and linguistic expertise of professionals recruited by the ETF, the knowledge of Community procedures, etc.

Interestingly, the case of the dockers shows that socialisation to European institutions through intense participation and consultation organised by the Commission not necessarily imply an ideological convergence with the dominant paradigms of the Commission; nor does it necessarily create a 'transnational ideological machinery' by which 'European trade unionism functions as a guarantor of the docility of dominated groups in the face of a social regression process impossible to implement on a State-by-State basis' (Pernot, 1998). European socialisation provides the adequate resources for trade union and political action in a European framework, both in terms of know-how and interpersonal skills. In other words, the typically European resources acquired by the ETF with the European Commission in a nascent state of relations can be turned, under certain conditions, against the latter. Resources only become efficient when they are repositioned by union representatives in a cleaved space, enrol potential allies and find an echo in a more favourable political and ideological climate.

In this case, the ETF no longer functions simply as a social partner to the Commission and as a transmission belt from the top (European) to the bottom (workers). On the contrary, it functions as an *entrepreneur* of European mobilisation that can contribute, together with certain MEPs, to reshape European political agendas.

For its affiliated national trade union organisations, ETF also functions as a supplier of European political resources. In return, this perspective allows the ETF to reintroduce itself and its affiliated organisations into negotiation processes based on new power relations.[17] From this point of view, the case of the port directives created a new awareness of the capacities of action and reaction to the Commission's projects for the trade unions as well as for their partners and opponents. These logics of learning and awareness are evident in the seminars and training workshops organised by ETF representatives within the European Conference of Trade Unions to explain and learn from the conditions that made the success of the mobilisation possible.[18] Hence, beyond short-term success of mobilisation, one can identify a sedimentation of successful repertoires, a gradual redefinition of roles and, more generally, a transformation of the rules of the game within the entire European political space.[19]

Parliamentary mobilisations and structures of political games in the European Parliament

Trade union mobilisations were not sufficient by themselves to overturn the Commission projects. As it turned out, these mobilisations produced concrete effects only through the mediation of MEPs and thanks to several elements: the existence of a context of high media visibility, the emergence of new political issues, and a set of actors in the parliamentary space who were ready to relay those issues, to give them credit and take advantage of their brokerage. The case of the port directives exemplifies the logics of European Parliament internal games and their consequences on political bargaining structures characteristic of the entire EU.

Although the routine functioning of the European Parliament works less along bipolar lines than on the basis of permanent give and take between political groups, the parliamentary space remains divided along several fractures, one of which is the divide between the 'mainstream' block – the EPP–ED and ESP with the liberal group – and the 'fringe' block made up of groups often referred to as 'small', such as the EUL, the Greens, sovereignists and the unregistered. The latter contest the institutional routines and a political game built around the dominant EPP–ESP pair.

While the dominant groups seek to stabilise internal relations in order to guarantee their role and the compromises on which they are based, the 'small' groups are more predisposed to conflict through a politicisation of issues. When there is right–left polarisation, the position of both the Greens and the EUL is notably reinforced. Apart from the fact that for them this politicisation is a way of 'existing' in the face of the duopoly, more 'political' modes of exercising the function also correspond to the dispositions and postures of the MEPs who compose these groups, both subjectively (their conception of political and representative action) and objectively. Coming more often from a political, trade union and associative militancy than from the socially and politically dominant circles, their resources are mainly 'militant' and 'political'.

For the same reasons, many left-wing MEPs, and particularly those of the EUL, are known for constantly seeking external sociopolitical support, likely to help rebalance unfavourable power relations, to set up, or replenish a stock of resources that can be mobilised in future struggles. Thus EUL MEPs (as well as the different actors associated with these groups, staff and officials) permanently seek to position themselves as institutional relays of the 'social movement' to which they refer endlessly. Numerous actors and organisations, while being marginalised in the Commission, led consultations on legislative projects and are more than ready to respond positively to such overtures coming from a section of the MEPs. Facilitated by permanent contacts with social movements, the EUL has adopted a 'spokesperson' posture taking numerous but characteristic forms: circulation of strategic information about the activity of European institutions; advice on successful political action within the EU; drawing up points of view and amendments either in Committee or in plenary sessions; invitations to hearings of groups and committees, etc. In fact, MEPs are as much recipients for external demands for access to the European scene as actors who contribute to build demand and generate it through various practices aimed at encouraging mobilisations which they can then capitalise on in interactions with other groups within the European parliament.

For reasons linked to their position within the European Parliament, their conception of political action and their trajectories or resources, EUL MEPs provide an explicit example of the possibility of alternative postures to the dominant figures of expertise and diplomatic repertoires. Further politicisation is therefore in the interests of these parliamentarians in order to move their (political and militant) resources towards the centre of the parliamentary stage. From this perspective, the 1999–2004 legislature was a somewhat exceptional moment with the breakthrough of 'small lists' and the arrival of new MEPs, combined with the greater visibility of anti-liberal protests. Of course, given that boundaries between political groups are not hermetic, characteristically EUL postures are also to be found in other groups, particularly within the ESP where trade union mobilisations have good chances of finding ready sympathisers. The activation of the networks created in the framework of 'trade union coordination' takes a whole new dimension here.

These political postures are found especially within a section of the French Socialist Party, confronted with the breakthrough of far-left parties and environmentalists in 1999, as well as the relative success of alter-globalist mobilisations and anti-liberals. The dispersion of the left-wing votes had favoured Prime Minister Lionel Jospin's defeat at the first round of the presidential elections of 2002, thus rekindling the internal rivalries over leadership and strategic choices. Faced with a susbsequent leadership crisis, many in the Socialist party, notably in the minority fringes, were tempted to adopt part of the alter-globalist rhetoric. Harlem Désir for example co-founded the 'Tobin Tax' inter-group of the European Parliament, while Laurent Fabius supported the 'no' vote in the referendum on the ECT. This approach is all easier to adopt for MEPs given the relatively peripheral position occupied by the European Parliament in the French political space which thus makes such stances less risky. Dependent on a context of strong trade union and far-left mobilisation, the port directives and their successive readings therefore constituted opportunities to put into practice the strategies of repositioning adopted partially by the French Socialist Party – strategies which reached their apogee a few months later with several party leaders calling for the rejection of the ECT.[20]

Rejection of the text and requalification of the port directives

It is mainly due to this new-found readiness to serve as institutional relays for the social protests of left-wing MEPs, that trade unions attempted to 'penetrate' the parliamentary arena, make their voice heard and try to win over MEPs of various groups, especially those of the ESP, which eventually united around the principle of supporting the demands made by trade unions representing all categories of port workers (stevedores, pilots, coasting-pilots, etc.). Trade union demands thus moved from the margins to the centre of the parliamentary debate, making it finally possible to redefine the problem and reject the directives. Relations in the European Parliament were very tense during the third reading due to the increased politicisation of the issue and the growing mobilisation of the entire left. Records of parliamentary proceedings give evidence of the hardening of positions, with the European Socialists converting to positions represented initially only by the EUL. While support for reform did not really weaken among conservatives and liberals, the technical nature and the reconciliatory tone of the first reading paved the way for clearly more belligerent pronouncements centred on the condemnation of social dumping, defense of working conditions or even the safety of persons and property.

The conciliation between the European Parliament and the Council succeeded only with a one-vote margin, given that the EPP–ED and ESP could not agree on a final position vis-à-vis the Council and the Commission. The latter stuck to their initial positions and to the more criticized dispositions (pilots and coasting-pilots remaining in the scope of the text as well as the principle of self-assistance, including for ground personnel). The EPP–ED wanted to see the draft text passed at all cost. However the rapporteur managed to reach a compromise with members of the Council, but at the price of compromising the ties that linked them to the ESP in the European Parliament. As such, the rapporteur was accused by his socialist partners of sacrificing parliamentary interests for those of the Council and the Commission,[21] which are rival institutions. The politicisation of the issue therefore compromised the duopoly between the EPP and ESP, thus making the results of the plenary vote less predictable. The EUL and the Greens hardened their positions even more when the text was sent to the plenary session.

The compromise text was finally rejected by 22 votes on November 20, 2003. The conservatives and liberals remained massively attached to the directive despite the defection of a section of their block. On the other hand, most ESP delegations as well as the shadow-rapporteur finally rallied to the initial opposition of the EUL, a section of the Greens and the Socialists. The politicisation of the issue led to a situation of great uncertainty within the European Parliament. The political games became fluid, thus resulting in more or less spectacular repositioning, later accentuated by the activation of inter-institutional competitions after the deposition of the second port package.

Encouraged firstly by the slim majority of the first rejection and secondly by the victory of the conservatives and liberals in the 2004 European elections, Commissioner de Palacio introduced a new text into the legislative circuit which was very similar to the previous one. Despite a more favourable majority in the European Parliament, the reframing of the issue proved to be durable. Indeed, this new proposal quickly raised unanimous opposition, with rejection of self-assistance, fears about the risk of social dumping and security issues proving to be more central than market liberalisation and efficiency in the framing of the problem. When consulted, the Commissions for the Internal Market and Social Affairs recommended the rejection of the text. There was so much uncertainty at the committee level that the rapporteur failed to have the whole text passed although he managed to push through various compromise amendments.

The opponents of the text mobilised one last argument during the plenary session: denial of democracy. They contended that the re-introduction of a text that had been rejected a few months earlier[22] constituted an act of contempt for the European Parliament. Although the version presented in the plenary session was the Commission's original text, there was a complete turn-around – it was massively rejected by 532 votes to 120. The text had lost all support both from the left and the right. Where 'healthy competition' was initially considered an essential component of the problem, it was now workers' conditions and the security of which they appear to be the guarantors which emerged as the key factors.[23]

Conclusion

The case of the port directives illustrates how, far from being dysfunctional, conflict is both a product of European processes and a contributing force to their dynamics. It is through the analysis of the shifting configurations of actors and organisations that we have sought to understand its logics and effects.

The case of the port directives was undoubtedly a relatively short political sequence dependent on the contextual opening of political and media spaces, as well as the increasing number of these conflicting configurations. However, the occasional success of social mobilisations may favour more sustainable processes of learning and problem redefinition through sedimentation, both within the parliamentary space and within political, associative and trade union organisations. In the former, the typically political and representative nature of the function is asserted, whereas in the latter, renewed attempts at self-assertion in European games are gradually being reorganised. In the case at hand, the mobilisation of 'Eurocritical' discourses targeted against the Commission paradoxically served as a strategy for legitimising and strengthening the positions held by trade union organisations (especially the ETF and its agents) or even by some MEPs. This mobilisation also contributed, through the socialising effects of conflict, to spread the belief that both the EU and the European Parliament are essential spaces for action and practice of political power.

Of course, it is difficult to anticipate the content of this power owing to the nature of European political games, the ever-shifting nature of alliances and repositioning in a multi-level setting where differentiated, if not contradictory, logics of action intertwine. Nevertheless, these 'experiences' and 'moments' of transactions between parliamentary actors and non-institutional actors, in spite of their temporary nature, facilitate more far-reaching and sustainable structural transformations that underpin the unpredictable creation of a European public space.

Notes

1   By political space we mean 'all the power relations existing in a given institutional order, and whose effect is to preserve and modify this order and the relationships between all persons who can use it' (Lagroye, 1997: 132).
2   This research draws on several years of work on the European Parliament and on a series of specific interviews with Commission officials, elected representatives, parliamentary staff, journalists and trade unionists as well as on documentary sources.
3   Green Paper, December 10, 1997, on ports and maritime infrastructures (COM/97/678). See the Port Infrastructure: Green Paper, at www.europa.eu /scadplus/leg/en/lvb/l24163.htm.
4   White Paper, European transport policy for 2010: Time to decide (COS/2001/2281).
5   COD/2001/0047: Port services: access to market and financing seaports.

6 COD/2002/0047: 13/02/2001-Commission/Council: initial legislative document, at www.europarl.europa.eu/oeil/.

7 A member of the ports unit of DG Transport who contributed to the directive explained: 'personally, as a European citizen, I cannot understand why ports should be the only sector of economic activity in Europe without a framework directive for applying the treaty. I just don't get it' (interview, Brussels, January 2007). Commissioner Palacio said: 'As far as I am concerned, I believe that in principle it is better to bank on healthy competition than on a monopoly situation. It is basically a matter of ideology ...: things work better when there is competition' (parliamentary debate, March 10, 2003).

8 In spite of their heterogeneity, the unity and identity of political groups in the European Parliament above all meet political convergences (the Right–Left axis) rather than considerations linked to pro-integrationist or Eurosceptic postures. Hence, the politicisation of the problem to which they are confronted is a classic strategy for crisis resolution (Hix and Lord, 1997).

9 See for example the words of Piecyk during the second reading, which were clearly more determined than his position two years earlier (parliamentary debate, March 10, 2003.)

10 References from the dossier 'Stop Ports Package 2' sent by the ETF to all MEPs just before the vote in plenary session on January 18, 2006.

11 See for example the declarations of Piecyk (ESP), Ainardi (EUL) and Vermeer (Liberals), on March 10 and November 18, 2003.

12 See for example the contributions of Markov (EUL) and Lancker (ESP) on November 18, 2003.

13 An ETF employee told us that the organisation had enlisted the services of marketing companies to design their poster.

14 The assistant of an ESP parliamentarian made the following remark: 'When the first directive was issued, they did not know the legislative procedures of the European Parliament. Subsequently, they proposed amendments. They were very organised ... Through the port directive, an insignificant profession gained access to the European Parliament and really understood how the system worked.'

15 'It functioned around a coordinating committee emanating from the "ports and docks" section. It was open to all members depending on their interests, with clearly identified interfaces, which relays information down to workers who are able to mobilise on the ground. It also played the important role of secretariat coordinating action in agreement with the section ... Brussels decides which actions to take in coordination with the various affiliates. Our action was mainly successful because we proceeded from the principle that each organisation must act within its own means ... if it is decided to suspend unloading in the port of Antwerp, the port of Rotterdam must do the same in solidarity. Otherwise, all ships are immediately rerouted, thus concentrating all activity on Rotterdam ... our action will then have very strong impact with obvious financial and economic repercussions.' Interview, January 2007.

16 These contacts, which also represent political resources, are particularly important in the recruiting procedures of ETF personnel based in Brussels. For example the head of the 'ports and docks' department is the former parliamentary assistant to a French ESP MEP.

17 Following the rejection of the second port package, the European Commission re-opened consultations for port sector actors in which trade union federations played a more central role than in 1999–2000.

18 The coordinator for the 'ports and docks' section thus participated in training programmes within the Economic and Social Council where he presented a paper

entitled: 'Towards a progressive balance of power in Europe: workers' mobilisation against the liberalisation of port services'.

19 Concerning the Euro-strikes that followed the closure of the Renault plant in Vilvorde, Lefebure and Lagneau noted that 'politico-media crystallisation can only be considered for what it is – a moment ... On the other hand, there are lessons to be learned when a political process is triggered by a sporadic event through interpellation: the European public space should not be seen as a structure but as transformation of political action' (Lefebure and Lagneau, 2002: 526.)

20 French Socialist parliamentarians were particularly virulent in the European Parliament. Thus Savary (ESP) denounced the 'social piracy' that the directive encouraged and the 'infernal price and salary-lowering machine' that the 'dockers saw coming' (parliamentary debates, March 10, 2003). Of course, political pressure linked to the context was all the more intense for parliamentarians originating from port areas.

21 See for example the contributions of Collado (ESP) or Blak (EUL) on November 18, 2003.

22 During the plenary debate, Savary (ESP) stated for example: 'It is a denial of democracy. The Commission must not be encouraged to reproduce the same texts each time Parliament votes against and fails to listen' (parliamentary debate, January 18, 2006).

23 Following this fiasco the Community administration opened renewed consultations in which trade unions, especially the ETF, appeared to be more closely involved. Through the TRUST programme financed by the European Commission, the 'ports and docks' section of the ETF adopted a more enterprising posture, encouraging its affiliates to take the initiative again and offer the Commission, ship-owners and port authorities a general vision of the entire ports sector.

Bibliography

Abélès, M. and Bellier, I., 'La Commission européenne. Du compromis culturel à la culture politique du compromis', *Revue française de science politique*, 46 (3), 1996, 431–456.

Beauvallet, W., *Profession: eurodéputé. Les élus français au Parlement européen et l'institutionnalisation d'une nouvelle figure politique et élective (1979–2004)*, PhD Thesis in Political Science, Strasburg, 2007.

Berger, P. and Luckmann, T., *The Social Construction of Reality: A Treatise on the Sociology of Knowledge*, Garden City, New York: Anchor Books, 1966.

Bourdieu, P., *La distinction. Critique social du jugement*, Paris: Editions de Minuit, 1979.

Cobb, R. and Elder, C., *Participation in American Politics: the Dynamics of Agenda-Building*, Baltimore: The Johns Hopkins University Press, 1972.

Costa, O., *Le Parlement européen, assemblée délibérante*, Bruxelles: Editions de l'Université de Bruxelles, 2001.

Costa, O. and Magnette, P. (eds), *Une Europe des élites?*, Bruxelles: Editions de l'Université de Bruxelles, 2007.

Georgakakis, D. (ed.), *Les métiers de l'Europe politique. Acteurs et professionnalisations de l'Union européenne*, Strasburg: Presses Universitaires de Strasburg, 2002.

Gobin, C., 'De la Communauté économique européenne à l'Union européenne. Aperçu d'une double histoire', in L. Mouriaux (ed.), *L'année sociale. Edition 1998*, Paris: Les éditions ouvrières, 1998, 153–174.

Hix, S., *The Political System of the European Union*, New York: Palgrave, 1999.

Hix, S. and Lord, C., *Political Parties in the European Union*, Oxford: Oxford University Press, 1997.

Hooghe, L. and Marks, G., *Multi-Level Governance and European Integration*, Lanham, MD: Rowman & Littlefield, 2001.

Jabko, N., 'Une Europe politique par le marché et la monnaie', *Critique internationale*, 4 (13), 2001, 81–101.

Judge, D. and Earnshaw, D., *The European Parliament*, New York: Palgrave, 2003.

Kauppi, N., *Democracy, Social Resources and Political Power in the European Union*, Manchester: Manchester University Press, 2005.

Kingdon, J., *Agendas, Alternatives, and Public Policies*, New York: Harper Collins, 1984.

Lagroye, J., *Sociologie politique*, 3rd edn, Paris: Presses de Sciences Po, 1997.

Lefebure, P. and Lagneau, E., 'Le moment Vilvoorde: action protestataire et espace public européen', in R. Balme, D. Chabanet and V. Wright (eds), *L'action collective en Europe*, Paris: Presses de Sciences Po, 2002, 495–529.

Marks, G. and Steenbergen, M. (eds), *European Integration and Political Conflict*, Cambridge: Cambridge University Press, 2004.

Mazey, S. and Richardson, J., 'Pluralisme ouvert ou restreint? Les groupes d'intérêt dans l'Union européenne', in R. Balme, D. Chabanet and V. Wright (eds), *L'action collective en Europe*, Paris: Presses de Sciences Po, 2002, 123–162.

Michel, H. (ed.), *Lobbyistes et lobbying de l'Union européenne. Trajectoires, formations et pratiques des représentants d'intérêts*, Strasburg: Presses Universitaires de Strasburg, 2006.

Pernot, J.-M., 'Une université européenne du syndicalisme? L'Europe des syndicats', *Politix*, 43, 1998, 53–78.

Robert, C., 'La Commission européenne dans son rapport au politique. Pourquoi et comment faire de la politique sans en avoir l'air', *Pôle Sud*, 15, 2001, 61–75.

Sabatier, P. and Schlager, E., 'Les approches cognitives de politiques: perspectives américaines', *Revue française de science politique*, 50 (2), 2000, 209–234.

Smith, A., *Le gouvernement de l'Union européenne: une sociologie politique*, Paris: LGDJ, 2004.

Wessels, B., 'Whom to Represent? Role Orientations of Legislators in Europe', in H. Schmitt and J. Thomassen (eds), *Political Representation and Legitimacy in the European Union*, Oxford: Oxford University Press, 1998, 209–234.

PART III

Constructing reality through policy instruments

Isabelle Bruno

9

From integration by law to Europeanisation by numbers: the making of a 'competitive Europe' through intergovernmental benchmarking

What does Europe construct? Let me tackle this question from the angle of means instead of ends. In doing so, the teleological problem of purpose gives way to a pragmatic one: how? Such a reversal implies that instruments should be taken seriously as fully-fledged actors of the European venture. Far from being polity-neutral, I posit that their technical mediation (Latour, 1999) brings about cohesive effects, in the sense that they collect and connect people and things, thus forming associations. Understanding how instruments operate is not merely a matter of effectiveness (i.e. is the chosen instrument the most efficient for reaching an objective?), it is about replacing them in a larger context in order to go beyond the utilitarian debate and gain new insights into European policy-making. Instruments inextricably interweave technical and social dimensions. Examining the linkages they promote helps us to understand the shaping of contemporary society and the underlying governmentality at work. In other words, opening the European black box and looking at its toolbox may help us specify this 'unidentified political object'.

Whereas European integration has historically been centred on producing law, it seems that the current momentum of Europeanisation proceeds from the making of comparable statistical figures. The nature of the bonds that hold together the entity 'Europe' has changed, indicating a shift in the means used to forge them. By focusing attention on the intergovernmental ties resulting from the benchmarking exercise, I will seek to shed light on the way the Open Method of Co-ordination (OMC) is adjusted to the Lisbon goal to 'become the most competitive and dynamic knowledge-based economy in the world' (EC, 2000: § 5). That this method fits the objectives and has proved to be effective is here beside the point. I will therefore not seek to assess progress towards the targets set by the European Council. Rather than framing the question in utilitarian terms, I would like to ask more generally how the OMC goes about coordinating member states without standardising their legislation. To do this, I assume that its *modus operandi* – based on benchmarking – is consistent with its purpose – international competitiveness first and foremost – inasmuch as benchmarking functions as a matrix of competitive relations. Strictly speaking, nothing proves that this instrument enhances 'European competitiveness'. What it does do however is implement a managerial scheme for arranging a 'competitive Europe' modelled on private corporations, as a normative model of the competitive organisation *par excellence*. In this respect, one needs to bear in mind that competitiveness is an idea and that 'ideas do not float freely' (Risse-Kappen, 1994): they are embedded in socio-technical apparatuses which lend them a tangible reality. Investigating the guiding rationality that underpins both the discourse on competitiveness and the recourse to benchmarking opens heuristic avenues in understanding how the latter performs the former. Therefore, what is at stake here is how the *competitiveness-benchmarking* couple fulfils neo-liberal governmental technology as theorised by Michel Foucault (2008).

Since its launch in 2000, there has been much ado about the Lisbon strategy in the European bureaucratic sphere as well as in the academic field. A huge number of publications have been devoted to the OMC, describing at length official process, the various experimentations and the set of stakeholders ostensibly associated with it. In reference articles which problematise it as a 'new mode of governance' through 'mutual learning', the imperative of competitiveness is taken for granted, and hence the need for benchmarking is self-explanatory.[1] This pivotal technique for coordinating national policies appears as a cure-all, useful for whatever goal may be pursued, be it economic growth, social inclusion or sustainable development. Moreover, even though practitioners and observers have recorded disappointing results, the method has not been abandoned. It has rather become the object of attempts for improvement through the 'streamlining' of implementation. My intention here is not at all to demonstrate its failures or to make recommendations to improve organisational problems which limit European competitiveness. However, I will stress its success in introducing the logic of competition in the Union as the driving *modus operandi* of intergovernmental cooperation. I set out to challenge the perception of benchmarking as a universal, all-purpose tool, respectful of sectoral idiosyncrasies. In contrast, I will point out how this managerial mechanism of polity-building through harmonising statistics, quantifying indicators and performance comparison renders completely disparate public services, territories and populations commensurable, thereby subjecting their administration to a unique homogenising competitive regime.

To examine these questions, I will proceed in three sections. I will first explore the process of emergence of a blueprint for a 'competitive Europe', surrounded by controversies, before international competitiveness was given top priority on the European agenda under Delors. Then I will briefly outline the genealogy of benchmarking, from Japanese industry in the 1950s to New Public Management (NPM) in the 1990s. Neither self-evident nor self-propagating, this technique was brought into widespread use by management experts, who theorised and simplified the principle of cooperation through competition ('co-opetition') that made its diffusion to private as well as public organisations possible. Following the analysis of this historical process which made recourse to benchmarking appear self-evident, I will finally consider how deeply it has affected the sense – both the meaning and the direction – of European construction. As the centrepiece of the Lisbon strategy, it is in a position to put into practice the 'indefinite discipline' (Foucault, 1977) that is latent in the discourses on competitiveness. Far from being a toothless gimmick, the mantra of competitiveness combined with the device of benchmarking thus achieves a new expression of the neo-liberal governmental technology, all the more powerful as it integrates the member states.

Discourses of European competitiveness: turning a floating idea into an overarching world-view

Ideas are not naturally in the air like seeds waiting to land and germinate. They are socially articulated in discursive practices which give them form, meaning and mobility. Once translated into intelligible words and sound reasoning, their ability to circulate and to format beliefs depends not so much on the weight of their evidence as on the social network that sustains their development and propagation. If there is no denying that discourses 'exist independently of the actors who draw upon them' and 'provide, as it were, an ideational context – a repertoire of discursive resources in the form of available narratives and understandings at the disposal of political actors' (Hay and Rosamond, 2002: 151), their felicity ultimately stems from a mutual agreement on their value and accuracy. In Risse-Kappen's words, the 'power' of ideas is due to their 'consensuality', i.e. to their social acceptance and approval. More precisely, he means that 'communicative processes are a necessary condition for ideas to become consensual (or to fall by the wayside, for that matter). Instrumental uses of ideas works, because their value has been previously established in discursive processes of persuasion and deliberation' (Risse-Kappen, 1996: 69–70).

The study of the spread of discourses on 'European competitiveness' should therefore combine ideational and sociological factors in order to grasp how shared beliefs and frames of reference are socially constructed, whilst forging collective as well as individual identities and interests. Rather than striving to distinguish between genuine and rhetorical uses, between cognitive and strategic deployments, I will focus on their multiplicity and recurrence. It is through repetition, diversification and streamlining that vague and disparate ideas about competitiveness have turned into an overarching 'paradigm through which social, political and economic developments might be ordered and rendered intelligible' (Hay and Rosamond, 2002: 151).

This section offers insights into how the matter of Europe's greatness has come to be thought of in terms of competitiveness. Following Foucault's approach of universals such as madness, disease, delinquency or sexuality, I do not aim to show how competitiveness was 'for a long time hidden before finally being discovered', nor how its discourses convey 'only wicked illusions or ideological products to be dispelled in the light of reason finally having reached its zenith'. Similar to Foucault's own objects, competitiveness is not an illusion 'since it is precisely a set of practices, real practices, which established it and thus imperiously marks it out in reality'. The point is then to wonder 'by what conjunctions a whole set of practices – from the moment they become coordinated with a regime of truth – was able to make what does not exist (madness, disease, delinquency, sexuality, etc.), and nonetheless become something, something however that continues not to exist' (Foucault, 2008: 19). Competitiveness is neither an innate quality, nor a fictitious entity. It is something hybrid, heterogeneous, made of conceptual and material elements, of persuasive notions and implicit assumptions, of tangible facts and dedicated databases. Competitiveness is indeed all the more real as it is constructed (Latour, 2003). Before considering the pyramid erected in its name by the European Commission, I will first go back to the 1970s when political debates, scholarly controversies and reporting activities kicked off in the United States.

From the 'competitive state' ...

According to Rosamond,

> the idea of competitiveness became a routine component of political vocabulary in the 1970s and was most extensively used to discuss the dilemmas of the American economy in the context of the breakdown of the postwar settlement and the rise of neoliberal political economy. (2002: 165)

The combination of stagflation and growing international competition indeed aroused a 'competitiveness threat', all the more pervasive as it was fuelled by publications like the first *Global Competitiveness Report* edited by the World Economic Forum in 1979. At the same time, the annual report released by the Joint Economic Committee of US Congress really set the ball in motion, insofar as it rejected a continuation of Keynesian management and instead advocated the implementation of a supply-side economic policy. In September 1980, the Office of Foreign Economic Research (US Department of Labor) followed suit by publishing the landmark *Report of the President on U.S. Competitiveness*. Later, the 1985 report of President Reagan's Commission on Industrial Competitiveness – better known as the Young Commission after its chairman's name – entitled *Global Competition: The New Reality*, listed a series of specific steps to be taken by public authorities on investment, learning, science and technology, and trade that set the broad outlines of the US competitiveness strategy (Commission on Industrial Competitiveness, 1985). It is important to note that all these reports called not so much for deregulation and liberalisation in keeping with neo-classical precepts, as for a reconfiguration of state interventions to foster economic performance by means of outward-looking and business-friendly policies.

The concern for national competitiveness was also inscribed into institutions. On the one hand, the Council on Competitiveness was founded in 1986 by a group of business, academic and labour leaders 'committed to the future prosperity of all Americans and enhanced U.S. competitiveness in the global economy'. This self-proclaimed 'non-partisan, nongovernmental organization' sees itself as 'a forum for elevating national competitiveness to the forefront of national consciousness'.[2] In order to shape the debate, it arranges conferences, seminars or special events, and widely disseminates findings to experts, policy makers, government officials, the media and the general public. It introduced to a wider public the principle of benchmarking national economic performance through its 'flagship product': the Competitiveness Index. On the other hand, the Omnibus Trade and Competitiveness Act of 1988 cast in a legal stone the broad strategic focus of the Young Commission and entrusted another advisory group, officially bipartisan, with the mission of expanding on it. Operational since 1991, the Competitiveness Policy Council was mandated to make recommendations to the President and the Congress. In its first report, significantly entitled *Building a Competitive America*, competitiveness was defined as 'the ability to produce goods and services that meet the test of international markets while citizens earn a standard of living that is both rising and sustainable over the long run' (Competitiveness Policy Council, 1992). However obvious this definition may seem, it is far from being self-evident.

The pertinence of discussing the national competitiveness of a country is much debated among economists. In his now famous *Foreign Affairs* article, Paul Krugman criticised the 'competitive metaphor' – i.e. the image 'that, in the words of President Clinton, each nation is like a big corporation competing in the global marketplace' (Krugman, 1994: 29) – as economically meaningless, politically misguided and socially damaging. His demonstration countered the progressively established orthodoxy, which made the design of a 'competitive state' consensual, desirable, and hence free of debate. More than economic nonsense, Krugman argued that it had in fact become a 'dangerous obsession'. How can one then explain the success of such flimsy rhetoric? Krugman advances three explanations: 1) 'competitive images are exciting, and thrills sell tickets'; 2) 'the idea that U.S. economic difficulties hinge crucially on our failures in international competition somewhat para-doxically makes those difficulties seem easier to solve'; 3) 'many of the world's leaders have found the competitive metaphor extremely useful as a political device. The rhetoric of competitiveness turns out to provide a good way either to justify hard choices or to avoid them' (Krugman, 1994: 39–40). However groundless they may be, discourses on national competitiveness exert an adaptive pressure by exploiting the 'thrill of competition' underpinning the transition 'from the Welfare State to the Competition State' (Cerny, 1990). Correlated with the neo-liberal vision of the state–society relationship, they instrumentalise international competition as a safeguard against internal interventionism. As Susan Strange puts it, 'competitiveness in the world market requires a competitive environment in the national market. This is an aspect of global structural change which has directly affected the responsibil-ities of national governments' (Strange, 1996: 80). Since public authorities conceive of economic competition 'as a struggle not between firms but between political jurisdictions (be it at national, regional or local scales)', it is up to them to develop sociopolitical strategies likely 'to fix mobile forms of capital investment within their boundaries' (Brenner, 2000: 320). Such 'loca-tional politics' reveals a fundamental change in the rationalisation of governmental practice which channels the exercise of political power into the building and the maintenance of a 'competitive space'. In other words, 'the role of the States today, when it comes to keeping up with the rest of the world, is to act as good landlords' (Strange, 1998: 113).

This changing governmentality spilled over American boundaries and gained momentum among opinion leaders throughout the world. In most member states of the OECD, advisory groups were modelled on the US Competitiveness Policy Council. Across the Atlantic, competitiveness strate-gies were deployed not merely at the national level but also on a European scale.

... to the 'European competitiveness' pyramid

Since its inception, European construction has fed on the shared belief in competition among economic and political elites. Competition is deemed valuable because it makes the market work, and competitive markets are thought to be the key to prosperity. Nevertheless, it was only in the 1980s, when Europessimism was at a high point, that a 'competitive Europe' as such became thinkable. Indeed, there is 'nothing intuitive or easily definable about "European competitiveness", especially in an era of stateless firms and global corporate strategies' (Rosamond, 1999: 662). This idea did not naturally emerge as a driving force, 'central to many of the discussions leading to the revitalisation of European integration'. It was socially constructed as the sole and necessary political answer to the economic crisis. As in the US, the rationale for deregulation and liberalisation was inseparable from the advocacy of public policies making societies, rather than just firms, competitive. It is generally held that the effective turn to competitiveness dates from 'the pivotal 1993 White Paper on Growth, Competitiveness and Employment' (Rosamond, 2002: 168).

Issued by the European Commission, this document purported to define 'the challenges and ways forward into the 21st century' (CEC, 1993). It laid out the means to fulfil the aspiration for reconciling both economic and social goals. The triangle of 'growth, competitiveness and employment' was supposed to create a virtuous cycle of mutually reinforcing processes in implementing potentially conflicting objectives. The centrality of competitiveness for the European project was defended by Jacques Delors, then president of the Commission, who 'didn't confront the problems of either the welfare state or the EMS'. He explained that 'the root cause of European unemployment was a lack of competitiveness with the United States and Japan and that the solution was a program of investment in infrastructure and high technology. It was a disappointing evasion, but not a surprising one' (Krugman, 1994: 28–29). In doing so, he agreed with the various proposals voiced by the European Round Table (ERT, 1993), an elite club gathering forty captains of industry. Keith Richardson, its Secretary-General from 1988 to 1998, testified that

> ERT staff worked in close liaison with the Commission. ERT ideas were evident in the Delors White Paper on Competitiveness, Growth and Employment, and also in the parallel Action Plan issued by the Brussels European Council in 1993, while the Essen European Council in 1994 formally endorsed the ERT proposal for a high level Competitiveness Advisory Group with powers to lay relevant issues directly before heads of government as well as the President of the Commission. (Richardson, 2000: 8)

Directly inspired by the US precedent, such a group was expected to turn 'competitiveness' from a malleable and elusive keyword in the public debate into a powerful lever to design and urge policy prescriptions (van Apeldoorn, 2000).

In pursuance of the recommendation made at the Essen summit, a Competitiveness Advisory Group (CAG) was established in February 1995 as an 'independent group', consisting of leading industrialists, trade unionists, politicians and academics. Its mandate was 'to produce a six-monthly report on the state of the Union's competitiveness and to advise on economic policy priorities and guidelines with the aim of stimulating competitiveness and reaping its benefits in terms of growth and employment'. Meant to be pragmatic, it adopted the so-called 'bottom up' approach, drawing lessons from the experience of national economies, sectors and firms, by benchmarking them to identify best practice. The four reports produced by the first CAG (1995–96) were published as a book, prefaced by Jacques Santer, then president of the Commission (Jacquemin and Pench, 1997). Besides stressing the need to complete 'the internal market for the free flow of goods, services and people', it strongly advocated the closing of the worldwide technology gap leading to 'the development of the information society in which workers are recognized as a major asset to be invested in'. The emphasis was indeed put on 'reaping human resources', reforming labour markets and building the 'learning society'. From the CAG's perspective, pursuing social ends and 'enhancing European competitiveness' were not conflicting objectives since the latter was not viewed as an end in itself, but as a tool for achieving the former. To quote its second report, 'competitiveness should be seen as a basic means to raise the standard of living, provide jobs to the unemployed and eradicate poverty' (CAG I, 1995).

Consequently, the CAG contributed to shaping the issue of European competitiveness as an overarching world-view embracing a wide range of concerns and sectors. It thus backed up the European Commission in broadening the scope of its sphere of activity. In a communication entitled 'Benchmarking the Competitiveness of European Industry' (CEC, 1996), the latter constructed a pyramid (see Figure 9.1) to graphically represent an all-encompassing policy paradigm.

The diagram explicitly included 'framework conditions', and thus paved the way for a potential extension of competitiveness-oriented actions beyond the industrial field towards demographic, social, knowledge or even fiscal domains. The Commission used this causal chain to deepen further the process of Europeanisation through a comprehensive competitiveness

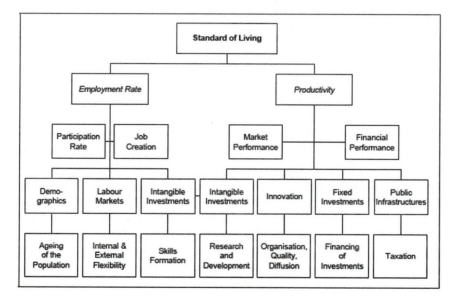

Figure 9.1   Competitiveness pyramid of the EU

Source: (CEC 1996: 4)

strategy. Significantly enough, the report on 'The Competitiveness of European Industry' (CEC, 1999) was renamed in the 2000 edition: 'European Competitiveness Report' (CEC, 2000a). Before considering in which sense the year 2000 marked the climax of 'competitive Europe' as an apparently depoliticised vision of society, we must show how the practice of benchmarking translates this idea into an organisational reality by activating the associative principle of competition.

Benchmarking, or how to put into practice a 'competitive Europe'

Benchmarking is a governmental technique first developed by Japanese industry in the 1950s, then codified by quality management in the United States. Imported into public administration by the NPM paradigm, this way of steering and monitoring organisations has been spread throughout the EU by its public and private promoters such as DG Industry or the ERT. It has generalised management by objectives based on benchmarks and schedules, comparable data and indicators, scoreboards and league tables. By mediating intergovernmental relations, it is designed to generate emulation and prompt decision-makers to arrange a business-friendly regulatory environment. This section follows a genealogical approach in order to historicise, and hence denaturalise, the workings of this coordinating device built around systematic quantification and comparison. My purpose is to distance ourselves from managerial discourses which posit its universal appropriateness and usefulness. On the contrary, I want to shed light on the ambivalent process of 'co-opetition'.

What genealogy teaches us about the ostensible universality of benchmarking
The roots of benchmarking could be traced back to Taylor's scientific management, insofar as this technique is about information centralisation and performance analysis. However, benchmarking departs in several ways from Taylorist principles, as it is part of a 'Total Quality Management' (TQM) seeking to go beyond the unique emphasis placed on high productivity. It is generally admitted that benchmarking was developed in the 1950s by a Toyota engineer – Taiichi Ohno – who gave his name to Ohnism. In short, this industrial paradigm sought to reinforce the performance of Japanese industry in the face of international competition. It moves beyond simple imitation and systematises the assessment of the industrial process and the need to be competitive at all levels of organisation. It consists in comparing performance with competitors and using objective criteria as a way to gain a competitive edge.

At the beginning of the 1980s, American managers – themselves confronted with intense Japanese competition – deemed this method of emulation useful to keep pace. In 1979, Rank Xerox initiated the first programme of systematic comparative assessment, which then spread under the name of benchmarking. From a success story, it became a classic case study in management textbooks. Robert Camp, the engineer who implemented the benchmarking device in Xerox, related his experience in a reference book published in 1989 under the title *Benchmarking: The Search for Industry Best Practices that Lead to Superior Performance* (Milwaukee, ASQC Quality Press). He schematised his *modus operandi* as a cycle made up of ten steps as shown in Figure 9.2.

Since then, business literature has identified benchmarking as a cornerstone of TQM. Working on the assumption of functional isomorphism between public and private organisations, NPM experts also recommended benchmarking in administrations as a tool to make them outward-looking, self-evaluating, even self-adaptive, and hence competitive. Since the 1990s, the OECD has actively and consistently promoted benchmarking as a policy-learning tool, consisting in exchanging best practices and learning from comparison in the drive to be competitive (Cave, Joss and Pollitt, 1994; OECD, 1997).

This way of steering and monitoring organisations spread in the EU through the Commission and the ERT. In 1996, DG Industry and ERT's Competitiveness Working Group organised a joint seminar to familiarise policy-makers with benchmarking, referred to as 'The Way to Competitiveness, Growth and Job Creation' (ERT, 1996). The following year, the Commission developed a flexible methodology in a communication entitled: 'Benchmarking: Implementation of an instrument available to economic actors and public authorities' (CEC, 1997). When the High Level Group on Benchmarking – which brought together politicians, managers and social partners – reported

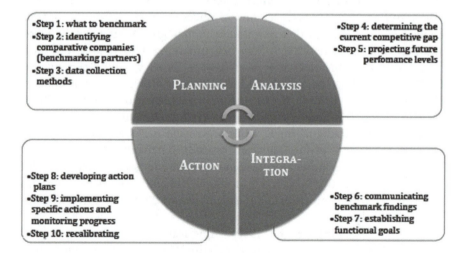

Figure 9.2   Steps in the benchmarking process

to the Commission in 1999 (HLGB, 1999), its intention was to promote the overall benchmarking of framework conditions, i.e. the generalisation of this managerial technique to non-market sectors such as national systems of social protection, employment, education or research and innovation. Jacques Santer perfectly expressed the *Zeitgeist* by exclaiming: 'We are all benchmarkers now!' (quoted in Richardson, 2000: 26).

Neither competition nor cooperation: 'co-opetition'

Strangely enough – for those who are unfamiliar with managerial reasoning – the guiding principles behind benchmarking are that 'one gets competitive through competition', and that 'competition is the most efficient coordination device'. Competition is neither natural nor self-regulating. Therefore, it needs to be arranged not only by laying down the rules of the game, but also by stirring a 'competitive spirit'. For this purpose, management consultants claim to offer specific solutions for policy-makers, more appropriate than economic and legal tools of government, which theorise perfect competition or regulate a competitive environment, but are portrayed as useless for solving problems of coordination. In order to deal with these problems, which are alleged to concern all human organisations, they endeavour to develop a 'calculative collective device' (Callon and Muniesa, 2005) which shapes intergovernmental coordination by mimicking market relations.

Benchmarking epitomises this effort. In the management literature, it was framed in terms of 'co-opetition', a generic word that blends cooperation with competition. More than a mere 'mixed metaphor' (Mann, Samson and Wolfram Cox, 1997), it is a hybrid mechanism of cooperation through competition supposed to convey a 'revolutionary mindset' (Brandenburger and Nalebuff, 1998). However paradoxical it may seem, benchmarking puts competition into practice as a matrix of social ties. It solves the 'paradox of the economic bond' which Foucault refers to as a 'principle of dissociation', or rather as a 'dissociative principle of association' (Foucault, 2008: 291 seq.). Its genealogy has thus shown us that it cannot be reduced to a policy-learning tool (Lundvall and Tomlinson, 2002), with politically neutral implications for the social order. I will now build on this characterisation of the tool to demonstrate how this technology of government actually constructs a 'competitive Europe' by creating union through competition.

The Lisbon strategy (2000–10): a pragmatic revolution

In March 2000, a special summit of the European Council was held in Lisbon. The fifteen Heads of State and Government set an all-embracing goal for Europe to assert itself by 2010 as 'the most competitive and dynamic knowledge-based economy in the world, capable of sustainable economic growth with more and better jobs and greater social cohesion' (EC 2000, § 5). The advent of the new millennium, the IT revolution, the dot-com bubble and the economic growth created a euphoric context reflected in the ambitious formulation of the strategic plan by jumping on the 'new economy' bandwagon (Rodrigues, 2002) and by giving grist to the mills to those in favour of a reinforced 'social Europe'. However ambitious and unprecedented the strategy was, its novelty resided elsewhere: in its method. As a consequence, this last section will not seek to evaluate policy outcomes measured against declared benchmarks. On the contrary, I will focus on its far-reaching effects on the European governmentality, inasmuch as the benchmarking exercise – through intergovernmental classifications, peer pressure and multilateral monitoring – underlies a shared competitiveness-oriented rationale for the shaping of public policy. I will finally elaborate on what we mean by the 'indefinite discipline' of competitiveness, and to what extent it derives from benchmarking.

The strength of a weak method
In 2000, the traditional Community method appeared to be in crisis. It was deemed too heavy-handed, too bureaucratic, not inclusive of stakeholders and difficult to implement in a context of deepening and enlargement. To overcome the declining returns of traditional EU instruments of coordination, the Portuguese Presidency sought to pursue European construction through intergovernmental cooperation rather than supranational integration. It streamlined and systematised the existing coordinating processes in fields where State sovereignty still prevailed (such as national systems of research, education or social protection). Even though the method had been used for several years in the European Employment Strategy, it seemed novel when given a new name: 'Open Method of Co-ordination' (OMC).

This method was described as 'open' because it was purported to be 'fully decentralised' and bottom up through the involvement of all significant stakeholders (public authorities, social partners, civil society), at all levels (Community, national, regional, even local), in compliance with the principles of subsidiarity and 'good governance' (EC, 2000: § 38). To get a handle on this multiplicity of actors, the Commission resorted to benchmarking as an iterative process in four stages, which are reminiscent of Camp's steps (planning, analysis, integration, action; see Figure 9.2):

1) 'fixing guidelines for the Union combined with specific timetables for achieving the goals which they set in the short, medium and long terms';

2) 'establishing, where appropriate, quantitative and qualitative indicators and benchmarks against the best in the world and tailored to the needs of different Member States and sectors as a means of comparing best practice';

3) 'translating these European guidelines into national and regional policies by setting specific targets and adopting measures, taking into account national and regional differences';

4) 'periodic monitoring, evaluation and peer review organised as mutual learning processes'. (EC, 2000: § 37)

Insofar as the prospect of a 'competitive Europe' was believed to entail a 'learning organisation', the template for the OMC device was logically the TQM approach. Benchmarking cycles were regarded as the obvious solution for 'spreading best practice and achieving greater convergence towards the main EU goals'. They were intended to initiate a continuous improvement process geared to 'help Member States to progressively develop their own policies' without top down standardisation. National policy-makers were not expected to follow the same path at the same pace, but to head in the same direction and to strive for excellence by learning from best practice. 'Peer comparisons among member states at variable territorial levels are meant to induce self-reflexive learning cycles, thereby speeding up the laggards and encouraging them to catch up with ongoing improvements' (Zängle, 2004: 6). Indeed, what was at stake in 'mutual learning processes' was not merely sharing knowledge, but reallocating power and legitimacy. Such processes were directed towards exerting peer pressure through 'naming, faming, shaming' among sovereign states, which is 'quite different from naming and shaming in the classroom. National pride, the protection of sovereignty and the dignity of the State are at play, with the players bargaining both over benchmarking targets, performance measurement, and benchmarking results' (Zängle, 2004: 10).

Concerning the benchmarking targets – i.e. the benchmarks – they refer to the best performance worldwide, used as yardsticks against which to judge one's competitiveness. In the OMC framework, they were negotiated by national representatives who demonstrated their political goodwill and commitment to the Lisbon strategy. Beyond this, they are bonds which tied them to measurable results. For example, the European Council decided 'to raise the employment rate from an average of 61% today to as close as possible to 70% by 2010 and to increase the number of women in employment from an average of 51% today to more than 60% by 2010' (EC, 2000: § 30). And as regards the project of the European Research Area (ERA), it was agreed at the Barcelona Summit in 2002 that 'overall spending on research and innovation in the Union should be increased with the aim of approaching 3% of GDP by 2010' and that '[t]wo-thirds of this new investment should come from the private sector' (EC, 2002: §47). To have an overview of the collective (EU) and individual (member states) progress towards these objectives, the European Commission was put in charge of the monitoring through regular reports based on grids of update statistics. To this effect, it equipped itself with a selection of 'structural indicators' provided by Eurostat which centralised and harmonised data collected at the national level. Once each country is reduced to such elemental figures, it becomes feasible to gather, order and rank them in graphic representations.

Jack Goody (1979) pointed out that such visible objects as tables, lists, maps or typologies, are not mere transcriptions of pre-existent discourse, but vectors which create new parallels, equivalences and assessments. The OMC technology perfectly illustrates this essential point. Colour charts, score-boards, league tables and the like that are published in the Commission's annual report make differentials in performance visible at a single glance. On the one hand, they materialise a 'field of visibility' which establishes the conditions of possibility of 'open co-ordination' though information exchange, mutual comparison and emulation. On the other hand, they keep a close watch on national results and, by inference, make policy choices vulnerable to peer judgement. Through the agency of the Commission, member states are able to graphically compare their performance. As Jens Henrik Haahr stressed,

> tables and graphs construct a set of *identities* which are continuously reproduced in the framework of the Lisbon process: the European Commission as an institu-tion capable of legitimately and authoritatively passing out grades to member states, thereby establishing their relative forwardness or backwardness in terms of achieving virtue; and member states as entities engaged in a process of moving towards the attainment of different targets and objectives. At the same time, the tables in themselves and the assessments upon which they often rely lend them-selves to comparisons and rankings. Indeed, the Commission itself actively promotes this competitive mentality. (Haahr, 2004: 223)

The well-known ERA benchmark of '3%' exemplifies this logic. In order to set into motion the benchmarking of national research policies, and thus to deepen the intergovernmental coordination in this domain, the relevant DG[3] released Key Figures from 2000 with a special focus on R&D invest-ments. The first edition devoted eighteen data tables and colour graphs to the question, with the focus being the worrying gap between Europe as a whole and its main competitors – the United States and Japan (CEC, 2000b: 18). No graphic representations of differences between member states were present so as not to offend national susceptibilities. The following year, Key Figures were used as a political stimulus to catalyse the benchmarking process by dissemi-nating national results against a set of 15 science and technology indicators to a wider European audience. Concerning R&D financing, statistical grids, hard to decipher for the uninitiated, were replaced by eleven charts which rendered the ranking of countries readily apparent on the Y-axis (see Figure 9.3). The reason why these Key Figures caused an uproar among national authorities was neither the disclosure of hitherto unpublished data (e.g. the R&D intensity[4] is a classical ratio calculated by statistical services worldwide), nor their deceptiveness, if not falseness. It was their publicity and transparency. They gained unusual media coverage which triggered competition to attempt to reach the pole position.

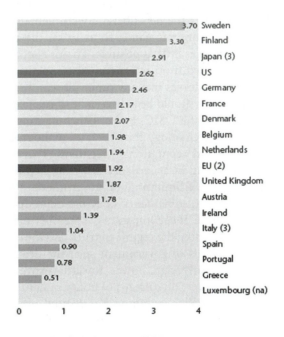

Figure 9.3   R&D intensity (%), latest available year
Data: Eurostat, member states, OECD, Japan (Nistep)
Source: CEC (2001: 18)

If mutual benchmarking among states is a politically sensitive exercise, it is not only because 'having to learn from other states is equivalent to making inferiority visible, which seems rather hard to bear for representatives of states and elected politicians' (Zängle, 2004: 11). It is also because, in practice, it entails publicly accessible databases and results in league tables, fit for publication and circulation, that are likely to make the headlines, and hence to become either an asset or a disadvantage both in the global race to attract investors and in internal political competition. Thereby, both peer and public pressure drives policy-makers to adopt an outward-looking state of mind. In order to be marked out from the poorest-performing countries and to catch up with the best ones, they feel compelled to arrange a 'business-friendly regulatory environment' conducive to increasing private R&D investments. Such reasoning sounds hackneyed but actually goes beyond free-market mantras by seeking nothing less than a 'cultural revolution'. More than cutting red tape or corporate taxes, it advocates improving the macro-economic as well as the socio-cultural framework conditions for business activities. Building a 'knowledge-based society' by means of benchmarking thus consists in developing both an administrative climate and a public mood more conducive to entrepreneurship and risk-taking. In doing so, the OMC typifies what Foucault refers to as an 'environmental technology' (Foucault,

2008: 259–260). It underlies the neo-liberal governmentality which acts on the environment of the economic game, so as to set the players as free as possible by governing them as little as possible. To this end, those who govern should no longer be shielded from international competition but should be exposed to its disciplinary forces like any other players. In other words, the exercise of sovereign power should be subservient to rules of the market.

As the cornerstone of the OMC device, benchmarking subjects policy-makers to a disciplinary technology that operates without law enforcement but with peer pressure and reputational incentives. Therefore, it shapes a European way of governing in accordance with the neo-liberal rationality whose principle is 'the self-limitation of government' (Foucault, 2008). Properly speaking, this governmentality does not reproduce the sovereign state at a supranational level. It encompasses EU member states as objects but it is strictly non-state regarding the regime of truth and the exercise of power. Nor does the neo-liberal art of government spell the death of the state. It harnesses and channels sovereign power towards exogenous targets, by leading political leaders to rely on calculus of utility rather than *raison d'État*. Such a utilitarian inclination is anything but natural or irrepressible, but results from conditioning, equipping and hence disciplining forces.

The 'indefinite discipline' of competitiveness

To sum up, benchmarking is a technique of management by objectives which enables government from a distance without resorting to legal constraints. By mediating inter-state relations, benchmarking makes national governments commit themselves to achieve as well as – if not better than – their peers. It is an incentive technology that not only spurs decision-makers on to act by encouraging emulation; it also gives them the means to legitimately act according to a certain kind of rationality. They remain free but it is 'a constrained and structured freedom' (Haahr, 2004: 220). In that sense, benchmarking in general – and the OMC in particular – combines technologies of involvement and of performance which govern conducts by framing practices of liberty. They equip policy-makers with scoreboards, indicators, key figures, and targets which enable them to systematically compare their results and do their utmost to hit the top of the charts, or at least not to lag behind. This governmental technology informs – and gives form to– a utilitarian reasoning based on calculations and action plans, striving towards efficiency and maximisation of performance as defined by the indicators, which themselves only take into consideration what is measured, or measurable, and thereby contributes to the framing of certain policy problems at the expense of others (see Rowell in this volume).

Even though benchmarking is devoid of coercive or legal force, it is not toothless. Within the framework of the Lisbon strategy, it underpins a competitiveness-oriented rationale for the conduct of state interventions and the shaping of public policies. Its exercise materialises the objective of competitiveness in benchmarks, and what is tangible cannot be easily ignored. In doing so, it exerts the 'indefinite discipline' of competitiveness. Why 'indefinite'? Because the norm of competitiveness is endogenous to the endless competition in which benchmarking engages its users. The benchmark, i.e. the reference point identified as a goal, is a moving target which cannot be reached once and for all. It is ideally fugitive, and hence unattainable, set only to be caught up and replaced by the latest 'best performer'. Setting competitiveness as the aim to achieve by means of benchmarking, which precisely consists in measuring gaps of performance so as to close them, amounts to strive to reduce a distance while reproducing it in(de)finitely. This expression of 'indefinite discipline' is taken from Foucault who coined it to refer to 'a procedure that would be at the same time the permanent measure of a gap in relation to an inaccessible norm and the asymptotic movement that strives to meet in infinity' (1977: 227).

Expert reports evaluating progress to reaching the Lisbon targets contribute to this disciplinary force. For example, the mid-term review, delivered by the High Level Group chaired by Wim Kok (CEC, 2004), depicted disappointing overall performance in reaching targets. With the help of statistical evidence, it foresaw that Europe would not reach the performance targets of its main benchmarking comparators – Japan and the United States – by 2010. However, the fault was not perceived to lie within the method itself, but rested on the lack of political will. Consequently, it called for redoubled national efforts as a moral obligation, and praised the virtue of mutual benchmarking. This kind of assessment is a fully-fledged part of the OMC technology. Considering disciplinary power at work within benchmarking and reporting mechanisms challenges the viewpoint regarding them as policy-neutral instruments, all the weaker as OMC is a so-called 'soft-law' governance method.

Conclusion

Wherever benchmarking is implemented, it requires a sound base of comparable data, a battery of reliable indicators and a consensus on the pertinent benchmarks. Its alleged universality indeed derives a great deal of its credibility and legitimacy from the ecumenical 'language of quantification' and the widespread 'trust in numbers'. As Ted Porter has pointed out, a 'decision made by the numbers (or by explicit rules of some other sort) has at least the appearance of being fair and impersonal. Scientific objectivity thus provides an answer to a moral demand for impartiality and fairness. Quantification is a way of making decisions without seeming to decide' (Porter, 1995: 8). Indeed, benchmarking helps decision-makers to reach consensus by translating political problems of collective action into statistical issues of quantification. This way of coordinating member states tends to Europeanise national policies through comparable figures rather than integrate them by supranational law. These statistical figures do not reveal a measurable degree of competitiveness which pre-exists the actual process of its measurement. They create the conditions for competition and make competitive relations possible. It is in that sense that the OMC effectively contributes to the emergence of a 'competitive Europe'.

The statistical feature of this technology suggests some new avenues of research to understand the European drive for competitiveness. Besides analysis of discourses or institutions, it speaks in favour of developing the sociology of quantification in European studies (Desrosières and Kott, 2005). Even if statistical figures have always been instrumental in the construction of the EU, the Lisbon device is unprecedented and much remains to be explored. In order to provide insights into these 'black boxes', a sociological research programme should try to disclose their 'trade secret' by looking into their making and their makers. On the one hand, it would help us to closely observe the strategic use of numbers, not only as a scientific proof backing up governmental measures, but also as action-oriented incentives which spur governments to redouble their efforts towards unattainable benchmarks. On the other hand, it would contribute towards a better understanding of the depoliticisation effects of consensual techniques such as benchmarking. Ultimately, what Foucault wrote about the panoptic principle could be applied to this coordinating technology: 'in appearance, it is merely the solution of a technical problem; but, through it, a whole type of society emerges' (Foucault, 1977).

Notes

1   A notable exception is Haahr (2004) who characterises the OMC as 'advanced liberal government'.
2   From the Council's website: www.compete.org.
3   More precisely, the initiative came from the unit for Competitiveness, Economic Analysis and Indicators of DG Research in close collaboration with the unit for Research and Development, Methods and Data Analyses of Eurostat, and under the aegis of the commissioners Philippe Busquin and Pedro Solbes Mira, respectively responsible for Research and Economic and Monetary Affairs.
4   Gross domestic expenditure on research and development as percentage of GDP.

Bibliography

Brandenburger, A. and Nalebuff, B., *Co-opetition: A Revolutionary Mindset that Combines Competition and Co-operation*, New York: Currency Doubleday, 1998.
Brenner, N., 'Building "Euro-regions". Locational Politics and the Political Geography of Neoliberalism in Post-unification Germany', *European Urban and Regional Studies*, 7 (4), 2000, 319–345.

CAG Competitiveness Advisory Group I, 'Enhancing European Competitiveness', *Second Report to the President of the Commission, the Prime Ministers and Heads of State*, 1995.

Callon, M. and Muniesa, F., 'Economic Markets as Calculative Collective Devices', *Organization Studies*, 26 (8), 2005, 1229–1250.

Cave, M., Joss, R. and Pollitt, C., 'International Benchmarking as a Tool to Improve Public Sector Performance: A Critical Overview', in OECD, 'Performance Measurement in Government: Issues and Illustrations', *Public Management Occasional Paper no. 5*, 1994, 7–22.

CEC (Commission of the European Communities), 'Growth, Competitiveness, and Employment. The Challenges and Ways Forward into the 21st Century', *White Paper*, COM (93) 700 final, December 1993.

CEC, 'Benchmarking the Competitiveness of European Industry', *Communication from the Commission*, COM (96) 463 final, October 1996.

CEC, 'Benchmarking. Implementation of an Instrument Available to Economic Actors and Public Authorities', *Communication from the Commission to the Council, the European Parliament, the Economic and Social Committee and the Committee of the Regions*, Com (97) 153 final, April 1997.

CEC, 'The Competitiveness of European Industry: 1999 Report', *Working Document of the Services of the European Commission*, Luxemburg, OOPEC, 1999.

CEC, 'European Competitiveness Report 2000', *Commission Staff Working Paper*, SEC (2000) 1823, October 2000a.

CEC, 'Towards a European Research Area. Science, Technology and Innovation', *Key Figures 2000*, Luxembourg: OOPEC, 2000b.

CEC, 'Towards a European Research Area. Indicators for Benchmarking of National Research Policies', *Key Figures 2001: Special Edition*, Luxembourg, OOPEC, 2001.

CEC, 'Facing the Challenge: The Lisbon Strategy for Growth and Employment', *Report from the High Level Group Chaired by Wim Kok*, Luxembourg: OOPEC, November 2004.

Cerny, P., 'Transnational Structures and State Responses: From the Welfare State to the Competition State', in *The Changing Architecture of Politics: Structure, Agency, and the Future of the State*, London: Sage, 1990, 204–232.

Commission on Industrial Competitiveness, *Global Competition: The New Reality*, Washington, DC: US Government Printing Office, January 1985.

Competitiveness Policy Council, 'Building a Competitive America', *First Annual Report to the President and Congress*, Washington, DC, 1992.

Desrosières, A. and Kott S. (eds), 'Quantifier', *Genèses*, 58, 2005.

EC (European Council), 'Presidency Conclusions', *Lisbon Summit*, March 2000, Nr: 100/1/00.

EC, 'Presidency Conclusions', *Barcelona Summit*, March 2002, Nr: 100/1/02.

Elissalt, F., 'La statistique communautaire au tournant du XXIème siècle: Nouveaux enjeux, nouvelles contraintes', *Courrier des statistiques*, 100, 2001, 41–51.

ERT (European Round Table of Industrialists), 'Beating the Crisis: A Charter for Europe's Industrial Future', *Action Plan*, 1993.

ERT, 'Benchmarking for Policy-Makers: The Way to Competitiveness, Growth and Job Creation', *Report Based on the Findings of a Seminar Organized by the European Commission and the ERT (21 March 1996)*, Brussels, 1996.

Foucault, M., *Discipline and Punish. The Birth of the Prison*, New York: Random House, 1977.

Foucault, M., *Security, Territory, Population. Lectures at the College de France, 1977–1978*, Basingstoke: Palgrave Macmillan, 2007.

Foucault, M., *The Birth of Biopolitics. Lectures at the College de France, 1978–1979*, Basingstoke: Palgrave Macmillan, 2008.

Goody, J., *La raison graphique. La domestication de la pensée sauvage*, Paris: Minuit, 1979.

Haahr, J.H., 'Open Co-ordination as Advanced Liberal Government', *Journal of European Public Policy*, 11 (2), 2004, 209–230.

Hay, C. and Rosamond, B., 'Globalization, European Integration and the Discursive Construction of Economic Imperatives', *Journal of European Public Policy*, 9 (2), 2002, 147–167.

HLGB (High Level Group on Benchmarking) (European Commission/DG III), 'First Report by the High Level Group on Benchmarking', *Benchmarking Papers*, no. 2, 1999.

Jacquemin, A. and Pench, L.R. (eds), 'Europe Competing in the Global Economy', *Reports of the Competitiveness Advisory Group*, Cheltenham: Edward Elgar, 1997.

Krugman, P., 'Competitiveness: A Dangerous Obsession', *Foreign Affairs*, 73 (2), 1994, 28–44.

Latour, B., *Pandora's Hope. Essays on the Reality of Science Studies*, Cambridge: Harvard University Press, 1999.

Latour, B., 'The Promises of Constructivism', in D. Ihde and E. Selinger (eds), *Chasing Technoscience: Matrix for Materiality*, Bloomington: Indiana University Press, 2003, 27–46.

Lundvall, B.-A. and Tomlinson, M., 'International Benchmarking as a Policy Learning Tool', in M.J. Rodrigues (ed.), *The New Knowledge Economy in Europe: A Strategy for International Competitiveness and Social Cohesion*, Cheltenham: Edward Elgar.

Mann, L., Samson, D. and Wolfram Cox, J., 'Benchmarking as a Mixed Metaphor: Disentangling Assumptions of Competition and Collaboration', *Journal of Management Studies*, 34 (2), 1997, 285–314.

OECD (Organisation for Economic Co-operation and Development), 'Performance Management in Government: Performance Measurement and Results-Oriented Management', *Public Management Occasional Paper no. 3*, Paris: OECD, 1994.

OECD, 'Benchmarking, Evaluation and Strategic Management in the Public Sector', *Papers Presented at the 1996 Meeting of the Performance Management Network of the OECD's Public Management Service*, OCDE/GD (97) 50, Paris: 1997.

Ohno, T., *Toyota Production System. Beyond Large-Scale Production*, Cambridge: Productivity Press, 1988.

Porter, T., *Trust in Numbers. The Pursuit of Objectivity in Science and Public Life*, Princeton: Princeton University Press, 1995.

Richardson, K., 'Big Business and the European Agenda', *Working Paper in Contemporary European Studies*, 35, University of Sussex, Sussex European Institute, September 2000.

Risse-Kappen, T., 'Ideas Do Not Float Freely: Transnational Coalitions, Domestic Structures and the End of the Cold War', *International Organization*, 48 (2), 1994, 185–214.

Risse-Kappen, T., 'Exploring the Nature of the Beast: International Relations Theory and Comparative Policy Analysis Meet the European Union', *Journal of Common Market Studies*, 34 (1), 1996, 53–80.

Rodrigues, M.J. (ed.), *The New Knowledge Economy in Europe: A Strategy for International Competitiveness and Social Cohesion*, Cheltenham: Edward Elgar, 2002.

Rosamond, B., 'Discourses of Globalization and the Social Construction of European Identities', *Journal of European Public Policy*, 6 (4), 1999, 652–668.

Rosamond B., 'Imagining the European Economy: "Competitiveness" and the Social Construction of "Europe" as an Economic Space', *New Political Economy*, 7 (2), 2002, 157–177.

Strange, S., *The Retreat of the State: The Diffusion of Power in the World Economy*, Cambridge: Cambridge University Press, 1996.

Strange, S., 'Who are EU? Ambiguities in the Concept of Competitiveness', *Journal of Common Market Studies*, 36 (1), 1998, 101–114.

van Appledoorn, B., 'Transnational Class Agency and European Governance: The Case of the European Round Table of Industrialists', *New Political Economy*, 5 (2), 2000.

Zängle, M., 'The European Union Benchmarking Experience. From Euphoria to Fatigue?', *European Integration Online Papers (EIoP)*, 8 (5), 2004.

$\mathcal{P}$HILIPPE $\mathcal{A}$LDRIN*

10

From instruments to the instrumentalisation of 'European opinion': a historical sociology of the measurement of opinions and the management of the public space

Through their very existence, European studies tend to reinforce the certainty that the European Union is the product and the matrix of an unprecedented political process – an exception to the rule laid out by classical theories on the institutionalisation of nation-states (Pierson, 1996). The supposed *sui generis* properties of the EU are largely responsible for the fact that traditional models of analysis of political phenomena are not applied to *European* political phenomena. However, the epistemological and empirical arguments to support the notion of a radical alterity of the political material – be it conceptual, human, administrative, legal – that has built Europe as a Community require closer examination. This chapter will argue that beyond the specific object of our study, the EU is a political object that requires the same sociological approaches as other political objects for which this approach seems only 'natural'. On the basis of a survey conducted in the services of the European Commission's Directorate General (DG) Communication,[1] I apply to the EU communication apparatus the same hypotheses that are commonly applied to more 'classical' political institutions (Georgakakis, 2004). This continuist stance (Dobry,1986: 14–28) in no way negates or underestimates the specificity of the 'culture' and decision-making procedures of the EU or of certain types of issues faced by the EU. By focusing on the frames[2] and the instruments of European communication policy – i.e. on Community instruments of measure, analysis of opinions and manage-

* Translated by Jean-Yves Bart

ment of the public space – I aim first and foremost to show how Community actors have historically assessed, constructed and handled the 'problem' of European public opinion.

In keeping with the perspective of this book, this chapter places emphasis on three of the most salient conclusions of the survey it is based upon. The historical account of the Commission's information-communication policy will retrace the historicity of 'European public opinion' as a perceived problem within the Commission services. This analysis points to the early presence, originating in the 1960s, of a conceptualisation, and of systems of evaluation and resolution of the problem. The success or full efficiency of the latter, as measured by the huge importance given to public opinion from the 1990s onwards, has more to do with the reconfiguration of the internal and external tensions of the European political game than with a feedback or spillover consequence of the integration process (Haas, 1958). The socio-historical analysis of the European Community's communication apparatus then reveals the extent to which its structuring conceptions are malleable. The redefinition of the objectives and the means of European communication – from the original sectoral approach ('the information policy of the Communities') to a more global approach ('a European communication policy') is linked to the conceptual and technical changes of the instrumental equipment of European public action. However, these changes were not specific to the EU, as the processes of professionalisation and rationalisation of the EU's communication apparatus followed the same pattern as local and national executives in Europe at the same time (Olivier-Yaniv, 2000). Lastly, studying the work of EC agents highlights the importance of policy entrepreneurship in the construction of opinion and communication as a 'European problem'. To some extent, this is a new illustration of the weight of the civil service within the dynamics of European public action (Peters, 1992) as they mobilise internal and external networks, and gain support and material resources in order to legitimise Commission initiatives and choices in the face of resistance from member states.[3] But the genealogy of the instruments used to achieve these goals – in particular the sophistication of the Eurobarometer tool and its uses – also uncovers the tentative, sometimes improvised, but systematically opportunistic character (Kingdon, 1984) of such undertakings, in contradiction with the strategist vision of a political decision centre marked by a unanimous representation of coherent EC goals and a shared will to achieve them.

I will then seek to describe and recontextualise the successive adjustments in the approach of the opinion 'problem' within EC institutions. At each significant stage of this redefinition of the 'problem', I will attempt to show the links between the conceptual evolution and the instrumental equipment of communication within the decision-making space by following the constructivist tradition of research that 'takes ideas seriously' and analyses instruments and their uses as 'tracers' of these ideas (Lascoumes and Le Galès, 2004).

The powerless condition of European Community communication

Contrary to what the advocates of a retrospective vision of its history claim, the EC has since its inception been attuned to the question of public opinion. Various elements show that EC officials did not wait for the political shift of the Maastricht Treaty (1991), the launch of the single currency (2002) or the electoral debacle of the constitutional treaty (2005) to become interested in public opinion. Immediately after the creation of the ECSC, EEC and Euratom, their executives established services that ensured the diffusion of information on their activities for journalists and the populations concerned. Very early on, administrative and political officials monitored media coverage of Community activity and financed opinion polls on public perceptions of the Communities in each member country. The Commission, which centralised an information service shared by the three Communities, created the Eurobarometer in 1973. It was an internal instrument (activating external service providers) of biannual measurement of opinions in member countries. Under the first Delors presidency, the Commissioners adopted the Priority Information Programmes (PIP), and launched fully-fledged 'marketing campaigns' (partnerships with sporting events, launch of the 'European Year') in order to make EC initiatives and policies widely known. The Commission was clearly supported by the European Parliament in this effort to inform and evaluate the attitudes of 'populations'. As early as 1972,[4] MEPs adopted very firm resolutions on the 'information policy' of the Communities, recommending an increased mobilisation of resources and the systematic recourse to the most modern communication techniques.[5] If the genesis of the EC's instruments of measure of opinions and management of the public space was present at the very start of European administrations and institutions, the sequential reconstruction of EC communication tends to show that, at least during the last two decades, both the range of these activities and instruments and the 'problem' they purported to solve have shifted on several occasions.

Although initially labelled as a 'policy' strictly speaking, the information activity of the Community was not, at least when it started, a supranational public policy. It had no vocation to serve a collective good, solve a social problem or meet the needs of a specific sector of the population. In the early stages of the Common Market, the objectives of this policy were to popularise the activities of EC institutions towards target populations. There was a first shift of this information activity – which was not however framed as a political problem – when the attitudes of 'European public opinion' became a question of democratic legitimisation. Indeed, the political order of the EC was progressively democratised from the late 1970s on, thanks to the direct election of MEPs in 1979, the extension of the Parliament's attributions and the increasing use of referendums for the national ratification of European treaties. For a unification process that had been until then based on diplomatic negotiations ratified by national political elites, the challenge of universal suffrage made opposition to Europe more visible, and probably also more politically coherent. While they realised that popular support for Europe was waning in ballot boxes and polls, the actors of the EC process noted the emergence of a critical discourse denouncing the 'democratic deficit' (Marquant, 1979), the 'stateless bureaucracy' of 'Brussels Eurocrates' under the influence of lobbies, ranging from occasional bursts of Euroscepticism to the politically organised Europhobia of sovereignists and anti-capitalist movements. The EC enlarged geographically and extended its capacity of intervention[6] in member countries. As a result, the issue of popular support, and consequently of the manifest proof – through votes or polls – of its democratic legitimacy, became more acute. The awareness of this new situation modified the dominant framing of the opinion problem. Convinced that informational pedagogy was no longer enough to ensure popular support, the EC actors who were the most dedicated to the defence of the unification process – MEPs as well as political and administrative Commission officials in particular – started taking numerous initiatives in order to attempt to curb indifference to, fear of or rejection of Europe (Baget Bozzo, 1986).

The information effort progressively led to a new institutional treatment of the problem, wherein the mobilisation of opinion was to be achieved with the tools of mass communication. This political stake, crystallised by the phrase 'the democratic challenge', became so important that it seeped into every aspect of the EC's structure from the late 1980s on. The initiatives aiming to increase the 'transparency' of decision-making processes,[7] to deepen 'institutional reform'[8] should be seen in this light, as well as all the actions aiming to formally democratise Europe. As the apathy of European citizens appeared to threaten the integration process at the turn of the 1990s, the *Community* information effort was thus rephrased as a *European* problem of democratic legitimacy.[9] Even if they had been developed since the early stages of the Communities, the EC's tools of management of the public space (spokesperson's service, publications, relays and networks, etc.) and of measure of opinions (the Eurobarometer), only became a political instrument when mass public support to the EC became a vital political issue for the Community. By outlining the socio-technical combinations that have successively determined the definition and treatment of this problem, we will see how the functional instrumentation of information (instruments aimed at informing the populations concerned and opinion leaders) has been replaced by a sectoral instrumentation of communication (instruments serving as a cognitive measure allowing the harnessing of cognitive benefits of mass opinion).

Early stages of the European communication apparatus
The common information service of the three Communities, set up in the early 1960s on the initiative of the EP, initially sought to build contacts with national and local media and spread information among the populations

concerned by EC action. Nevertheless, each of the three executives still had their own press speaker, who interacted with the media present in Brussels and Luxembourg, enabling them to be reactive and keep sensitive issues under control. The merger of the executives in 1967 forced Community officials to find a new rationality in the organisation of external relations. A Spokesman's Service (including the press speakers of the various Commissioners) in charge of relations was created with accredited journalists present in Brussels under the direct authority of the President of the Commission[10] (Baisnée, 2001). With the merger, the Information Service became the Directorate-General of Information and Communication (DG-X), a fully-fledged administrative subdivision of the Commission.

The 'information policy' structured in the 1960s covered various services holding very traditional functions of public relations such as press relations and editing documents on the activity of Community institutions. From the very start, the institutional conception of European information was inspired by trendy scientific theories on public space, societal tendencies and social influence, as well as by strategic and technical progress in the field of communication. The sacralisation of the press briefing – for which former journalists were already responsible at that time, under the direct authority of the President of the Commission – as a major act of communication is symptomatic of this 'age' of political communication (Blumler, 1995). The choices that structured the organisation and the equipment of the Community's communication apparatus until the 1980s attest to this reactivity to contemporary debates and innovations, notably on two aspects that would become central: relations with the press and the media on the one hand, opinion polls on the other.

In the post-war years, government management of the media in western European countries was mostly limited to the setting-up of administrative services in charge of drafting press releases and reviews for government members.[11] Assimilated with propaganda of the totalitarian regimes, communication campaigns organised by governments were then few and far between, dealing only with politically neutral themes (combatting social scourges such as alcoholism; civic messages). Ministries and their specialised administrations limited themselves to spreading technical and practical information to 'their' audiences (agricultural workers, industrials, CEOs, teachers, etc.) (Olivier-Yaniv, 2000). The Communities' relationships with journalists – and their relationships with populations – partake in this cybernetic approach to communication: the institution provides information through various channels, and then receives feedback on that information thanks to press reviews and opinion polls. Public institutions only started making a systematic use of interviews, press tribunes or rented space in mass media in the 1980s, when commercial sponsors themselves resorted increasingly to institutional communication, thereby making the audience familiar with a form of communication where the message is not exclusively centred on the promotion of a product, but on the identification with values or projects. The founding principles and the evolution of European information thus strictly follow the models of communication techniques used by member states.

The Information Service was at first a small administrative apparatus in charge of informing and observing the media (Rabier, 1993). Symptomatically, its size and scope would mirror the evolution of the integration process itself and more generally reflect the rise and fall of the authority of the Commission within the institutional game. The organisation and the objectives remained identical when the Information Service was transformed into a Directorate-General of Press and Information after the merger (1967) and, subsequently, when it turned into a Directorate-General of Press and Communication or DG-X (1973). Two main principles guided the organisation of these services. First, the staff was dispatched to central services (the Commission headquarters in Brussels) or external offices. Secondly, efforts were concentrated on audiences perceived as priority targets: journalists (to ensure contact with the general public), and 'determined audiences', i.e. professional categories concerned by Community policies (professional organisations, trade unions, agricultural workers), as well as the milieus expected to be interested in the Community's project of integration (teachers at all levels). The Information Service employed about 100 people at its creation and over 200 when it became a DG. The information policy instruments remained basic as most of the activity consisted in drafting and disseminating informative brochures and magazines, and in putting together press reviews for the cabinets of Commissioners. DG-X's work was therefore no different from that of the nascent press and information services that were being created in other DGs (Joana and Smith, 2002).

Europeans and Europe ... before the invention of 'European public opinion'

The political and administrative officials of the Information Service were influenced by the dominant trends in social sciences on public opinion issues. As post-war European sociology was openly disinterested in social phenomena related to opinion; the scientific knowledge on the mechanisms of opinion formation emanated mainly from theories derived from experimental American psycho-sociology based on polling techniques. The few European scholars interested in opinion, such as Jean Stoetzel in France or Elisabeth Noelle in Germany, acted as mediators for the American science of opinion and introduced polling techniques in their national academic spaces.[12] This psycho-sociological approach to opinion would deeply influence Jacques-René Rabier, a high-ranking Commission official who played a crucial role in the first institutionalisation of the services and logics of the European opinion policy. Indeed, he was the director of the Information Service from the beginning, and then Director-General of DG-X and founder of the Eurobarometer (see Box 10.1). In the mid 1960s, almost ten years before the Eurobarometer was officially introduced, Rabier put forward a very precise assessment of opinion-related issues for the Communities and of the communication tools necessary to face them. Strongly influenced by Lazarsfeld's theory, this conception was certainly not typical of high-ranking officials at the time, but it is nevertheless an extremely enlightening indication of the clarity of vision of one of the main entrepreneurs of European communication policy even at that early stage. In a lecture on 'The Information of Europeans' given at the Institute for European Studies in Brussels, the head of the Information Service provided one of the most revealing contributions on the future European communication. Referring to the works of such specialists as Jean Stoetzel, David Easton[13] and especially Paul Lazarsfeld, he highlighted 'resistance, processes of protection and selection' of media messages,[14] always 'transmitted in a more assimilable form, with affective connotations' by relatives, and argued in favour of a relativisation of the 'mass' concept. On the basis of these observations, he emphasised the advantages of polling, portrayed as the only technique likely to overcome the usual quibbling and biased interpretations of opinion.[15] On the basis of polls conducted in 1962 (*Public Opinion and the Europe of Six*, a poll sponsored by the EC and conducted by Gallup International) on civic attitudes and in 1963[16] on consumer behaviour in the six member states of the EEC, Rabier noted a 'widespread adhesion of the public to the European idea' but 'little curiosity for the steps of Europe's construction'. Without mentioning it explicitly, Rabier borrowed Lazarsfeld's classifying principles of political interest.[17] Using data from these polls, he defined three categories of 'attitudes towards political life and the unification of Europe in the EC'. These categories were indexed to socio-professional status, levels of income and education, and distributed according to the following groups: 'well informed, interested and generally favourable' (20 to 30%), 'weakly politicized and generally favourable' (40 to 60%); 'relative or absolutely apathetic' citizens (20 to 30%). For Rabier, the results of these first polls 'undeniably' mark the beginning of a 'European consensus' produced by a 'relative homogeneity of the natural and technical conditions of production', as well as the resemblance of the 'attitudes towards life, shaped by a long history of cultural exchanges, cooperation and conflicts' (Rabier, 1965: 18). In light of these results, the director of the Information Service and thereafter the director of the DG-X wrote:

> A European information policy's goal would be to support and 'boost' favourable attitudes of active minorities; raise the interest level and increase the information of citizens who are both favourable and badly informed, or not very interested, and of those who are on a more or less vague level of consensus. (Rabier, 1965: 32)

Ideally, the EC's strategy would be to direct communication towards the socially 'better integrated groups and milieus' who would in turn act as relays, translators and information multipliers among their peers according to the 'two-step flow of communication' (Lazarsfeld and Katz, 1955). But Rabier immediately went on to explain why this would not work:

These institutions (the EC's) are hampered by a series of factors: 1. The integration process is recent and the image of its reality has difficulty emerging against
national imagery or ideological representations of a generous but vague interna-
tionalism. 2. It follows that the most apparent forms and results of European
integration, in the economic field, are quite technical, involve numerous and
complex institutions bearing obscure acronyms. 3. [...] The participation of
citizens in European integration is indirect and covert: as citizens of an emerging
Europe, they do not even have the right to vote. 4. The system of psychosocial
conditioning occurs almost exclusively to the national sphere – in the fields of
(notably, civic) education or information. 5. Furthermore, the very resources of
European institutions, except the ECSC, are provided by member states (whose)
attitude is often reluctant and suspicious. (Rabier, 1965: 63)

One by one, Rabier had pointed out the intrinsic flaws of the EC's institutions and of the system of intergovernmental constraints that limited their
leverage in terms of communication. Overcoming the EC's communication
problem would entail two types of solutions. There was a material one,
consisting in increasing the means of analysis (of media and opinions) and of
transmission of information. The other was political and consisted in giving
more freedom and range of action to the information services, i.e. to the
Commission. In order to do so, states had to be persuaded, as they were in
control of the budget and granted competences to EC institutions.

A few years after Rabier's remarks, in 1974, the Eurobarometer brought
the hypostasising power of numbers to something that used to revolve around
debatable considerations and impressions. The instrument replaced the
multitude of subjective visions and controversies with a supposedly objective
and unequivocal statement based on a supposedly unquestionable form of
expertise resulting from a methodology resembling a scientific protocol. The
Eurobarometer was presented as a scientific objectivation of 'European public
opinion', to which it instantly conferred an almost tangible reality. But this
was not enough to transform the issue of opinion into a European problem,
i.e. a problem shared by member states and the EC's institutions. This only
happened when the EU entered the realm of 'democracy of the public'
(Manin, 1996) and the legitimacy of its action was correlated to popular
support. Until then, the Eurobarometer remained confined to the periodical
examination of the attitude of Europeans towards the European project.

The instrumentalisation of opinion in building legitimacy for EC action

A new institutional problematisation of the issue of European opinion took
place at the turn of the 1980s–1990s, transforming the place of the issue and
hence the place of the communication staff within the EC's decision-making
space. Despite the precocity of Rabier's assessment, the EC's communication
apparatus remained structurally embryonic and in charge of secondary tasks
until well into the 1980s. The original principle of division of information

tasks was maintained: the spokesmen were in charge of the management of 'sensitive' information and daily relations with accredited media, while the DG-X was responsible for the management of the Commission's network of representations (mostly in member countries), for the contacts with the relays of information, as well as for the drafting and diffusion of brochures. DG-X's confinement to mundane tasks of institutional communication was masked by the integration of the Spokesman's Service within DG-X in 1977. From then on, DG-X was often directed by a very high-ranking political official (often a former Head or Deputy Head of Cabinet of a Commissioner) who paid particular attention to the management of the Spokesman's Service. The resilience of these traditional conceptions illustrates the low level of interest expressed by high-ranking officials and members of the Commissioners' college for the type of information-communication policy outlined by Rabier twenty years earlier. From the 1960s–1970s, each institution and each division of the Brussels administration set up its own communication service (Joana, Smith, 2000). As a result it gave a sectoral, fragmented character to the EC's information task, which fulfilled the Commission's aspirations for autonomy without dramatically challenging member states who were wary of open intervention in their public spaces.

DG-X's vocation is not to produce directives; it does not have the legitimacy conferred by the institutionalisation of a link with professional groups,[18] unlike other DGs where agents are involved in regular transactions and act as mediators between Brussels and 'the field'. For this reason, DG-X was perceived as weak within intra-institutional games, in contrast with the big 'historical' DGs such as Internal Market, Competition, Secretariat-General or Agriculture, which had more power (normative competences, 'clienteles'), means (budgets, human resources) and a reputation for competence (staff training and diplomas, close contact with political reality).[19]

However, this situation changed radically between 1985 and 1995 due to several congruent factors. First, a new configuration of relationships between member states and the Commission characterised the Delors Era. It contributed to increase the authority of the EC through the revival of the integration process, wider competences and increased political cooperation between member states (Maastricht Treaty), given the perspective of a vast enlargement following the collapse of the Soviet Bloc. In addition, Jacques Delors was highly interested in opinion issues. Delors's interest in opinion issues and communication can be explained mainly by his quest for success in his great endeavour: the advent of the Single Market in 1992 (Ross, 1995).

In 1988, the Commission developed the Priority Information Programmes (PIPs) in order to concentrate information-communication resources on priorities determined by the Commission. At the same time a '92 Market' information unit (notably in charge of the monthly *Objectif 92* magazine) was created within the DG-X. Remarkably, after a long struggle against DG-III (Internal Market), DG-X obtained the management of 'audiovisual policy' (Polo, 2001) and launched the first MEDIA programme (1991–95). As the Maastricht Treaty provided the EC with new competences in culture and audiovisual medias – within the limits of the subsidiarity principle – DG-X was for the first time in its history able to issue directives and negotiate with professionals and representatives of the major media firms of member countries. The political determination to improve communication, as well as the will to strengthen administrative resources, would find an opportunity for expression during the first real democratic 'crisis' of the European project.

The reinvention of 'European public opinion': instruments of opinion to face the 'democratic challenge'

In the early 1990s, a succession of events favoured the expression of this new voluntarism in EC communication. The Maastricht Treaty, which turned the EEC into the EU, was rejected in the June 1992 Denmark referendum[20] and was only accepted by a narrow margin by French voters in September.[21] The referendum's failure echoed the relative drop in 'public support for the EU' measured by the Eurobarometer since autumn 1991[22] and the chronically weak participation in European elections. At the same time, academics pointed to the 'half-hearted' support for Europe (Percheron, 1991) and the end of the 'permissive consensus' (Lindberg and Scheingold, 1970) for a European project driven by political elites (Feather, 1994). Without the support of the citizens of member countries, who had become European citizens with the ratification of the TEU, it would be difficult for the EU to confront the looming political challenges: economic and monetary union; integration of the former 'popular democracies'; and providing security for the European continent. The Commission seized the opportunity provided by the mounting grievances and controversies around the 'democratic challenge' to launch communication campaigns. In January 1993, Delors entrusted Portuguese Commissioner João de Deus Pinheiro with the Commission's communication policy. Around the same time, Belgian MEP Willy de Clercq was asked to write a report on EC communication. With the help of senior officials, such as the Director-General of DG-X Colette Flesh, and professionals of political communication, such as President Mitterrand and later Jacques Chirac's communications guru Jacques Pilhan, de Clercq interviewed numerous communication and media specialists. In March 1993, he came to an uncompromising conclusion of the shortcomings of EU policy:

> After many years of growing impatience, '1992' came and went in an enigmatic silence. Politicians and officials of European construction complain that they are misunderstood. However, they confine their communication efforts to formal, dry and rational information, apparently thinking that someone else will make their messages 'livelier' for the public. But journalists (who are essential mediators of communication) cannot turn boring information into engrossing news items. The main reason for this crisis situation lies in the fact that the

Commission and some of the member states are trying to 'sell' the wrong 'product'. The product that should be 'sold' to the public is not the Maastricht Treaty ... Trying to 'sell Maastricht' instead of selling the positive effects that the EU will have on everyone is a mistake. (de Clercq, 1993: 3–4)

There were mixed official reactions to the report due to the phrasing used to describe the course of action ('sell the good "product" to "target audiences"') and the solutions deemed necessary ('regain lost credibility', 'show the common sense and usefulness of the decisions', 'make the proposition relevant'). It did however have consequences, especially the on 'good instruments' such as the Eurobarometer which, better used, could be used to evaluate 'the changes in the public's awareness and attitude following information campaigns' (de Clerq, 1993: 37). The Eurobarometer tool, which up to that point had only been an experiment developed and debated by academics (see Box 10.1), became a factor of political exchanges and even a policy instrument.

Since the 1970s, every report, resolution and written question related to the information policy has recommended the extensive use of this tool. But due to the absence of a strong political will, the tool remained for a long time limited to biannual polls sponsored by the Commission providing a reflection of popular opinion towards Europe in member countries. Thanks to the stability of its methodology[23] and its frequency, the tool offers a longitudinal comparability which mostly interested specialists of opinion. The politicisation of the 'European opinion' issue however upset both the tool and its uses. The first indicator of this evolution is the increasing number of thematic *ad hoc* polls conducted at the request of particular DGs on specific issues (inflation, languages, energy policy, agricultural policy, single currency, etc.). 68 special Eurobarometers were conducted between 1974 and 1992 (i.e. 3.5 per year on average), whereas 219 were conducted between 1993 and 2007 (more than 14.5 per year). The second indicator is the appearance and subsequent multiplication of the Flash Eurobarometers. Conducted by phone, they can focus on a single country or category of people (CEOs, agricultural workers, youth). 235 surveys of this kind have been conducted at the time of writing. In addition, the European Continuous Tracking Survey (CTS) was launched between 1994 and 1997 in order to provide monthly monitoring based on 200 phone interviews in each member state. From 2001 onwards, 'qualitative surveys' were added based on the focus group method.

From the 1990s, the Eurobarometer tool was not only 'a valuable feedback element on what affects citizens the most',[24] but it was also a precious instrument for public policy. It enabled decision-makers to have a snapshot of opinion on a given question and to evaluate their leverage or windows of opportunity for a particular policy proposal, as well as develop campaigns directed to relevant audiences or to the general public. We can even say that in the political configuration and shifts in the structures of the institutional game between 1985 and 1995, the tool pursued three separate

Box 10.1   J.-R. Rabier, the entrepreneur and his entreprise

Former Head of Cabinet for Jean Monnet in the ECSC's High Authority, J.-R. Rabier became Director-General of the Information Service in 1960 until the latter was transformed into a Directorate-General in 1967. He was appointed as Director-General of DG-X in 1970 but was replaced by an Irish official after the first enlargement (1973). The new French President of the Commission, François-Xavier Ortoli, granted him the title of Honorary Director-General, which allowed him to remain a member of DG-X, where his mission was to systematise opinion polls on the integration process. With very few resources (he had only one agent at his disposal), he coordinated the Eurobarometer's biannual surveys until the mid 1980s, with the support of a small group of academics interested in the international comparison of political attitudes and values.

From the 1950s, Rabier was closely in touch with J. Stoetzel and Hélène Riffaut, specialists of opinion and heads successively of IFOP and the Faits et Opinions institute which was in charge of the Eurobarometer during the first fifteen years of its existence (from no. 0 to no. 31). A small team of researchers grew around them, mainly from the Political Science Department of the University of Geneva created in 1969. Along with Dujan Sidjanski, the founder and director of the department, there was a PhD student from Barcelona, Anna Melich (who would then be in charge of the Eurobarometer), and a young American political scientist from the University of Michigan, Ronald Inglehart, who was a visiting professor in Geneva in 1969–70, and who collaborated with Eurobarometer over several years. The tool's conception was strongly influenced by these researchers' scientific agenda, in particular by Inglehart who at the time was studying post-materialistic values and their effects on the attitudes of European populations (Inglehart, 1971). He played a crucial part in the construction of surveys and the elaboration of analytical indicators.[1] The links between Rabier and these academics led to a series of scientific publications (Rabier, 1964; Inglehart and Rabier, 1984; Reif and Inglehart, 1991).

1 R. Inglehart's theoretical model can be found in Inglehart, 1977.

goals which have contributed to the transformation of the *Community* information problem into the *European* opinion problem. The first goal is the symbolic creation of a 'European public opinion', i.e. an audience specific to Europe, expressing its expectations and fears about European decisions. The tool 'organically' produced the appearance of a transnational public opinion through powerful instruments of objectification such as numbers, percentages, statistical tables, and graphic representations (histograms, linear curves, pie charts, geographic representations, etc.).[25] The second objective is the justification of the ongoing supranational project. Without excessively pushing the orientation of the questions and the interpretation of the results, the tool induces an apparent desire for Europe among the pollees questioned on their agreement with positively connoted attitudes towards dialogue and cooperation between member states. The third underlying objective, related to the second, is the legitimisation of the Commission's increased communication effort vis-à-vis member states and the Parliament – the Commission being the only institution capable of responding to the lack of information on Europe recorded by Eurobarometer surveys (see Box 10.2). Seen in the light of the Eurobarometer results, the apathy of Europeans towards Europe was interpreted as the consequence of a lack of information, of communication, and thus presented as a problem which could be solved through an extension of the capacity of Brussels to 'talk' directly to the populations of member states.

From the 'information policy of the Communities' to the 'European communication policy'

Since the 1990s, Commission communication has made good use of its instruments and their intrinsic legitimacy. Without a clear legal foundation, the Commission's communication apparatus has acquired ever more sophisticated means and has became progressively desectorised, even giving up the traditional discourse of the duty to advertise political action in order to become a transversal repertoire of the EU's legitimisation task. Year after year, the functions – and therefore the technical, financial and human resources – attributed to the task of information have been officially requalified in terms of 'communication strategy'[26] and 'governance'. The 'governance' concept, officially theorised in a Commission White Paper (European Commission, 2001), links two logics: informational transparency and the participation of relevant citizens – stakeholders – in the decision-making process. The institutional theory of governance laid the foundations for a participatory shift in opinion management, later completed by the 'communication strategy' adopted by the Commission in 2002 (European Commission, 2002), and confirmed in subsequent programmes.[27]

Each European crisis has been the occasion for the Commission to increase its authority within the EU on the 'European opinion' problem. If the resignation of the Santer College in March 1999 temporarily weakened its capacity for action and initiative, the failure of the Rome II treaty (TEC) in the French (May 2005) and Dutch (June 2005) referendums paradoxically gave the Commission an opportunity to regain the upper hand. The results of these referendums immediately revived the debates on the 'democratic challenge' around a new imperative: 'closing the gap with citizens'. Even before the advent of this new crisis, President Barroso, while setting up his

Box 10.2   The structural pro-Europe effect of Eurobarometer surveys

Because of the biases in the formulation of the questions and the limited range of possible answers available, the famous 'trend questions' tend to artificially produce the existence of a 'European public opinion', as well as the idea of a strong adhesion to European integration. For example, the following question, used to measure the respondent's support to their country's adhesion to the EU – 'Taking everything into account, would you say that (our country) has on balance benefited or not from being a member of the European Union? Benefited – Not benefited – Don't Know' – has since 1974 invariably received 50% of positive answers or more.

More generally, the choice of words, the tone of the questions and the implicit alternative in the question create a pro-Europe effect on the latitude respondents have in their answers. The following question shows this effect: 'For each of the following areas, do you think that decisions should be made by the (national) government, or made jointly within the European Union? Fighting crime / Taxation / Fighting unemployment / Fighting terrorism / Defence and foreign affairs / Immigration / The educational system / Pensions / Protecting the environment.'

For such serious issues, clearly perceived as transnational (but not necessarily European), answers appear as an unconditional support for a common resolution implicating the EU. 79% of respondents believe that decisions on fighting terrorism should be made jointly within the EU, 71% for protecting the environment, 70% for scientific research, 64% for defence and foreign affairs, 62% for support to regions. The authors of Eurobarometer reports hastily claim that 'Europeans continue to favour decision-making at European level'.

Source: EB 69, Spring 2008.

College in November 2004, had expressed the wish that communication constitute a portfolio in its own right in order to favour the ratification of the TEC. This mandate – exceptional in the Commission's history – was entrusted to Swedish Commissioner Margot Wallström, symbolically appointed Vice-President of the Commission in charge of the 'communication strategy and inter-institutional relations'. The recognition of the Commission's role in the resolution of European opinion problems was made clear in the conclusions of the June 2005 council, which called for a 'period of reflexion to allow for a broad debate' on the future of the EU in which the Commission was mandated to lead a 'mobilising debate' on Europe. During summer 2005, it had already adopted texts recommending that DGs professionalise 'European communication' by systematically integrating public expectations, fears and perceptions, as well as communication goals (preparing budgets, planning and communication strategy) in the first stages of the chain of normative or legislative production. The *Action Plan to Improve Communicating Europe by the Commission* states:

> Commissioners and their DGs will insure that communication aspects are included right from the beginning of all policy formulation [...] Key proposals will be accompanied with a 'layperson's summary' explaining the personal and societal benefits of the policy. A communication plan will be prepared by the DG concerned when the topic so necessitates. Clear, simple and precise drafting of Commission proposals is essential if they are to be transparent, readily understandable and their rationale fully endorsable by citizens and business. 'Eurojargon' or 'Eurospeak' is confusing, complicated and often elitist. (European Commission, 2005a: 7)

A few months later, the 'Plan D' adopted in October 2005 by the Commission on M. Wallström's initiative announced the organisation of debates and participative forums throughout Europe and set up a new frame of action involving all partners of the European institutional game:

> Any vision of the future of Europe needs to build on a clear view of citizen's needs and expectations [...] The Commission will present a specific Eurobarometer survey on the future of Europe, assessing citizens' views on the future of the European project as well as citizens' support for and expectations of European policies and actions. (European Commission, 2005b: 2 and 10)

Beyond the calls for more rationality, coordination and professionalism, the Commission now possesses the authority to assess and address the problem of 'European communication'. It defines the objectives and the lines of action with its expert instruments. As we have seen, this shift is primarily the result of a gradual shift in perspective of the institutional framing of the opinion problem which took place in various stages mainly through a dramatisation of the supposed 'democratic deficit' and a changing use of the Eurobarometer. Following this line of thought, we can wonder if the White Paper on a European communication policy published in February 2006 by the Commission is a sign of a final evolution in this process of affirmation of Brussels' legitimate role in the communication within member states' public spaces, as one of the main proposals of the Commission suggests: 'Communication should become an EU policy in its own right, at the service of the citizens' (European Commission, 2006: 4). The reception of this proposal by other EU institutions has probably played a part in this White Paper's relative failure (Aldrin and Utard, 2008), temporarily sidetracking the proposal, at least until the next European crisis.

Notes

1 This article is based on archives of the EU and on interviews with the actors of the EU's communication policy.

2 By 'frames', we refer to the order of signification, the certainties, the concepts that guide discourses and actions of European actors. These frames can be identified in the phrasing and justification of action ('political', 'strategic', 'plan of action'). Frames can be used as prognoses, diagnoses and justifications for common principles of action. See Benford and Snow, 2000, and on political choices Rein and Schön, 1991.

3 On this general perspective, see Sabatier, 1998.

4 On the basis of the Dutch MEP Wilhelmus Schuijt's report (Schuijt, 1972).

5 For the 'creation of the Community's image', 'We can ask ourselves whether the possibility of renting airtime or newspaper space should be ruled out' (Schuijt, 1972: 18, 10).

6 The ratification of the Single European Act (1986) paved the way for the construction of the Single Market (1986–92), causing a considerable increase in legislative initiatives.

7 See 'Institutional Declaration on Democracy, Transparency, and Subsidiarity' (1993).

8 See the dispositions in the Maastricht and Amsterdam treaties to reinforce the EP's attributions.

9 On the useful distinction between a 'Community problem' and a 'European problem', see Smith, 2004.

10 Bino Olivi was put in charge of the Spokesman's Service of the unified Commission.

11 The Federal press office in FRG, the Central Office of Information in England and later on the *Service de liaison interministériel à l'information* in France.

12 Jean Stoetzel worked in New York with Paul Lazarsfeld's team and founded the (first) French Institute of Public Opinion (1938). He shed light on the American roots of his axiological and methodological approach to public opinion in Stoetzel, 1963.

13 Easton, 1957.

14 Numerous references are made to Lazarsfeld, Berelson and Gaudet, 1944.

15 We find here the theme of an 'alliance' between polls and democracy put forward by the American (Elmo Roper, George Gallup) and French (J. Stoetzel) advocates of the method (Blondiaux, 1998: 211–226).

16 *Products and People*, published by *The Reader's Digest Association* in 1963.

17 On the political predisposition index, see Lazarsfeld, Berelson and Gaudet, 1944.

18 On connections with 'client groups' as a power resource in the EU's sectoral bureaucracies, see Richardson, 1996.

19 The prosopographic study of the highest-ranking European officials shows that having worked in one of these 'historical' DGs confers 'institutional credit' to European careers (Georgakakis and de Lassalle, 2006).

20 50.4% voted against the ratification of the TEU.

21 Only 51.04% of votes were cast in favour of the TEU, with more than 30% abstentions.

22 See Eurobarometer 36, 1991.

23 Some questions have remained almost unchanged since 1974, hence their labelling as 'trend' questions. Along with other questions, they act as indicators on the 'climate of opinion'.

24 Jorge de Oliveira e Sousa, Director-General of DG Press and Communication, in 2003.

25 This 'reality effect' is produced by the method and the modelling it enables

(Bourdieu, 1984: 222). Moreover, the theme imposed (Europe) increases the 'feeling of incompetence' of the pollees with the remote, abstract character ('disconnected from everyday issues') of the problems posed and the political bias of the questions (Bourdieu, 1979: 466–467).

26 See de Clercq, 1993.

27 This procedural legitimisation contrasts with the analysis that limits the EU's capacity of legitimisation to its outputs, thus caught in a 'negative integration' trap which makes it more efficient in the correction and harmonisation of national policies, especially market distortions, than in the elaboration of new public policies (Scharpf, 1999).

Bibliography

Aldrin, P. and Utard, J.-M., 'The Ambivalent Politicisation of European Communication. Genesis of the Controversies and Institutional Frictions Surrounding the 2006 White Paper', *GSPE Working Papers*, 10/2008 (http://prisme.u-strasbg.fr/workingpapers /WPAldrinUtard.pdf).

Baget Bozzo, G., *Rapport sur la politique d'information de la Communauté européenne*, Parlement européen, A 2–111/86, 1986.

Baisnée, O., 'Les relations entre la Commission et le Corps de presse accrédité auprès de l'Union européenne: crise en renouvellement des pratiques', *Pôte Sud*, 15, 2001.

Benford, R. and Snow, D., 'Frame Processes and Social Movements: An Overview and Assessment', *Annual Review of Sociology*, 26, 2000.

Blondiaux, L., *La fabrique de l'opinion. Une histoire sociale des sondages*, Paris: Seuil, 1998.

Blumler, J., 'Three Ages of Political Communication', *Revue de l'institut de sociologie Bruxelles*, 1–2, 1995, 31–45.

Bourdieu, P., *La Distinction. Critique sociale du jugement*, Paris: Minuit, 1979.

Bourdieu, P., 'L'opinion publique n'existe pas', in Bourdieu, P., *Questions de sociologie*, Paris: Minuit, 1984, 222–235.

de Clerq, W., *Réflexion sur la politique d'information et de communication de la Communauté européenne*, Bruxelles: édité par la Commission européenne, 1993.

Dobry, M., *Sociologie des crises politiques, La dynamique des mobilisations multisectorielles*, Paris: Presses de la Fondation nationale des Sciences politiques, 1986.

Easton, D., 'An Approach to The Analysis of Political Systems', *World Politics*, 9 (3), 1957, 383–400.

European Commission, *Gouvernance européenne. Un livre blanc*, COM(2001) 428 final.

European Commission, *Une stratégie d'information et de communication pour l'Union européenne*, COM(2002) 50 final/2.

European Commission, *Plan d'action relatif à l'amélioration de la communication sur l'Europe*, Bruxelles: OPCE, 2005a.

European Commission, *Contribution de la Commission à la période de réflexion et au-delà. Le Plan D, comme Démocratie, Dialogue et Débat*, IP/05/1272, 2005b.

European Commission, *White Paper on a European Communication Policy*, COM(2006) 35.

European Parliament, *Rapport sur les problèmes de l'information dans les communautés européennes* (doc. 89), 1960.

Feather, K., 'Jean Monnet and the "Democratic Deficit" in the European Union', *Journal of Common Market Studies*, 32 (2), 1994, 149–170.

Georgakakis, D., La *République contre la propagande. Aux origines perdues de la communication d'Etat en France 1917–1940*, Paris: Economica, 2004.

Georgakakis, D. and de Lassalle, M., 'Genèse et structure d'un capital institutionnel européen. Les très hauts fonctionnaires de la Commission européenne', *Actes de la Recherche en Sciences sociales*, 2007, 166–167.

Haas, E., *The Uniting of Europe. Political, Social, and Economic Forces 1950–1957*, Stanford: Stanford University Press, 1958.

Inglehart, R., 'The Silent Revolution in Europe: Intergenerational Change in Post-Industrial Societies', *American Political Science Review* 65 (4), 1971, 991–1017.

Inglehart, R., *The Silent Revolution. Changing Values and Political Styles Among Western Publics*, Princeton: Princeton University Press, 1977.

Inglehart, R. and Rabier, J.-R., 'La confiance entre les peuples: déterminants et conséquences', *Revue française de science politique*, Année 34 (1), 1984, 5–47.

Joana, J. and Smith, A., *Les commissaires européens. Technocrates, diplomates ou politiques?*, Paris: Presses de Sciences Po, 2002.

Kingdon, J., *Agendas, Alternatives, and Public Policies*, Boston: Little Brown, 1984.

Lascoumes, P. and Le Galès, P. (eds), *Gouverner par les instruments*, Paris: Presses de Sciences Po, 2004.

Lazarsfeld, P., Berelson, B. and Gaudet, H., *The People's Choice*, New York: Columbia University Press, 1944.

Lazarsfeld, P. and Katz, E., *Personal Influence: The Part Played by People in the Flow of Mass Communications*, Glencoe, IL: The Free Press, 1955.

Lindberg, L. and Scheingold, S., *Europe's Would Be Policy. Patterns of Change in The European Community*, Englewood Cliffs: Prentice Hall, 1970.

Manin, B., *The Principles of Representative Government*, Cambridge: Cambridge University Press, 1996.

Marquant, D., *Parliament for Europe*, London: Jonathan Cape, 1979.

Ollivier-Yaniv, C., *L'État communiquant*, Paris: Presses Universitaires de France, 2000.

Percheron, A., 'Les Français et l'Europe: acquiescement de façade ou adhésion véritable? Note de recherche', *Revue française de science politique*, 41 (3), 1991.

Peters, G., 'Bureaucratic Politics and the Institutions of European Community', in A. Sbragia, (ed.), *Euro-Politics, Institutions and Policy-Making in the 'New' European Community*, Washington: The Brookings Institutions, 1992, 75–122.

Pierson, P., 'The Path to European Integration: A Historical Institutionalist Analysis', *Comparative Political Studies*, XXIX, 1996.

Polo, J.-F., 'La relance de la politique audiovisuelle européenne: les ressources politiques et administratives de la DG X', *Pôle Sud*, 15, 2001, 5–17.

Rabier, J.-R., 'Comment les peuples européens se voient et voient les autres', *Revue de psychologie des peuples*, 1, 1964, 22–32.

Rabier, J.-R., 'L'information des Européens et l'intégration de l'Europe', Institut d'études européennes, Université libre de Bruxelles, document reprographié, 1965.

Rabier J.-R., 'La naissance d'une politique d'information sur la Communauté européenne (1952–1967)', in F. Dasseto and M. Dumoulin (eds), *Naissance et développement de l'information européenne*, Berne: Peter Lang, 1993, 21–32.

Reif, K. and Inglehart, R., (eds), *Eurobarometer. The Dynamics of European Public Opinion. Essays in Honour of Jacques-René Rabier*, London: Palgrave, 1991.

Rein, M. and Schön, D., 'Frame-Reflective Policy Discourse', in Wagner P. et al. (eds), *Social Sciences and Modern States. National Experiences and Theoretical Crossroads*, Cambridge: Cambridge University Press, 1991, 262–269.

Richardson, J. (ed.), *European Union. Power and Policy-Making*, London: Routledge, 1996.

Ross, G., *Jacques Delors and European Integration*, Cambridge: Polity Press, 1995.

Sabatier, P., 'The Advocacy Coalitions Framework. Revisions and Relevance for Europe', *Journal of European Public Policy*, 5, 1998, 98–130.

Scharpf, F., *Governing in Europe. Efficient and Democratic*, Oxford: Oxford University Press, 1999.

Schuijt, W., *Rapport sur la politique d'information des Communautés européennes,* Commission politique du Parlement européen (246/71), 1972.

Smith, A. (ed.), *Politics and the European Commission,* London: Routledge, 2004.

Stoetzel, J., *La psychologie sociale,* Paris: Flammarion, 1963.

Romuald Normand

11

Expert measurement in the government of lifelong learning

The European lifelong learning policy has been the object of many studies in the international research literature. The different sequences of the European political agenda have been closely scrutinised since the European Commission White Paper 'Teaching and Learning – Towards a Cognitive Society' was published in 1996. Scholars have since described the different cycles of negotiations between the Commission and member states, and policy implementation following the European Council's conclusions or those adopted by the Ministers of Education during their successive meetings in Lisbon, Bologna or Copenhagen. Their reading does not differ much from those of the Directorate-General for Education and Culture (DG EAC) in explaining the success or failure of a particular recommendation or directive and its implementation (Ceri Jones, 2005; Green and Leney, 2005). However, some researchers seek to distance themselves from the Commission's online texts, reports, and documents, to offer a meta-analysis of its political rhetoric and to reveal concepts related to a neo-liberal ideology (Mahieu and Moens, 2003; Cusso, 2005). Some have suggested that the actors of this European policy – experts and policy-makers – circulate in transnational spaces and share the same principles (Lawn and Lingard, 2002).

Only recently has research focused on statistical features of the European construction of education and training, especially the role played by indicators (Dale, 2006; Lingard and Ozga, 2007). This is part of a larger research agenda centred on instrument-driven public action and the institutionalisation of knowledge systems and new forms of collective action (Lascoumes and Le Galès, 2004). Pioneering works have demonstrated the importance of public statistics in the building of different modes of government and types of representations of society (Hacking, 1990; Desrosières, 1993; Porter, 1995). In parallel, the Actor-Network Theory (ANT) and science and technology studies have shown the importance of social representations in the measurement activity of researchers, as well as the effects of scientific activity on the arts of government (Latour, 1987; Callon, 1989; Rosental, 2003). European government also includes a policy of formatting information even in the area of education and training (Thévenot, 2007). This involves building standards for classification, codifying practice and creating instruments of objective measurement around particular forms of information and knowledge. Far from being neutral, this policy contains moral and political implications in terms of justice, in the sense that it shifts the scales of definition of the common good from the regulatory state to more transnational modes of coordination (Thévenot, 2001; Boltanski and Thévenot, 2006).

However, this European process of standardisation does not automatically imply a standardisation of education and training policies in each member state. The idea of a convergence or harmonisation of European educational systems is debated within the educational research community. Some researchers claim European construction is part of a larger globalisation movement which mobilises diverse actors and multiple levels of regulation and governance (Novoa and Lawn, 2002). At the European level, the subsidiarity principle apparently gives leeway to member states for the implementation of Commission directives and recommendations. Other studies argue that national and local contexts, fearing a hegemonic imposition from above, constitute solid obstacles to further European integration in education (Dale, 2000; Antunes, 2006). In all cases, since the Lisbon strategy was launched and the Open Method of Coordination adopted, EU member states have adopted common principles for the convergence of their education and training systems.

This harmonisation is not a legislative regulation and it would be false to consider it as a process tending towards binding supranational legal norms. In fact, the European harmonisation of education and training policies is built step by step, with failures and successes, but also with compromises between states following different cycles of negotiation. But what observers often overlook is that these procedures have been accompanied by often irreversible measurement instruments designed by international expert networks. A new metrology (new conventions and tools related to the measurement of education and training) has progressively taken root at the heart of policy-making. It is part of a method of government which remains under the responsibility of member States but closely associates the Commission's internal operations management, and networks of actors involved in European education and training programmes.

It is the articulation between instruments of measurement, a European government, and international expertise that I would like to describe in this chapter. Empirically, the analysis developed here rests not only on a careful reading of official reports from the European Commission but also on a detailed study of technical documents, a source neglected by all but statisticians. In addition, data were analysed with Pajek software to map the main actors and international networks involved in measurement expertise. The mapping reveals a number of epistemic communities that contribute to designing instruments at European and international levels. Finally, my participation in a series of international meetings as an expert has also provided food for thought.

Nomenclatures, classifications and statistical indicators: a European metrology

The harmonisation of statistical information systems at the European level is arduous at best because of the profound structural differences between national educational systems (West, 2003). Statistical data are heterogeneous and are produced in different ways. The International Standard Classification of Education (ISCED) designed by UNESCO in 1997 aspired to contribute to the development of international comparisons but was poorly fitted to the European Commission's ambitions. Similarly, the OECD's international indicators only partially meet the requirements for the coordination of education and training policies across Europe. In fact, the production of European statistics is subject the essential requirements of metrological realism (Desrosières, 2003) which forces statisticians to design measurement instruments that are the least biased possible, relevant, reliable and accessible to potential users such as policy-makers and stakeholders in a public discussion. However, as suggested below, these European statistics shape a particular representation of education and training in relating technical instruments (nomenclatures, classifications, indicators) to new categories of knowledge and action within the lifelong learning policy.

The harmonisation of statistical classifications and nomenclatures
In their study on the International Classification of Diseases managed by the WHO, Geoffrey Bowker and Susan Leigh Star suggested that lists are a very effective means to coordinate information and practice widely distributed across time and space (Bowker and Star, 1999). But classification schemes and statistical nomenclatures lead to conflicting definitions because the different stakeholders – civil servants, statisticians, experts, researchers – invest them with different values and political conceptions. These systems are the result of a permanent negotiation and evolution and depend not only on the resolution of technical problems but also on the will to better reflect reality. Classifications and nomenclatures are technologies which impose universal categories by ordering information gathered from very heterogeneous areas of social practice. Three examples in the area of education and training will illustrate this point.

The 2001 'Report of the Eurostat Task Force on Measuring Lifelong

Learning' identified the principles of a statistical classification of learning activities related to formal, non-formal, and informal education (Eurostat 2001). This classification has since been used in a handbook published by Eurostat's Education and Culture unit (Eurostat 2006). Lifelong learning is regarded as an intentional activity performed by young or adult individuals to improve their knowledge and skills in a more or less formalised environment. *Formal education*, the first statistical category, characterises intentional learning on the basis of a set schedule and duration in a hierarchical structure with successive course levels and enrolment requirements within established educational institutions. *Non-formal education*, the second statistical category, includes all types of learning activities on a teacher–student(s) basis, occurring not necessarily with spatial or temporal proximity. The last category, *informal learning*, corresponds to self-learning within the family, in the workplace or in everyday life.

According to Eurostat, the UNESCO-designed international classification – ISCED97 – is helpful to classify formal and non-formal education but it fails to cover all lifelong learning categories. The classification promoted by Eurostat aims to measure the time and money spent in learning and to combine these data with information gathered on informal learning as perceived by individuals. As of 2001, Eurostat departments planned surveys on how individuals invested their spare time in learning (Time use surveys) and on its share of household budgets (Household budget surveys). Time use surveys ask respondents to estimate the average time spent in activities as varied as attending seminars, conferences and exhibitions, use of a computer and the Internet, listening to the radio or watching TV, or learning with colleagues or friends. In parallel, household budget surveys collect information on the personal financial investment devoted to learning. Data collection should ideally be extended to both private individuals and companies in order to cover all lifelong learning categories. For Eurostat, these data should be oriented towards learners and take into account all forms of formal, non-formal and informal knowledge acquisition.

The second example concerns the review of the architecture of qualifications at the European level (Deane, 2005). For Eurostat statisticians, the classification of learning activities is closely related to the classification of qualifications. The Commission has for several years argued for the accreditation of non-formal and informal learning and has encouraged member states to adopt common principles and procedures. The idea is to link the accreditation of learning to the expression of individual rights via a capitalisable credit transfer system. In 2006, The European Qualifications Framework (EQF) laid the foundations for the accreditation, transfer, and recognition of formal, non-formal and informal skills. This accreditation is regarded as a process leading to the identification, assessment and recognition of a comprehensive range of skills that individuals develop throughout their lives in different areas (education, work, leisure). It is based on learning outcomes, standards from which assessments are designed, and a procedure to define the criteria of validation. For formal education, they take the form of exams or tests. For informal education, accreditation hinges on interviews with individuals, the building of a skills portfolio, skills check-ups, observations or simulations of an activity, evidence of professional practices, etc. This relation between the classification of learning activities and the classification of qualifications reduces the centrality of diplomas in the validation of skills. It also marks a deep transformation of how certification is perceived and represented.

Consequently, there have been intense discussions under Eurostat leadership to create a new nomenclature of professions at the European level. This classification has been directed by several statistical agencies (UK, Sweden, and the Netherlands) and is inspired by the work of two sociologists – Erikson and Goldthorpe (Erikson and Goldthorpe, 1992). It has had profound consequences in several national contexts, for example in France where the nomenclature of *Professions et Catégories SocioProfessionnelles* (PCS) was the result of a social and political compromise which related the definition of occupations to the recognition of skills and the certification of qualifications by the state (Desrosières and Thévenot, 1988). This nomenclature also contributed to a particular statistical representation of professional groups in linking the nomenclature to collective conventions and to a typically French conception of equal opportunities in education.

This new European nomenclature rests on principles that are different from traditional French statistical data collection (Brousse, 2007). It identifies and distinguishes two forms of employment – 'service relationship' and 'labour contracts' – inspired by the British model. In this nomenclature, workers hold different social positions according to the degree of subordination to their employers, hence two main types of contracts: on one side, workers in a strict subordinate relationship and on the other side those who are in a more flexible, informal, and autonomous relationship with their employers. Under the 'labour contract', employment is characterised by the completion of tasks over relatively short periods of time on piece or time rate with no social protection. This classification is marked by flexibility and low job security. The other employment relationship corresponds to an exchange of services over a long period, greater job security, higher employability, payment in the form of a wage, and possibly social insurance.

The European nomenclature is divided into nine classes which reflect different employment relationships. At the top (Class 1), there are highly skilled and qualified individuals (entrepreneurs, professionals, etc.) and at the bottom (Class 9) individuals with little human capital who perform simple execution tasks (cleaners, drivers, packers, etc.). Class 2 features lower-ranking executives and managers (including teachers), Class 6 corresponds to 'supervisors', i.e. mid-rank workers who perform some management tasks; Class 7 gathers office employees and Class 8 skilled workers. In a word, individuals are classified along their positions in a management hierarchy and their proximity with executive power, and not according to collective bargaining conventions or a civil servant status. Similarly, the divide between the employed and the self-employed is particularly transformed just as the categories of workers and employees are revised to be extended or combined. Finally, company managers hold a dominant position within the classification. Despite criticism from some experts about the methodological and epistemological questions that this new nomenclature raises, over the past several years it has structured cooperation between national statistics agencies working towards a harmonisation process at the European level. Statistical classifications of jobs, qualifications, and learning are combined and contribute to the complete shift from the traditional forms of the training–employment relationship to a lifelong training policy with new requirements for wage earners: individual responsibility, accountability, individual contractualisation, flexibility and mobility (Boltanski and Chiapello, 2007).

European indicators, comparisons, and international surveys

Another form of convergence of education and training systems lies in the progressive design of European lifelong learning indicators largely inspired by the OECD while at the same time diverting its founding principles (Normand, 2004; Bottani, 2006). The OECD started developing indicators in the early 1970s in order to produce cost–benefit analyses as well as assess teaching and learning outcomes. The interest in these educational indicators was linked to the Programming Planning Budgeting System, a tool for the rationalisation of public expenditures. Within the OECD's Education Committee, experts presented performance indicators on knowledge and value transmission, equal opportunities, social mobility, the satisfaction of economic needs and individual development. However, this initiative did not succeed because of the profound disagreements between member states.

It was not until the 1990s that a global network of experts was structured around the INES (International Indicators of Education Systems) project with the support of the USA's National Center for Education Statistics and the OECD. The objective was to enhance the effectiveness and equity of educational systems through the development of a system of international comparisons likely to foster cooperation and exchange of best practices (Hutmacher, Cochrane and Bottani, 2001). Albert Tuijnman, one of the contributors to the project and has since contributed to the European Commission's thinking on the design of lifelong learning measurement instruments (Tuijnman, 2003). According to this economist, the development of skills implies a distribution of scarce resources in a learning process designed to produce skills. This process is based on a mathematical model linking inputs (physical, financial, human capital) to outputs (measurement of success in different skills, values and attitudes).

Lifelong learning represents a sort of insurance policy minimising 'market risks' related to uncertain costs and risks of the investment in human capital. Using the categories of non-formal and informal learning, Tuijnman considers that it is important to develop a systematic knowledge of skills acquisition and of the allocation of qualifications among the working population in order to devise a pertinent policy of human resource development. He regrets that the skills of the labour force cannot be directly observed, that statisticians and researchers resort to approximations, and that conventional measures of achievement remain imperfect because they are said to impede a genuine measurement of human capital. He recommends a skills-based approach at the heart of the European statistical system as a prerequisite to progress in the European lifelong learning policy.

In his eyes, the European statistical system has to confront five major challenges. First, it has to measure the learning process to reform instruction in formal education. The second challenge is to develop more adequate statistics to cover all aspects of lifelong learning, especially those related to courses offered, funding, recruitment, diplomas, adult education and further vocational training. The third challenge concerns the measurement of the cumulative effects of formal, non-formal, and informal learning activities on the indicators of human, financial, and social capital through a longitudinal approach. Tuijnman also recommends the end of UNESCO's ISCED monopoly because he deems it too oriented towards educational programmes and unable to take into account the variety of learning contexts and the flexibility of the labour market. Finally, he advocates the development of international surveys for the direct measurement of skills (following the example of the International Adult Literacy Survey (IALS) or the Programme for International Student Assessment (PISA)) that would enable policymakers to use data to build and maintain adult skills.

Some of the statistical data gathered by international organisations were instrumental in defining an architecture which new measurement instruments for education and training policies built on. They constitute an epistemological framework shared by human capital economists and school effectiveness researchers seeking to identify the effects of context, input, output and process in educational systems (Scheerens, 1995; Fitz-Gibbon, 2004). In linking quality to a measurement of performance, these studies legitimise the development of benchmarking procedures which allow the comparison of standards and practices between countries (Scheerens and Hendricks, 2004). The European Commission, in cooperation with Eurostat, the OECD and UNESCO, has defined comparison indicators used in the Open Method of Coordination and a task force on the measurement of lifelong learning has worked for several years to improve existing tools (EC, 2000, 2001, 2002, 2004, 2005).

The central role played by international comparisons such as PISA in the implementation of this European government of education and training could come as a surprise in the light of their substantial shortcomings (Normand, 2003). Despite their flaws, these data are nonetheless considered by the economists of human capital as a direct measurement of labour productivity. According to them, education enhances the human capital and hence the productivity of the labour force. It fosters innovation and the production of new knowledge necessary to economic growth. Hanushek and Wössman, prominent spokesmen of this economic paradigm, have argued that these large international surveys provided a significant statistical and economic measurement of the quality of education (Hanushek and Wössmann, 2007). The measurement of individual cognitive skills seems more effective to them, in terms of impact on economic growth, than the quantity of additional resources that educational systems may provide.

In consequence, they believe that supply policies – a lower number of students per class, improved pay for teachers, further school expenditure – are unlikely to improve performance. In their eyes, the quality of teachers is the essential factor in improving the performance of educational systems. Similarly, more school choice and financial incentive schemes are identified as influential factors. Efficient markets are also seen as a good means to improve the effectiveness of educational systems and individual skills. Fiercer competition, more power given to parents as consumers, more autonomy given to school managers and accountability to identify performing schools should lead to improved teaching quality. An attentive reader will have recognised the promotion of accountability and standards policies implemented in the USA from the publication of the report *A Nation at Risk* (1983) to the No Child Left Behind Act of 2001 (Normand, 2005). This does not come as a surprise, as Eric Hanushek is a member of the Hoover Institution, a think tank which has supported New Right policies in the area of education. He and Ludger Wössman are also influential spokesmen of the European Expert Network on Economists of Education, a think tank sponsored by DG EAC to help policy-makers formulate recommendations for member states.

The Open Method of Coordination: networks of experts and governance based on measurement instruments

We have so far characterised the epistemology behind the building of a new European statistical architecture in education and training. It suggests that the human capital paradigm plays a crucial role and that the equation between initial training, diploma-based qualifications, and occupational position have been revised along a neo-liberal line promoting a contract-based approach and individual rights. Equity is not absent from the reflection of DG EAC and has indeed led to the building of specific indicators to combine both competitiveness and social cohesion (Demeuse and Baye, 2007). However, this conception is essentially centred on outcomes, as promoted by international comparisons like PISA under a metrology measuring the effectiveness of national education systems, even if issues of gender, ethnicity, and handicap inequalities, special needs and social inclusion have been progressively introduced (Tomlinson, 2001; Ball, 2007). But, as we will see below, the demographic challenge is equally important for the European Commission in the design of their lifelong learning policy. It is reminiscent of the concerns of policy-makers in the 1950s who wished to feed economic growth by increasing the talent reserve, thereby contributing to the emergence of an arithmetic of inequality measurement and an unprecedented expansion of secondary and higher education (Normand, 2007). However this policy is now aligned with the European Employment Strategy (EES) based on a specific indicator – the employment rate (and not the unemployment rate) – seeking to encourage member states to a greater mobilisation of their labour force. The lifelong learning policy is largely embedded in a knowledge-centred policy extended to the areas of employment, social welfare, and research, mobilising networks of experts in the quest for a legitimate evidence-based policy (Normand, 2006).

The European political agenda for 2020: demographic challenges

While the European lifelong training policy is central to the Lisbon strategy, it is also linked to a particular conception of demographic challenges that member states are expected to face by 2020. The first challenge concerns the ageing of the working-age population. Eurostat's forecasts suggest that the number of children under 14 will decrease by 15 million in the 25 EU member states considered at the time of the study (Eurostat 2007). During the same period of time, the 55–64-year-old population will increase by 4 million while the number of those aged 80 and over will double between 2005 and 2050. According to experts close to the Commission, this situation will lead to the reduction of the working-age population and to a rise in the number of pensioners. It is therefore deemed necessary to adjust educational and training systems at all levels through a complete review of how resources are allocated, especially between public and private sectors or between urban and rural areas, in order to make them more efficient. It also implies targeting policy towards the increasing numbers of older workers.

An ageing population may indeed affect the labour supply and the employment rate, two items at the heart of the Lisbon strategy. The human capital theory (whose premises are accepted by DG EAC) holds that investing in the training of older workers is a powerful lever to boost their productivity and to retain them in employment. According to DG EAC experts, postponing the legal retirement age may also encourage this population to invest in their own training without raising public expenditure, as they are less likely to face financial problems than younger workers. Experts close to DG EAC are also concerned with ageing teachers because they are regarded as one of the key factors in improving educational quality. The ageing of this population implies updating their skills, while retirement will bring about shortages that will have to be compensated for by extensive recruitment and training.

Emigration is another challenge, particularly of young graduates to the USA. This brain drain is considered a threat to European competitiveness at a time when a knowledge economy is Europe's ultimate objective. One of the Commission's objectives is to attract the best talents and build poles of excellence as part of its higher education and research policy (Corbett, 2005). The economic development of China and South-East Asia raises additional fears as a qualified labour force is in great demand there.

Raising labour skills in a globalised economy marks another commitment of European policy. DG EAC pays particular attention to reducing the rate of early dropouts, especially among working-class and immigrant children. It is also deemed crucial to provide a quality educational environment in early life as it later on contributes to improving workers' ability to learn throughout their lives, according to human capital economists. They argue that it is in the first school years that educational rates of return are highest. The mobility of workers and students within the EU is equally crucial in enhancing the overall quality of the labour force. Finally, the Commission also seeks to favour the promotion of women in scientific or technological disciplines where they are underrepresented.

Indicators and benchmarking policy

The Open Method of Coordination is an additional step towards setting up a measurement instruments-based European educational and training policy (Ertl, 2006). Education ministers showed interest in quality indicators during the Prague meeting in 1998 and agreed to set up a working committee of national experts in charge of developing a limited number of indicators and benchmarks in addition to the assessments of educational systems at the national level. This committee, chaired by Anders Hingel, then head of the 'educational policy' unit at DG EAC, was responsible for identifying comparative fields between countries, exchanging experiences, mapping good practice, and defining policy orientations (Hingel, 2001). The report *Sixteen Quality Indicators for Educational Systems* published in May 2000 argued for the necessary definition of indicators and performance thresholds in order to provide policy-makers with recommendations on knowledge, decentralisation, resource management, social inclusion and data comparison. The report specified that benchmarking was expected to provide insight on the performance of educational systems at the local, regional and national levels.

However these benchmarking instruments only became effective when the Lisbon European Council launched the Open Method of Coordination (OMC), seeking to promote a global and coherent strategy for lifelong learning. The OMC has been the opportunity for the Commission to make recommendations to member states and to set a timetable for the implementation of reforms in education and training. This new method makes it possible to compare the performance of member states with international rivals, and evaluate progress on the basis of periodic reporting and peer-assessment. It attenuates the rigidity of the subsidiarity principle as the EU can set specific targets and exert normative pressure on member states through the use of league tables, indicators measuring progress towards different targets, comparisons to a European average, the average of the top three countries, or comparisons with the performance of the USA and Japan.

Let us now examine these instruments more closely. The indicators and benchmarks are centred around eight policy domains, each being related to one or more indicators: making education and training fairer; promoting efficiency in education and training; making lifelong learning a reality; mastering key skills for the youth; modernising school education; modernising vocational education and training; modernising higher education; improving employability. At first, this categorisation seems to be an attempt to modernise education and training but in fact it is really focused on economic objectives. In order to understand the scope of these indicators, it is necessary to place them in relation to demographic challenges and to the employment strategy, which strongly contribute to orienting the lifelong learning policy.

In this light, participation in pre-school education (equity) and the completion rate for upper secondary education (lifelong learning) are aimed at boosting the productivity of young people until they reach adulthood. Similarly, investments in education and training (efficiency and modernisation) and the returns in terms of employability are inspired by human capital theories. The participation of adults in lifelong learning and skills development reflects the objective of sustaining the productivity of older workers. The educational attainment of the population, the rate of higher education graduates and transnational mobility of students (modernising higher education) translate the Commission's desire to develop and strengthen the reserve of talents in the context of global competition. The indicators of literacy in reading, mathematics, science, ICT, etc. (key skills for young people) fulfil the needs for international comparisons of educational achievement, regarded by economists as the appropriate measurement of productivity and the quality of educational systems.

Five benchmarks have also been set as part of the OMC and presented as targets to be reached by 2010: the proportion of early school-leavers should be limited to 10%; 85% of young people should complete upper secondary education; 12.5% of the adult population should participate in lifelong learning. The number of low-achieving 15-year-olds in reading is to be reduced by at least 20% as compared to the 2000 level. The number of university graduates in mathematics, science and technology is targeted for a 15% increase over the same period. These benchmarks, just as the indicators above, suggest that they correspond to the Commission's concerns over demography and labour supply. However, the Commission has progressively noted in successive reports that progress towards the achievement of these objectives has been slow. These documents nonetheless show that the development of indicators and the collection of statistical data are now part and parcel of policy-making.

Expertise networks and evidence-based policies: a connexionist Leviathan

As expressed by Giandomenico Majone's 'regulating state' concept, Europe is a supranational entity because it breaks away from two basic principles of the nation-state – the redistribution or transfer of resources from one group to another and the preservation of satisfying levels of economic growth, inflation rates and employment (Majone, 1996). He specifies that the European Leviathan can be analysed as a network of more or less independent regulatory agencies that strive to compensate market imperfections or failures; European legislation guaranteeing the security and health protection of consumers or the environment are cases in point. However the network metaphor may fall short of explaining the characteristics of the European government. Andrew Barry suggested that it is necessary to take into account the connections between technological areas beyond national frontiers because they produce transferable standards or measurement instruments bridging space or time (Barry, 2001). This standardisation process, whether it applies to statistical items or to other technologies, remains essential to the harmonisation of European policy and to the construction of a 'space of calculation'. Therefore European institutions do not have sole command of the harmonisation process. The European Commission delegates responsibilities to other actors by accepting that standards and measurement instruments develop on a voluntary basis (Thévenot, 1995). The harmonisation process does not give rise to a centralised European government but relies on scattered institutions and agencies both in the public and private sectors such as research laboratories, expert groups or networks, standardisation committees or ministerial departments (Borraz, 2004).

The Centre for Research on Lifelong Learning (CRELL) provides a striking example. This centre, based in Ispra (Northern Italy), was set up by DG EAC's statistical unit to develop indicators and benchmarks for member states to make progress on the Lisbon objectives at a time when the Commission reported insufficient progress. CRELL econometrists and statisticians are high-level experts who have already worked for the Commission or major international organisations or sometimes have an affinity with human capital economists. There are also close links between CRELL and EENEE (the European Expert Network on Economics of Education) set up by DG EAC. CRELL provides its expertise to DG EAC and helps prepare their annual reports, and write briefs that, in turn, DG EAC uses with its groups of experts. CRELL also organises seminars, conferences or workshops specialised in the measurement of lifelong learning in cooperation with the OECD. EENEE is a European think tank created by the European Commission to improve decision-making in education and training policies at the European level. Led by Ludger Wössmann, it provides advice and supports the European Commission in analysing economic aspects of policies and reforms. These experts have also worked for other international organisations: the World Bank, OECD, UNESCO, etc.

CRELL is also coordinated by the EC's Joint Research Centre (JRC). JRC management is placed under the aegis of the European Commissioner for research and consists of institutes spread all over Europe. JRC is in charge of bringing scientific support to research programmes aligned with European policies in fields as varied as environment, health, energy, technology, conducting materials, etc. JRC considers that econometric and statistical tools are essential to assess the efficiency of European policies in areas such as growth, competitiveness, internal market and education. Building on the competences it has developed in data analysis, modelling and information quality, it claims its effective contribution to statistics, macro-economic modelling, financial econometrics, knowledge and multi-criteria social assessment.

CRELL is hosted by the Econometrics and Applied Statistics Unit which belongs to one of the JRC's networked institutes: the Institute for the Protection and Security of the Citizen (IPSC). The Econometrics and Applied Statistics Unit is in charge of developing econometric tools for the analysis and assessment of European policies in conjunction with several DGs (Economic and Financial Affairs, Internal Market and Services, Research, Information Society and Media, Enterprise and Industry). The mission of the Institute for the Protection and Security of the Citizen (IPSC) is to provide research results and to support EU policy-makers in their effort towards global security and towards protection of European citizens from accidents, deliberate attacks, fraud and illegal actions. To that end, it develops information technologies and sophisticated engineering systems for the development of international data analyses.

This transformation in the modes of production of knowledge makes the frontiers between expertise and research more porous. It involves new actors, especially technicians, engineers and policy-makers as well as new institutions and agencies that are more distant from academic research (Gibbons, 1994; Derouet and Normand, 2008). This new organisation extends to educational research policies at the international level (OECD 2007; EC 2007). It is endorsed by DG EAC that has set three challenges in the promotion of an evidence-based knowledge policy in education and training: the production of scientific knowledge based on the collection and analysis of quality data, implementation of evidence-based knowledge by policy-makers and practitioners, especially through capacity building, and mediation between knowledge production and knowledge application.

DG EAC policy is actually based on a number of programmes tested in several English-speaking countries (New Zealand, the USA and the UK) and research conducted by a number of international networks under the umbrella of the OECD's Centre for Educational Research and Innovation. This evidence-based policy aims at providing frameworks or standards for methods in educational research and, in turn, enhancing efficiency and quality. Researchers are expected to provide 'neutral' and 'accurate' findings and make a systematic census of objective and rigorous data to identify effective teaching methods and promote them as 'good practice' and 'quality standards'. These methods are borrowed from the medical field where they have been used in therapeutic studies: first meta-analyses, then systemic literature reviews, randomised controlled trials, cohort follow-ups, case studies and finally expert advice (Dodier, 2003). DG EAC plans to further the development of such brokerage agencies whose tasks are to link policy and research and to make recommendations in terms of quality assessments. Another objective is to better recognise the different stakeholders – practitioners, policy-makers, the media, think tanks or firms – and strengthen their relations in data production, sharing, and use, in the form of cooperation or partnerships.

Conclusion

To what extent is a country with strong centralised institutions and traditions of measurement such as France influenced by the gradual emergence of a measurement instruments-based European government in education and training? The seminar 'Education and Training in the Lisbon strategy' organised in January 2007 by the *Centre d'Analyse Stratégique* (CAS) provides some insight. CAS is an agency directly under the authority of the Prime Minister whose mission it is to assist the government in defining and implementing its economic, social, environmental and cultural policies. Building on the European strategy towards lifelong training, human capital development, and the adaptation of labour needs, CAS focused its work on European indicators and benchmarks. Their analysis was strongly influenced by human capital economists belonging to the network of experts set up by DG EAC.

CAS has since engaged in the charting of good practices in the assessment of structural reforms in France and Europe. The design of new methodologies is regarded as central to a differentiated and coordinated implementation of the Lisbon strategy across nations. This is why CAS has also attempted to identify the different methods with their assets and drawbacks (micro-econometrics on individual data, Real Business Cycle models, sectoral dynamic models, international macro-economic models, etc.), in order to identify good national practices and prioritise reforms. As the emergence of a knowledge economy was the priority of the Lisbon strategy, CAS aimed to identify obstacles to the improvement of the quality of educational and training mechanisms and their funding, and link them to other policies, particularly employment policy. CAS has also planned to work more specifically on higher education, migration and gender equality in the labour market and the lengthening of the professional life cycle. All these topics echo the EC's demographic concerns and attest to the alignment of the French reform agenda with European goals.

We could mention other examples of the strategic orientations of French organisations for the production of statistical information in education and training or the production of territorial governance by the *Délégation Interministérielle à l'Aménagement et à la Compétitivité du Territoire* (*DIACT*). These large-scale transformations call for the application of a broad research programme to better appreciate the relations between these different forms of instruments and government at local, national, and supranational level. In this perspective, it might first be helpful to study the local sites that contribute to the development of global structures, like the identified calculation centres (Latour, 2005) and then put the delegation and global-to-local interpretations to the test. It will subsequently be necessary to map the information formats and standardisation processes that participate in the same measurability and comparability processes.

Bibliography

Antunes, F., 'Globalisation and Europeification of Education Policies: Routes, Processes and Metamorphoses', *European Educational Research Journal*, 5 (1), 2006, 38–54.

Ball, S., *The Education Debate*, Bristol: The Policy Press, 2007.

Barry, A., *Political Machines. Governing a Technological Society*, New York: The Athlone Press, 2001.

Boltanski, L. and Thévenot, L., *On Justification: Economies of Worth*, Princeton: Princeton University Press, 2006.

Boltanski, L. and Chiapello, E., *The New Spirit of Capitalism*, London: Blackwell, 2007.

Borraz, O., 'Les normes: instruments dépolitisés de l'action publique', in P. Lascoumes and P. Le Galès (eds), *Gouverner par les instruments*, Paris: Presses de Sciences Po, 2004, 123–161.

Bottani, N., 'Le niveau d'huile, le moteur et la voiture: les enjeux d'une évaluation de la qualité de l'enseignement par les indicateurs', in R. Normand (ed.), *De la formation à l'emploi: des politiques à l'épreuve de la qualité, Education & Sociétés*, no. 18, Paris: INRP/De Boeck, 2006, 141–161.

Bowker, G.C. and Star, S.L., *Sorting Things Out. Classification and its Consequences*, Cambridge: MIT Press, 1999.

Brousse, C., 'Le projet de nomenclature européenne des catégories socio-économiques', *Idées*, 147, 2007, 6–14.

Callon, M., *La science et ses réseaux. Genèse et circulation des faits scientifiques*, Paris: La découverte, 1989.

Centre d'Analyse Stratégique, 'L'éducation et la formation dans la stratégie de Lisbonne : des priorités aux modalités d'application', séminaire no. 3, Paris: La documentation française, 2007.

Ceri Jones, H., 'Lifelong Learning in the European Union: Whither the Lisbon Strategy?', *European Journal of Education*, 40 (3), 2005, 247–260.

Corbett, A., *Universities and the Europe of Knowledge. Ideas, Institutions and Policy*

Entrepreneurship in European Union Higher Education Policy, 1955–2005, New York: Palgrave Macmillan, 2005.

Cusso, R., 'La rhétorique de la société de la connaissance et l'Europe: vers un rétrécissement de l'espace public', in A. Van Haecht (ed.), 'Education et formation. Les enjeux politiques des rhétoriques internationales', *Revue de l'institut de sociologie, Bruxelles*, ULB, 1–2, 2005, 75–92.

Dale, R., 'Globalization and Education: Demonstrating a "Common World Educational culture" or Locating a "Globally Structured Educational Agenda"?', *Educational Theory*, 50 (4), 2000, 427–448.

Dale, R., 'Construire l'Europe en bâtissant un Espace Européen de l'Education', in R. Normand (ed.), *De la formation à l'emploi: des politiques à l'épreuve de la qualité, Education & Sociétés*, no. 18, Paris: INRP/De Boeck, 2006, 35–53.

Deane, C., 'Transparency of Qualifications: Are we There Yet?', *European Journal of Education*, 40 (3), 2005, 279–293.

Demeuse, M. and Baye, A., 'La Commission européenne face à l'efficacité et l'équité des systèmes éducatifs européens', *Education & Sociétés*, no. 20, Paris: INRP/De Boeck, 2007, 105–119.

Derovet, J.-L. and Normand, R., 'French Universities at a Crossroads Between Crisis and Radical Reform. Towards a New Academic Regime?', *European Education*, 40 (1), 2008.

Desrosières A., *La politique des grands nombres. Histoire de la raison statistique*, Paris: La découverte, 1993.

Desrosières, A., 'Comment fabriquer un espace de commune mesure? Harmonisation des statistiques et réalisme de leurs usages', in M. Lallement and J. Spurk (eds), *Stratégies de la comparaison internationale*, Paris: CNRS Éditions, 2003, 151–169.

Desrosières, A. and Thévenot, L., *Les catégories socioprofessionnelles*, Paris: La découverte, 1988.

Dodier, N., *Leçons politiques de l'épidémie de sida*, Paris: EHESS, 2003.

Erikson, R. and Goldthorpe, J.H., *The Constant Flux. A Study of Class Mobility in Industrial Societies*, Oxford: Clarendon Press, 1992.

Ertl, H., 'European Union Policies in Education and Training: The Lisbon Agenda as a Turning Point?', *Comparative Education*, 42 (1), 2006, 5–27.

European Commission, *European Report on the Quality of School Education. Sixteen Quality Indicators. Report Based on the Work of the Working Committee of Quality Indicators*, Brussels: DG EAC, 2000.

European Commission, *The Concrete Future Objectives of Education and Training Systems*, Brussels: 2001.

European Commission, *European Report on Quality Indicators of Lifelong Learning. Fifteen Quality Indicators*, Brussels: DG EAC, 2002.

European Commission, Commission Staff Working Paper, *Progress Towards the Common Objectives in Education and Training. Indicators and Benchmarks*, Brussels: DG EAC, 2004.

European Commission, Commission Staff Working Paper, *Progress Towards the Common Objectives in Education and Training*, Brussels: DG EAC, 2005.

European Commission, Communication, *A Coherent Framework of Indicators and Benchmarks for Monitoring Progress Towards the Lisbon Objectives in Education and Training*, Brussels: 2007.

European Commission, Commission Staff Working Document, *Towards More Knowledge-Based Policy and Practice in Education and Training*, Brussels: DG EAC, 2007.

Eurostat, European Commission, *Report on the Eurostat Task Force on Measuring Lifelong Learning*, Luxembourg: Office for Official Publications of the European Communities, 2001.

Eurostat, European Commission, *Classifications for Learning Activities-Manual*, 2006.

Eurostat/F-4, European Commission, Education, *Science and Culture Statistics*, Luxembourg: Office for Official Publications of the European Communities.

Eurostat, European Commission, *Europe in Figures: Eurostat Yearbook 2006–2007*, Luxembourg: Office for Official Publications of the European Communities, 2007.

Fitz-Gibbon, C.T., *Monitoring Education: Indicators, Quality and Effectiveness*, London: Continuum, 2004.

Gibbons, M., *The New Production of Knowledge*, London: Sage, 1994.

Green, T. and Leney, T., 'Achieving the Lisbon Goal: The Contribution of Vocational Education and Training', *European Journal of Education*, 40(3), 2005, 262–278.

Hacking I., *The Taming of Chance*, Cambridge: Cambridge University Press, 1990.

Hanushek, E. and Wössmann, L., *The Role of Education Quality in Economic Growth*, World Bank Policy Research Working Paper 4122, February 2007.

Hingel, J., *Education Policies and European Governance: Contribution to Interservice Group on European Governance*, Brussels: DG EAC, 2001.

Hutmacher, W., Cochrane D. and Bottani N., *In Pursuit of Equity in Education. Using International Indicators to Compare Equity Policies*, London: Kluwer Academic Publishers, 2001.

Lascoumes, P. and Le Galès, P. (eds), *Gouverner par les instruments*, Paris: Presses de Sciences Po, 2004.

Latour, B., *Science in Action*, Cambridge: Harvard University Press, 1987.

Latour, B., *Re-Assembling the Social. An Introduction to Actor-Network Theory*, Oxford: Oxford University Press, 2005.

Lawn, M. and Lingard, B., 'Constructing a European Policy Space in Educational Governance: The Role of Transnational Policy Actors', *European Educational Research Journal*, 1 (2), 2002, 290–307.

Lingard, B. and Ozga, J. (eds), *The Routledge Falmer Reader in Education Policy and Politics*, Oxford: Routledge, 2007.

Mahieu, C. and Moens, F., 'De la libération de l'homme à la libéralisation de l'éducation. L'éducation et la formation tout au long de la vie dans le discours et les pratiques européennes', in E. Charlier (ed.), *L'influence des organisations internationales sur les politiques d'éducation, Education & Sociétés*, no. 12, Paris: INRP/De Boeck, 2003, 35–55.

Majone G., 'A European Regulatory State?', in J. Richardson (ed.), *European Union: Power and Policy-Making*, London: Routledge, 1996.

Normand, R., 'Les comparaisons internationales de résultats: problèmes épistémologiques et questions de justice', in E. Charlier (ed.), *L'influence des organisations internationales sur les politiques d'éducation, Education & Sociétés*, no. 12, Paris: INRP/De Boeck, 2003, 73–89.

Normand, R., 'La formation tout au long de la vie et son double. Contribution à une critique de l'économie politique de l'efficacité dans l'éducation', in Van Haecht (ed.), *La posture critique en sociologie de l'éducation, Education & Sociétés*, no. 13, Paris: INRP/ De Boeck, 2004.

Normand, R., 'De l'accountability aux standards: la traduction européenne des politiques de la performance', in Van Haecht (ed.), *Education et formation. Les enjeux politiques des rhétoriques internationales, Revue de l'Institut de Sociologie*, Bruxelles: ULB, 2005/1–2, 2005, 56–74.

Normand, R., 'Les qualités de la recherche ou les enjeux du travail de la preuve en éducation', in R. Normand (ed.), *De la formation à l'emploi: des politiques à l'épreuve de la qualité, Education & Sociétés*, no. 18, Paris: INRP/De Boeck, 2006, 73–91.

Normand, R., 'En quête d'une mesure des inégalités: genèse et développements d'une arithmétique politique en éducation' in P. Batifoulier, A. Ghirardello, G. de Larquier, and D. Remillon (eds), *Approches institutionnalistes des inégalités en économie sociale*, Tome 1, Paris: L'Harmattan, 2007.

Novoa, A. and Lawn, M., *Fabricating Europe: The Formation of an Education Space*,

Dordrecht: Kluwer, 2002.

OECD, *Evidence and Education: Linking Research and Policy*, Paris: 2007.

Porter, T.M., *Trust in Numbers.The Pursuit of Objectivity in Science and Public Life*, Princeton: Princeton University Press, 1995.

Rosental, C., *La trame de l'évidence*, Paris: PUF, 2003.

Scheerens, J., *Measuring the Quality of Schools*, Paris: OCDE-CERI, 1995.

Scheerens, J. and Hendricks, M., 'Benchmarking the Quality of Education', *European Educational Research Journal*, 3 (1), 2004, 101–114.

Thévenot, L., 'Emotions et évaluations dans les coordinations publiques', in P. Paperman, and R. Ogien (eds), *La couleur des pensées. Emotions, sentiments, intentions*, Paris: EHESS, 1995, 145–174.

Thévenot, L., 'Organized Complexity: Conventions of Coordination and the Composition of Economic Arrangements', *European Journal of Social Theory*, 4 (4), 2001, 405–425.

Thévenot, L., 'The Plurality of Cognitive Formats and Engagements: Moving Between the Familiar and the Public', *European Journal of Social Theory*, 10 (3), 2007, 413–427.

Tomlinson, S., *Education in a Post-welfare Society*, Buckingham: Open University Press, 2001.

Tuijnmann, A.C., 'Measuring Lifelong Learning for the New Economy', *Compare*, 33 (4), 2003, 471–482.

West, A., 'Comparer les systèmes éducatifs: débats et problèmes méthodologiques', in M. Lallement and J. Spurk (eds), *Stratégies de la comparaison internationale*, Paris: CNRS Éditions, 2003.

Jay Rowell

12

The instrumentation of European disability policy: constructing a policy field with numbers

Over the past several years the European Union has produced an increasing number of action plans, targets, communications, discussion papers, statistical indicators, and policy recommendations on disability. This proliferation has been driven by the disability unit within DG Employment, the creation of a high-level group in 1996, interservice groups, and research tendering, all of which point to the increasing role of Europe in a policy area which remains officially within the competences of member states. Mainstreamed into a variety of established policies (transportation, built environment, anti-discrimination, new technologies, employment), the goal of improving the social and economic integration of disabled Europeans has become a constant preoccupation in what is, at least at face value, an essentially consensual policy field. One European official interviewed rhetorically asked 'if anyone can possibly be against improving the social and economic integration of people with handicap'.[1] While care has been taken to avoid imposing rigid policy recommendations and targets, the Commission, national representatives and disability interest groups have managed to forge a common representation of disability as a European problem accompanied by a wide-ranging set of 'soft' policy instruments. While this consensual framing of the problem appears to be intrinsically linked to the nature of the problem of supporting the most vulnerable in society, at closer inspection, the consensus is not as evident as one may think.

Disability is a category of action shaped by social norms and state action deeply anchored in national histories (Stone 1984; Buton, 2003). National policies geared towards social and economic insertion, rehabilitation, education and, more recently, non-discrimination are therefore tightly linked to responses forged in each context to the problem of identifying and compensating legitimate forms of labour market exemption. In this respect, disability brings into play the fundamental and highly divisive question of defining normality and deservingness of claims to collective solidarity.

Disability policy is nowhere tidily subsumed within one body or organisation. Policies are financed through different mechanisms, implying social policy dimensions as well as labour market regulations and fiscal policy. It mobilises actors in the fields of health, education and social services and touches on questions of human rights. At the European level, disability policy has been mainstreamed into a variety of policies run by DGs ranging from Employment to Regional policy, Transportation, SANCO and ECFIN, as well as Enterprise and Competition. The terminology used to designate disability (for example disability, disadvantage, differently-abled, deficiency, incapacity, invalidity, handicap, long-term illness, chronic illness)[2] is highly variable and compounded by linguistic diversity and the breathtaking scope of measures used to identify, sort and compensate individuals.

Despite this diversity, the EU has nonetheless successfully promoted a broad range of policy proposals and has taken a leading role in stimulating reforms of national policies and negotiating international norms. By which mechanisms did European actors manage to build legitimacy for *European* action in this field? Were common policy problems at the national level simply 'uploaded' into European arenas or can the dynamics of building a European policy be seen as being largely independent of national preoccupations?

In this chapter we will not attempt to measure the effects of European policy. In keeping with the general orientations of this volume, the essential question will be to understand how disability was recast at a European level through the creation of common cognitive categories, analytical tools, scales and forms of intervention. The institutionalisation of a European disability policy required the creation of a minimal consensus on the definition of the problem to be addressed and the hypotheses of causation (Jacobsson, 2004: 360). We will focus primarily on the role of knowledge instruments and in particular quantification in defining policy frames and institutionalising categories, policy tools and shared cognitive categories. Despite their technical and politically neutral appearance, the construction, the choice and the integration of numbers into causal chains produce powerful framing effects (Desrosières, 1993; Lascoumes and Le Galès, 2004). In this respect, the aim is to go beyond discourse analysis and try to understand the mechanisms by which discourse is 'hardened' and inscribed into institutional and social configurations (Henry and Rowell, 2007).

The rise of disability on the political agenda of the EU: translations from a national to a European context

The timing of agenda-setting and problem definition suggests that the inscription of disability on the European agenda can neither be reduced to the sum of national preferences, nor to the uptake of a successful national model. Activity on disability within the Commission began in the early 1980s through the monitoring of compliance to the UN Charter on Equal Opportunities of 1981. The issue became increasingly salient in the run-up to the Amsterdam Treaty. With mounting political pressure for a reinforced 'social Europe', the identification of the disabled as a particularly deserving and emblematic population demonstrated that European institutions were responsive to political and social demands. It proved to be an excellent political opportunity and Article 13 gave a legal basis for the EU to take measures to fight all forms of discrimination (Mohanu, 2007). The question of disability began to progressively appear in different loci of the European institutions in the late 1990s but only became a recurrent subject of preoccupation following the Treaty of Lisbon and the declaration of a European Year of Disability in 2003. If the symbolic mobilisation of the disabled as a demonstrative social 'poster child' provided political impetus, the uploading of disability into European arenas was not a sum of national preferences.

The rise of disability on the European agenda followed a decade of increasing pressure to reform disability provisions in member states. Contrary to other historical periods such as the aftermath of the two world wars when societies sought to compensate and rehabilitate a highly 'deserving' population of disabled war veterans, the re-emergence of disability as a social and political problem was a more gradual process in which the criteria of deservingness became more controversial. The decline of heavy industry, chronic unemployment and tightened access to unemployment benefits created a combination of push and pull factors which caused the rolls and costs of disability benefits to rise sharply throughout the 1980s and 1990s. The disappearance of swaths of industry led gatekeepers to make a liberal use of disability status, particularly for older unskilled workers (Alcock et al., 2003). Until the early 1990s, the increase of disability and early retirement seemed to be an acceptable price to pay to pull workers with skills in low demand out of the workforce as a means to keep the politically sensitive unemployment figures under control.

But by the early 1990s, increasing disability expenditures collided with stricter budgetary discipline, in part driven by European monetary union. Expenditure on disability benefits far outstripped unemployment benefits in most countries. In the UK, the number of persons claiming long-term sickness and disability benefit rose from 570,000 in 1981 to 2.88 million by 1999 (Vicar, 2005: 8), more than double the number of registered unemployed. Perhaps more worrying and enigmatic was the fact that the robust growth of the late 1990s did not result in a return to the labour market for the disabled (OECD, 2003). On the contrary, despite the tightening of eligibility criteria, the numbers of disabled on benefits remained stable or even rose.[3] Not only did there seem to be a particular difficulty in reversing the mechanism which had drawn surplus labour out of the labour market, but also the percentages of the active population with disabilities in the labour market fell steadily: in the United States, for example, it dropped from 80% in 1970 to less than 60% in 1992, a percentage that has fallen further since (Burkhauser and Stapleton, 2003: 10).

In the mid to late 1990s, eligibility criteria were tightened in most countries, benefits were reduced or increasingly means-tested, beneficiaries were submitted to more frequent health evaluations, and recipients of disability benefits were increasingly expected to develop individual plans for return to work, engage in skills training or participate in the labour market to continue to claim benefits.[4] The supposed fluidity between early retirement, unemployment and disability in the minds of policy-makers and large segments of the public had several consequences. The idea that different types of benefits could be used (and abused) interchangeably attenuated the legitimacy of replacement income and transformed the image of the disabled as possible 'free riders' (Schneider and Ingram, 1993: 336). To use the expression of Robert Castel, the invalidation of valid workers of the 1980s was replaced by a validation of invalids (Castel, 1995). Secondly, through the extension of the logics of activation to the disabled, combined with the stigmatisation of benefit traps, the disabled were perceived as rational actors calculating the costs and benefits and ultimately responsible for their own destiny. Finally, the idea that disability was a disguised form of unemployment softened the borders between aptitude and inaptitude.[5] This made the extension of supply-side labour market policies based on mutual obligations and responsibilities to the field of disability both possible and, to some, evident. A Commission document of 2005 stated that 'nearly all aspects of the European employment strategy are pertinent for the employment of people with disability' (CEC, 2005: 7). While policy-makers remained more guarded in their discourse on the disabled than on the unemployed to avoid being seen as insensitive,[6] the problems of labour market integration of people with disabilities became tightly linked to active labour market policies.

The 'jump' from national political agendas to the European agenda was neither linear, nor automatic. If the Amsterdam Treaty created a potential space for the development of EU policies in the field of disability, policy formulation remained firmly anchored in member states with implementation increasingly transferred to regional, local or private actors. The expanded and diversified European discourse on disability from the late 1990s onwards shares many of the basic causal assumptions which characterise evolutions on the national level. Keywords such as inclusion, activation, mutual obligations and responsibilities, benefit traps, and making work pay are omnipresent. At both levels, disability policy has been integrated in a general grammar of welfare reforms which mobilises the semantics of the individual (projects, lifelong learning, adaptation, contractual arrangements and conditionality) rather than collective categories based on professions, rights and compensation (Rowell and Zimmermann, 2006). However, the inscription of disability onto the European agenda differs from national frames in several important ways, in part due to differing budgetary constraints and the distribution of responsibilities between the levels of government.

As disability was seen as a way to reinforce the legitimacy of broader policy objectives, policy entrepreneurship required the integration of disability into more general pre-existing policy frames.[7] As such, this multifaceted policy problem was more than just a mere problem awaiting a policy response, it was also a political and institutional resource to be seized upon. The analysis of official documents and the activism of the Commission in creating working groups and structuring interest groups[8] enable us to identify two essential moments of institutionalisation of disability at the European level.

The first concerted integration of disability into the European political space occurred between 1996 and 1998. The 1993 White Paper on growth, competitiveness and employment opened the path for an increased role of the EU in welfare reform, but focused mainly on employment, representing both the most politically important issue and a policy field at the confluence of social and economic policy. The 'European social model' insisted on 'less passive and more active solidarity' and public intervention centred on 'preventive rather than reparative' policies (CEC, 1993: 15). Monetary union, budgetary constraints, and limitations on industrial policy deprived member states of essential macro-economic policy tools. Emphasis therefore shifted to labour supply (Jepsen and Pascual, 2005: 237). The rhetoric of reconciling economic competitiveness and social justice created a consensus both on the right, as emphasis was placed on modernising and streamlining welfare provisions, and on the left, as care was taken to present active labour market policies as a step to the empowerment of individuals, focused on lifelong learning (see Normand in this volume), capacity-building and combating social exclusion.[9]

Within this context, the launching of the European employment strategy in 1996 was followed closely by a Commission communication on Equal Opportunity for people with Disabilities and the creation of a High Level Group on Disability in December 1996 in order to both diversify the employment strategy and address the specific problems faced by people with disabilities. As one of the first major Commission documents on the employment of the disabled put it:

> In addition to the particularly low employment rate, member states indicate that most people with disabilities of working age are out of the labour market altogether and heavily dependant on disability benefits. These benefits can often

reinforce recipients' exclusion from the labour market – creating a benefit trap
[...] access to education and training, reviewing the design of income support'.
(SEC, 1998: 2)

The promise of emancipation and self-empowerment also fitted well with
the objectives of interest groups representing people with disability who
contested the marginalisation of the disabled in society by placing emphasis
on ability rather than disability as a way to integrate into the social mainstream. To fight exclusion it was deemed necessary to replace benefit systems
which 'compensate a state of exclusion and harden the social fracture' by
moving from 'passive solidarity to measures promoting social and economic
integration' (CEC, 1997: 11).

Compared with the framing of the issue at the national level, much less
attention was however paid to social and health services, deinstitutionalisation, budgetary impact, public health and improved workplace safety. If
concerns about budgetary discipline and the sustainability of welfare state
provisions are voiced by DG ECFIN, European discourse is far less centred on
expenditures than is the case in national contexts. The European discourse
made the assumption that nearly all disabled people were willing to undertake
and capable of undertaking, some kind of gainful employment on the open
labour market. The Commission positioned itself as an advocate for the
disabled, a champion of a cause hampered by well-meaning, but essentially
patronising and stultifying national welfare provisions. Despite these first
inroads, disability remained a minor chapter of the employment strategy and
beyond the relatively toothless anti-discrimination directive of 2000, there
was little concerted effort to go further.

The second important moment for the institutionalisation of disability in
Europe followed the Lisbon Summit, with the generalisation of quantifiable
targets as central tenets of a new method of policy coordination. The Lisbon
package produced new opportunities going in two separate, but complementary directions. On the one side, the creation of OMC-inclusion created a new
arena of discussion where health, disability and long-term illness were integrated within a battery of statistical indicators of exclusion (Atkinson et al.,
2002). Similarly, the emphasis on new communication technologies and
lifelong learning created a new space for policy entrepreneurship for interest
group representatives and commission officials to integrate the disabled into
these topoi. Finally, the use of quantifiable targets and the shift from unemployment rates to rates of workforce participation as a central benchmark of
employment policy focused new attention on the disabled as an untapped
labour reservoir.

By placing the percentage of working-age Europeans in employment
at the centre of policy preoccupations and fixing the target of 70% of
15–64-year-old men and women by 2010 (starting from 61% in 2000), the EU
sought to equal the performance of the United States, presented as both the
chief economic rival and a model in a knowledge-based global economy.

Potential growth of total employment in the EU was thereby estimated at 30 million persons, double the number of the registered unemployed (CEC 2001: 2). Alarming projections on the ageing workforce and the sustainability of welfare systems placed labour supply at the forefront of employment policy and was perceived as a key to improving competitiveness. The corollary of the promotion of the employment rate as the central structuring objective was to bring 'underachieving' populations into the limelight. National action plans and joint reports not only recorded overall progress, but also targeted specific populations. As the percentage of men between the ages of 24 and 55 had employment rates as high or higher than the US and Japan, a particular target of 50% was set for older workers and women (60%) to close the overall gap. The disabled were designated in official documents as a 'labour reserve' (CEC, 2006: 73), an 'untapped potential' of labour and skills to feed the growing demand for labour and to reach the EU's goal, but no firm targets were set. What was missing was numbers to back up these claims and mainstream the activation of the disabled into a concerted effort to achieve both global employment targets and goals of social inclusion.

The quest for the authority of numbers

The Lisbon strategy expanded and firmly anchored a culture of measurement into European policy-making, in particular in fields where the EU could not command 'harder' policy tools (Jacobs and Manzi, 2000: 90).[10] Given the importance of comparisons, ranking and target-setting in policies relying on 'naming and shaming', mutual learning and benchmarking (Bruno, 2008), the creation of statistics to reflect reality, guide and evaluate public policy and control policy images through 'empirical facts' (Baumgartner and Jones, 2005) and 'marshalling evidence' (Peters, 1994: 13) became essential. Official documents therefore invariably called for improved statistical indicators. The role of quantification in the European polity is encapsulated by Atkinson, a leading figure in quantifying social inclusion:

> The use of a common set of indicators has the potential to bring about significant change in the way policy with respect to social inclusion is framed [...] gives policy makers a basis on which starting points and progress can be reliably compared. (Atkinson, Marlier and Nolan, 2004: 65)

The task of quantifying a group as heterogeneous as the disabled proved to be daunting. Already problematic at the national level, the problem was (and is) further compounded on the European level by heterogeneous and largely incommensurable national statistical categories. What were the possible solutions to shift the scale of knowledge production to the European level?

The spiralling benefit rolls and expenditures were powerful tools used in national contexts to demonstrate the urgency of reform. European statistics could have potentially been created by adding these available national figures. However powerful these numbers were in national contexts, they were not adapted to European arenas. Budgetary constraints were not a direct concern for the EU even if the sustainability of social protection was, and remains, a concern. Moreover, using numbers of benefit recipients did not provide an accurate picture as they excluded the estimated 40% of unregistered disabled persons who were not drawing benefit or in employment (OECD, 2003: 42). These indicators therefore left out two essential pieces of information: the overall number of disabled and the activity rate. Finally, huge national variations in definition of disability did not provide a sound basis for comparison. The quest for an objective and comparable measure of the reality of disability and its link to other social problems – such as economic inactivity, poverty and an ageing society – would paradoxically come from surveys based on self declaration.[11]

Survey items on disability were included into two existing statistical survey systems providing the EU with a specific and independent basis of knowledge upon which to build 'evidence-based policy'. A specific disability module was inserted into the 2002 Labour Force Survey (LFS), while a more limited set of indicators was integrated into the Survey of Incomes and Living Conditions (EU-SILC) of 2004. Two types of questions, responding to two slightly different definitions of disability, were used, both built upon established international experience. The first option used in the LFS consisted in asking respondents if they had suffered from a long-standing illness or condition over the last six months, then went on to ask if this condition 'restricts the kind of work that can be done', 'the amount of work' and mobility to and from work. The question used in the EU-SILC relates more particularly to the effects of a health condition on daily activities and does not directly ask respondents if they suffer from a long-term health problem. In both surveys answers were graded from 'highly restricted' to 'some restrictions' to 'no restrictions'. If each measure provides slightly different overall numbers, both allow the identification of consistent trends over time and give comparable proportions between subsets of populations (nationality, age, gender, educational attainment and profession).

The number generated by the LFS was dramatic and provided the central number of EU disability policy. The number of 44.6 million Europeans with disability and the percentage of Europeans of working age with disability (16%) is the starting point of nearly every subsequent policy document, even if only 57% of those reporting a condition went on to declare some form of restriction in the kind of work they could do, the amount of work (55%), or in their mobility (30%) (Ward and Grammenos, 2007: 10). The fact that the number is limited to 15–64-year-olds (whereas the EU-SILC covered all age groups) points to the emphasis on employment and the choice to forgo a higher overall figure by including the over-65 age group. Although statistical indicators were available on a wide series of connected 'problems' such as the need for social services, income and poverty rates, statistics were integrated into a causal story focused nearly exclusively on employment and took the form of a recurring twofold argument.

The first was based on humanist values of inclusion in society constructed around the following syllogism: 1) The social inclusion of the disabled is a question of basic human rights; 2) employment, while not being the only form of social inclusion, is essential to social inclusion and the best means to fight poverty; 3) policies encouraging increased labour market participation are therefore the best solutions. The LFS module was not equipped to record links between disability and poverty or income, unlike the EU-SILC survey. The power of the syllogism making employment the ultimate objective blended out the problem of poverty in two ways. By postulating that work was the most effective – if not exclusive – means to combat poverty, issues such as imperfect uptake of disability benefits, increasingly restrictive access, means testing and benefit reduction which affected poverty rates among the disabled took second seat. Secondly, as income replacement was disqualified as a 'passive' expenditure and part of the benefits trap, the poverty rate among the disabled was regarded as a mechanical consequence of low employment rates and, by consequence, as a residual problem to be solved through increased labour market participation.

The second argument echoed the more collective premises of the employment strategy and insisted on the necessity of raising employment levels to counter the effects of an ageing workforce. From this starting point, the disabled became, along with women and older workers, a 'reservoir' for increasing the overall level of employment (COM, 2005: 3). A policy paper of 2002 on active inclusion of the disabled not only sought to close the wide gap in activity rates but to 'bring the employment rate of people suffering from a handicap to the same level as persons without a handicap by 2010'. (CEC, 2002: 5) A more measured paper produced by the network of experts on disability targeted 2 to 3.5 million disabled Europeans for economic reintegration, contributing 1 to 2% to the overall European target of 70% (EIM, 2001: 12).

The statistical unification of the disabled therefore instituted a specific population as an object of European policy, but at the same time made the assumption that disability could no longer be systematically considered as a legitimate ground for decommodification. This placed the disabled on an equal footing with other social categories, both in terms of rights and expected outcomes. While specific provisions were made to help attenuate physical and social barriers (workplace accommodation, the authorisation of wage subsidies for employment in the open labour market, the pending anti-discrimination directive, positive discrimination in public tendering), the essential tools for increasing labour market participation were common to all employment policies.

The problematic 'hardening' of disability into 'soft' policy instruments

While the overall numbers were essential to create legitimacy for European policies, disability has not been the object of a specific OMC procedure and has proved to be difficult to mainstream into policy instruments used in the employment strategy or the OMC social inclusion. The theme is only occasionally mentioned in national action plans or joint reports, usually as pilot projects or examples of good practice. National governments have been averse to setting or accepting hard targets, and while interest groups are important venues for the diffusion of best practices (EASPD or MHE for example), there has been little headway in benchmarking disability policy. Commission documents do carefully express preferences, for example the priority given to open rather than sheltered employment, but these recommendations are rarely, if ever, backed up with hard statistical indicators which are particularly important in a polity where evidence-based policy-making has become a categorical imperative.

If the figure of 16% of the labour force with a disability was essential in establishing the necessity of a European approach, the solidity of this indicator and beliefs in its utility remain weak despite the continued investments by Eurostat and research tendering to improve and refine methodology.[12] This is particularly true for top civil servants in the DG ECFIN who thought the numbers wielded by DG Employment overstated the case, that 'it just wasn't credible and hurt its case'.[13] But this opinion is also shared by officials within DG Employment who admit that if the figure clearly indicates that the problem is important, it remains based on 'some sort of self assessment'.[14] This sceptical appraisal of a 'subjective' statistical source weakens the solidity of this indicator and leaves policy-makers with the impression that they are dealing with something imprecise, 'soft'; the implicit belief being that 'true' disability remains more limited than the numbers might suggest.

Contrary to other target categories for increasing labour market participation with less contestable and discrete boundaries such as gender and age, disability remains a category where membership is always open (Titchkosky, 2003: 525), based on subjective self-assessment defined in relation to social definitions of 'normality'. However, the limited solidity of this indicator also derives from the legitimacy of the actors who wield it. Even if many high-level civil servants of DG Employment are also trained economists, civil servants of DG ECFIN use their legitimacy based on their uncontested command of economic expertise to downplay the validity of knowledge instruments used by DG Employment. DG ECFIN sees its role as providing the 'overarching story' of the European project based on evidence and econometric modelling deemed necessary to 'put limits on other DGs who are perhaps sometimes captive of their clienteles', one interviewee going so far as to question the economic competence of other DGs.[15] Part of these claims are based on the quality and methodology used for producing convincing 'evidence': DG ECFIN relying on widely accepted statistical inputs and time-tested indicators such as the fiscal burden, public expenditures and demographic projections, while other DGs rely largely on surveys and more qualitative indicators where cost–benefit analysis remains problematic.

Furthermore, interest groups do not commonly have recourse to statistical arguments to make their claims. Their place in policy forums is both based on their representation of stakeholders and their practical expertise. As European interest groups are umbrella organisations which retain members by helping them access European funds, provide training and organise exchanges of best practice, they tend to put emphasis on their expertise in policy implementation when dealing with Commission officials. They 'provide examples to illustrate problems on the ground' (EPR), anticipate difficulties or anomalies in applying proposed EU regulations in specific national contexts or present innovative practices on the ground which the EU could generalise.[16] Predominantly trained in public affairs, policy officers of interest groups focus on implementation at the national level and practical dilemmas, but do not appear to regularly use numbers to state their case.

The subjective stigma of disability statistics is further compromised by the huge national variations in survey results. The distributions around the European average of 16% range from 6% to 32% of the working-age population, a dispersion which cannot be explained through demographic or public health differences (Ward and Grammenos, 2007: 20). Furthermore, the countries on the low or the high end do not fit with oppositions commonly used to read differences in Europe (North/South; new and old member states; continental, Nordic or liberal welfare systems, etc.) as on the low end one finds Romania (6%), Italy (7%), Spain (8%) and Lithuania (9%) and at the high end Finland (32%), the UK (27%), the Netherlands (25%), France (25%) and Estonia (24%). One could have expected a lower dispersion of respondents declaring 'considerable restrictions' with most of the variations concentrated in the 'looser' categories of those declaring 'some' or 'no restrictions' in the type and intensity of activities they can perform. However, despite some variations, all three categories remained largely proportional to the general figures, with European averages of 5.2% declaring a condition but no restrictions, 4.1% some work restrictions and 6.3% considerable restrictions in the amount of work that can be done (Ward and Grammenos, 2007: 27).

National discrepancies are masked by averages and are not presented in policy documents destined for the general public, but their existence undermines beliefs in the commensurability of disability statistics among policymakers.[17] Similar inconsistencies beleaguer statistics on employment rates. Respondents declaring a condition without restrictions (5.2% of 15–64-year-olds) have a higher employment rate than the European average: 68% versus 63% at the time of the survey! The percentage drops to 62% for those declaring some limitations, a number just under the European average, but only 28% for those declaring considerable limitations (6.3% of the workforce). This evidence points to the fact that the 'potential' to increase labour market participation is perhaps less than what is often claimed, as potential progress is concentrated in the segment of the most severely disabled. The figure also tends to indicate that the distinction between the 'truly' disabled and those who are disqualified from the workforce and mildly impaired but 'trapped' in disability benefit is difficult to maintain, as only those reporting significant impairments have a large gap in activity rates.

A breakdown by national context provides even more puzzling results, as the percentage of those with considerable restrictions in work ranges from under 10% in Slovakia and Estonia to 40% in the Netherlands and even 58% in Belgium (Ward and Grammenos, 2007: 113). This makes the task of ordering, ranking and identifying successful national models based on an accepted interpretation of a desirable outcome nearly impossible. Should a low rate of self declaration be interpreted as a reflection of a strong social stigma, an 'underdeveloped' disability benefits system or a result of a successful policy to combat stigma and make even those with an acute condition feel that there are no significant obstacles to their integration? How should countries such as Slovakia or Italy, with a low percentage of self declared disabled but also with a low percentage of market participation be compared to countries such as Sweden, the Netherlands or Finland, which are high on both counts, but where the number of economically inactive disabled people is significantly higher? On the question of the economic integration of the disabled, there is no universally recognised example of a successful model. Member states commonly identified as models in employment policy such as Finland, Sweden, Denmark, the Netherlands, and the UK actually have quite poor results, depending on the indicator one looks at.

The ability of percentages of disabled in the workforce to provide clear benchmarks was further weakened by the absence of a clearly defined target outside the EU. If Commission documents insisted heavily on the performance differential with the United States for 15–24-year-olds (37% employment rate in Europe vs. 52%), for women between 25 and 54 (63% vs. 74%) and for older workers between 55 and 64 (36% vs. 57%) (CEC, 2001), the poor and declining performance of the United States[18] in integrating the disabled into the workforce made it impossible to find a fixed exterior target to attain or emulate. While indicators provided an idea of the magnitude of the problem and made the existence of a European policy evident and desirable, they were difficult to integrate into argumentative chains as they neither produced a clear indication of the sources of the problem nor facilitated the identification of successful policy responses.

The framing effects of knowledge instruments

Statistical conventions were powerful enough to symbolically unify a hetero-geneous set of social and national situations, yet not solid enough to set into motion an autonomous 'evidence-based' policy process. Should this lead to the conclusion that uses of disability statistics are limited to a mainly symbolic function of legitimation? If the actual effects of the European disability strategy are next to impossible to ascertain, it can be argued that statistical indicators and their uses have had far-reaching effects by orienting problem definitions in one direction at the exclusion of other possible problem constructions. The analysis of the inscription of particular problem definitions into seemingly neutral instruments can reveal as much about which social problems are ignored as about those which are targeted for public action (Rowell, 2007).

Naming the problem

European statistical indicators set a premium on inclusion in the workforce rather than focusing on other potential problems. Other available or possible statistical conventions could have brought problems such as the financing and access to social and health services, assisted living, public health moni-toring and prevention to the fore. Much of the 'soft' European policy is based on identifying gaps between the performance of a target population and European averages as a means to make problems visible. As we have shown above, break-downs by the severity of impairment generate highly differential deviations from the statistical average ranging from next to no ascertainable effects to highly significant ones not only in activity rates, but also in income and poverty rates. These questions were rarely addressed in policy documents on disability even if figures from the EU-SILC were readily available. Finally, the refusal to statistically distinguish between possible causes of disability has far-reaching policy implications. Some policy documents include claims that the majority of conditions are linked to work conditions and employment history, which, if explored, would quite radically transform the primary direction of policy from the disabled themselves, to a tighter regulation of working conditions and safety. This causal story would however imply a strengthening of regulations on employers and shift the focus from the indi-vidual, a step which would meet with stiff opposition from a number of member states and organised interests. In the end, the refusal to statistically deconstruct the population avoids politically explosive problems such as distinguishing between the 'truly' disabled and the 'less deserving', refusing to make distinctions between visible and easily diagnosed conditions and more elusive, but rapidly growing categories of disability such as mental disorders or muscular-skeletal disorders which represent up to 50% of all causes of handicap.

The individual as the unit of analysis and action

Despite the prevalence of the 'social' definition of disability, the tools used to measure disability remain firmly centred on the individual and medicalised in their logic. Breaking down social and physical barriers have both found their way into EU policy through recommendations on the built environment and transportation, research funding on assistive technologies and the proposal to reinforce obligations on employers for workplace accommodation. However, the statistical instruments used to evaluate these obstacles remain individual and are blunt; limited to asking respondents if they have restrictions in mobility, or are benefiting from some sort of support or require such support. As a result, despite the insistence on the social model, the locus of policy is the individual in what remains an evaluation of individual deficiencies. The emphasis on the individual is not just a statistical artefact. It reflects both the increased attention to personally tailored service provision and a diffuse political discourse stressing individual rights and obligations.

The disabled person is constructed as a utility maximiser responding to policy stimuli seeking to 'overcome barriers preventing people from making the right choices' (Schneider and Ingram, 1990: 517) or, in the words of a senior Commission official, to 'push the disabled into work, perhaps for their own good. It's what we call in England, tough love'.[19] The borders of disability as a specific social condition are blended with the more general category of employability, placing the individual in direct competition with other populations considered to be more or less employable, as the category of the employable mechanically creates its negation, the unemployable (Rudischhauser and Zimmermann, 2004: 252). The universal 'unit' of the more or less employable (or disabled) individual overshadows other sociological characteristics of this population, as disability is strongly correlated with age, blue collar professions and low educational attainment. All things equal, these sociological characteristics place the disabled not only at the back of the queue in employment centres, but also at a disadvantage in obtaining scarce resources in job training and individualised support, as agencies tend to concentrate resources on those who most closely correspond to the expectations of potential employers (Ebersold, 2001). However, because physically demanding professions are perceived to belong to the 'old economy', there has been little or no attempt to link disability to professional status and little policy discussion on capacity-building in the transition from blue collar professions to service professions requiring high levels of cognitive, communications and interpersonal skills.

Mechanisms of causation

The discourse on capacity-building and activation has focused on incitation but has remained more guarded when addressing more coercive measures. Disability is therefore a policy problem without a clear image of causation and even less of blame, as the statistical construct and the consensual policy style of European institutions make it difficult to go beyond the 'naming' of the problem to 'blaming' and 'claiming' (Felstiner, Abel and Sarat, 1981). Without uncontroversial 'evidence-based' indicators of causation and assignation of 'blame', European policies on disability adopt a 'scattergun' approach with some measured and euphemised responsibility assigned to the disabled themselves (passivity, failure to properly see the benefits of employment), a criticism of misguided welfare policies and some general discourse on 'awareness raising', information and fighting discrimination, with no formal identification of the authors of discrimination.

The labour market has continued however to be particularly harsh for the disabled. If restricted access to benefits has in most cases stopped or slowed the growth in the numbers of benefit recipients, little or no progress has been made in increasing labour market participation. All attempts to evaluate policy outcomes, whether by the OECD or the EU, come to the conclusion that no headway has been made, that the measurable effects of activation policies have been next to nil, and that there is no measurable correlation between expenditure on active programmes and outcomes (OECD, 2003: 58 and 119). This poor performance remains a puzzle to all EU officials and most representatives of interest groups interviewed, as general employment rates have risen for all other target groups. Despite the evidence to the contrary, the expectations remain that an ageing workforce and activation will sooner or later produce effects.

With statistical indicators centred on the individual, the characteristics of the labour market have remained largely outside of the field of vision. If the disabled are portrayed as rational actors responding to policy stimuli, the discourse on employers insists on a lack of information and awareness, thereby failing to consider the possibility that employers make rational anticipations on the potential costs of hiring a disabled person (sick leave, health care costs, lower productivity, etc.). Policies directed toward employers are for the most part voluntary, including 'awareness raising' or the authorisation of public wage subsidies of up to 60% of labour cost to employers. More binding policies such as sheltered employment or a quota system for the employment of people with disabilities such as those practised in France and Germany are portrayed in EU documentation as being largely counterproductive.

The conception of the labour market as a neutral and undifferentiated entity has failed to take into account market segmentation which hinders the uptake of disabled workers. A first level of segmentation is territorial, with high variations in activity rates between employment basins both within Europe and within each member state. As regionalised research in the UK has shown, inactivity rates for working-age men, largely linked to disability, vary greatly, ranging from 10% in economically dynamic regions to over 30% in the 'rust belt' (Alcock et al., 2003). This regional 'blind spot' has also been identified in indicators on social inclusion, thereby reinforcing their individualist bias (Atkinson et al., 2002: 338). Similarly, while the decline of the European manufacturing industry and the intensified use of robots and improved ergonomics have reduced the proportion of the workforce exposed to dangerous conditions, outsourcing, intensification of work and the multiplication of physically and cognitively demanding positions in the service industries are obstacles to retaining or hiring workers with physical or mental illnesses, questions that have been given little if no attention at the European level.

Conclusion

Not only do statistics reflect a particular reality, but to a certain degree statistical indicators create and institute reality by providing actors with a common language to designate a problem and a target population assumed to have empirically verifiable and discrete boundaries. This cognitive instrumentation of disability policy isolates and identifies a group and gives purchase to policy-makers to act (Desrosières, 2003: 164–165). Cloaked with the aura of numbers-based legitimacy, the figure of 16% of the working-age population and 44 million disabled workers provided an authoritative argument for action by certifying the dramatic scope of a European problem. Tied into the Lisbon targets for increasing activity rates in the face of the challenges of an ageing population and the sustainability of welfare provisions, the employment of people with disability both focused attention on the specific problem of economic integration and implied that the problem and the possible solutions could only be found within the individual, thereby excluding alternative problem definitions and public policies.

Notes

1   Interview, Commission official, 11.12.2007.
2   In 1981 the WHO produced an influential integrated classification of handicap by distinguishing between deficiencies, defined as a loss or an abnormality of a physiological, psychological or anatomical function, incapacity defined somewhat tautologically as a an incapacitating limitation to accomplish activities considered to be normal for a human being, and handicap understood as a social disadvantage resulting from an incapacity preventing normal activities for a given age, gender, cultural or social situation (ILO, 1998, 15-16; CEC, 2004, 24).
3   Reductions in the levels of benefits in the Netherlands brought the costs down from 4% to 2.5% of GDP between 1995 and 2005 but did little to reduce overall numbers. (De Jong, 2004: 182).
4   In this paragraph we seek to sketch out some general trends which cover the national contexts most often cited in European documents. The pace and contents of reforms varied, but the direction of reforms of the 1980s and 1990s followed the same general direction.

5   This process can also be linked to the diffusion of the social definition of handicap adopted by most international organisations. Incapacity is not intrinsically situated within the individual but is seen as a product of interactions with the environment. The same person can be considered disabled in one context and not in another and even the most able-bodied can theoretically be considered disabled in some circumstances.

6   During interviews, Commission officials pointed to high numbers of Europeans on benefit and the extreme variations between countries to imply the subjectivity of disability but did not go so far as to claim that many of the disabled did not have a legitimate health concern.

7   This mechanism of frame extension is similar to the process of integrating an external shock (September 11, 2001) into existing EU policy frames (Rhinard, 2007).

8   Interest group representation was largely transformed at the end of the 1990s, simultaneously reflecting the work of the Commission to support and even create stable and representative organisations, and the pull factor linked to the increasing activity of European institutions in the field (see H. Michel in this volume). The umbrella group European Disability Forum was created in 1997, the European Association of Service Providers for Persons with Disabilities in 1998, Mental Health Europe in 1998.

9   In many ways this political consensus is reminiscent of the neo-classical revival in the United States in the 1950s and 1960s in its application to social policy. Productivity gains are seen as aggregated individual choices rather than the product of institutional factors such as unions, government policy and firm practices. This idea attracted interest from the right as a way to reduce big government and from the left as it justified increased spending on education and training (O'Connor, 2001: 140-143).

10   Georgakakis and de Lassalle have documented the rise of economic expertise and the relative decline of diplomatic careers and legal expertise among top civil servants in the EU. This sociological shift explains in part the rise of the culture of numbers as opposed to a more regulatory and legal approach (de Lassalle and Georgakakis, 2007).

11   This paradox is all the more acute as policy recommendations on procedures used to identify the disabled insist on the need to restrict self-declaration and certification by 'complacent' personal physicians in order to obtain more consistent and equitable outcomes.

12   If disability statistics meet the requirement of salience and political neutrality theorised by Peter Haas, they have yet failed to meet the criteria of usefulness in policy-making, credibility (belief that the figures are a true reflection of a problem) or scientific legitimacy (Haas, 2004: 574).

13   Interviews, DG ECFIN, December 10, 2007.

14   Interview, DG Employment, December 12, 2007.

15   Interview, DG ECFIN, December 10, 2007.

16   Interviews with policy officers of EASPD, MHE, Workability Europe, 2007.

17   Interview with a member of the Cabinet of DG 5, December 11, 2007.

18   In the US, the number of benefit recipients increased by 43% in the 1990s despite dynamic job growth. Employment rates of the moderately and severely disabled were lower than in all other OECD nations but the UK (OECD, 2003: 34 and 61).

19   Interview, Commission official, 11.12.2007.

Bibliography

Alcock, P., Beatty, C., Fothergill, S., Macmillan, R. and Yeandle S., (eds), *Work to Welfare. How Men Become Detached from the Labour Market*, Cambridge: Cambridge University Press, 2003.

Atkinson, A., Marlier, E. and Nolan B., 'Indicators and Targets for Social Inclusion in the European Union', *Journal of Common Market Studies*, 42 (1), 2004, 47–75.

Atkinson, T., Cantillon, B., Marlier, E. and Nolan, B., *Social Indicators. The EU and Social Inclusion*, Oxford : Oxford University Press, 2002.

Baumgartner, F. and Jones, B., *The Politics of Attention: How Government Prioritizes Problems*, Chicago: Chicago University Press, 2005.

Bruno, I., *A vos marques, prêt, cherchez!*, Paris: Éditions du Croquant, 2008.

Burkhauser, R. and Stapleton, D. (eds), *The Decline in Employment of People with Disabilities: A Policy Puzzle*, Kalamazoo: Upjohn Institute for Employment Research, 2003.

Buton, F., 'L'Etat et ses catégories comme objets d'analyse socio-historique. Principes, modalités et limites de la production étatique des "handicapés sensoriels" au XIXᵉ siècle', in P. Laborier and D. Trom (eds), *Historicités de l'action publique*, Paris: PUF, 2003, 59–78.

Castel, R., *Les métamorphoses de la question sociale. Une chronique du salariat*, Paris: Fayard, 1995.

CEC, 'White Paper on Growth, Competitiveness and Employment', 1993.

CEC, 'Moderniser et améliorer la protection sociale dans l'Union Européenne', communication de la Commission, 102, 1997.

CEC, 'Les politiques communautaires au service de l'emploi', 2001.

CEC, 'Programmes actifs du marché du travail pour les personnes handicapées', DG Emploi et affaires sociales, 2002.

CEC, 'Définitions du handicap en Europe: Analyse comparative', DG Emploi et affaires sociales, rapport de l'Université Brunel, 2004.

CEC, 'La situation des personnes handicapées dans l'Union Européenne élargie: Plan d'action européenne 2006–2007', COM 2005 (604 final), 2005.

CEC, 'Indicators for Monitoring the Employment Guidelines Including Indicators for Additional Employment Analysis', Compendium, 2006.

De Jong, P., 'New Directions in Disability (Benefit) Policy: The Dutch Experience', in B. Marin, C. Prinz and M. Queisser (eds), *Transforming Disability Welfare Policies: Toward Work and Equal Opportunity*, Burlington: Ashgate, 2004, 175–194.

de Lassalle, M. and Georgakakis, D., 'Genèse et structure d'un capital institutionnel européen: les très hauts fonctionnaires de la Commission européenne', *Actes de la recherche en sciences sociales*, no. 166/167, 2007, 38–53.

Desrosières, A., *La politique des grands nombres: histoire de la raison statistique*, Paris: Éditions la découverte, 1993.

Desrosières, A., 'Comment fabriquer un espace de commune mesure? Harmonisation des statistiques et réalisme de leurs usages', in M. Lallement and J. Spurk (eds), *Stratégies de la comparaison internationale*, Paris: CNRS Éditions, 2003, 151–169.

Ebersold, S., *La naissance de l'inemployable ou l'insertion aux risque de l'exclusion*, Rennes: Presses Universitaires de Rennes, 2001.

EIM Business and Policy Research, 'The Employment Situation of People with Disabilities', commissioned by DG Employment and Social Affairs, 2001.

Felstiner, W., Abel, R. and Sarat, A., 'The Emergence and Transformation of Disputes: Naming, Blaming, Claiming . . .', *Law and Society Review*, 15 (3–4), 1981, 631–654.

Haas, P., 'When Does Power Listen to Truth? A Constructivist Approach to the Policy Process', *Journal of European Public Policy*, 11 (4), 2004, 569–592.

Henry, E. and Rowell, J., '*La construction des problèmes publics en Europe: perspectives de recherche*', in A. Campana, E. Henry and J. Rowell (eds), *La construction des problèmes publics en Europe*, Strasburg: Presses Universitaires de Strasburg, 2007, 205–222.

ILO, *Vocational Rehabilitation and Employment of Disabled Persons*, Geneva: ILO, 1998.

Jacobs, K. and Manzi, T., 'Performance Indicators and Social Constructivism: Conflict and

Control in Housing Management', *Critical Social Policy*, 20 (1), 2000, 85–103.

Jacobsson, K., 'Soft Regulation and the Subtle Transformation of States: The Case of EU Employment Policy', *Journal of European Social Policy*, 14 (4), 2004, 355–370.

Jepsen, M. and Pascual, A.S., 'The European Social Model: An Exercise in Deconstruction', *Journal of European Social Policy*, 15 (3), 2005, 231–245.

Lascoumes, P. and Le Galès, P. (eds), *Gouverner par les instruments*, Paris: Presses de Sciences Po, 2004.

Mohanu, A., 'L'institutionnalisation du secteur du handicap: entre intégration européenne et européanisation', in O. Baisnée and R. Pasquier (eds), *L'Europe telle qu'elle se fait*, Paris: CNRS Éditions, 2007, 245–262.

O'Connor, A., *Poverty Knowledge. Social Science, Social Policy, and the Poor in Twentieth-Century U.S. History*, Princeton: Princeton University Press, 2001.

OECD, *From Disability to Ability*, Paris, 2003.

Peters, G., 'Agenda-setting in the European Community', *Journal of European Public Policy*, 1 (1), June 1994, 9–26.

Rhinard, M., 'Le cadrage de la politique antiterroriste de l'Union Européenne', in A. Campana, E. Henry and J. Rowell (eds), *La construction des problèmes publics en Europe*, Strasburg: Presses Universitaires de Strasbourg, 2007, 83–108.

Rowell, J., 'Knowledge and Power in State Socialism: Statistical Conventions and Housing Policy in the GDR', *Journal Policy History*, 19 (3), 2007.

Rowell, J. and Zimmermann, B., 'The Eclipse and Rebirth of "Civil Society" in a Historical Perspective: The Case of Germany from the Wilhelmian Era to the GDR', in P. Wagner, (ed.), *The Languages of Civil Society*, Oxford: Berghahn Books, 2006, 100–130.

Rudischhauser, S. and Zimmermann, B., 'De la critique à l'expertise. La modernisation de l'action publique: le cas du chômage en France et en Allemagne', in B. Zimmermann (ed.), *Les sciences sociales à l'épreuve de l'action. La savant, le politique et l'Europe*, Paris: Éd. Maison des Sciences de l'Homme, 2004, 247–285.

Schneider, A. and Ingram, H., 'Behavioral Assumptions of Policy Tools', *Journal of Politics*, 52 (2), 1990, 510–529.

Schneider, A. and Ingram H., 'Social Construction of Target Populations: Implications for Politics and Policy', *American Political Science Review* 87 (2), 1993, 334–347.

SEC, 'Raising Employment Levels of People with Disabilities. The Common Challenge', *Commission Staff Working Paper*, 1998.

Stone, D., *The Disabled State*, Philadelphia: Temple University Press, 1984.

Titchkosky, T., 'Governing Embodiment: Technologies of Constituting Citizens with Disabilities', *Canadian Journal of Sociology*, 28 (4), 2003, 517–542.

Vicar, D., 'Why Have Disability Benefit Rolls Grown so Much?', *School of Management and Economics, Queens University Belfast, Working Paper*, August 2005.

Ward, T. and Grammenos, S., 'Men and Women with Disabilities in the EU: Statistical Analysis of the LFS ad hoc Module and the EU-SILC', Final report, study financed by DG Employment, 2007.

Academy of international law of The Hague 83
Actor-Network Theory 225
agenda 6, 13, 75, 110, 128, 130, 135, 148, 150, 166, 171, 187, 225, 239, 245
Aldrin P. 220
alter-globalist 170, 175–176
Association des régions européennes pour les produits d'origine 157

Bachelet F. 99
Ball G. 85n.18, 233
Barroso J. M. 31, 218
Barry A. 236
Beach D. 48, 60
Beauvallet W. 165
benchmarking 185–187, 189, 191–199, 200–202, 231, 234, 249, 252
Berger P. 19n.2, 131, 166
Boissieu (de) P. 61–62
Bolkestein directive 170
Bonn A. 79, 81
Bourdieu P. 11, 25, 91, 129, 133, 137, 165, 221n.25
Bowker G. 227
Bruno I. 129, 249
bureaucracy 2, 46–47, 209

Cabinets of Ministers 30
Calmes C. 50–54, 65n.7
Camp R. 194, 196

Caporaso J. 4
Castel R. 246
causal story 251, 255
Centre d'Analyse Stratégique (CAS) 238
Centre d'Etudes Européennes (Nancy) 102
Centre for Educational Research and Innovation 238
Centre for Research on Lifelong Learning (CRELL) 236–237
Charter of Fundamental Rights 115–117, 122, 130, 132, 135–137, 142
Checkel J. 10, 111
Chirac J. 95, 215
Christiansen T. 5, 48, 68, 88
Cini M. 28, 58
Clercq (de) W. 215, 222n.26
code of good administrative behaviour 63
Coleman R. 38, 40, 44n.13
College of Europe 36
Committee of the Regions 94
Common Agricultural Policy (CAP) 151, 158–159
Common Foreign and Security Policy (CFSP) 47–48, 59, 60, 62
community competence sectors 29
community doctrine 156
competitive Europe 186–187, 190, 193,

195, 197, 202
Competitiveness Advisory Group (CAG)
    191–192
Competitiveness Index 189
constitutional system (EU) 119
constitutional treaty project (the) 46
constitutional value 141, 143n.18
constructivism 1, 5, 6, 9, 10–11, 13,
    15–16, 13, 131–132, 146–149, 151,
    153, 155–157, 159, 160n.1, 207
Costa A. 43
Costa F. 72
Costa J.-P. 124n.11
Costa O. 94, 120 150, 164
Cottrau A. 75, 78
Council of the European Union
    Commission of Coordination In
        Luxemburg (COCOR) 50
    Committee of Permanent
        Representatives (COREPER) 51,
        54, 57, 62
    Competitiveness 189
    Directorate for 'General Political
        Questions' 62
    Economic and Social Council
        179n.18
    External Relations DG 37–38, 40, 59,
        61–62
    General Affairs Council (GAC) 52, 62,
        65
    Justice and Home Affairs DG 29, 48,
        59
    Policy Planning and Early Warning
        Unit (PPEWU) 61
    Political and Security Committee
        (PSC) 61
    Presidency 47, 51, 57, 65
    Schengen secretariat 59
    Secretariat of the EU council 51
    Secretariat's delegations 64
    Secretary-General 29, 47, 49, 50–59,
        60–63, 65, 191
    Special Council of Ministers of the
        Staff Committee 54–55,
        65n.9
crisis of the empty chair 1

Declaration of the Rights of Man and
    the Citizen 138
Delors J. 6, 31, 40, 57, 187, 191, 208,
    214, 215
democratic deficit 18, 209, 220
departmental councils 95, 98, 100–101,
    103
depoliticising effects 129
Diez T. 6
Duran P. 94–95

Easton D. 212, 221n.13
EC Legal advisers 70, 74–76, 79
EC Service directive 70
ECHR jurisprudence
    Dangeville case 118
    SA Gras 118
    Senator Lines 117
ECJ jurisprudence
    Costa V. ENEL 72–73
    Van Gend en Loos 72
Ecole Nationale d'Administration 35,
    42, 102
Elias N. 112, 146
Erika catastrophe 170
Ersboll N. 55–59, 62
EU Agency for Fundamental Rights
    131
Euratom 51, 54, 84, 208
Euro Parties
    European People's Party – European
        Democrats (EPP–ED) 168–169,
        170, 174, 176–177
    European Socialist Party (ESP)
        168–169, 170, 174–177
    European United Left (EUL) 169, 170,
        174–176
Eurobarometer 152, 207–209, 211, 213,
    215–219, 220
Eurocrats 209
Euro-law 71, 75–76, 80–82, 85n.16,
    114–118, 124n.6, 148, 150
Euro-lawyers 69, 70, 77, 79, 83–84, 109,
    110
Euro-litigants 72, 74, 80–81, 83
Euro-litigation 69, 70–71, 73–79, 82–84

European Central Bank (ECB) 42
European citizens 209, 215, 237
European Civil Service
  'A' rank officials 54
  Deputy Directors-General 28, 31,
    35–36, 38, 40
  Director General of the Commission
    27, 206
  EC Civil Service 70, 73, 79
  Senior Civil Service 35
European Coal and Steel Community
  (ECSC) 42, 50–51, 76, 79, 80, 208
  213
  ESCS's High Authority 47, 217
European Commission
  Admin DG 29, 44n.3
  Advisory Committee 29
  Agriculture DG 31, 34, 37, 44n.12, 56,
    151, 154–158, 162n.20
  Commission delegations 64
  Commission's Legal Service 40, 79
  Commissioner 28, 30, 39, 40, 170,
    202n.3, 208, 210–211, 214, 220
  Commissioner's cabinet 26, 28,
    34–35, 37, 39
  Competition DG 40, 159
  Credit and Investment DG 37
  Development DG 29, 31–33
  Economic Affairs DG 31–34, 36–37,
    42, 244, 248, 252–253
  Education and Culture DG 225,
    232–234, 236–238
  Employment DG 41–42, 243, 252
  Energy DG 40
  Environment DG 40
  External Relations DG 29, 32–33,
    36–8, 40, 64
  General Secretariat of the European
    Commission 43n.1
  Health and Consumer Protection DG
    38, 40
  Industrial Affairs DG 36, 40, 44n.12
  Information and Innovation DG 39
  Information and Communication DG
    206, 210, 211–212, 214–215,
    217

  Market DG 44n.12, 154, 214
  Personnel DG 40–41
  Research DG 37, 202n.3
  Social Affairs DG 40–41, 177
  The College of commissioners 40
  Trade and Industry DG 40, 44n.12,
    193–194
  Transport DG 40–41, 179n.7
  Vice president of the Commission 64,
    66n.16, 219
European confederation of property
  managers 143n.6
European Constitutional Treaty (ECT)
  99, 170, 176
European constitutionalism 115
European Convention 115–116, 121,
  138
European Cooperation Policy 66n.11
European Councils
  Cologne European Council (1999) 60,
    135
  Fontainebleau Council (1984) 56
  Helsinki European Council (1999) 60,
    62
  London Council (1981) 56
  Seville Council (2002) 62
  Tampere Council (1999) 59
European Court of Human Rights
  (ECHR) 111, 113, 116–119,
  120–123
European Court of Justice (ECJ) 12, 69,
  70–79, 81–83, 109, 111, 113,
  115–119, 120–123, 152–153
European Courts
  CFI Court of First Instance 113, 118
  Court's Advocate General 74
  European judges 109, 111–113,
    115–117, 119, 120–124
European crisis 218, 220
European Defence Community 1
European elections 177, 215
European elites 1, 4, 11–12, 15, 25–26,
  28, 36, 42–43, 73–74, 84, 110–111,
  152, 190–191, 208, 215
European Employment Strategy 19, 196,
  233, 246–247

European Expert Network on
  Economics of Education (EENEE)
  236
European External Action Service 64
European Federation of National
  Organisations working with
  Homeless (FEANTSA) 137
European Housing Forum (EHF) 142
European identity 8, 111
European indicators/statistics 227, 230,
  238, 250
European Landowners Organisation
  (ELO) 130, 137, 139, 140–141
European law firms 76–77
European legal capital 82, 85n.16
European milieus 102, 211–212
European Monetary System (EMS) 191
European Movement (The) 35
European opinion
  European public opinion 210–211,
    213, 216–219
  Instruments of measure 92, 152, 206,
    208, 220, 231
  Priority Information Programmes
    (PIP) 208, 214
European Parliament
  Groups 57, 69, 84, 174
  MEP 38, 60, 134, 179n.16, 215, 221n.4
  Presidents 44n.1
  Quaestors 44n.1
  Regional Politics and Transport
    Committee 168
  Urban Housing Parliament inter-
    group 130
  Vice-Presidents 44n.1
European Political Cooperation (EPC)
  59
European Property Agency (EPAG)
  143n.6
European Qualifications Framework
  (EQF) 228
European Research Area (ERA) 190,
  197–198
European Round Table (ERT) 191,
  193–194
European schools 102

European Security and Defense policy
  (ESDP) 48, 61–63
European social capital 71, 80, 84, 91,
  100, 102–103, 231
European Social Fund (ESF) 103
European social model 247
European statistical system 231
European Structural Funds 93, 95, 97,
  157
European Union of Developers and
  House Builders (UEPC) 141,
  143n.6
Europeanisation of local authorities 94,
  96
euroscepticism 209
Eurostat 41, 197n., 227–229, 231, 233,
  252
Euro-Strikes 180n.19

Fédération internationale pour le droit
  européen (FIDE) 85n.16
field
  academic 186
  administrative 26
  economic 213
  Euro-litigation 83
  European 6
  industrial field 192
  policy field 95, 243, 247
  theory 11
Fligstein N. 2
Fonds Européen de Développement
  Régional (FEDER) 97
Fonds Européen d'Orientation et de
  Garantie Agricole (FEOGA) 97
Foucault M. 18, 63, 186, 188, 195,
  200–202
French AOC 150, 155
French Constitutional Court 138, 141,
  143n.10
French referendum 176

Galanter M. 75
Gaudet M. 75, 79, 221n.14–n.17
General Agreement on Tariffs and Trade
  (GATT) 59

Georgakakis D. 26, 29, 38, 91, 112, 164, 206
Giddens A. 9
Global Competition 81, 189, 235
Global Competitiveness Report 188
globalisation movement 226
governance 68, 88–89, 94, 104, 109, 111, 114, 120, 129, 130, 164, 186, 196, 201, 218, 226, 232
Granger M.-P. 76, 111
Green paper 167, 178n.3
Groupement Européen des Fédérations intervenants dans l'Immobilier (GEFI) 130–132, 137, 139, 141–142
Guiraudon V. 8, 142

Haahr J. H. 198, 202n.1
Haas E. 48, 111, 128, 207
Haas P. 259n.12
Hacking I. 7, 225
Hall P. 146
Hallstein W. 52, 84n.9
Hay C. 6, 187, 188
Hecke (van) G. 79, 81, 83
High Level Group on Benchmarking (HLGB) 194–195
High Level group on Disability 247
High Representative for Foreign Affairs and Security Policy 64
Hommel N. 55, 57, 60
Hood C. 16
Hooghe L. 25, 89, 90
Hoover Institute 232
Human rights 109, 113–119, 121–123, 138, 244, 251

Iglesias R. 120
incomes and living conditions 250
informal learning 228, 231
Inglehart R. 217
Institute for International Law 85n.16
Institute for the Protection and Security Citizen (IPSC) 237
institutional architecture 57, 109, 123
institutional orders 148, 154–155
institutionalisation 26, 48–49, 63, 89, 103, 111, 131, 146, 148–149, 150–152, 156, 207, 211, 214, 225, 244, 247–248
institutionalism 10, 17, 48, 146
instruments 2, 6, 9, 11, 16–17, 148, 150, 154, 185, 196, 206–207, 209, 211, 243, 244
intellectual property protection 156
interest group 2, 13–15, 63, 130–132, 138, 141–143, 248, 252–253, 257, 259n.8
intergovernmentalism, 4, 18, 59, 68, 88, 110, 112, 186
Interim Committee for the Rome treaties 51
International Indicators of Education Systems (INES) 230
International Labour Organisation (ILO) 42
International Law Association 83, 85n.16
International Monetary Fund (IMF) 42–43
International Standard Classification of Education (ISCED) 227, 231
International Union of Property Owners (IUPO) 134, 143n.8

Jacobs F. 120, 122, 124n.14
Jones H.C. 42, 60n13
journalists 170, 178, 208, 210–211, 215
Jullien B. 146, 148, 159, 160n.1

Kallestrup M. 6
Kauppi N. 165
Keller-Noellet M. 56, 62
Kinnock N. 28, 44n.6
knowledge instruments 244, 252, 255
Kok W. 202
Krugman P. 189, 190–191
Kuhn T. 5

Labour Force Survey (LFS) 250–251
Lagroye J. 49, 91, 148, 178n.1
Lassalle (de) M. 26, 29, 40, 130
law clerks 112, 122

law professors 70, 74, 79, 85n.16, 112, 115
Lazarsfeld P. 212, 221n.12
League of Nations 52
Lebaron F. 42
Lefebure P. 180n.19
Levits E. 122, 124n.9
Lewis J. 48
liberalisation 167
lifelong learning 225, 227–229, 230–231, 233–237, 247–248
Lindberg L. 25, 128, 215
Lisbon Strategy 167, 186–187, 195, 197, 200, 226, 233, 238
Lisbon summit 248
lobby *see* interest groups
London School of Economics (LSE) 102
Luckmann T. 19n.2, 131, 166

MacGowan L. 150
Majone G. 128, 236
Makarczyk J. 122
Mangenot M. 48
Marcussen M. 5–6
Marx G. 88, 90
media/press 170, 174, 178, 189, 198, 209, 210–215, 238
Michel H. 132, 137, 165, 259n.8
Monaco R. 80, 85n.10
Monnet J. 50–51, 85n.18, 217
Moravscik A. 3
multi-level governance 88–89, 94

national Civil Services 34, 37, 39
National Federation of Farmland Owners (FNPA) 137
National Institute of Designations of Origin (INAO) 152, 155, 158, 160n.2
national jurisconsults 70, 74, 76
national parties
  CDU 35
  Conservatives 176–177
  French Socialist Party 175–176
  Labour 35, 42
  SPD 35

Greens (the) 174, 177
national preference 2, 4, 68
neo functionalism 3, 112, 128–129, 147, 160
network 9, 18, 30, 34–35, 69, 81–84, 90–91, 99, 102, 123, 134–137, 150–151, 157, 167, 214, 236, 251
New Public Management (NPM) 187, 193–194
New Right policies 232
NGO 112
Noël E. 30, 37
Normand R. 230, 232–233, 237, 247
North Atlantic Treaty Organisation (NATO) 51, 60

Olsen J. 3
Open Method of Coordination (OMC) 63, 196, 200–202, 226, 231–232, 234–235, 248, 252
Organisation for Economic Co-operation and Development (OECD) 41–43, 51, 190, 194, 230–231, 236–237, 257
Ortoli F.-X. 42, 66n.16, 217

Padoa-Schioppa T. 37, 42
Palacio (de) 177, 179n.7
Pasquier R. 89, 90, 95, 97
permanent representations 29, 34, 50, 113
Pescatore P. 85n10, 124n14
Peterson J. 4
Piecyk W. 168, 179n.9
Pierson P. 146, 206
Piris J.-C. 60, 66n.15
policy sectors 8, 9, 19, 29, 36, 130, 132–133
port directives 166–167, 173–174, 176, 178
Port Package 165, 167–168, 171, 177, 179n.17
Prestige catastrophe 170
private international law 85n.20
private legal practice 76
Programme for International Student

Assessment (PISA) 231, 233
Programming Planning Budgeting System 230
Property Rights 130, 132, 139, 140–142
Protected Geographical Indications (PGIs)
  Appellations d'origine contrôlée (AOC) 150, 155
  Bayonne ham 157, 161
  Feta 152–153
  Parma ham 149, 152–153, 156, 160
  Roquefort cheese 152–153
  Slakis 153
  wine industry 150
public opinion 207–208, 211–213, 215, 217, 219, 221
Puchala D. 48
Puissochet J.-P. 102, 124n.13

Quermonne J.-L. 54

R&D investments 198
Rabier J.-R. 37, 211–214, 217
Radaelli C. 6
regional councils 97
regional funds 13
regional public planning units (France) 97
regulating instruments 150
regulation policy (in the EU) 128
repeat player 73–75
resilience (of European institutions) 214
Reuter P. 79
Richardson J. 8, 130, 171
Richardson K. 44n.13, 191, 221n.18
Rifflet R. 41
Risse-Kappen T. 187
Robert C. 124, 165
Roemer K. 85n.9
Rosamond B. 187–188, 190–191
Rosas A. 120–121
Rowell J. 147, 200, 244, 247, 255
Rumford C. 10

Santer J. 1, 191, 195

Savary T. 180n.20–22
Scharpf F. 13, 222n.27
Scheeck L. 114, 116–117, 124n.5
Schmidt V. 6
Schuman's declaration (09/05/1950) 49
Science of opinion 211
Secretary-General of the Western European Union (WEU) 61
Secrétariat Général pour les Affaires Régionales (SGAR) 93
Sidjanski D. 217
Simmel G. 113
Smith A. 69, 89, 91, 93, 129, 148–149, 150, 154, 164, 211, 214, 221n.9
social Europe 41, 196, 245
social mobilisations 113, 178
Social Policy 41, 244, 259n.9
Social Rights in Europe 141
socialisation 25, 39, 109, 110–115, 119, 173
Solana J. 60–61
Spielmann D. 124n.14
Stoetzel J. 211–212, 217, 221n.12
Stone Sweet A. 70, 111
Strange S. 190
structural funds 93–98, 100, 102–103, 157
subsidiarity 140, 154–156, 196, 215, 226, 235
supranational entrepreneurs 48, 74

Thatcher M. 56
Tobin Tax 170, 176
Total Quality Management (TQM) 193–194, 197
Toulemon R. 36, 44n9
trade unions
  Dockers' union 170, 172–173, 180n.20
  European Conference of Trade Unions 174
  European Transport Workers' Federation (ETF) 171
  International Transport Workers' Federation 172
treaties
  Amsterdam treaty (1997) 47, 59,

61–62, 64, 245–246
Lisbon treaty (2007) 64, 109
Maastricht treaty (1992) 47, 58–59,
    208, 214–216
Nice treaty (2001) 47
Paris treaty (1951) 50
Rome treaty (1957) 41, 55
Single European Act (1986) 124n.2,
    150, 221n.6
Trondal J. 25–26
Trumpf J. 57, 59, 60
Tuijnman A. 230–231

Unites Nations Educational, Scientific
    and Cultural Organisation
    (UNESCO) 136, 227–228, 230, 237
UNICE 138
Union nationale de la propriété
    immobilière (UNPI) 132–139,
    140–142

United Nations (UN) 39, 42–43, 51, 59,
    152, 245
Universal Declaration of Human Rights
    (the) 138

Vanhoonacker S. 48
Vauchez A. 69, 72–73, 75, 84n.1, 109,
    111–112, 129

Wallström M. 220
White J. 83
White paper 130, 167, 178n.4, 191, 218,
    220, 225, 247
Wiener A. 5
Wildhaber L. 120, 124n.10
Workability Europe 259n.16
World Bank 237
World Trade Organization (WTO)
    154–156, 159
Wössman L. 232, 237